AF208054

CORA DU BOIS

Cora Du Bois

Anthropologist, Diplomat, Agent

SUSAN C. SEYMOUR

UNIVERSITY OF NEBRASKA PRESS
Lincoln and London

Library of Congress Cataloging-in-Publication Data

Seymour, Susan C.
Cora Du Bois: anthropologist,
diplomat, agent / Susan C. Seymour.
pages   cm.—(Critical studies in
the history of anthropology)
Includes bibliographical references and index.
ISBN 978-0-8032-6295-9 (cloth: alk. paper)
ISBN 978-0-8032-7428-0 (epub)
ISBN 978-0-8032-7429-7 (mobi)
ISBN 978-0-8032-7430-3 (pdf)
1. Du Bois, Cora Alice, 1903–1991. 2. Women
anthropologists—United States—Biography.
I. Title.
GN21.D84S49 2015
301.092—dc23
[B]
2014038949

Set in Lyon by Lindsey Auten.
Designed by N. Putens.

To the two most significant men in my life

Laurence Drell Graham

and

Elliot Close Graham

CONTENTS

ILLUSTRATIONS

SERIES EDITORS' INTRODUCTION

Stephen O. Murray and Regna Darnell

Cora Du Bois's life trajectory was cursed with all-too-interesting times, from the Boer War (in which her father lost everything) through the Vietnam War (which she warned U.S. officials against entering). Within American anthropology, Du Bois came close to being like Saint Bonaventure's God with periphery everywhere, though her center focused on individuals in culture, and more specifically how nonmodal personalities were accepted (or not) in various societies.

Having had special access to her biographical subject, decades before combing the archives in which the often remote-seeming Du Bois left unvarnished material about her feelings, Susan C. Seymour has fashioned  an exemplary biography of a woman who succeeded within a sexist and homophobic academic culture though her lesbian relationships were open secrets, if secrets at all. In 1954 she became the first female full professor at Harvard. She became the fifth woman president of the American Anthropological Association in 1968 and took on transforming it into a more democratic organization. As chief of research and analysis for the Southeast Asia Command in Ceylon (now Sri Lanka), she was the only woman to head a branch of the Office of Strategic Services during the Second World War.

Her *People of Alor* remains one of the most intensive works of psychological anthropology; like Edward Sapir, she examined individuals in society rather than "culture and personality" and insisted on taking seriously intracultural variation rather than focusing on any culture's particular "modal personality type" (in contrast to the writings of Du Bois's first anthropological mentor, Ruth Benedict). She carried out important ethnographic and ethnohistorical research on Native California, and, at Harvard, headed a large research project on social change during the 1960s in the ancient temple city of Bhubaneswar, capital of the state of

Odisha (formerly Romanized as "Orissa"), India, a project on which Seymour worked and which she eventually took over.

In her biography, which contextualizes Du Bois within the concurrent expansion of academic anthropology and the expansion of U.S. attempts to manage the world, Seymour balances the personal, the professional, and the historical context with aplomb. Seymour explores some of the travails and humiliations visited on women of even the most signal accomplishment.

To anyone who thinks that the personal biography is a posthumous invasion of privacy (as in the much-discussed case of the letters of the most famous Nebraska-born-and-raised writer, Willa Cather, who clearly opposed such delving), we would respond (as Seymour does within the book) that Du Bois arranged for her letters and diaries to be archived rather than destroying them. Thus it is reasonable to conclude that she hoped the records of her living a life of dignity despite the prejudices against same-sex love would be made public in a less hostile time than that in which she lived.

PREFACE

Cora Du Bois began life in 1903 as a lonely and awkward girl who liked being a distant observer of humankind. She matured into a formidable woman whose intellect, curiosity, and presence helped take her on a remarkable journey—a journey that culminated with an appointment at Harvard. There she would become the first woman to receive a tenured professorship—the Zemurray-Stone-Radcliffe chair in the Departments of Anthropology and Social Relations. Along the way, in addition to getting a PhD in anthropology and doing pioneering research in the field of culture and personality, she served as a high-ranking intelligence officer during World War II and as a Southeast Asia expert in the State Department following the war. In the State Department she opposed actions of the U.S. government that led to the Vietnam War and stood up for civil liberties during the McCarthy era when, as a "liberal" and lesbian, she was repeatedly investigated and harassed by the FBI.

This is a book about a twentieth-century "first woman." For the general reader, it is a chronicle of that life, one that intersected major events of the past century. Du Bois was one of the few women of her generation who succeeded in having a career that included both university teaching and government service. We tend to think of Margaret Mead as the public face of anthropology during much of the twentieth century and assume that anthropology was a discipline welcoming to women. It was not. Although in the first half of the century women were admitted into certain graduate programs, few were able to obtain jobs commensurate with their degrees. This included Mead, who, unlike Du Bois, never had a full-time academic appointment.

This book is also about the development of American anthropology as viewed through the life of one individual. Du Bois studied with Franz Boas, the founder of American anthropology, and with some of his most eminent students—Ruth Benedict, Alfred Kroeber, and Robert Lowie.

For both the anthropologist and the general reader, I have tried to make that period accessible and engaging. It was a time when lone sociocultural anthropologists undertook long periods of fieldwork with peoples whose language they had to decipher while trying to understand and record their social organization and cultural practices. What made Du Bois's early research of particular interest was her focus on the individual *in* culture rather than on broad cultural patterns that did not acknowledge intracultural diversity. In the late 1920s and early 1930s, she began considering such questions as: How do individual members of a society come to share certain cultural practices and ways of thinking and believing? And how are they unique?

These interests moved Du Bois into the midst of what became known as the "culture and personality movement" within American anthropology—a convergence of sociocultural anthropology, psychiatry, and personality psychology. As described in more detail in chapter 4, this period was what anthropologist Robert A. LeVine has characterized as "arguably one of the most exciting intellectual explorations launched by American social science in the 20th century." I begin that chapter with the historic meeting, in 1909, of Franz Boas and Sigmund Freud at Clark University and the discussions about the relationship of culture to personality that ensued. Du Bois's role in those theoretical debates is then introduced. Chapter 5 follows Du Bois on a voyage to collect empirical data to test some of the theories and proposed methodologies that had emerged from these debates. It was a voyage to the remote island of Alor in the Indonesian Archipelago, then part of the Netherlands East Indies, where she spent eighteen months among a group of former headhunters. The result of that expedition was her pioneering work, *The People of Alor: A Social Psychological Study of an East Indian Island* (1944).

When the United States entered World War II, Du Bois was recruited into the Office of Strategic Services (OSS)—the country's first intelligence organization—as a Southeast Asian expert (chapter 6). There she rose to become the only woman to head one of the OSS branches of intelligence. She became chief of research and analysis for the Southeast Asia Command in Ceylon (Sri Lanka), working closely with both the military and other branches of intelligence. It was in this setting that she became friends with such persons as Lord Louis Mountbatten, the British supreme commander, and the not-yet-world-famous chef Julia Child (then Julia McWilliams), who at the time was an OSS clerk and record keeper. Du Bois's position was one of great responsibility, and it provided her with unusual opportunities for a woman.

In order to try to contribute to the formulation of postwar American policy, Du Bois joined the State Department after the war as chief of the Southeast Asia Branch of the Division of Research for the Far East (chapter 7). In that post, from 1945 to 1950, in addition to overseeing research, Du Bois tried to educate State Department officials about the cultural heritage and contemporary realities of the emerging nations of South and Southeast Asia. She, along with some others, anticipated the risks associated with American involvement in France's efforts to maintain Indochina as a colony. However, fears of the spread of communism prevailed and the result was the Vietnam War.

Du Bois returned to academe in 1954 when she received an appointment at Harvard (chapter 8). To this point Du Bois had spent most of her career in settings where the majority of her colleagues were men. She had learned to successfully navigate gender issues and thought little about them. Becoming the only female full professor at Harvard, however, was a different experience. During her years at Harvard, Du Bois initiated a long-term study (1961–72) of sociocultural change in India—a different kind of anthropological endeavor from the one she had undertaken in Indonesia. Chapter 9 addresses how and why her interests shifted from psychological anthropology to issues of change and development and how a project of this kind required a large number of personnel—Indian research assistants and a diverse set of PhD graduate students who could examine change in Bhubaneswar, India, from the perspectives of different disciplines. It was no longer solo anthropology.

An issue that affected Du Bois's life, and that is consequently woven through the book, is how she handled her sexuality in an era when the word "lesbian" was not used and when to be homosexual was considered deviant. One strategy was to keep her public and private lives separate—a compartmentalizing of life that, over time, had some pernicious effects (chapter 10). It also compelled her to censor the personal documents that she left behind, such as correspondence with her longtime partner, Jeanne Taylor. Fortunately, however, just as Du Bois opened the door of her home to trusted friends and students, she has revealed aspects of her private life in her poetry, journal entries, and letters to friends and relatives.

Because Du Bois was an eloquent and prolific writer of both private and professional works, her own voice will appear often throughout this biography and will help to illuminate the events in which she participated. For example, Du Bois's extensive correspondence with Benedict, Kroeber, and Lowie about issues of culture and personality (chapters 4 and 5) provides insight into her processes of thinking about these issues as well as the flavor of her prose. Her acerbic cables and reports from Ceylon to Washington headquarters during World War II help to evoke that era. Finally, Du Bois's poetry illustrates her more intimate and humanistic side—a part of her that never became fully integrated with her scholarly self.

Some of Du Bois's biographical notes and journal entries indicate that she had contemplated writing a personal account of the twentieth century as she had experienced it. Such a memoir does not exist. As her biographer, I have tried to incorporate as many of her thoughts about each stage of her life as possible. Although I was a student, advisee, and, ultimately, a friend of Cora Du Bois (see prologue), this undertaking has been one of exploration and discovery. Du Bois rarely spoke of her childhood, never spoke about her OSS years, and only occasionally mentioned her research in Alor. While I have personal knowledge of Du Bois's research project in India and of her later years, I have approached my examination of her life as a fellow anthropologist, someone trained to move back and forth from a distanced perspective on others to a more intimate one. To signal that both perspectives are present, throughout the book I have alternated using the more familiar "Cora" with the more distant "Du Bois" and the more formal "Cora Du Bois." If in the course of this biography I sometimes sound like an admirer of Cora Du Bois, it is because I am.

Research for this biography dates back to the summer of 1984, when I interviewed Cora Du Bois at her home in Cambridge for a short biographical chapter that appeared in *Women Anthropologists: A Biographical Dictionary*. She made available to me a copy of her vita, along with other documents—in her words, "from unrecognizable to dubious relevance, to relevance to [your] biography"—that she was sifting through before giving them to the Tozzer Library of Anthropology at Harvard University. Du Bois saw and commented on drafts of that article. At about the same time, Beatrice Whiting, then a professor of anthropology in the Harvard Graduate School of Education, tape-recorded several interview sessions with Du Bois. Whiting had been asked by the editor of the *American Ethnologist* to write an article about Du Bois for the journal. Between Whiting's increasing deafness and Du Bois's worsening memory, however, it was not a successful endeavor, and in 1988 Whiting sent me the rough interview transcripts, asking me to take over—a project that I, too, never completed. Both endeavors, however, have provided me with special access to information about Du Bois and have prompted this biography.

Du Bois's letters, journals, writings, research, and teaching materials are located in two places. Most of them are archived as the Cora Alice Du Bois Papers at the Tozzer Library of Anthropology at Harvard University. However, all of her Harvard-Bhubaneswar, India, Project materials, including pertinent correspondence with graduate students and Indian friends and colleagues, are housed at the Regenstein Library at the University of Chicago. I have consulted both archives extensively thanks to the hospitality and helpful assistance that I have received at both libraries. In particular, I want to thank Lynne M. Schmelz, Janet Steins, and Gregory A. Finnegan at Tozzer Library. Their help and support throughout this project has been invaluable: At the University of Chicago, James H. Nye, Daniel Meyer, and

Susan Summerfield were helpful in giving me access to the Cora Du Bois Papers that are part of the library's special South Asia collection.

I consulted the A. L. Kroeber Papers and the Robert Harry Lowie Papers, together with the records of the Department of Anthropology, all of which are archived at Bancroft Library at the University of California, Berkeley. These collections have provided invaluable information about Du Bois's graduate student years and ongoing relationships with Kroeber and Lowie. The Ruth Fulton Benedict Papers, archived at Vassar College, provided important correspondence between Benedict and Du Bois. The Wilbur Kitchener Jordan presidential records at the Schlesinger Library, Radcliffe Institute, provided valuable information about the Zemurray-Stone Professorship at Harvard as well as interesting correspondence between President Jordan and Cora Du Bois. Also located at the Schlesinger Library is the "Oral History of Tenured Women in the Faculty of Arts and Sciences at Harvard University," collected by Judith Walzer, which includes taped interviews with Du Bois.

In addition, I have consulted the Papers of the American Anthropological Association at the National Anthropological Archives, Smithsonian Institution, Washington DC, for documents that would provide insight into Du Bois's presidency (1969–70) during a rancorous period when the association was forced to consider professional ethics during wartime.

In order to understand the details of what Du Bois was doing during World War II, when she served in the Office of Strategic Services (OSS), I examined documents housed at the National Archives in Washington DC, some of which had only recently been declassified by the CIA when I read them in 2007. In particular, two archivists, John E. Taylor and Lawrence H. McDonald, were knowledgeable about OSS documents and very helpful. In addition, Sameer Popat and Jack Lopez helped me copy pertinent documents at the National Archives and find yet other materials after I had returned home to California.

I am grateful to David H. Price, who supplied me with copies of Du Bois's FBI records that he had acquired for writing his book, *Threatening Anthropology: McCarthyism and the FBI's Surveillance of Activist Anthropologists*. His generosity saved me a lengthy process of requesting them directly from the FBI.

Finally, and most importantly, I want to thank members of Cora Du

Bois's family who generously provided me with their time and pertinent family documents and who took a special interest in my enterprise. They are Carol Schreiber Bollinger, Gérard and Pat Du Bois, Peter Du Bois, and Helga Kaussler-Du Bois. In addition, Lisa Schlingerman, the niece of Jeanne Taylor, has been helpful in providing information about Taylor, her family, her art, and her book illustrations.

In the course of my research, I have visited all of Du Bois's childhood residences in the United States, France, Germany, and Switzerland. I knew her Cambridge residence well and have seen the exterior of her post–World War II home in Georgetown. In addition, her letters provide drawings and descriptions of her residences in Berkeley as a graduate student and her Georgetown home. Her Atimelang "house" in Alor, Indonesia, is well documented in letters, publications, and photographs.

Many persons kindly agreed to be interviewed for the purposes of this biography and were invaluable resources. They include several of Du Bois's former OSS colleagues, former Harvard colleagues and other anthropologists who knew her, a handful of personal friends, and numerous former students. I want to express my appreciation to each of them and, below, I have tried to acknowledge them in alphabetical order:

Hannah Ansel, Hetty Baets, Frederic G. Bailey, Burton Benedict, Philip K. Bock, Christopher Boehm, Amanda Bowen, Jean Briggs, Thomas Buckley, Sally Cole, Roy D'Andrade, G. N. Dash, Eric Davis, Irven DeVore, George DeVos, Alice G. Dewey, Nicholas B. Dirks, Joe Elder, Carole Farber, Drew Gilpin Faust, Ben Finney, Noël Riley Fitch, James Freeman, Hildred Geertz, James Gibbs, Walter Goldschmidt, Barrie Grenell, Peter Grenell, Karl Heider, Sonia Hodsen, Frank Hutchins, Richard Hyland, Robert Jay, David K. Jordan, Alice Kehoe, Jane Kelly, Pauline Kolenda, Louise Lamphere, Harry M. Lasker, Sabra Lee, Robert A. LeVine, Elliott Leyton, Socrates Litsios, Nancy Lurie, Joan Mark, Kim Marriot, Guy Martin, Elizabeth P. McIntosh, Peter Metcalf, Antonia Mills, Robert Lee Munroe, Rhodes Murphy, Laura Nader, Sally Nerlove, Eugene Ogan, Hannah Papanek, James Peacock, Herbert Phillips, David Plath, James Preston, Michael Prokosch, Robin Ridington, Joseph Alan Sable, J. David Sapir, Nancy Schmidt, Richard Shweder, James Siegel, Sam Smith, Melford Spiro, George Stocking Jr., Richard Taub, Robert Textor, Margaret Trawick, Sylvia Vatuk, Emilie Wellfelt, Elvi Whittaker, and Stephen Williams.

Finally, I want to thank the readers of various drafts of my book manuscript. My Pitzer College colleagues Robert L. Munroe and Claudia Strauss read and usefully critiqued some early chapters. My husband, Laurence Graham, read and made useful editorial suggestions throughout the writing process. My son, Elliot Graham, read the manuscript, chapter by chapter, and gave me useful comments and encouragement. I am greatly appreciative of two outside reviewers for the University of Nebraska Press, Louise Lamphere and David Price, who provided me with any author's coveted reward—much praise. And I want to thank Regna Darnell and Stephen O. Murray, who, as the editors of the Critical Studies in the History of Anthropology series, offered their strong support.

PROLOGUE

Cora and Me

With head erect and shoulders back, Cora Du Bois strode into the Peabody
Museum classroom at Harvard. As she gazed at us with vivid blue eyes,
everyone's attention was riveted on her. *"Formidable"*—with the French
pronunciation—was how Harvard students described her, and formidable
she was, with a chiseled face, prominent nose, and sonorous voice. It was
the fall of 1962, when I had just begun graduate work in anthropology at
Harvard, and I had fortuitously registered for Du Bois's course, Peoples
and Cultures of India. All I knew about her was that she was the author
of the classic work in culture and personality *The People of Alor* (1944), of
which I had read parts as an undergraduate. I had no idea that she was one
of only two tenured women professors in the School of Arts and Sciences
and the first woman ever to hold such a position at Harvard University.[1] I
was also ignorant of the prestigious chair she held—the Zemurray-Stone
Professorship in Anthropology—but I did recognize that I was in the presence of a distinguished woman scholar. Later I learned that she had been
a distinguished World War II intelligence officer who was awarded the
Exceptional Civilian Service Award by the U.S. Army and the Order of
the Crown of Thailand by the Thai government.

My first one-on-one exchange with Du Bois came several weeks into
the course, when she returned our first set of papers. I had written about
the matrilineal Nayars of South India, and my paper had a note on it asking
me to come see her. By then I knew her reputation for trenchant critiques
of student papers and, accordingly, entered her office with some trepidation. Peering at me across her large desk, Du Bois said, in her deep voice,
"While you might have expanded your discussion of the Nayars and the
Nambudiri Brahmins some, this is an excellent paper and I would like you
to present it to the class next week." I should have felt elated, I suppose,
but instead I was petrified at the thought of lecturing to a class of forty-
five Harvard undergraduate and graduate students. This was the first of

a series of trials by fire—special opportunities—that Cora Du Bois would offer me during my graduate career.

As I think back, I now see the risk that she was taking in turning the class over to a new student. But Du Bois, I learned, made quick, and usually insightful, assessments of people. She knew that I had adequate material for a lecture and, as she assured me, I had a better command of the Nayar literature than she did. Beneath her outward presence, I would discover, she was self-effacing and, at times, highly self-critical.

At the end of the semester I received a brief, handwritten note from Du Bois—in her tiny, precise penmanship—inviting me to join the Harvard-Bhubaneswar Project that she had just established. It would become a twelve-year, interdisciplinary study of sociocultural change in a town in Odisha, India. The note said, "I would like you to join the Bhubaneswar Project. Go get trained by the Whitings." This was shorthand for, go learn from John and Beatrice Whiting, two Harvard psychological anthropologists who had pioneered the systematic, cross-cultural study of childrearing practices. I was to adapt their techniques to a study of children and their families in Bhubaneswar, India.[2] Du Bois was making another quick assessment. She knew I was interested in India, but she had to intuit my as-of-yet unarticulated predilection for psychological anthropology. With this invitation, my immediate future was laid out for me if I wanted to accept it, and, happily, I did.

Cora Du Bois lived at 20 Coolidge Hill Road in Cambridge. There she kept a repository for materials on India, the state of Odisha, and its new capital city, Bhubaneswar, along with field notes that were arriving with some regularity from a set of Indian graduate students who were working on different aspects of the project. These materials were being housed and filed in "the Annex," a room attached to the back of her home, and students who joined the project were given keys to an outside entrance so that they might peruse the files at their convenience. In the spring of 1963 I worked in the Annex on Friday afternoons. Inevitably, at about 5:00 p.m., Cora would come to the Annex to invite me into the kitchen for a drink—usually straight gin, accompanied by Goldfish crackers—and then into the living room for conversation. The living room, which opened onto a garden of flowers and fruit trees, was an airy room decorated with old Indian Mogul paintings and modern abstracts by her partner, Jeanne Taylor.

In this setting I came to realize that Du Bois was both an intensely public and an intensely private person. In public she was a prominent professor with a forbidding presence. At home, sitting comfortably in her armchair, dressed in casual slacks and a sweater—with a drink in one hand and a cigarette in the other—she became openly loquacious. For those invited into this private sphere, Du Bois was elegant without being formal, eloquent, and perceptive. Her blue eyes lit up with pleasure when I told her, in response to her query, that I had grown up on Mount Tamalpais, in the San Francisco Bay Area, a terrain she had enjoyed hiking while she was in graduate school in Berkeley. Soon she had elicited a family history from me. Her public austerity belied an inquisitive and caring person who enjoyed drawing out her interlocutors. Her curiosity was infectious, and her eyes twinkled when she wanted to register approval. In this private realm, a guest became a friend. It was in this setting, during my second semester at Harvard, that Du Bois invited me to address her as "Cora."

This biography is, in part, the product of special relationships with Cora Du Bois. Officially, she was my advisor as a graduate student, and because I was part of the Harvard-Bhubaneswar Project, I worked closely with her. She visited Bhubaneswar while I was beginning my fieldwork there; she sent me letters with comments and queries about *all* my field notes, which were sent to her from India at regular intervals for filing in the Annex; and she scrutinized every line of my dissertation. She was both an attentive advisor and a mentor and friend. Our friendship lasted until her death in 1991.

Du Bois cultivated friendships, as will be evident in the course of this biography. As a youth she wrote poems about friendship. And as a Harvard professor, she taught a yearlong graduate seminar that examined friendship cross-culturally. From my personal perspective, however, what Cora offered was friendship and solicitude, combined with exacting mentoring. My ideas and writing were, at times, subjected to the same severe critiques that other students experienced.

Du Bois demanded clear, precise thinking and also believed that writing should have some degree of style and elegance. She regularly referred students to Strunk and White's *Elements of Style* and to the *New Yorker*. In Washington Du Bois had a reputation for acerbic cables and memos that was established during her World War II service. When she was serving in the State Department after the war, Talcott Parsons, then a Harvard sociologist, sent her a paper with his ideas on government. She returned the paper, saying that she would consider it when he rewrote it in English. Those who know Parsons's Germanic style of writing will understand, and only a Cora Du Bois would have the hubris to tell him.

Friendship included stays in Cora and Jeanne's guest room—a cheerful room on the second floor of the house that always had a vase of flowers and a bowl of fruit. In the fall of 1968, when I returned from my fieldwork in India too late to find housing, Cora invited me to use the guest room temporarily. I used that room on a number of occasions—once during Boston's historic spring snowstorm in 1970. I had been visiting Cora on a Sunday afternoon to discuss my thesis, and when I tried to leave, my car was buried in snow. Cora urged me to spend the night, and one night became four as we—Cora, Jeanne, and I—waited out the storm. Cora, turned commander, set her alarm clock at regular intervals each night so we could get up and shake snow from the fruit trees in their garden to prevent branches from breaking. Fortunately, the house was well provisioned. Cora, who was the principal cook, always had a soup stock brewing on the back burner, an excellent brie under glass on the kitchen counter, and good homemade salad dressings. Accordingly, we spent the four days removing snow from fruit trees, working on our various projects, talking, and consuming lots of good food and drink.

Once I finished my PhD and began teaching in California, Cora and Jeanne's guest room became my haven whenever I visited the Boston-Cambridge area. Cora's standard welcome was, "The guest room, liquor closet, and icebox are at your disposal." One evening when my husband and I and our six-month-old son, Elliot, were visiting, we had dinner plans with other friends in Boston. Cora insisted that we leave Elliot behind in her and Jeanne's care. "Cora," Jeanne exclaimed, "we have never taken care of a baby!" "There's nothing to it," Cora responded in her calm, authoritative voice. Baby Elliot remained with them for the evening to no ill effect.

During the spring of 1969, the second semester of my first year back in Cambridge after two years in India, I had housing without kitchen privileges. As I began work on my thesis, I regularly visited Cora at 20 Coolidge Hill Road for discussions, after which I was frequently invited to stay on for drinks and dinner. Wanting to reciprocate, one evening I suggested that I prepare dinner for the two of them at their house, an offer they accepted. Cora soon phoned to set a date and to mention that they wanted to invite some guests. A few days later Cora phoned to say that the guests would be Julia and Paul Child. The Childs were old friends of Cora and Jeanne's, dating back to when they all had served together in the OSS in Ceylon during World War II. Of course, by this time Julia Child had become a famous chef, author, and television personality. It was another trial by fire: I survived; the meal and selection of wines were applauded; the company was delightful; and I had a story for a lifetime—exactly, I suspect, what Cora wanted to provide. All of Cora's gifts came with high expectations.

CORA DU BOIS

CHAPTER 1

Tomgirl

> Cora was a real tomboy and, in later life, the star of the family.
> —George Straub

Cora Du Bois—the woman who was to become the Zemurray Professor of Anthropology at Harvard University, renowned for her eloquent English prose—began her writing career in English with a simple, charming, but also revealing diary that she began keeping in 1913, when she was nine years old. Although born in the United States, she and her family lived in France during her first years of schooling, and French was her first language. As she reported later in life, she had been a slow talker who, after her family moved to France when she was four and a half, had not learned English. Instead, she had developed a jargon that only her mother and aunt understood. "It was my own language. You had to be broken into it. When I first began speaking comprehensively, it was French."[1]

Cora's parents were fluent in English, French, and German, and they maintained a French-speaking household while living in France. So when the Du Boises returned to the United States, Cora did not know English and was held back two years in school until her English skills improved. This undoubtedly motivated her to try hard and, at her parents' suggestion, to begin to keep a diary in which to practice English.

Cora named her diary—"Diary of a real Tom-girl"—and decorated it with drawings of family members and of herself. Why "tom*girl*" rather than "tom*boy*"? Probably this reflected her lack of command of colloquial English, but it is clear that she wanted to identify herself as a tomboyish girl—a girl who enjoyed outdoor sports and other male-defined activities. One of the drawings on the back of the diary shows Cora building a fort with another girl, her friend Helen. There are two other drawings, of her playing the piano and walking to school, but there are no drawings of more stereotypical girls' activities such as playing with dolls, cooking, or playing "house." There are also no such journal entries. Rather, Cora frequently mentions going out to play basketball or going fishing down on the wharves.

The drawings on the inside cover of "Diary of a real Tom-girl" are intriguing. The top figure is a man turned sideways. He is dressed in a black jacket with striped pants and is holding a sword, upright, in his left hand—an overtly male figure that is labeled "PAPA." Surely this is intended to be Cora's father, Jean Du Bois. His position above the other figures puts him in a dominant position as head of the household, but Jean was also the family member whom Cora most liked. Below him are two abstract figures that have both male and female features. One is considerably larger than the other, and together they are labeled "no good." It is likely that they represent the remaining two members of Cora's immediate family, her mother and older brother—the two antagonists in her childhood.

The first entry in Cora's diary, which is written on lined paper in a large, carefully formed, schoolgirl-type script—very different from the tiny, precise handwriting of Cora's later years—reads as follows (without corrections):

> 1913
> January 10   Cloudy no rain
> Friday   Have a muscik lesson.
> And I found a girl
> that could speak French
> in school. Trided to write
> a story but could'nt
> If got to take may
> muscik lesson so good by.[2]

She begins with the weather and ends by saying, good-bye because she has to run off to a piano lesson. In between, however, she mentions two significant things: First, she has met a girl at school who speaks French—someone with whom she can really communicate and who might help make her feel less isolated and alone. Second, she mentions having been unsuccessful in writing a story *in English*—presumably a school assignment. The latter may have provided the final impetus to practice her English skills by keeping a diary.

The Beginning: Family Background

The relationship of a person to his or her society and culture is deeply affected by his or her family—something that Cora Du Bois was instrumental in studying in the 1930s as part of the culture and personality movement in American anthropology. The family—in whatever form it takes—is the principal context in which children learn about their world and begin to form their sense of personhood, self, and identity. So it is appropriate and necessary to begin with a brief account of the rich family heritage that, combined with extensive international travel and intercultural experiences, helped form the young Cora Du Bois.

Cora Alice Du Bois was born into an international, entrepreneurial family on October 26, 1903, the second child of Jean Jules Philippe Du Bois and Gertrude Martha (Mattie) Schreiber Du Bois. If all had gone according to plan, she would have been born in Johannesburg, South Africa, as had her older brother, Claude, five years earlier. However, historical events had intervened—as they would numerous times in Cora's life—and, instead, she was born in Brooklyn, New York, not nearly so romantic sounding a birthplace as Johannesburg, the center of both diamond and gold rushes in the late nineteenth century. But the outbreak of the Second Boer War (1899–2002)—one of the first major military clashes of the twentieth century—would force her family to flee southern Africa and seek temporary refuge with her mother's father, stepmother, and siblings in Brooklyn.[3]

Cora's parents had met in Heidelberg, Germany, in 1895. Jean—a stylish young multilingual Swiss explorer and entrepreneur—had recently returned from the Transvaal in southern Africa to visit family members in Switzerland and Germany. While visiting friends in Heidelberg, he was introduced to Mattie Schreiber, a very attractive young American woman traveling with her German American father, American stepmother, and younger siblings. (Her own mother, Cora Horton Schreiber, had died in

1890 when Mattie, the first of four children, was twelve.) It was love at first sight, and the couple was married in Heidelberg soon thereafter. On the back of a photo of her mother from that time period, Cora penned, "Perhaps in year she and Father spent 'cutting capers all over Europe' after their marriage."[4] Following their European honeymoon, Jean took Mattie back to the Transvaal in southern Africa. He was twenty-six and Mattie seventeen.

Cora grew up hearing the stories of her parents' sojourn in Johannesburg. In 1891 her father had followed his older brother Philippe to the Transvaal, the northeast part of southern Africa where the Boers had established a republic. Jean was the second son of prosperous parents from the French-speaking canton of Neuchâtel, Switzerland, and was studying law at the University of Neuchâtel when his brother enticed him to southern Africa. Philippe, with the help of his father and other Swiss investors, had leased land from Cecil Rhodes—the British diamond miner, financier, and statesman—to run cattle, develop salt plants, and explore for minerals. Due to the discovery in the Transvaal of huge diamond deposits in 1868, and gold in 1886, many young Europeans were flocking to where fortunes could be made in these valuable minerals and related trades.

Jean, at the age of twenty-three, joined his brother and spent several years exploring the Limpopo River basin in what was then the northeast corner of the Transvaal and the southwest corner of Portuguese Mozambique, looking for phosphate deposits and other minerals.[5] In 1895, having accumulated some wealth, he took a trip home and met Cora's mother. When they returned together to Johannesburg, it was to a town that had grown to more than one hundred thousand residents, only a small fraction of whom were citizens due to the recent waves of immigration by foreign adventurers and speculators.[6] Mattie, at seventeen, was put in charge of a large home with numerous African servants while her husband and brother-in-law traveled, scouring the countryside for gold and other minerals.[7] It must have been both exciting and challenging for this adventurous, young American woman with only a grammar-school education. Despite her lack of formal schooling, Mattie was fluent in both English and German, knew some French, had been exposed to other cultures through travel, and was a person of strong will. She also had a sister-in-law living

1. Jean Du Bois as a young man. Cora Alice Du Bois Papers (SPEC.COLL.ETHG.D852C), Tozzer Library, Harvard College Library, Harvard University.

2. Mattie Du Bois as a young woman. Cora Alice Du Bois Papers (SPEC.COLL.ETHG. D852C), Tozzer Library, Harvard College Library, Harvard University.

nearby. Philippe had married the preceding year in Durban, Natal, and he and his wife also lived in Johannesburg.

In 1897, two years after their arrival in the Transvaal, Mattie gave birth to their first child, Jean Claude, Cora's older brother. What was intended to be a prolonged sojourn in this part of the world, however, where both Du Bois brothers would make their fortunes, was abruptly eclipsed by the outbreak two years later of a treacherous three-year war between British imperial forces and Boer guerrilla soldier-farmers. The diamond and gold rushes had produced tensions between Britain, which was competing with other European powers for control of southern Africa, and Boer settlers who, together with native populations, inhabited this suddenly valuable region of Africa. Britain decided to take steps to control the entire region.

Only fragments of information remain about Jean and Mattie Du Bois from this period. When the British invaded the Transvaal, Jean and Philippe put their wives and infant sons on a ship back to Europe to get them out of harm's way, but not long thereafter they also had to flee, leaving behind their land and investments. Arriving back in Europe penniless, they were not popular with their Swiss relatives who had invested in their South African enterprises.[8] Probably with the help of his younger brother Georges, Philippe was able to find work in London, where he and his wife lived permanently. Jean also went to London temporarily but then found employment, in 1900, with a French company that was mining phosphate in Florida and Tennessee, which brought him to the United States for the first time. Meanwhile, Mattie and Claude had sought refuge with her father, stepmother, and younger siblings in Brooklyn, where Mattie's father, a prosperous dentist, also owned a restaurant and department store. Once Jean arrived in the United States, Mattie and Claude accompanied him to Florida and Tennessee for several years. However, when the mining operations did not materialize into a secure job, the Du Boises returned to Brooklyn, where Mattie's father helped Jean find a job as a bank clerk; hence their residence in Brooklyn when Cora arrived in 1903.[9]

Cora Alice Du Bois may have arrived during an unsettled and economically difficult period for her parents, but she was born into two strong family lineages—one based in the United States and the other in Europe.

3. Cora Du Bois as a baby with brother, Claude, Brooklyn, 1903. Cora Alice Du Bois Papers (SPEC.COLL.ETHG.D852C), Tozzer Library, Harvard College Library, Harvard University.

The Du Bois family from which Cora is descended has roots that can be traced back for centuries in the canton of Neuchâtel, Switzerland, but it also has branches that have spread worldwide. It is a family of merchants, watchmakers, and international explorers, businessmen and professionals who have traveled the globe, and yet with many remaining rooted in one small town, and surrounding vicinities, in Switzerland. The town is Le Locle, located within a few miles of the French border in the Jura Mountains of northwest Switzerland and renowned for its two centuries of watch- and clock making. In fact, in 2009 it became a UNESCO World Heritage site. There is evidence of Du Boises living in Le Locle since the early sixteenth century, probably having migrated there from southern France for religious reasons. An impressive family genealogy and history traces its roots back to a Jaquet DuBoz in 1507 and works its way forward to 1986.[10] Although Cora took only a minimal interest in her family genealogy, she grew up knowing many of her Swiss relatives and hearing tales of their adventures. She visited them as a young child and again when she graduated from high school, and she maintained correspondence with many of them throughout her life. Cora always said that her inclinations to travel and explore the world came from her Swiss side.

Cora's father, Jean, grew up mostly in Le Locle, today one of Switzerland's smallest cities with a population of just over ten thousand residents. It still has the feeling of a village, with churches, shops, and restaurants clustered together in a narrow valley surrounded by homes perched on mountain slopes. Two Du Bois homes remain intact—one, a nineteenth-century manor set high on a hill overlooking the town; the other, a four-story, eighteenth-century home-cum-watchmaking-atelier located mid-town, across from a central square with an imposing church and clock tower. The former, the Chateau des Monts, has become a premier horological (clock and timekeeping) museum. The latter, known locally as "La Maison Du Bois," has recently been turned into a small bed and breakfast that is owned and operated by the wife of the last male descendant of Philippe Du Bois & Fils, the oldest watchmaking firm in Switzerland.[11] It was built in 1785 to house the family on its upper two floors, reserving the second floor for business offices and the first floor for assembling watches. Until watchmaking factories were introduced, watch parts were made by individual farmer-craftsmen scattered throughout the surrounding hills and mountains. The parts would then be gathered together and assembled into watches in Le Locle and, once assembled, would be exported to such commercial centers as London, Amsterdam, and Frankfurt, which required travel by this branch of Du Boises.

Although Cora's father, Jean, was not a member of the watchmaking branch of the Du Bois family, his father—Philippe Henri Du Bois—was engaged in commerce that took him regularly to Frankfurt am Main, which was a free city until 1881 and hence an attractive location for international business. In fact, Jean's mother—Louise Philippine Andreae—was from Frankfurt and several of his seven siblings were born there. Philippe Du Bois & Fils kept a home and offices in Frankfurt, which still stand today and which served as a family base for various members of the Du Bois clan. Eventually, Jean's younger brother Georges would also settle in Frankfurt, marrying a member of the Andreae family, and would provide yet another home for visiting Du Boises, including Cora when she was seventeen.

Jean and his four brothers lived international lives. As already mentioned, his older brother Philippe settled permanently in London after fleeing southern Africa. Jean would make several international moves during his lifetime. Albert, the third-oldest Du Bois brother, who had a degree in agriculture from the prestigious Swiss Federal Institute of Technology, spent twelve years in Santo Domingo, the Dominican Republic, overseeing the cocoa and sugar plantations that supplied the Suchard chocolate manufacturing company in Neuchâtel. When he returned home, he became the technical director of the Suchard chocolate plant in Lörrach, Germany—the first Swiss chocolate factory to be established abroad, in this case just across the border from Basel, Switzerland.

The fourth-oldest Du Bois brother, Georges, was perhaps the most distinguished. He first studied at the Royal Academy of Mines in Freiberg, Germany, during which time he participated in a three-year expedition to Surinam, where he gathered geological and ethnographic collections now housed in museums in The Hague and Neuchâtel. Then he completed a PhD in chemistry at Rostock University in Germany, followed by travels to much of Asia, including stops in North America on the way home to visit mines in California, Nevada, Utah, and parts of Canada. In 1905 Georges settled in Frankfurt am Main, Germany, where he married and became a director of the Deutsche Gold-und Silber-Scheideanstalt. Later known by the acronym DEGUSSA, it was a metallurgical and chemical company founded in 1840 by Friedrich Ernst Roessler in the then–Free City of Frankfurt. In addition to his business responsibilities, Georges became a diplomat and was in charge of the Swiss consulate in Frankfurt. He and his family resided there in an imposing home facing the Main River until his retirement in 1933, when he returned to Switzerland. He and his wife settled in his parents' home, the Villa Montperreux, next door to his brother Albert, in Peseux—a small town perched on a hill overlooking the city of Neuchâtel with its spectacular setting on the banks of Lake Neuchâtel. These stately homes, with lovely views of the lake, had gardens that sloped down to vineyards, which grew on the hills surrounding the town and lake. Peseux is not far from the family's origins in Le Locle and is where Cora visited her grandparents when she was a young child and, again, in her youth.

Jean's youngest brother, Hugues, also had a successful business career, in Frankfurt, Paris, and New York City, but died, unmarried, at a relatively early age at the onset of the First World War. Of Jean's three sisters, one also died young. The other two both married—one to a Protestant minister and the other to a medical doctor—and settled permanently in Switzerland. It was an era when sons, not daughters, went abroad to study and make their fortune.

The Schreiber Family

By contrast with her paternal lineage, which can trace its roots back to the sixteenth century in one small town in Switzerland, Cora Du Bois's maternal lineage is, in many respects, typically American. Her maternal grandfather, Henry William Schreiber I, was born in Germany in 1856, emigrated to New York as a youth with only a third-grade education, became apprenticed to a dentist, and married into an already established American family of British and Scottish Presbyterian ancestry. He became a self-made man who by the time of Cora's birth was well established in Brooklyn with several business enterprises. Despite his limited formal education, he became the commissioner of education for the city of Brooklyn.[12]

Becoming a dentist in the nineteenth century was very different from today. There were no schools of dentistry; instead, one became an apprentice and learned by doing—that is, by extracting, drilling, and filling teeth in an era before electricity or anesthetics. And one traveled to one's clients in the countryside by horse and buggy, rather than expecting them to come to offices in the city. On one such trip to Englishtown, a small rural settlement in the borough of Monmouth, New Jersey, Henry met the woman who, in 1877, would become his first wife, Cora Horton.[13] Henry was twenty-one and Cora was seventeen—the same age that her daughter Mattie would be at the time of her marriage eighteen years later.

There is nothing comparable to the detailed Du Bois family history and genealogy for the Schreiber family, which was a blend of different immigrant groups in the nineteenth-century United States. It is noteworthy, however, that Cora Horton's family dates back to prerevolutionary times in this region of New Jersey and that one of Cora Du Bois's first cousins was, accordingly, able to join the Sons of the American Revolution. He remembered, as a young man, that Cora's mother, Mattie, had been invited to join the Daughters of the American Revolution but had refused when she learned that, in 1939, the group had refused permission for Marion Anderson to sing to an integrated audience in their Constitution Hall in Washington DC. "Aunt Mattie," he reported, "said, 'I don't want to have any part of that organization if they did what they did to Marion Anderson. That's the end [of the discussion].'" The same cousin went on to say, "[Aunt Mattie] was the most independent character in the entire family."[14]

It seems that the family was filled with independent women—from Cora Horton, who married a poorly educated German immigrant and moved with him from her rural home in New Jersey to Brooklyn; to Mattie Schreiber, who, while vacationing in Germany, married a Swiss explorer-entrepreneur and traveled to an adventurous life in South Africa; to Cora Du Bois, whose career as an anthropologist and World War II intelligence officer would take her to many different parts of the world and, ultimately, to a prestigious, groundbreaking appointment at Harvard University. Cora's strong will and thriftiness, she said, came from her mother's side of the family.

Henry Schreiber and Cora Horton had four children—Mattie, Lisa, Henry II, and George, all of whom married and lived in the area during portions of Cora Du Bois's childhood. Thus she had a close set of relatives in Switzerland and Germany, whom she came to know when her parents moved to France during her early childhood, and another set in New York when her parents returned to the United States when Cora was eight.

Early Years in St. Quentin, France

Cora's first years were spent in Brooklyn, where her family resided in a brownstone close to her Schreiber relatives. She had only two poignant memories from that time period: one, the death of two pet rabbits that she had been given one Easter; the other, her family's departure for France when she was four and a half. Both were unsettling memories—the grief of losing pets and the uncertainty of moving to an unknown land from which she might not return. More specifically, the latter memory was of Cora's mother telling her, as their ship pulled out of New York Harbor and passed by the Statue of Liberty, "This is the Statue of Liberty. You may not see this again." It was a sufficiently disturbing remark for a small child that Cora remembered it in old age and viewed the voyage to France as a transition to a "new, perplexing, lonely" world.[15]

A photo of Cora and her older brother, Claude, taken shortly before their departure in April 1908 belies the apprehension she felt. It shows a young, smiling child dressed smartly in a dark coat decorated on the front with four big white buttons. On the back of her head is a large, puffy, beret-style hat that accentuates her short, wavy brown hair, which is decorated with a big white bow. On her feet Cora wears shiny black patent leather shoes over white leggings. Looking stylish and ready for adventure, she gazes directly at the camera. Next to her, with his arm on his sister's back, stands an unsmiling, ten-year-old Claude, dressed in a well-cut dark suit, with short pants and a tie. While he may be touching his little sister, his gaze is averted from both her and the camera.

For Cora's parents, it must also have been an unsettling moment. They were setting off to an uncertain job and future in an unfamiliar town in France, and what might have been just another adventure together was complicated by the presence of two young, school-age children. They were, however, well feted by the Schreiber clan, who gave a gala farewell dinner in their honor, with printed menus and a bon voyage card signed by all.[16]

4. Cora and Claude Du Bois about to board ship in New York City, 1908. Cora Alice Du Bois Papers (SPEC.COLL.ETHG.D852c), Tozzer Library, Harvard College Library, Harvard University.

What took the Du Bois family to St. Quentin, France, in the spring of 1908 was the opportunity for Cora's father to oversee the building and management of a chemical factory there called Produits Chimiques de l'Aisne, a subsidiary of Deutsche Gold-und Silber-Scheideanstalt, the company for which his brother Georges was now a director in Frankfurt. Georges had helped arrange for this opportunity, and for several months Jean would live for a while in Frankfurt with Georges and his family and then alone in St. Quentin while permits for factory construction were finalized. First, however, upon landing in Le Havre, France, Jean took his wife and children by train to Switzerland to stay with his parents in Peseux. It was to be a difficult period of separation and adjustment for all of them.

Jean's letters to his wife, Mattie, have survived from this period and offer a glimpse into these family arrangements.[17] Mattie was unhappy and homesick much of the time, and Jean wrote her frequent letters of solicitude, encouraging her to be patient while he got affairs settled in St. Quentin. In a combination of fluent English and French, he described in detail what that city was like, the difficulties he was having with the French bureaucracy in getting permits, the kinds of housing and schooling arrangements he was trying to make for his family, and his worries about their finances. He gave Mattie advice about how to dress for a Swiss wedding so as not to look too ostentatious and wealthy, which they were not, and how to handle certain difficult people whom she would meet. And he tried to reassure her about his health when he was suffering from bronchitis and having some difficulty breathing. In what would be prophetic, Jean reported that the doctor who treated him in Frankfurt had told him that the Andreae family, his maternal side, suffered from this indisposition because they smoked too much. The doctor's advice was to take up smoking a few cigars a day and no cigarettes.

Mostly, however, Jean was concerned about the well-being of his wife and children. He regularly asked about the children and how their French lessons were coming along in preparation for attending school in St. Quentin. He urged Mattie to have Claude keep a daily journal that he could send as a letter to his father at the end of each week. In addition, Jean wanted to see his son use longer sentences so that he could "better shape his ideas" and "develop coherence of thought." Little Cora he warmly referred to "as a pet."

After two months of living alone in St. Quentin, Jean grew impatient with the numerous obstacles he faced with the French government bureaucracy in getting permits for construction of a new factory. On July 19, 1908, he wrote to Mattie, "Now it is war! And we have to fight to the finish. You know how much I have at heart to be successful; it means our meeting so much sooner—and our whole future. Therefore, you can realize that I will leave nothing undone." The opportunity of managing a chemical factory in St. Quentin was Jean's second chance at financial and professional success after losing his fortune in South Africa. While living in the United States, he had just eked out a living and had had to borrow money from his father and his brother Georges to make the move to France. Financial difficulties were very much on his mind as he struggled over which house to lease in St. Quentin and how to furnish it, but he kept Mattie engaged in the process by teasing her about furniture decisions that he claimed to be making, knowing full well that she would object. And she did. He also worried about hiring a maid for her—an expense that they could ill afford at first but that he believed his wife would need to maintain a three-story house without American amenities, such as running water on the upper two floors. On August 4, 1908, Jean wrote to Mattie, happily announcing that the permit papers had finally been signed and that he was making arrangements for her and the children to come to Paris by train, where he would meet them and bring them to St. Quentin. The family's three-month separation was to end.

St. Quentin is a small industrial city, with a population today of fifty-five thousand, situated in the Picardy region of northern France, equidistant from Paris to the south and Brussels to the north. It sits on a low hill overlooking the Somme River. A massive gothic cathedral (the Basilica), severely damaged from two world wars, sits on top of the hill, together with an impressive city hall that opens onto a large plaza from which narrow streets radiate out and downward. As Jean described it to his family in 1908, the town was "old without being ancient, and with the exception of the city hall, the courthouse, and two theatres, it was not very architecturally interesting." At the top of the hill, the streets are lined with a mixture of multistory shops and residences that become increasingly residential as they fan out down the hill. Houses do not sit independently but share walls and have tiny gardens in the back. It is a pleasant working- and middle-class city with no luxury stores, hotels, or restaurants and no overt signs of wealth.

From 1908 to 1911 the Du Bois family lived in a comfortable, three-story home, the layout of which Jean had sketched and sent to Mattie in Switzerland—something that, in later life, Cora would also do. (She always sent her mother a sketched layout of the house in which she lived and, ultimately, a floor plan of her own home in Cambridge, Massachusetts.) It was a larger and more expensive house than Jean would have preferred to rent, but their residence had to be consistent with his new managerial position and their social status in town. Soon after their arrival Claude began attending a local French lycée (secondary school), headed by a Protestant minister whose name was Monsieur Saint d'Afrique—something Jean joked about in a letter to Mattie. "This is his actual name," he wrote. "What do you think of a Protestant minister to be called a 'Saint.'" The headmaster, Jean continued, had assured him the school would adequately prepare Claude for his baccalaureate (the equivalent of an American high school degree), which would gain him entrance to any university. Clearly Jean was very concerned with his son's education and professional future.

Cora's schooling seems to have been less a concern to her father, but then she was a much younger child and also a girl, who was not expected to be preparing for a profession. She was enrolled in a private Catholic girls school where, as she reported in later life, she felt shunned by the other children.

> I was isolated there from anybody my own age. In the school, I was treated snubbingly, I would say, by the little girls in my class, though the teacher was perfectly fair and kind. There was no attempt at conversion, but you were given your "bon point" if you made a good recitation. You got a little card, which was a religious scene, and when you got 10 of those, you got something else. And it was customary in those French schools, when the year ended, everybody got a prize of some sort or the other, so I got my prize. Mother didn't help the situation at all. You wore a black coverall apron to school. Mother didn't think that was healthy or something, and so I had a white one that just made me stand out even more explicitly.[18]

Not only did Cora wear an inappropriately colored apron, but she had trouble with the gender of French nouns, which, to her great embarrassment, produced laughs from the other children. "To this day," she reported, "I don't know whether it is *le tortu* or *la tortu* [tortoise], but anyhow I got the wrong gender and titter, titter, titter."[19] Nonetheless, the immersion-style schooling, combined with her parents' use of French at home, soon made Cora fluent in French.

At home, the Du Bois's French-speaking maid, Alice, became Cora's closest friend and nurturer during these lonely years. Claude was too much older to be much of a playmate, and he was experiencing adjustment problems that manifested themselves in fights with boys at school and disobedient behavior at home. Mattie was a severe disciplinarian who was not averse to using corporal punishment. One of Cora's early, painful memories from this period was seeing her mother physically beat her naked brother while he was on his hands and knees.[20] Her father, she recalled in later life, was not a disciplinarian.[21] That he was aware of Mattie's use of physical punishment, however, is reflected in a solicitous but teasing letter that he sent to her in Switzerland upon learning that she had broken her wrist. "I know you are well cared for but that does not alleviate the pain which must be terrible. How did it happen? You don't say a word about it. Not in slapping Claudy's face? Why, you won't be so quick anymore in the future about your slaps, right and left, of which you were so proud, owing to the promptness with which they were delivered."[22]

During these years in St. Quentin, Cora's father, a seemingly kind and caring man, was preoccupied with his enormous responsibilities in establishing a new chemical company, which would be critical to his and his family's future. The weight of those responsibilities was even heavier knowing that the success of the factory would also reflect on his brother Georges, to whom he was greatly indebted. Meanwhile, Mattie was undoubtedly under the strain of managing a home and family in a new country, and in a different language and culture, where she was required to entertain her husband's business associates in a suitable manner. As a consequence, Cora felt somewhat abandoned by her parents and turned to Alice, the family maid, for comfort.

Alice, a rural Picardy peasant who was married but whose three-year-old daughter had recently died, quickly took over mothering Cora. In her reminiscences of this period, Cora wrote, "Alice and I loved each other. . . . Alice was my solace in those three formative years."[23] Cora recalled riding on Alice's shoulders down the main boulevard of St. Quentin to see the French cavalry and marching soldiers, while singing the "Marseillaise," in celebration of the end of the French-Prussian war. Alice also took Cora to see the Catholic bishop when he visited St. Quentin and to kiss his ring. And Alice introduced her to mushroom hunting in the woods outside her home village. These were some of Cora's special recollections of Alice.

Mostly, however, Alice was Cora's friend and surrogate mother, and it was with Alice that she spent time every day when she returned home from school. They missed one another deeply when Mattie took Cora and Claude to Switzerland for summer vacations. For example, in a July 1910 letter that Jean sent to his family, he wrote, "Alice wants to write you a letter too, but she says she does not know how to express her wishes. I told her to write what was in her heart without troubling about correct sentences and orthography. Poor girl, she is not consoled yet and seems very lonely. She says, 'Cora always used to come straight to the kitchen when she arrived from school, and after being a while upstairs she came back to me, and we used to talk all the time; now I have nobody to talk to.'"[24]

Despite her loneliness at school, Cora flourished academically and received all "firsts" (the top grade) on her annual report card. Claude received a "first" in German, three "mentions," and a note of commendation that seemed to satisfy his father. In July of that year Jean wrote to his wife, who was vacationing in Switzerland with the children, to report on "Claudy's yearly report" and to say, "please let the children have a couple of weeks entire holiday if the weather permits, and not bother them with lessons and piano exercise."[25] Clearly, he was deeply engaged with their schooling and knew how strict Mattie was inclined to be with their lessons.

For three years the Du Bois family settled into life in St. Quentin, France, with visits to relatives in Switzerland during vacation periods and the expectation that their future would be in France. Then came rumblings of war—Germany's buildup to World War I—and the closure of Produits Chimiques de L'Aisne in France. Jean was transferred to the United States, where another subsidiary of DEGUSSA was located, and in 1911 the Du Boises left France for Perth Amboy, New Jersey. It was a fortunate move because in September 1914 the Germans invaded St. Quentin, and the city endured a harsh occupation throughout the war.[26]

Once again Cora's family was displaced by war, but this time they returned to the United States with greater economic security. And once again the young Cora Du Bois had to shift allegiances from one country, language, and culture to another, but these would not be her biggest challenges.

The Move to Perth Amboy, New Jersey

Upon the family's return to the United States in 1911, Jean Du Bois joined the Roessler and Hasslacher Chemical Company, an American subsidiary of Deutsche Gold-und Silber-Scheideanstalt that had been established in Perth Amboy in 1885. One of its major products was a preparation called "liquid gold"—a viscous liquid suitable for applying to porcelain and enamel, a profitable venture in an era of Victorian decoration.[27] Jean became the company's business manager, a position he would hold until his untimely death in 1922. In the course of those years he would also become vice president of the Perth Amboy Board of Trade, director of the New Jersey Manufacturers Casualty Insurance Company, and a leader in the development of the Perth Amboy waterfront.[28] In addition, he finished the law degree that he had never completed when he left the University of Neuchâtel to seek his fortune in South Africa. For Cora's father the years in Perth Amboy were ones of professional success and economic prosperity.

The move to Perth Amboy, New Jersey, put the Du Boises in another small industrial town not unlike St. Quentin, France. It had a population, in 1911, of about thirty-five thousand. (A century later, it has grown to only forty-eight thousand.) Instead of being situated on a river, however, Perth Amboy is a seaport, with deepwater docks, located directly across from Staten Island and Manhattan, New York. Driven by the railroad and coal industries in the early twentieth century, Perth Amboy became an attractive location for a variety of industries, such as the Guggenheim copper refineries, that required transporting ores and manufactured goods by both railroad and ship. Between 1900 and 1910 Perth Amboy grew by 80 percent as it attracted many such industries and an immigrant labor population.[29] Today Perth Amboy remains a working-class town, although some of the waterfront that once housed boat docks, ship building, and factories has, with the skyrocketing value of waterfront property, been turned into homes and condominiums.

Initially, after their arrival back in the United States and until they found suitable housing in Perth Amboy, the Du Boises stayed in Brooklyn with Mattie's brother and sister-in-law, Henry and Anna Schreiber, and their two sons, Henry and William. Cora's cousin Henry would become one of her favorite playmates. And once the Du Boises acquired their own lovely home, it would become the center of Schreiber family gatherings.

For the remainder of Cora's childhood, the Du Boises would reside at 105 High Street in Perth Amboy. High Street is a broad tree-lined avenue that rises up from the waterfront to the top of a small hill where the town's eighteenth-century city hall sits on a square with a set of imposing homes. Unlike St. Quentin, however, there is no grand basilica and open plaza. The Du Bois home would have, in its day, been considered large and imposing. A three-story Victorian—surrounded on all sides by big verandahs and set in a large garden—it is still standing on the second block above the waterfront. It was a spacious home with an enormous dining room that had hand-hewn wooden beams and provided an excellent place for Schreiber family holiday parties and other entertaining. It also had hidden stairwells to upper floors where Cora and her cousins could play hide-and-seek and other games.[30] Furthermore, it stood next door to the Roessler home, putting the family in an elite neighborhood, separate from immigrant labor families. When Cora reflected on this stage of her childhood, she recalled that there were few suitable friends for her either in the neighborhood or at school.[31]

Cora's parents disagreed about which schools their children should attend. According to Cora, her father was reluctant to send his children to public schools in this somewhat rough, working-class town, but Mattie prevailed. She wanted her children to experience an American-style, democratic, public education. Accordingly, Cora was enrolled in the local grammar school, where she was placed in the first grade—two grades below her age-mates.[32] Once again, but only temporarily, she was an outsider with inadequate language skills. Cora's diary—"Diary of a real Tom-girl"—indicates that she advanced rapidly during her first year of school, getting moved to the fourth grade, and by 1915, when she was eleven, she was in the seventh grade. In her April 21, 1915, journal entry—in

5. The Du Bois family home in Perth Amboy, New Jersey. Cora Alice Du Bois Papers (SPEC.COLL.ETHG.D852c), Tozzer Library, Harvard College Library, Harvard University.

greatly improved penmanship—Cora proudly wrote, "I was in fourth grade when I began my diary, I'm in seventh now, I skipted [*sic*] fifth grade so I am even with Helen [a school friend]. I've been in her class two years. Mother is giving me a cent every time I write [in my diary] so I'll get seven cents a week plus fifteen cents for pocket money. . . . Father gives me five cents for every 'one' I get on my report card and ten off for every 'three' and nothing for 'twos.' I got a quarter on my last card."[33]

Cora was being rewarded for academic excellence as well as for practice in writing—something that her father considered very important. His conviction that skilled writing helped to shape one's ideas and to develop coherent thought was something that became well instilled in Cora Du Bois and that she, in turn, tried to instill in her students.

Cora's diary also provides glimpses into her tomboyish inclinations. She frequently mentions playing basketball with neighborhood boys and going fishing down on the wharves. During one summer, when away at camp, Cora wrote home asking that her basketball be sent to her.[34] Occasionally, her outdoor activities and explorations would get her into some kind of difficulty. For example, in her April 21, 1910, diary entry, Cora wrote, "Just two weeks ago I had my finger wedged in Mrs. Dills [*sic*] barn out at Woodbridge between the ax and the wall and was kept in the barn an hour that way, a few days later I got a fish hook in the same finger on the other hand and I had to go to the doctors [*sic*] to have it taken out." That particular journal entry continues with a disappointed description of going fishing but catching only shrimp that "clung to the bait."[35]

One of Cora's playmates, her cousin Henry, recalled that they built forts together, climbed trees, and went swimming. According to Henry, on one occasion Cora climbed so high into a tree that she had trouble descending and the fire department had to be called to help her down. On another occasion, Cora, who was three years older than Henry and a strong swimmer, grew impatient with her cousin's fear of the water and reluctance to swim, so she pushed him into the water, saying, "Darn you, swim!" And he did. Henry remembered Cora as a "real tomboy" and, in later life, as "the star of the family."[36] A love of the outdoors and of athletic activities, together with a willingness to take occasional risks, would characterize much of Cora Du Bois's life.

Henry remembered his Aunt Mattie as a wonderful cook and entertainer but also as a strict disciplinarian. For example, if any of the children did not finish the food on their plates, it returned for the next meal and the next, until it was consumed. Another Schreiber cousin remembered her as quite stern. "She was actually giving the back of her hand to the children very often. That was her method of discipline. She wouldn't stand for anything. She was a super person. We had so much respect for her, every one of us, I think. But we didn't like her so much."[37] Clearly these nephews had mixed feelings about their stern aunt, but they also had fond memories of family dinner parties that she put on, with the help of a Danish maid, and they were impressed by her informative conversations. "Conversations with Aunt Mattie were generally on an intellectual plane. She didn't have much to do with small talk. It always had to be something important that she talked about. She could discourse at considerable length on many subjects."[38] One gets the impression from these memories of a no-nonsense woman who was both respected and feared by her young nephews.

Mattie was a woman with little formal education but considerable experience. And her role as the wife of a prominent business manager in St. Quentin, France, and then Perth Amboy, New Jersey, had trained her to be an able cook, entertainer, and household manager. However, like her cousins, Cora did not find her mother particularly congenial. "Mother was a person to whom I related much less warmly than I did to my father," she recalled. In fact, Cora used even harsher language, characterizing her mother as "a street angel and a home devil"—that is, someone who, like her own father (Cora's maternal grandfather), was pleasant with outsiders but a tyrant at home.[39]

Cora's relationship with her mother was a complex and ambivalent one that was deeply affected by her mother's inconsistent and harsh treatment of her brother, Claude, and by her occasional insensitive treatment of her daughter. The memories of loneliness and abandonment by her mother in St. Quentin, together with the anxiety produced by her mother's physical beating of her brother, lingered with Cora into old age. And in her adolescence other mother-daughter problems emerged.

Meanwhile, however, Claude was exhibiting increased behavioral problems, for which his mother would punish him but then try to protect him when Cora's father became engaged in disciplining his son. A handsome photo of the family standing together on the steps of their imposing home belies the evolving interpersonal dynamics of their home life. Cora, instead of having an older brother whom she could admire and who, in turn, would be protective of her, had an increasingly antisocial sibling—one whom she would later describe as "a psychopathic personality."[40] Claude was exhibiting the antithesis of the Protestant ethic that Cora says her family tried to instill in them. Instead of working hard at

6. The Du Bois family on the steps of their Perth Amboy home, ca. 1912. Cora Alice Du Bois Papers (SPEC.COLL.ETHG.D852c), Tozzer Library, Harvard College Library, Harvard University.

school and helping at home, he refused to do his homework much of the time, was uncooperative at home, got into fights with other boys, and began to steal things. As an adult, he emerged into a small-scale con man—someone who, seemingly lacking in conscience, wrote bad checks and tried to deceive others into lending him money or investing in bogus operations.

Cora's uncle Albert Du Bois may have intuited something about Claude's nature when he reported to his brother Jean, after first meeting Claude in Switzerland in 1910, that it was "too bad he's a boy who is not more open and trusting." At the time Jean responded defensively. As he reported in a letter to Mattie, "I answered him immediately that if Claudy was such, it was due to circumstances preceding his birth and that I was more responsible for his character than himself."[41] Little did he know how problematic Claude was to become.

For Cora, Claude became the antagonist against whom she defined herself. If he was going to be the bad child who gave his parents undue trouble, then she was going be "the good little girl" who tried to please them. If he refused to do his schoolwork, then she would do hers thoroughly. As she reported later in life, "I formed myself in opposition to this naughty boy, and I was going to be a good girl, by heavens."[42] So Cora excelled at school, dutifully practiced the piano, and wrote in her diary, but she also found ways to escape. Outdoor, "boyish" activities that took her away from home became one form of escape. Another was learning to distance herself emotionally from her brother's antagonistic behavior and her mother's tirades.

As Cora once related it to me, "I became something of a distant observer of human affairs and found a kindred spirit in Sir Roger de Coverley."[43] To watch rather than engage in the emotional dramas between her mother and brother became a goal—one well suited to her later vocation, anthropology, as well. While still in grammar school, she discovered Sir Roger de Coverley in a small book to which the local Perth Amboy librarian had introduced her. Entitled *Days with Sir Roger de Coverley*, it is a set of witty, fable-like morality tales written by two late seventeenth- to early eighteenth-century writers, Joseph Addison and Richard Steele, and published in their British daily, the *Spectator*, in 1711–12. For the purpose of satirizing landed country gentlemen of that era, Addison and Steele created the character Sir Roger de Coverley, a benign knight who lived on his country estate surrounded by devoted servants and local parishioners. His family consisted of "sober and staid persons" who did not include a wife or children. He preferred to surround himself with "person[s] of good sense and some learning."[44] It is likely, however, that the "kindred spirit" that Cora alluded to was not so much Sir Roger de Coverley as it was the authors' fictional narrator, Mr. Spectator, who describes and comments on the habits, foibles, and social faux pas of his fellow citizens—in this case, country gentry. What Cora liked about these stories, I suspect, was their emotionally distanced and ironic tone, a voice that she would learn to cultivate.

Despite Cora's efforts to distance herself emotionally from her mother and brother, tension in the family built. In 1916, upon the recommendation of a physician, Claude was sent to a military-style boarding school for boys and Cora was sent to Arkansas for a two-month period to stay with a close family friend. On January 18, 1916, when she was twelve, Cora typed the following entry in her diary: "This is an introduction to my [diary]. I have not kept it for quite a while, so I am starting again as mother and I are going south for two months. I intend to study down there. Sister Fay is going to tutor me. The teacher said that every two weeks she would send me the schedule of the work done by the class. I think I will be able to keep up."[45]

The trip to Monticello, Arkansas—a small, rural town with a population of about twenty-four hundred people—was intended to give everyone some emotional relief. Claude would be in a more formally structured environment without his familiar antagonists, and Cora would get to visit a family friend to whom she felt "passionately devoted."[46] "Sister Fay" seems to have been the nickname that Cora used for a woman whom the Du Boises had met on ship during their return to the United States in 1911. As a single woman who owned and managed her own farms in Arkansas, she provided Cora with a different role model, that of an independent woman. This period of family separation was also intended to provide Cora's father with some quiet time during which he could get medical attention for throat and lung problems that he was experiencing.

Unfortunately, Cora seems not to have maintained her diary while in Arkansas, but we do know something about her stay there from existent correspondence with her father. On March 6, 1916, for example, Jean wrote the following to his daughter:

Dear Little Cora:

I thank you very much for your "jumbled" letter of the 29th of February and I am very glad to see that you [are having] such a good time in Monticello. I am also glad to know that you are doing well with your school lessons and your drawing lessons; I am anxious to receive some drawings of yours which were sent, according to Mother's letter of the 3rd, under separate cover. I will write again as soon as I receive them.

It is indeed very lucky for me that you were not here when I went hunting in the back yard of the Club [Jean's men's club, where he resided during his family's absence]; otherwise you would have surely spanked me as you say in your letter.

Now I am going to tell you about my trip to Peddie Institute last Saturday afternoon . . . where I went to see Claude to make arrangements for his Easter holidays.

Jean proceeds to tell his daughter about how Claude is doing academically and otherwise at his new boarding school, including sending Claude's report card to share with her mother, and concludes,

I will not say to you to be a good little girl as I know that you do all you can to please your parents.

With love and kisses,
Your old father, Jean Du Bois.[47]

The letter illustrates the warmth and intimacy of this father-daughter relationship. Jean teases his daughter about her imperfect, "jumbled" prose, once again emphasizing the importance of clear writing, but at the same time he praises her schoolwork and art. The letter also contains humor with regard to his hunting proclivities, of which he knew Cora did not approve. Cora's father also treats her as a confidante in discussing with her Claude's adaptation to his new school and in seeking her opinion of the Easter vacation arrangements that he is making for her brother. And he concludes by praising her for being such a good daughter to her parents.

Cora enjoyed this stay in Monticello, Arkansas, with Sister Fay. While there, among other things, she learned to horseback ride—a sport that she would return to as a graduate student at UC Berkeley. This period of familial separation did not, however, resolve Claude's problems. The following year, in 1917, he dropped out of school and joined the war effort—first enlisting in the army, from which he was quickly discharged, and then joining the merchant marines. Among Cora's family photos is one of her parents vacationing in Bermuda in 1917, labeled "a bad time for them due to Claude's difficulties."[48]

World War I was on everyone's minds. The Roessler and Hasslacher Chemical Company, as a German-owned company, came under suspicion and was legally transferred to American ownership in February 1917, just a few months before the United States officially entered the war. Fortunately, this did not affect Jean Du Bois's position in the company. By 1915 he had become an American citizen and had been approached by the U.S. government to do intelligence work in Europe. There is evidence that he traveled to France that year and again to France and Switzerland in June and July 1919—when the Treaty of Versailles was being signed to end the war—but what clandestine work, if any, he may have done is not known.[49]

Cora, who had begun writing poetry in grammar school, wrote about the war. One poem is about soldiers "meeting their fate in the battlefields of Europe." It also alludes to "the tortures" of war. Another poem, entitled "Christmas This Year," is about the irony of celebrating such a holiday in "a stricken world, an earth in chaos hurled" and one where "Our feast and joy a mockery seems."[50] A young Cora Du Bois had already learned to recognize, and express in poetry, some of the deep ironies of life—in this case, the ability to celebrate a religious holiday safely in the United States when so many other people in the world, including her own relatives in Europe, were suffering.

Following the war, Claude lived mostly away from home, returning periodically to ask for money or to have bad checks covered. Cora reported that her father "was much incensed by this behavior, but always bailed him out for the sake of family pride."[51] In the spring of 1921, when Cora was a senior in high school, Claude married Birdie Katherine Luedecke in Manor, Texas. The marriage lasted only a short time.

Coming of Age

In the fall of 1916 Cora turned thirteen, moving into adolescence and, the following year, into high school. Without the ongoing distraction of Claude, Mattie became more focused on her daughter and her daughter's physiological development. Cora continued to excel at school, but she also continued to be tomboyish in behavior, preferring outdoor sports and activities with other girls in the Campfire Girls—an organization in which she had become active—to trying to be attractive to boys or dating. According to Cora, her mother became deeply disconcerted about her daughter's physical and sexual maturation and even consulted a physician. From her mother's perspective, it seems, Cora was not emerging into a stereotypical pretty, young woman such as she, Mattie, had been, so she insisted on dressing Cora in fancy, frilly clothes, trying to make her look more overtly feminine. There is, for example, a portrait of Cora from this time period in which she is seated in a satin chair, wearing a long-sleeved dress with a lace shawl around her shoulders. Her wavy, light-brown hair hangs down to the middle of her back. The pose, dress, and hairstyle give Cora a demure look—that of an attractive girl on the edge of womanhood. However, from Cora's perspective, this was not an authentic look. These forms of maternal attention, coming at a particularly vulnerable age, made her "feel ugly"—an assessment that she thought her mother agreed with—and they made her "all the more stubborn and negativistic."[52] Cora, who had always been the good child, began to grow more strong-willed and antagonistic with her mother.

Cora left no diary for her high school years, but two poems that she wrote during this period offer some insight into the emotional turmoil she was experiencing. Not surprisingly, the topic of her poetry had shifted from war and other issues to love and friendship. They were handwritten, and I present them without any corrections:

UNTITLED
Love roams self-willed, inconstant, prey of time.
Without reason she shifts her searing flame
But to vanish more quickly than she came;
Her truest life is a poor poets rhyme.
Friendship grows more slowly, is strangely wise.

7. Cora Du Bois in adolescence, 1918. Cora Alice Du Bois Papers (SPEC.COLL.ETHG. D852c), Tozzer Library, Harvard College Library, Harvard University.

Love must surmount her very pinnacle
To aspire to the other's citadel;
For peace lies only in her profound eyes.
More holy Friendship than she born of foam,
Nurtured in cultured Greece and pass'nate Rome.
Love's deepest hope is that she yet may be
Capable of Friendships deep constancy;
Ah! Friendship is the only wedded whole
Of a purged love, lofty mind, and calm soul.[53]

UNTITLED
Orpheus! Inspire me with some faint breath of magic
That in Friendship's sacred name I may strike such cords
    Upon the Human heart
As those of Milton in resonant Lycidas;
For I too would humbly praise that stainless Goddess
    As Man's purest deity.
Bards have immortal made Rolland and Oliver;
Minnesingers and minstrels caroled silvered song
    To glory Friendship's name.
With us yet dwells the grey-eyed Goddess of the soul's love;
More holy she than treacherous Venus conceived
    In cultured, passionate, Greece.
Friendship walks ever with her head high above clouds,
Holds earth more firm than yore in meditative step,
    Raising high souls of men
Our modern cycle with shallow frivolous youth
Struggling madly, insatiably, for bitter dust,
    Has yet redeemed itself;
For that Goddess of man's best passion walks with us yet
Undeserted—nay more poignantly vigorous
    She sustains us ever.
Calm and unconcerned she abides joyfully here
· More imbedded than e'er before in human loves;
    She is a guiding star,
In whom my youth would gloriously wrap itself.

> To whom my age would confidently turn itself
>   For a most perfect peace.[54]

Underlying these rather abstract, emotionally distanced verses, there is evidence of emotional turbulence.[55] The poems provide a glimpse of a young, highly literate young woman who is struggling with the early vagaries of passionate love and who has seemingly chosen the safety of "calm" friendship over such love. In the second poem, for example, Cora characterizes youthful love as "shallow" and "frivolous," "struggling madly, insatiably, for bitter dust"—suggesting either unattainable or unrequited love that may have motivated her to "purge" passion in favor of "unstained" friendship. Given Cora's emerging sexual orientation—that of a lesbian—expressions of love for another young woman would have been socially dangerous, and such feelings would likely have produced conflicting emotions in her, especially given the pressure from her mother to become more overtly feminine and attractive to males.[56] This may be why she characterizes love as a dangerous emotion—"self-willed," "inconstant," and "without reason"—while romanticizing friendship as "strangely wise," profound, and calm. Friendship is even elevated to the status of a goddess—"Man's purest deity" and "man's best passion." Furthermore, Cora writes, "She [friendship] is a guiding star, In whom my youth would gloriously wrap itself." Friendship becomes both guide and solace—especially friendships with older women, such as Sister Fay and teachers who admired her intellect. Relationships with such women may have provided Cora a safe haven during these tumultuous years when she was coming to terms with her sexuality and was forging her sexual and gender identities.

The poems also contain interesting, even ironic, uses of gender. For example, love and friendship are both feminized—even to goddess status in the case of friendship—suggesting a precocious feminism. Although in later years Cora was not sympathetic to the feminist movement of the 1970s and 1980s, in these poems she has used the feminine pronoun throughout for both the emotions and the relationships that she was addressing.[57] Ironically, however, only male examples of friendship are cited. John Milton's poem "Lycidas," for example, mentioned in the second poem, is a memorial to a close male friend who died young. Similarly, the reference to Roland and Oliver is to the epic poem "Song of Roland," in which Oliver is Roland's best friend. Even the lofty references in both poems to friendship nurtured in "cultured Greece" are to the celebrated male, not female, friendships of ancient Greece that could also be homosexual. In this respect, the poems open a veiled door to same-sex love, but they do not provide suitable models for a young woman seeking alternatives to heterosexual love.

I examine these poems with some trepidation, not wanting to read too much into them. However, they—together with some notes from her high school history classes—are all that Cora left for any future biographer trying to understand this period of her life. They seem to suggest an internal struggle about what it is to be a young woman desirous of love, but not heterosexual love. These two poems contain no evidence of heterosexuality, except perhaps in the generic reference to "shallow frivolous youth." Rather, the author redirects her conflicted emotions to a safe, idealized notion of friendship that can occur between sets of women or sets of men. In selecting male examples of friendship, Cora may have felt that to use examples of female friendships would have been too self-revealing, or perhaps male ones were simply more accessible to her from high school readings.

What we do know with certainty is that the topic of friendship became a lifelong interest of Cora Du Bois and that she, unlike many other women of her era, never succumbed to social pressures to appear heterosexual by dating or marrying men.[58] She would, however, develop many deep friendships with men during the course of her life. High school was made bearable because her teachers treated her as "a pet"—a rare student in this small working-class town who was bright, came from a "good" family, and was college-bound. "I was considered pretty snotty by the run-of-the mill student there," Cora recalled. "I was . . . somebody apart."[59]

Return to Europe

In September 1921 Cora returned to Europe. She was seventeen and a recent high school graduate. The voyage was supposed to have been made together with her parents, who wanted to reintroduce their daughter to France and to her Du Bois relatives, but Cora's father's declining health intervened. As a consequence, they hired a chaperone—Virginia Wittens, a young professor of French at Smith College—to accompany Cora by ship to Europe to tour some of Holland, Belgium, and France, where there were friends and relatives to visit, and to deliver Cora safely to her uncle Georges and aunt Wally Du Bois in Frankfurt, Germany, where she would spend several months before going to visit her grandparents in Switzerland. It was, in several respects, a critical journey for the young Cora Du Bois.

Serendipitously, Cora's parents selected a chaperone who was not only a highly educated, French-speaking college professor but also a sensitive young lesbian.[60] Probably for the first time in her adolescence, Cora had someone with whom she could relate intimately. Many years later, when she was residing in Washington DC following the Second World War, Cora recorded the following in her journal after having received a phone call from Virginia Wittens:

> She [Virginia Wittens] took an ill-at-ease, springy but unrealized 17 year old "child" and gave her the delicate but unmistakable affection, the intellectual and the esthetic stimulus that only an unfamiliar adult can give at that age. A slow sea voyage and Paris permitted the delicacy of the relationship to take root in soil that was receptive but only slightly less than barren from a decade of malnutrition. What was planted or cultivated has only partially fruited. The intellectual stimulation has gained the upper hand—for this was what was already most congenial and advanced. The affection was persistent and displaced. The esthetics have been always a recalcitrant growth. This I regret in increasing measure. Yet it was with Virginia Wittens at Chartres from which I date the first of my rare "esthetic experiences."[61]

Like much of Du Bois's journal writing, this is written in an abstract, distanced voice, as if she were examining another person—not unlike the narrator in *Sir Roger de Coverley*. Yet these sentences are laced with intense personal meaning. She remembers Virginia Wittens as the person who befriended her at a critical stage of childhood—as a "malnourished" seventeen-year-old who was receptive to the "delicate but unmistakable affection" of an unfamiliar adult. In this case, the adult was a young woman who shared Cora's emerging sexual orientation and whom she found intellectually and aesthetically stimulating. In fact, Cora traces

her first great aesthetic awakening to a visit to Chartres Cathedral with
Virginia Wittens. At a critical moment in her adolescence, when she was
troubled by her home life and her emerging sexuality, Cora was befriended
by an ideal person—a sympathetic, highly educated, professional woman.
Cora also credited Virginia Wittens with providing her with her first real
taste of French culture—through visits to museums, cathedrals, theaters,
and restaurants. It was a brief but significant coming-of-age sojourn.

The trip to Europe also provided a young Cora Du Bois with an
opportunity to develop skills as an evocative travel writer and prescient
ethnographer. Each week she sent her parents lengthy letters describing what she was seeing and whom she was meeting, and in the course
of these writings she honed her powers to capture the essence of places
and people. The latter is particularly evident in her descriptions of "the
folks here in Frankfurt"—her aunt Wally, uncle Georges, and their four
daughters, with whom she lived for three months:

> Aunt Wally just makes me chuckle all inside of me—I don't know why
> but she does. She is an awfully good sort—not in the least old fashioned
> or narrow for others but rather that way with herself. She is terribly
> practical and exact—is somewhat brusk and therefore not in the least
> sensitive and when she steps on anyone's toes and they show it, she
> becomes most contrite. I like very much her simplicity and the way she
> gives me jobs and expects me to pile right in on such occasions as the
> arrival of big crates of vegetables from Keoningstein.[62]

> [She] is awf'ly nice and immensely amusing without meaning to be
> so I have to keep a straight face but honest t'mama it is hard when one
> sees her scoot down the steps with her little hat perched on the top of
> her head and a circular ostrich feather tied around her neck with a big
> black bow.[63]

> Uncle Georges is most kind and indulgent toward me, in fact we have
> gotten to the stage where he calls me "ma poule" [little chicken] and
> I pull his ears if he pesters me too much when I come down stairs to
> say good evening. He is home so very little that Aunt Wally really has
> charge of everything but Uncle G has but to whisper a suggestion and
> it's done.[64]

Concerning my cousins—Well they're not what I had expected at all. First and foremost I am more than ever impressed that the well bred European child is a pretty myth of yester-year used to torment the American youngster. Ruthie [twelve years] and Ellen [eight years] are my favorites. Louison [thirteen years] is too bossy and cock-sure of herself and anyway she doesn't give me an instant's peace. Irene [five years] is a typical undernourished puny colorless war baby but seems fairly intelligent. Her sisters just think she's perfect and as a result she is a spoiled youngster, not too obedient and decidedly whiny. Ruthie is rather quiet and studious and is much more intelligent than Louison who is frankly stupid. Ellen is the funniest chubbiest eight-year-older imaginable, full of fun and energy.[65]

There is also the youngsters' governess—Fraulein Platt—who is most violently German—north German at that and the battle-royals we have most every day must be a soothing syrup for jazzified ears. Both of us try to be liberal but we can't get around to see the other fellow's point of view. However she is a good enough sort and is especially decent in the pains she is taking to teach me German—we really have tackled Goethe's lyrics which, as Mother would say, is overreaching ourselves.[66]

By comparison with these family portraits, Cora's description of her reunion with Alice—the Du Boises' former maid and the woman who befriended her during her lonely years in St. Quentin ten years earlier—is more straightforward and less judgmental. What is missing, however, is any sign of the deep affection that we know Cora felt for Alice.

The Mater in her last letter made some suggestions about my telling of the people I have seen. . . . Alice comes next—well about her I scarcely know what to say except that she seemed much younger than the picture I had formed of her while I was in the U.S.A; her husband I didn't remember in the least but he seems to be a funny meek little duck who takes most quietly the twits that Alice still throws him about his size. She—Alice—was as proud as punch to show me around the town and to present me to a slew of people. She had apparently talked about my coming for most every other cat waylaid us and talked. . . . At present they live out in Roquecourt and the best things were [laid] out for me in the shape of towels, dishes, etc; they even finished some precious wine on account of me. They certainly were nice and it was touching to see how much they think of us.[67]

In letters home, the emotional attachment that Cora felt both to Virginia Wittens and to Alice remained unexpressed. Rather, Cora's quick characterizations of people for public consumption were not unlike what, many years later, she would put in the appendix to her book *The 1870 Ghost Dance* (1939), where she quickly described all of her informants.

Cora's emerging prowess as an evocative travel writer is perhaps best captured in the letter home in which she describes her visit to Basel, Switzerland, to visit her uncle Albert. "I can tell you how much it [Basel] pleased me! It pleased me more than any town approaching its dimensions which I've seen to date in Europe for it is quaint without being hopelessly antiquated. Its old buildings and brightly colored glazed tiled roofs, its exterior paintings, the Rhine which is such a rich shade of jade green, its white heavy arched bridges and its striking cleanliness in comparison with the German towns, combined to give it a most delightful sensation."[68] The next day Cora explored Basel's cathedral. The following excerpt is part of a seven-page letter to Cora's parents—handwritten, in ink, without any corrections—in her small, mature penmanship. I quote her description of the cathedral in full in order to capture the flow of Cora's prose and the way she builds tension.

First I walked thru the old streets, then I went to the Munster which appealed to me immensely as [a] cathedral. The exterior isn't very handsome, rather, interesting. The back, which is arranged for a cloister and is built on a terrace which almost overhangs the Rhine, was by far the most beautiful point of its exterior. For the interior I went across the way for the concierge, who, once having let me in, went about her housework leaving me in perfect liberty to explore that perfectly beautiful cathedral at will with nothing more harmful in sight than a little cleaning boy. The glasses [stained glass windows] were superb, most fair in comparison with the Parisian ones. The vaults and general lines were much those of St. Denis but the glass was more like that of Notre Dame, of course not as abundant, but of excellent quality, it seemed at least to my inexperienced eye. I climbed up the blackest staircase imaginable which was a hollow column and led to the triforium. As for narrowness, my shoulders touched either wall. It was my first close range introduction to a triforium and to the rose windows. It was thrilling, I assure you, especially in the half light and appalling silence of an empty cathedral. But, in no way daunted, I even ventured up the bell towers on rickety ladder like stairways past the tower clock who broke the silence by its inevitably ominous tick. Farther up the wind began moaning among the bells suspended above my head; a few steps upward and I bent double to pass under the heavy hammer of the largest bell. As I went up the belfry the bells became smaller until suddenly I emerged into the lacy steeple which characterizes the cathedral. I was breathless from excitement and from the whipping wind but immensely exhilarated by the keen air and the vigor of a city spread out at my feet. . . . The Rhine was more green than ever, the bridges more white, the roofs more mottled with the bright colors of the porcelain tiles and the moss of centuries. But one can't live on the peaks, neither literally nor figuratively. That attractive little tea room I can just discern there snuggled up against the third bridge would serve excellently the purpose of a "dix heure." The spell is broken by the inner man! Yet the bells have begun tolling under my feet while far under me I see the black line of a funeral. Hurriedly I clamber down the stone steps to the wooden ones of the "clocher," the bells in there are still ringing yet the noise is not deafening as one might suppose; rather it is enveloping. One feels oneself losing identity until one becomes but a throbbing vibration. It is more stirring than powerful organ music but partakes of the same nature of emotion. It saps one's strength, imperceptibly, until one tries to proceed. My knees were weak as water when I finally stumbled out into the street.[69]

When she wrote this animated description of Basel's cathedral, Cora had recently turned eighteen and had gained command of the English language. Her adventures in Europe were providing her an opportunity to write evocatively and to share experiences with the parents who could not accompany her. Undoubtedly she wanted to sound upbeat to her ill father, but she was also having profound experiences exploring Europe as a young woman. For her birthday, her aunt Wally helped her shop for a fur piece—a blue fox—that her parents wanted her to have. Then Uncle Georges took her on a delightful outing into the countryside where they "ran across three itinerant musicians with their stringed instruments slung about their necks and bedecked with long streamers. It was most picturesque to see these three men march along those winding country roads along whose side lie red roofed villages nestled in the shadow of ruin crowned hills."[70]

On December 1, 1921, Cora's father sent her a Christmas/New Year's letter to Frankfurt, probably the last one she was to receive from him. Opening with, "My dear Pussy Cat!" Jean goes on to say that he hopes the letter reaches her in time. "We would surely feel very bad, should our good wishes not reach you *in time* for the first Xmas you pass away from home. We know, however, that you will enjoy the festivities at Uncle Georges', if for no other reasons than that it will be something new to you, which is part of the education you are getting and for which you were bundled up and shipped with a 'mixed' cargo to Europe." He adds that he has instructed his brother to purchase a Christmas present for her. "The reason your mother and I decided to let Uncle Georges buy you whatever he thought best, with the recommendation that it should be in line with the cost of presents given to his own children, is due to the fact that we do not want, *under any circumstances*, to appear to spend more money than they do, because we are Americans and can afford to do it on account of the exchange." Jean also tells his daughter how much he and Mattie enjoy her letters, that they are "our Sunshine" and that they indicate she has "absorbed" what she is seeing. He closes with, "Once more a thousand good wishes from your old, decrepidated (?)old father."[71]

Christmas Eve in Frankfurt was a huge celebration with the combined Andreae and Du Bois families. Cora reported that, in addition to all the food she consumed, she had enjoyed everything "from the wine thru the cigarette! Yes I had a cigarette to keep Tante Henriette company, so that was alright [*sic*]. Do you see oh Best Beloveds?" On the following day, Christmas, she was plied with champagne. "I was scheduled to get back in time for a dinner at which the grandparents were to be present and which was to be graced with champagne, opened upon the excuse of my never having tasted any. The men folks insisted upon my having two glasses under which I stood up like a man, never even feeling a tremor."[72] In adulthood, a cigarette, together with a good glass of wine—or something stronger—would become one of Cora Du Bois's pleasures in life.

Following the Christmas festivities in Frankfurt, Cora traveled to Switzerland, where her uncle Albert escorted her to Basel and then on to Neuchâtel, arriving on New Year's Eve to stay with her grandparents at the Villa Montperreux in Peseux. "As my New Year's celebration I sat up in bed, horrible to relate, and read my magazines to the munch munch of some Suchard [the chocolate that her uncle Albert's factory made]." The next morning Cora got her "first glorious re-glimpse of the Alps and the lake" and made plans with "Tante Alice" [one of her father's two sisters] to visit Geneva and Lausanne and then to go see "Tante Cecile" [her father's other sister], where they could "do a bit of winter sports. Hot Dickity Dog!!!" In her letter home relating these plans, she concluded with "my bestest love and my deep hope for Dad's throat."[73]

That trip never transpired because on January 12, 1922, Jean Du Bois died of throat cancer. When the news reached the family in Neuchâtel, Cora remembered that her grandfather began weeping on her shoulder—a shoulder of unusual strength and fortitude.[74] Soon thereafter she packed and took a train to Paris, where, on January 16, she sent her mother a Western Union cablegram that said, "Arrive 27th on America Heartbroken."[75] Cora's trip to Europe had been terminated early, and she returned home to a fatherless household and an uncertain future.

CHAPTER 2

Escape and Resolve

> [Ruth Benedict's] favorites were usually the "deviants" like Jules
> Henry, Ruth Landes, Regina Flannery, and Cora Du Bois, the
> women, homosexuals, and Jewish students whom she mentored
> as she had mentored Margaret Mead.
> —Hilary Lapsley

Cora Du Bois's return trip to Europe, which followed her high school graduation and ended with the death of her father, effectively marked the conclusion of her childhood. She returned home to the United States twenty pounds lighter and grieving for her father but, at the same time, burning with ambition. The trip—made independently of her parents—had whetted her appetite for travel, self-exploration, and intellectual stimulation. "I was extraordinarily insensitive and self-centered, which I have been all my life."[1] This is the self-deprecating Du Bois speaking, whose personal ambition, wit, and critiques of others were frequently tempered by self-criticism. In this remark she was alluding to having enjoyed her European sojourn in spite of the knowledge that her father was dying. But her father had insisted that she take the trip, not wanting his daughter to witness his slow and painful death from throat cancer.

At eighteen, Cora returned home significantly changed. The weight loss had occurred while she was residing with her aunt and uncle in post–World War I Germany, where food was scarce and expensive. But the transformation was more psychological than physical. It was built upon a childhood of deeply disturbing but equally enriching circumstances: the loneliness and outsider status associated with the moves between countries, cultures, and languages; the struggles with an antagonistic brother and a mercurial mother that resulted in a young girl's assumption of the role of "good daughter," on the one hand, and of "curious observer," on the other; and the gradual coming to terms with her stigmatized sexual orientation.[2] Until this point, the constant positive forces in her life had been a benign and caring father, regular scholastic success, and mastery of the pen. For the young Cora Du Bois, lucid and insightful writing had become a means of exerting some control in a life in which family circumstances were disorderly and emotionally trying. Writing was also a tool of academic achievement and a form of self-expression. She returned from Europe with increased self-confidence and the desire to apply her skills and dispositions to a new stage of life—attending college and finding a career. In addition to her ambition, she recognized that the traditional roles for women in her era, which were based on marriage and childbearing, were not suitable for her and that she would have to pursue a nontraditional life for an early twentieth-century woman.

Cora's ambitions, however, were put on hold while she helped her mother tend to business affairs, clear out and sell their Perth Amboy home, and move to a smaller home in Red Bank, New Jersey. This was a small town, southeast of Perth Amboy, to which her parents had considered retiring. Contrary to her self-depiction mentioned above, Cora *did* continue to be a good daughter, convinced that she should attend to her mother during this period of bereavement. Cora's brother, Claude, upon learning of his father's death, also returned home but was then permanently banished. Mattie, in a fit of emotional upset and temper, told him to get out of the house and to never return, and he never did.[3] Surprisingly, he never even came back to collect his inheritance from his father.[4]

Although Cora's educational ambitions would seem to be the natural outgrowth of a childhood in which educational achievement was emphasized and rewarded by her parents, in actuality the situation was ambiguous. If we reexamine aspects of her childhood, it becomes clear that her parents' educational goals for their daughter were uncertain and, to her, probably confusing, and even exasperating. Initially it was Claude who was expected to have a university education and a profession, but Claude dropped out of high school. Although Cora continued on to high school, it was only after completing a second year of the eighth grade. Mattie, in another effort to feminize her daughter, had insisted that Cora spend an additional year in grammar school taking a special program that stressed cooking and sewing for girls who, according to Cora, "had no plan [to continue] onto four years of high school." Cora, with some irony, reported that her mother had accurately assessed her lack of skills and aptitude for such womanly domestic activities. "She was quite right on that score, if a bit old fashioned even for those days."[5]

In the next year Cora did continue on to high school, taking a college-preparatory program that included three years of Latin, physics, chemistry, mathematics, modern languages, history, and English literature, all of which whetted her appetite for further education.[6] When she graduated in 1921, she belonged to the relatively small cohort of American youth (18 percent) who had attended and completed high school.[7] And she belonged to an even smaller set of students who had graduated with honors and, in her case, the senior-year prize for overall academic excellence. This, she reported, was "the beginning of my arrogance."[8]

Cora's years in high school coincided with a significant moment in the women's rights movement in the United States. The late nineteenth- to early twentieth-century first-wave feminism and suffragist movement culminated, in 1920, with American women gaining the right to vote. Cora was just completing her sophomore year in high school when, on Thursday, June 5, 1919, the *New York Times* announced, "SUFFRAGE WINS IN SENATE; NOW GOES TO STATES." Even though she, unlike her future anthropology colleague Margaret Mead, did not grow up in a feminist-oriented household, it is hard to imagine that this event would have passed unnoticed.[9] Furthermore, her awareness of such historical events would have been enhanced by a high school course that she took entitled U.S. History—Problems of American Democracy, for which she kept clippings from the *New York Times*. And, as a promising college-bound student, she would have been made aware of colleges that were established in the late nineteenth century to serve women with ambitions such as hers.

At home, however, Cora had received mixed messages. Her parents had wanted her to do well in school, but they also had no experience with higher education or professional ambitions for women. There existed, then, what Margaret Mead, in later years, would call "the generation gap."[10] Mattie, it must be remembered, had not even completed grammar school, much less attended high school. New York City, in fact, did not have any public high schools until 1878, and it was not until 1910 that public secondary schools began to spread throughout much of the United States.[11] So when Cora graduated from Perth Amboy High School in 1921, she had already surpassed her mother educationally. Furthermore, although Cora's Swiss father came from a highly educated line of men, he retained European ideas about women's education. He wanted his daughter to attend a finishing school in Switzerland for a year or two, where, according to Cora, "young women were sent to learn embroidering and good manners."[12] Neither of her parents, it would seem, was attuned to the rapidly changing circumstances for women in the United States and the influence they were having on their talented and ambitious daughter.

Her father's will, however, offers a different perspective. Jean Du Bois may have liked the idea of a Swiss finishing school for his daughter, but he nonetheless allocated in his will significant funds—up to $10,000—for her to use either for further education or to buy a business. By the time he made his last will, when he knew he had inoperable throat cancer, he provided for his daughter's educational and professional future as part of the trust fund that he established for his wife. The stipulation in the will reads, "To apply to the education of my daughter, Cora Alice Du Bois, or to use for her benefit in the purchase of a business or an interest in a business, a sum not exceeding $10,000 . . . [but only] upon the written request of my wife, Mattie C. Du Bois."[13] So, ultimately, Cora's father *did* anticipate and provide in his will for his daughter's educational and professional ambitions, even though her use of these trust funds would require the written approval of her mother.

There was no comparable bequest for Claude. Jean's will did leave to his son "all my jewelry, articles of wearing apparel and personal effects . . . *excepting my Swiss Chronometer, which I give and bequeath unto my daughter, Cora Alice Du Bois.*"[14] The personal item that Jean most prized, a Du Bois pocket watch and family heirloom, was left to Cora. According to the will, Claude would, however, receive some portion of his father's estate—although significantly less than Cora—upon the death or remarriage of his mother.

After her return from Europe, Cora postponed—for a year and a half—her dream of attending college while she helped her mother relocate to Red Bank and while her father's will was in probate. Upon the recommendation of the local Red Bank public librarian, with whom she became friends, Cora found some work with a branch of the New York Public Library. This employment helped to occupy her during a period of bereavement and gave her some time away from her mother, who, at forty-four, was a relatively young and intensely unhappy widow.[15]

Barnard College

In the fall of 1923 Cora enrolled at Barnard College. It appears that what enabled her to begin college was not the stipulation in her father's will, which may still have been in probate, but rather the delayed receipt of a $3,000 inheritance from her uncle Hugues Du Bois, Jean's youngest brother and Cora's godfather, who had died at the beginning of World War I.[16] Cora, still loath to leave her mother despite their "abrasiveness with one another," selected a college to which she could commute from Red Bank.[17] Barnard was the logical choice. Founded in 1889 as a woman's "annex" to Columbia University, it was both prestigious and located nearby in New York City. By 1900 it had become a separate legal entity with its own faculty and curriculum. Nonetheless, there was ongoing collaboration with Columbia. Barnard seniors, for example, could take courses at Columbia together with male students, and many graduate programs were open to women, which meant that Barnard undergraduates could have contact with graduate women who could serve as role models for them. The setting in New York City also meant that Barnard attracted a more ethnically and economically diverse set of students than most other women's colleges that required travel and had board and room expenses. Furthermore, its location also put Barnard women in the heart of the United States' fastest-growing city, which was also the capital of employed women.[18]

The first three years at Barnard—before she was able to move onto campus in her senior year—required a complex balancing act for Cora. She spent a total of four hours each day commuting, returning home at night to her "dolorous" mother, while trying to study and engage in college affairs with other students on campus. In old age, Cora remembered this period of life as "painful and tiring."[19] Nonetheless, she prospered scholastically and, in 1927, graduated Phi Beta Kappa. The commute, however, prevented her from participating in late-afternoon sports—something that she would have enjoyed. Instead, in order to fulfill Barnard's physical education requirement, she had to enroll in gym every year, and she became "an expert" in leading others in marching drills, performing on trapezes, and rope climbing while dressed in bloomers and middy blouses. "And so I became the pet of the gym teachers, because here was somebody who really enjoyed gym, presumably, and so, by the time I was a junior or senior, I had gone through this rigmarole two or three times."[20]

A more characteristic and feisty Cora emerges in her recollections of a sex education and hygiene course that first-year students were required to take. When a paper was assigned, Cora wrote what she thought was a humorous satire of the course material. Instead of being amused, the instructor "called me up and gave me hell." This may have been Cora's first experience with not receiving praise for her work from teachers, and she reported, "I was sort of crushed by it."[21]

Campus Life

Despite her commute, Cora was able to make friends, participate in some campus life, and even engage in school politics. In her diary, for example, she wrote about helping a friend run for class president. "These school 'politics'!" she wrote sardonically. "What perplexing diplomacies. It is so amusing to see and share in grave consultations, vote getting, etc. Now Marian Wadsworth has been suggested by Helen Robinson—and she will split the vote which we so laboriously built up against Margery Meyers. A storm in a tea-kettle! Grave consultations again. . . . And to think that some of the girls called 'brilliant' by their contemporaries have spent most of their college leisure with such stuff."[22]

Cora's more serious voice, however, is reflected in her account of the following incident at Barnard. During her senior year, Cora was able to move onto campus and was selected to serve on the student Honor Board, a body that heard cases brought by the administration against students for infractions of college rules. A case was brought against a senior who had "filched" books out of the library and then, afraid of getting caught returning them, had "foolishly" dropped them into a garbage can. They were found and traced back to the student, whose case was then brought before the board. Cora reported that "this group of her peers who were on the Honor Board just summarily, out of hand, said, well, she's got to be thrown out. Expelled. This was in her senior year, and this was a girl who came from, I imagine, a rather simple family where both money and education were terribly important for her. Earning her living and at the same time also having an educational experience. They just voted her out, and I was furious with them, and put in my resignation."

Dean Gildersleeve, who was the academic dean of Barnard at the time, called Cora in to ask why she had resigned. "I told her why. I said I don't like this mindless sense of justice [and] egoism." Cora also found it ironic and disturbing that the chair of the Honor Board, the one behind this seeming injustice, was U.S. Chief Justice Charles Evans Hughes's granddaughter.[23] In this college incident the deeply principled and fair-minded side of Cora Du Bois was becoming evident—the woman who was to become renowned for her forthright positions and communications during World War II, for her principled resistance to McCarthyism in the postwar era, and for her fair-minded participation in Harvard faculty politics.

Intellectual and Personal Growth

Not surprisingly, intellectual and personal growth was the hallmark of Cora's four years at Barnard (and a fifth year at Columbia, where she completed a master's degree in medieval history). Her diary, which she kept irregularly during these years, provides small glimpses into this period of maturation.

For example, in the spring of 1926 Cora took the overnight train from New York City to Washington DC to visit, for the first time, Virginia Wittens—the woman who had accompanied her to Europe when she was seventeen—and Virginia's "intimate friend," Mary Scott. The two women had lived together for five or six years and both taught French at a local college. Cora recorded the reunion as follows:

> To the extent that I have grown, V. W. seems to have shrunk. That seems to be a pain and disillusionment inevitably attendant upon growth. I waver between regret and an exultation in my growing sense of power and breadth. But no amount of intellectual growth on my part will ever make me attain V. W's bigness of character, her calmness and kindness

which seem to arise from being so much at peace with herself. One can be only selfish and self-engrossed without being self-sufficient until that truce has been made with oneself. Within the individual, peace and superiority are complementary; but only if peace has been dearly bought. And in the common meaning of the word, there is little success in superiority or peace.[24]

Here Cora's recognition of her personal and intellectual growth is tempered by regret that she may have outpaced her former mentor and by expressions of admiration for Virginia's character and peace of mind. The latter was something that, given her ambition, Cora was not sure she would ever attain.

Cora also described her first meeting with Virginia's friend, Mary Scott: "The first impression is not very favorable. She is a bit too abrupt, too brusque. Her manner toward V. W. wavers between a peremptory and a wheedling tone. Also she, like most self-assertive people, lacks delicacy and sensitiveness in estimating situations. However she is so devoted to V. W. and so willing and anxious to do all within her power to make her happy that one can forgive her many shortcomings."[25] Again, one sees in Cora a quick and incisive evaluation of another person. Of particular interest is her comment about "self-assertive people," since this also referenced herself, or the person that she was becoming. She preferred that assertiveness be tempered by a sensibility to others and their situations—something that she herself would strive for but not always achieve.

Another interesting glimpse into Cora's developing selfhood is apparent from this same trip. After accompanying Virginia and Mary to an evening communion service at St. Paul's Episcopal Church in downtown Washington DC, she wrote in her diary,

It has been six years since I have been to church and during that time I have lost all religious faith, all of that blind belief in the soul and immortality. So the whole ceremony seemed particularly detached from me. I took communion because not to have done so would have been to offer offense to my hostesses and Mary Scott with whom I was sitting. Yet at the very time that I was dipping the wafer in the cup of wine (what a strange half-hearted degeneracy of symbolism) I was amused almost to the point of openly smiling. Were I a little older, the meaning of the mummery to others would prevent me from treating it too litely; but at present I am so irrepressibly relieved at having shaken off the dead weight of god, soul, and immortality that my first reaction is one of delight to find myself free from that which has made slaves of so many millions.[26]

This is the first mention of any religious practice that Cora experienced while growing up, other than some limited exposure, as a young child, to Catholicism when she attended a Catholic school in St. Quentin, France. Both sides of her family were Protestants, but how observant they were is unclear. One of Cora's childhood friends in Perth Amboy was the daughter of the local Episcopal minister, so perhaps she had at times attended church with that friend. Clearly, religious belief and practice were issues that she had thought about and had, at this point in her life, rejected. When she discovered anthropology the following year, she would become captivated by the not-yet-famous Columbia anthropologist Ruth Benedict's lectures on different cultural systems of religious belief and practice.

A recurring theme in Cora's journal is that of the individual in society—a topic that she would address many years later as a professional anthropologist writing about American values.[27] At this stage of her life, however, she was struggling with finding her own sense of self in an academic setting where, remarkably for one so young, she recognized that much knowledge is socially constructed. For example, in 1926, as a junior, she wrote in her diary,

The mind, and the individual, finds itself in a hopeless quagmire of institutions which are the hallmark of many generations, of many minds. Life becomes more complex without becoming more profound. The scholars, after they have covered survey courses of this subject, exhaust and ramify purposeless digressions. To live in an intellectual milieu with one's fellow men in this confusion, one must acquire similarly distorting complexities of thought, of action, of speech. Then if one's constitution is able to bear the strain—one succeeds! Succeeds in what? I have often asked myself—Certainly it is not in the self-realization of the individual. The profound fundamentalities [*sic*] of life are lost. Life, death, and birth—love, hatred, and pain, are counted or juggled, and if the scholar restates them in meaningless terms he thinks he has explained them. Classify knowledge and call it science if you will. It is desirable and laudable. But do not try to arrive at meaning by totaling.[28]

Two things are noteworthy here: First is the lament that the individual is mired in "a hopeless quagmire of institutions." By the late 1930s Cora would become a pioneer in helping to develop and test a theoretical model for examining the interrelationships among individuals, social institutions, and culture. Second is Cora's skepticism about classifying and quantifying acts of human behavior in a search for meaning—something to which she had a lifelong antipathy.

This early expression of skepticism and ambivalence about academe and intellectualism would become a recurring theme in Du Bois's life. Nonetheless, by the time she graduated from Barnard, she had decided to pursue an academic career. As she was sailing for Europe in June 1927, she wrote,

> Taking stock of myself I find I am now definitely molded to an intellectual life—with all the inadequacies and artificialities of such an existence. At 23 I find that I have known little else but study and schooling and realize that in this type of life I can be happy and productive, yet matters are never so simple and I see plainly that I must struggle against the narrowing influence of the academic. I must be active in many fields—which should not be difficult since my interests and enthusiasm [are] omnivorous. Also I must love—must avoid hatred and indifference as destructive forces. I must not let my mind atrophy my emotions and I must avoid the conceit which maintains that reasons can motivate and dominate a person.
>
> All that reason can, and should do, is merely temper behavior.[29]

Throughout her subsequent career, Cora found ways to remain reasonably broad and omnivorous in her intellectual pursuits, many of which were interdisciplinary.

Love and Friendship

Cora's journal reveals little about her more intimate life during her college years—the life of love and emotions that she alludes to in the remarks above. By this time she had matured into a handsome young woman with many of her father's features—an oval face punctuated with a long aquiline nose, intense blue eyes, and short, dark, bobbed hair—the fashion of the day. The photo of Cora in her Barnard senior yearbook is of a serious-looking young woman wearing glasses with large round lenses and wire rims, whose look is that of a budding intellectual.

Scattered among Cora's diary entries are casual references to women friends in various contexts—from her electioneering work mentioned earlier, to postgraduation traveling companions in Europe, to occasional dinner companions, as in the excerpt below, which also reveals her more analytical and distanced voice: "On the evening of March 31, Trudy, Jean, Marian Howard, Florence Stuart and I had supper with Moyetta White. It was very pleasant, not very exciting—the company has little in common but from force of habit and because of mutual friendships we have these little festivals from time to time."[30]

Cora's more sensuous and humanistic side was generally revealed in poetry—the medium she used for expressing her more intense and personal emotions. (There would be a lifelong tension between these two sides of her persona and in her modes of writing.) Cora's college love poems reveal a newfound comfort with her sexual identity. These poems, unlike her high school poetry, are not fraught with the emotional turbulence and sexual uncertainty that characterized the latter but, rather, are openly expressive of her love for other women. Below are three short love poems, named for different women, and one longer, more sensuous untitled poem that were written at the conclusion of her Barnard/Columbia years.

TO BARBARA
  Love
Is a sacrament of beauty
Like flowers springing from the
    floor of a pine forest
Like white clouds caressing
    a blue sky
But in whose loveliness is not
    compelling necessity

8. Cora Du Bois, Barnard yearbook photo, 1927. Cora Alice Du Bois Papers (SPEC.COLL. ETHG.D852c), Tozzer Library, Harvard College Library, Harvard University.

TO MARGARET
    Love
Is exquisite formal gesturing
Like Chinese carvings in white jade,
Like the intricately patterned snow flake
Which is obliviated in the shift of
    Cultured considerations.

TO MARION
    Love
Is a mad lawless seeking
Like wind blowing over a hot
    desert
Like a red flame consuming that
Which long aridity has rendered
    into tinder.

UNTITLED
Beloved, let us part in the blackness of night
Before this dream too is blemished by the tyranny of
    time.
Let us leave to memory
Your body which cut darkness
Like a sword of white fire,
Molten metal pulsing thru our veins.
The maddening fire of cool flesh;
On a sated dawn
Will blur like some careless cutter of gems
The intaglio of our illusion.

For you I would know the music of song.
For you I would break the brittle shell of a
    mind
And pour the profligate riches of its hidden
    recesses
Out into sunlight.
I have feared beauty

But now I am made brave
By the reckless confidence of love.[31]

It is important to examine this evidence of Cora's emerging sexual identity in a historical context. When she entered college, the cultural ideology that defined women's intimate relationships with one another had recently shifted from one of presumed innocent romance, in the nineteenth century, to a more sexualized perspective in the twentieth century.[32] In the late nineteenth and very early twentieth centuries a culture of "smashing" was common at girls' schools, where younger women often developed crushes on older ones—crushes that they later defined as a first, intense love that for many helped pave the way for subsequent heterosexual relationships.[33] These were passionate friendships that involved physical expressions of affection as well as emotional infatuation and that were accompanied by the exchange of such tokens of love as bouquets of flowers, locks of hair, and love letters. Such crushes resembled, in an all-girls context, romantic courtships between young men and women. And despite overt touching, fondling, and kissing, such relationships were presumed innocent because the idea of genital contact between women was, at the time, foreign.

This presumed innocence began to change, however, with the emergence of publications by late nineteenth- to early twentieth-century sexologists such as Havelock Ellis, whose book *Sexual Inversion*, after being banned in England, was published in Philadelphia in 1901. The book addressed same-sex relationships, including those between women, and argued that bisexuality and homosexuality were inborn characteristics, not social perversions. While Ellis, on the one hand, tried to normalize homosexuality, and in particular, lesbianism—a term that had by then been introduced into the literature—he also saw lesbians as a danger to society. They were growing in numbers, he asserted, with the expansion of women's roles, opportunities, and institutions, especially among the middle-class intelligentsia.[34]

But the writer and thinker who, in the early twentieth century, had the greatest impact on popular ideas about sexuality in the United States was Sigmund Freud. Although some of Freud's ideas about psychoanalysis and human sexuality were already being taught in American universities, a series of lectures that he gave at Clark University in 1909 accelerated their impact. Freud's theory that humans move through a series of universal psychosexual stages that included heterosexual relationships in adulthood—with homosexual ones being defined as abnormal—captured the American imagination. "By the 1920s, Freudian theories of sexual development as well as writings of other sexologists had completed the redefinition of same-sex pairings as homosexual, and labeled them morbid and pathological."[35] Such theories were also being used to discredit many ambitious single women—professionals, reformers, and educators, including Barnard's Dean Gildersleeve—all of whom had to learn to carefully veil their personal lives.[36]

As it happens, then, Cora's sexual maturation occurred during an era when intimate same-sex relationships were becoming socially stigmatized. She would have been aware of this from the popular literature of the day and also, quite likely, from an introductory psychology course that she took at Barnard where Freud's ideas were probably presented. In any case, as an intensely curious and omnivorous reader, she would likely have explored Freud and other sexologists on her own. Further, she was a student in a large, cosmopolitan city, where discussions of Ellis, Freud, and others would not have been uncommon and also where there was a fair amount of sexual experimentation going on in the 1920s.[37] The decade of the 1920s, following the First World War, was a period of economic prosperity in the United States. With this prosperity, New York City became the center of a cultural rebirth that was reflected in everything from the art deco movement to jazz and the Harlem Renaissance. And New York's Greenwich Village was a center of poetry readings, music, and the flapper age, where women, who had removed the trappings of the Victorian era—quite literally, with the removal of corsets—dressed in short, loose, sleeveless dresses. In addition to a more general symbolic freedom, this clothing enabled them to dance more freely with men and with one another. Ironically, it was both a time of open sexual expressiveness and experimentation *and* also one of increased disapproval of what were now being labeled "homosexual" and "lesbian" relationships.

Cora was not a fan, at least initially, of New York City's youth culture and wrote disparagingly about it, and of her own emerging intellectual identity, in her diary. Nonetheless, and with some irony, she recognized that she was becoming a product of this city and its historical era. "I realize that the revulsion which I felt so strongly last year—a revulsion against the metropolis of New York and against the intellectual and artistic activities which I saw on all sides, was the natural revolt of youth which finds itself born into a decadent megalopolitan civilization. It is an uneasiness which cannot long endure. I shall soon be old enough and sufficiently intellectualized to feel at home in the 'cold clear intellect' and 'art craft' of an age of which I am a product."[38]

Yet it seems likely that she would have found Barnard and Columbia a comfortable environment for exploring her emerging gender and sexual identities and that such comfort would have been enhanced during her senior year when she discovered anthropology. "Tabooed or not, homosexuality, as well as bisexuality, flourished at Columbia in the 1920s and 1930s," according to the historian Rosalind Rosenberg.[39] While this is undoubtedly an exaggeration, it was the case that Barnard's own dean of students, Virginia Gildersleeve, lived with another woman throughout much of her career, and that the anthropology professor Ruth Benedict was exploring different cultural ideas about heterosexuality and homosexuality in both her research and her teaching.[40] And we now know that Benedict and her student Margaret Mead were avidly discussing these topics and engaging in what would now be labeled a lesbian love affair.[41] Nonetheless, these and other professional women knew it was prudent to keep their intimate relationships quiet—something that Cora also learned to do. As a professional woman, she would keep her private and public lives separate.

The Summer of 1926: Escape

A pivotal summer for Cora—that of 1926—was sandwiched between her junior and senior years at Barnard. In the previous two summers she had escaped briefly from home by serving as a camp counselor and swimming instructor at a YWCA camp on the Hudson River. But in the summer of 1926 she crossed the country by train to be a counselor at a Campfire Girls camp, Camp Sweyolaken, in Idaho. She relished the changing landscapes that she saw for the first time. "I have never felt before so much soothing spacious loneliness," she wrote in her diary.[42] Once again, she was on a voyage alone that nourished her appetite for new landscapes and for adventure.

On the way, Cora stopped for a few days in Denver to explore and hike in the Rockies and, through an acquaintance, accepted a blind date with a young man. "I went rather gladly because I have little contact with the male youth of this generation. (I know Mother's attendants very well indeed, though) . . . It was my first experience with the male of the species [who tried to kiss her] and I was very surprised to find that I was enormously amused rather than annoyed as I would have supposed I would be."[43]

From Denver, Cora took the train to California, where she wrote rhapsodically about an evening spent in Santa Barbara. The description is joyous and romantic, and it uses feminine imagery.

We stopped for the night at a beautiful hostelry (I can't call it anything less romantic) the Samarkand which means in Persian "Hearts Desire." In the evening in the light of a lingering afterglow and of a pale crescent moon, it lay solitary upon its hillside. In back rose the gray mountains of Santa Barbara, in front the sea spread out calmly. Between them both the Samarkand, with its two long wings, embraced a jewel like garden of water and flowers and lawns. Never has a building seemed so alive, so much like a beautiful woman lying with bared arms and shoulders among the draperies of her couch. And like a beautiful woman she gazed fondly down at her own reflection appearing a dozen times, a dozen ways, in the mirror lakes of her terraced garden.[44]

From Santa Barbara, Cora traveled north to San Francisco and then northeast to Idaho, arriving in July to work with 150 girls at Camp Sweyolaken. During this period she had her first experience with Native Americans when she attended the Second Annual Indian Congress in Spokane, Washington. She wrote, "There were over 700 Indians from 18 different tribes represented. Their names alone suggested all the romance of the settling of the west which in 70 years has already become provincial. There were tepees of the Blackfeet, Nez Perce, Coeur d'Alene, Umatillas, Colvilles, Yakimas and a dozen others."[45]

Another trip to Yellowstone inspired her evocative travel writing, accompanied by a self-critique of such inadequate symbolic efforts.

[T]he climax of the day was Old Faithful with the flash lite playing on it. That great jet of steam playing and sparkling at a height of over 150 ft. like a gay wraith is too beautiful to mar with word symbolism. That is the difficulty with all symbolism—it either undervalues or overvalues. It casts glamour upon the trivial, or detracts from the perfection of reality. The Campfire girl ceremonial, for instance, assumes an unwarranted importance and becomes desirable in itself—a condition contradictory of the purpose of symbolism. While an attempt to describe Old Faithful at nite would be so inadequate as to destroy the mental image I now possess—or at least to overcast it. Were it sufficiently artistic it might create a poor vicarious counterpart in another person's mind, which would be legitimate enough were I writing for another's eyes.[46]

The Campfire Girls administrators recognized in Cora an able leader and, by the end of the summer, offered her a permanent position as assistant to the executive head of the organization with, in addition, the assurance of a future sabbatical year to complete her college education. Cora wrote to her mother about this opportunity. "In sum—if I go into girls work it would be an ideal job but—it means I maybe will never finish college and I shall be signing myself away for a good long period to life in provincial districts."[47] While it was tempting to have paid employment with an organization she liked, Cora decided to return to Barnard to complete her undergraduate education forthwith. That summer's experience did, however, lead to her very first publication, in 1927, "How to Make a Totem Pole for Your Camp."[48]

But the most exciting news of the summer was Cora's mother's announcement of her engagement and plans to marry, in the fall, Richard Bicknell, an acquaintance of Cora's father. "I was free!" Cora exclaimed.[49] This meant that she could cease being the "good daughter" to her mother and move onto campus at Barnard for her senior year. Furthermore, it meant that she would become economically independent. Jean Du Bois's will stipulated that if Mattie died or remarried, Cora would inherit a sum equivalent to the value of all the real estate sold following his death and that she and Claude would divide the remainder of his trust fund. The upshot of this was that on September 30, 1926—the date of her mother's wedding—Cora began to receive the income on her inheritance of $30,750.[50] This inheritance enabled her to continue her education and her explorations of the world when, several years later, the country moved into a serious economic depression.

Discovering Anthropology

In her last year at Barnard, upon the urging of her history advisor, Cora enrolled in a yearlong course in anthropology taught by two Columbia professors, Franz Boas and Ruth Benedict, and in which Margaret Mead, then a graduate student, served as a teaching assistant. These three are now iconic figures in the history of American anthropology. Boas had founded the Department of Anthropology at Columbia in 1896 and, by 1927, at the age of sixty-nine, had already become the dominant figure in American anthropology. He had trained many of the next generation of significant anthropologists, including Alfred Kroeber and Robert Lowie, with whom Cora would study in graduate school. Boas was, then, not only a leading figure in American anthropology but also a well-known intellectual whose two books, *Changes in Bodily Forms of Descendants of Immigrants* (1911) and *The Mind of Primitive Man* (1911), had powerfully challenged racial theories and racial classifications in the United States that were based on notions of fixed racial traits. He did this by demonstrating, in the first book, the plasticity of physical types that characterized different racial categories. Then he popularized his conclusions in the second book, in which he also argued that values many people assume are absolute are, in fact, culturally determined.

Benedict, on the other hand, had only recently completed a PhD under Boas, in 1923, and was holding a series of one-year appointments as a lecturer at Columbia and Barnard. Columbia, at the time, was resistant to hiring women but ultimately, with prodding from Boas, made Benedict an assistant professor in 1931. In 1926–27, at the age of forty, Benedict was teaching the course with Boas because Gladys Reichard—another one of Boas's female protégées, who held Barnard's only anthropology position at the time—was on leave.[51] Mead, during Cora's senior year, had recently returned from her first fieldwork in Samoa and, with Boas's efforts, had an appointment at the Museum of Natural History in New York City, where she would remain for the course of her career. She was three years older than Cora and a Barnard graduate who would complete her PhD under Boas in 1929. So Cora had her first exposure to anthropology with three of the great figures in the field, two of whom were women.

"I was snagged," Cora reported about the course, which had a broad scope and covered history, archaeology, physical anthropology, cultural areas of the world, social organization, religion, and linguistics.[52] At first, Cora viewed anthropology as a way of becoming less culture bound as she traversed the world. Traveling was in her blood, she said, and anthropology "annealed both the academic aspirations that I subsequently developed and the travel." More important, she was captivated by Ruth Benedict's persona and lectures. "Benedict was an enormously challenging person. Her painful stammer, her curiously inappropriate dresses—chiffon gowns that sort of hung around in wrong directions, her vision of the human condition . . . and world view, as contrasted to culture bound history to which I had been exposed, were a challenge."[53] Cora described Benedict as "eccentric, sloppy, yes. [But] a beautiful woman, [with] a beautiful face."[54] With her large, sorrowful eyes, prematurely gray hair, and an enigmatic smile, Benedict was undoubtedly an alluring figure. Despite Benedict's odd clothing and problematic stutter, Cora found her lectures "fascinating" and "electrifying." Once a lecture got underway, Cora reported, the students sat there "goggle-eyed." By contrast, Cora found Boas's lectures on Eskimo grammar and myths mystifying. No one, she asserted, understood what he was talking about until his final, "brilliant" lecture on linguistics. "The subject matter was the principal obstacle. But Boas' accent, compounded by a dueling scar that left one cheek partially paralyzed, added to our incomprehension."[55]

Boas lectured once a week and Benedict twice a week. Not only did Ruth Benedict, the person, fascinate her, but Cora found the content of her lectures both intellectually intriguing and personally meaningful, especially presentations about sexuality and deviance in different cultural contexts. These were topics that Benedict was thinking about at the time and that she would incorporate into her 1934 bestselling book, *Patterns of Culture*—a book that has now introduced generations of Americans to the concepts of culture, cultural variation, and the impact of culture on

9. Ruth Benedict, ca. 1930. Photograph by Arthur Muray.

the individual. In retrospect, Cora wrote, "I remember only that even as a history major, the range of human thought and behavior of which she spoke with ethnographic intimacy and directness (particularly in respect to sexual behavior) *shook* that rather smug sense of knowing just about everything which is often so characteristic of the bright college senior."[56]

Extrapolating from Benedict's *Patterns of Culture* and from her 1934 article "Anthropology and the Abnormal," we can surmise what some of the ideas and ethnographic data were that so fascinated Du Bois at the time. Benedict argued that, in the great arc of human potential, each culture selects some behaviors over others to emphasize and to develop in elaborate detail, and it is these selected behaviors, and their associated institutions, that give a culture its particular pattern. In such selection processes, however, there are patterns of behavior that fit some individuals better than others, and there are some behaviors that are labeled deviant. But deviancy is culturally relative. What might be considered aberrant behavior in one culture might be valued in another. For example, Benedict cited trance and catalepsy as abnormal behaviors in American culture, whereas these behaviors were valued human capacities in other cultures. Indeed, such ecstatic experiences were not only highly appreciated in some cultures, but they were even deemed supernatural or divine. This, she pointed out, had been true for Catholicism at one stage of its history.[57] Similarly, Benedict used homosexuality as another example of a human behavior that was treated in different ways by different cultures through time and space. She cited Melanesian and Native American societies where homosexuality was not considered deviant but, rather, conferred special status, and where homosexual behavior was, in some cases, a cornerstone of social institutions. Furthermore, Benedict used such cross-cultural evidence to critique American society and its restrictive values.

One can well imagine a youthful Cora Du Bois's fascination with such lectures. During the course of this year, she participated in a discussion section led by Benedict where a range of ideas about religious practices were discussed, including psychological hypotheses about fasting, self-torture, artic hysteria, and shamanic performances.[58] She was, accordingly, introduced to an early stage of psychological thinking about such cultural phenomena—what today we would call psychological anthropology. For one of her course papers, Cora—the history major—compared some of the religious practices of the Ekoi of West Africa with aspects of sixteenth-century Europe. Both societies, she asserted, had "a religion steeped in fear of sorcery . . . and witchcraft." Examples abounded:

> Ordeals [among the Ekoi] are used to try cases, and witchdoctors have ornate procedures to detect the malefactors of the community. Strangely, it is often the closest kin who is suspected. Yet in Europe too we find that husbands frequently accused wives of riding off to witch meetings on broomsticks in the dead of night.
>
> It matters little that the leopard is substituted for the wolf. Also affinities are frequent and Talbot's story, repeated in Lowie, of the tree whose voice called the native to it in the dead of night, is psychologically not far different from Joan of Arc's voices.[59]

The paper was marked "Excellent" by Benedict.

Following her Barnard graduation in June 1927, Cora and several women friends traveled to Europe, where, having been inspired by a course in Romanesque and medieval art, Cora made "a pilgrimage" to the major Romanesque and medieval monuments in England and France. Also, inspired by her introduction to anthropology, she spent a week in Les Eyzies, France, touring prehistoric sites. Despite these new interests, in 1927–28 Cora continued in history by undertaking a master's degree at Columbia where she wrote "an aberrant thesis on what we would now call socio-cultural change from Hellenic to Hellenistic Greece."[60] Her exposure to anthropology may have affected her selection of a topic—a topic that she later described as "a ludicrously arrogant enterprise" because of its breadth and her inadequate language skills to do research in classical Greek and Latin.[61]

During that year Cora audited two courses that had a profound effect on her. One was History from the Middle Ages through the Eighteenth Century, which addressed Asian influences on Europe and "planted the seed of the culture-bound quality of our own western history."[62] The other was Primitive Religion, an evening seminar taught by Ruth Benedict. In the latter course, "we were required to read solid monographs like James Mooney's *1890 Ghost Dance*—a vast volume of the Bureau of American Ethnology."[63] The course also included in-person field reports from Margaret Mead on Samoa and from Ruth Bunzel on the Zuni. Consequently, Cora had an unusual degree of exposure to women in anthropology.

By the end of the year, Cora asserted, "I was stuffed to the gills and in a drop-out mood."[64]

Return to Europe: Resolve

From early childhood, significant periods in Du Bois's life were punctuated by travel, and a trip to Europe in the fall of 1928 was no exception. Having completed her MA in history, Cora returned alone to Europe to contemplate her future. She needed to decide between a career in history or in anthropology. Travel to Europe by ship allowed for a period of decompression and contemplation—a liminal time that we have lost in the era of jet travel. On board the SS *Colombo*, between New York and Europe, Cora reflected in her diary upon the intensity of the past year's work and social life: "As a result, the first day of solitude on board ship left me restless and distressed. The next day and night there blew a strong wind whose insistent ecstasy swept me bare of all those petty corrosions of affection. Now once again I can turn inward and find freshness, vigor, even exaltation. It comes so easily and naturally I wonder that people ever seek it in others, especially when mutual exhaustion is often the price paid."[65]

Also, with her curious observer's eye and newfound anthropological language, she described such shipboard events as the celebration of the Fourth of July: "Last night the Fourth of July was celebrated with wine and free champagne and much noise. Legalized license—anthropologists call it in primitive society. The immodest behavior of the American Anglo-Saxons quite shocked the Italian demi-mondaines. Fancy living so cramped an existence that one feels the necessity of organized non-restraint."[66] Cora went on to note that even "civilized people" fence themselves in with taboos that occasionally need to be broken.

Once in Europe, Cora divided the next five months between Heidelberg and Berlin, trying to resolve her personal conflicts about which academic field to pursue as a profession. Why these particular cities? She was using German resources to explore the feasibility of a topic that Franz Boas had proposed to her for a possible PhD dissertation in anthropology. "Papa Boas," as he was known by his women protégées, had encouraged

Cora to join the anthropology program at Columbia and, recognizing her strengths in history, had encouraged her to do a thesis that would make use of those skills. What he had suggested was a study of the medieval contacts between Western Europe and East African societies. So Cora spent time in the university libraries of Heidelberg and Berlin examining relevant historical and ethnographic sources to determine how viable this project was. Also, while she was in Berlin, she audited a seminar given by the German ethnologist Richard Thurnwald, a professor of anthropology and sociology at the University of Berlin.

Cora enjoyed Berlin, which she characterized as having "something of a mixture of the elegance of Paris and the modernity of New York."[67] In addition to visiting libraries and classrooms, she explored Berlin's museums, in particular the Neues Museum with its famous collection of ancient Egyptian artifacts. Here she discovered the iconic bust of the ancient Egyptian queen Nefertiti, which inspired a highly romanticized and feminist entry in her diary: "My visit to Berlin would have been justified by having seen Nefertiti alone. What unbelievable graciousness, charm, humor: She is as sensitive as a flower, and as strong as womanhood. She is more real to me than anyone I have ever known, because she is more ideal. Having been dead three thousand years nothing will make her less so for me. The world is full of blessings."[68]

At a Heidelberg museum, Cora had a different but also profoundly affecting experience with a particular piece of art. For years, she wrote in her diary, she had been haunted by the memory of a portrait of a distinguished middle-aged woman of the seventeenth century: "She wore a white curled wig, had large full eyes, a sensitive curling mouth, beautiful throat and softly curving breasts which her deeply cut white dress revealed. The dark grey background brought out the light luminous color in which the figure itself was painted. I had no idea where I had seen this portrait, and little by little the association connected with it became more tenuous until I forgot the frame and the background and this person became a living being that I felt I must have seen somewhere, sometime."

Upon rediscovering the portrait, Cora recalled that she had previously made a hasty visit to this museum with her Du Bois kin in 1921, when she was seventeen. She wrote, "I recalled passing hurriedly thru that very room and casting only a glance at that particular picture; yet yesterday I felt myself in the presence of an old friend, a person whose every detail was known to me, and yet withal one who remained shrouded in a certain fascinating mystery."[69] One wonders whether, at seventeen, Cora was attracted to "the grey lady" (her name for the portrait) as a sensuous, mature woman and, at the same time, a benign mother figure. She did recognize her own mother's beauty but, we know, did not find her benign.

Interestingly, Cora's diary entry the next day was about her mother. Looking at the Heidelberg Schloss reminded her of a photo of the castle that hung in her mother's room and that she had seen throughout her childhood. Thinking of her mother, Cora wrote, "She once lived in Heidelberg, was married here. She has seen the same things, walked the same paths, probably thought the same thoughts. Here I am, her flesh and blood, intimately associated with her, yet all this is strange and new."[70] This was one of the rare instances in which Cora overtly identified with her mother.

Thoughts of her mother also brought back painful memories of her father:

Before leaving for Europe I emptied a trunk in the attic of its old papers. It was full of father's school note books, pictures, briefcases, letters, and all such treasures as I myself cherish as an integral part of my individuality in its physical and outer manifestations. It was dreary sentimentality to cherish longer the contents of the trunk; yet as I burned them I felt guilty and sick at heart as though I had helped to bring father one step nearer to complete death. Paradoxically, immortality is transient, exists only in the memory of those who remember, and yet here I deliberately wiped out some of the last *visible* claims that my own father has to even a brief remembrance. He has disappeared so achingly swiftly as it is.[71]

The act of burning these mementoes, which she had treasured, was a dramatic one. It was a highly symbolic effort to rid herself of the pain and sorrow associated with the loss of her father as she moved into a new stage of life.

Cora's months in Germany, as she contemplated her future, constituted a period of self-reflection. She explored libraries and museums, and she also practiced some ethnography. In her diary she recorded descriptions of German social and cultural behavior that she observed. And from these observations she began to formulate ideas about broader sociocultural patterns, along with their underlying psychological implications, that she could then compare with patterns she had observed in the United States. The following entry from her diary is evidence of an incipient psychocultural anthropologist:

> A broad fertile plain dotted right and left with little round villages—but never an isolated farm house. No wonder they [the Germans] fail to understand our American policy of isolation. For centuries their social life, tradition and history has motivated against isolation. It is an American, at least a new world, luxury. Privacy is perhaps the individual aspect of the same problem. I am convinced the individual has far more privacy and seclusion in the States than in Europe. Life in the large cities tends to limit them of course. The hue and cry we set up over this loss is proof how dear they were to us.
>
> The independence, self-reliance, and accompanying self-respect so much admired in America seems no necessary part of a young European's character equipment. Women readily admit their inferiority to men. Young men seek the patronage of men who have arrived. Families are widely drawn upon for prestige. Flattery, logrolling and snobbery are rife. Of course the same vices exist in the States but I think are not so blatant in their use. There is a feeling that there is something a little disgraceful in such methods. Here that feeling seems not to exist—which of course makes the procedure here far more legitimate than it does in the States.[72]

By November Cora had made up her mind. She would pursue a career in anthropology, and so she wrote to Ruth Benedict for advice, asking for alternatives to Columbia for graduate work. She had decided that Boas's proposed dissertation project was not what she wanted to do and, furthermore, that she did not want to become one of his female "handmaidens" and "emotional daughters," a role from which she had only recently escaped.[73] And although she greatly admired Benedict, she knew that Boas ruled the department and that she would be forced to work with him rather than with Benedict. Benedict responded to Cora's letter, recommending that she study with Alfred Kroeber and Robert Lowie at the University of California, Berkeley. Cora wrote to them and received cordial replies from both Kroeber and Lowie, inviting her into the program. "In those days there was no need to be cagey about administrative procedures."[74] She was admitted into the graduate program in anthropology, beginning in January 1929.

During this same period, Cora also decided that she was more American than European and that "western Europe was going to pieces and I should turn to the Far East."[75] Her views, she reported, had been influenced by Oswald Spengler's *The Decline of the West* (1922), a book she had read in college and had reread in German during her months in Germany. Furthermore, she decreed, "the U.S. should face the Pacific rather than the Atlantic."[76] Little did she know how prophetic, both for herself and for her country, these thoughts would be.

Cora returned to the United States in time to celebrate Christmas with her mother and stepfather. Then, on December 30, having said farewells to family and friends, she boarded a train for San Francisco and her new life at the University of California, Berkeley. This voyage, as she put it, marked "the end of my late adolescence."[77] As she crossed the Continental Divide, she composed the following poem that expressed her own emotional "divide" as she left the familiar eastern side of the continent for new adventures in the West.

CONTINENTAL DIVIDE, COLORADO
Great piles of confused rock,
Boulders of variegated shape and color,
Massed into peaks and canyons
On whose precipitous slopes
Mesquite struggles to defeated victory.

Mad confusion of color
Even under the dull grey of a winter sky,
Madden confusion of form
Even under the leveling pressure of a vast
    solitude
In frenzied passion severs a continent in two
With a great bloody gash turned
    outward toward the sky.[78]

CHAPTER 3

Becoming an Anthropologist

[Miss Du Bois's] PhD examination was unquestionably one of
the most brilliant I have ever attended.
—A. L. Kroeber

"Open vistas" would be a suitable metaphor for the next stage of Cora
Du Bois's life. Moving to the West Coast in 1929, she not only faced out
across the Pacific but, as she later reported, she also learned to *look* outward. Berkeley and the San Francisco Bay Area were filled with hills and
mountains so that one could climb up and view the landscape from a
perspective that she had not experienced in the East.[1] The vistas were
huge and open. At the same time, the study of anthropology provided Cora
with a broad, new intellectual vista—a view of the world, and its many
different cultural inhabitants, throughout time and space. For the rest of
her life, she would savor these years of study and exploration.

After arriving in Berkeley in early January 1929, Cora wrote to her
mother providing her new address—a family hotel on Telegraph Avenue, one block from the university—and her first description of her new
locale: "The town is nice enough; the campus quite lovely; the weather
even more admirable than a native son paints it. Roses and callow lilies,
spring clothes and what not. Lowie and Kroeber have been charming.
They gave me long and personal attention. The technicalities here are
just as bad as at Columbia but at least Lowie and Kroeber do all they can
to minimize them."[2]

In coming to the University of California at Berkeley for graduate work in anthropology, Cora was joining the westernmost branch of a relatively new discipline in the United States. In 1901 UC Berkeley established the first anthropology program west of the Mississippi and hired Alfred Louis Kroeber as the program's first instructor and curator-custodian of what would become, much later, the Phoebe A. Hearst Museum of Anthropology. Kroeber, Franz Boas's first graduate student, had, in 1901, just completed a PhD in anthropology at Columbia. Like his mentor and many other early anthropologists, he would become intensively involved with simultaneously doing ethnography, collecting cultural artifacts, publishing, managing a museum, and building an academic program. And like its counterparts elsewhere—Harvard, Columbia, the University of Pennsylvania, and the University of Chicago—UC Berkeley's anthropology program would be closely linked with the establishment of a museum, in this case one to house, initially, its benefactor's collection.

Phoebe Apperson Hearst—a wealthy San Francisco philanthropist, UC regent, and the mother of William Randolph Hearst—provided the funds with which to build a temporary "museum" at the university, pay the salaries of two anthropologists, and underwrite some local and international archaeological and ethnological research expeditions. In addition, she covered the part-time salary for Frederic Ward Putnam, the famed director of Harvard University's Peabody Museum of Archaeology and Ethnology, to serve temporarily—and mostly in absentia—as director of the new museum. The first museum building, which was intended to be temporary but which lasted nearly sixty years, was a sixty-by-eighty-foot, two-story warehouse built of corrugated iron and known as the "Tin Bin."³

By the time Cora arrived in the spring of 1929, the museum had been moved to San Francisco and the Tin Bin turned into the Anthropology Department offices, library, and classrooms.⁴ The anthropology faculty had grown from two to three and one-half positions, now funded by the university, with additional monies provided for visiting anthropologists, research fellows, and some limited fieldwork by graduate students. Kroeber was chair of the department and director of the museum. Robert H. Lowie, another Boas-trained anthropologist from Columbia, and Edwin Meyer Loeb, with a degree from Yale, were the other two full-time

10. Alfred Kroeber. POR 36, Courtesy of The Bancroft Library, University of California, Berkeley.

professors of anthropology. Edward Winslow Gifford served as the museum curator and a part-time instructor. It was a small and intimate program situated in an unusual but intimate space.

Cora's first meeting with Alfred Kroeber was memorable. Kroeber was fifty-three and, by then, a renowned anthropologist and administrator, who, like his own mentor Boas, was somewhat Germanic and authoritarian in style. He asked Cora what she was interested in, and she responded, "You know, I have been reading Oswald Spengler's *Decline of the West* and am much influenced by him. I think this is an important but not a definitive book, but it is eventually the kind of thing I want to do. Meanwhile, I realize that I have to acquire a certain amount of technical training in anthropology, so I'm perfectly willing to sit down and do any ethnography [written description of a culture] that you think I should do." And Cora continued with her reminiscences: "I still remember Kroeber, who was quite a handsome man, with a short gray beard. He was sitting in what we called the Tin Bin—an old storage shed that had been turned into the Department of Anthropology. He sat there, stroking his beard, which was a very characteristic gesture, and looking out the window, doing his damnedest not to laugh."[5]

In actuality, Kroeber's response was probably both a mixture of amusement at this new graduate student's chutzpah and an appreciation of her particular ambitions—to learn enough worldwide ethnography, in historical context, to attempt something as grandiose as Spengler's work, however flawed it may have been. What Cora did not know at the time was that Kroeber had similar ambitions and that two years later he would begin to draft his 882-page *Configurations of Cultural Growth* (1944), a book not unlike what Cora had in mind and that addressed a formidable question: how and why do major cultural achievements of human civilizations tend to rise, cluster, and then decline?

Robert Lowie was the second in command in the Department of Anthropology at the time. He had completed his PhD in anthropology under Boas in 1908 and had then served as a research curator at the American Museum of Natural History in New York City before coming to UC Berkeley in 1921. Cora's first meeting with Lowie was quite different from the one with Kroeber: "Robert Lowie didn't get the same sort of high-toned aspirations that I was voicing to Kroeber, but he was delighted to have a graduate student arrive in Berkeley who would take both the French and German exams, which were required, right away on arrival. . . . He was German, a Viennese, actually, by extraction. Very much attached to the Vienna of his childhood and his notions of what Vienna was like, and to have someone come in and be given something to read and to translate—right there and then—I was his darling ever after."[6]

Unlike Kroeber, who had recently remarried and was expecting his first child, Lowie was a forty-six-year-old bachelor who enjoyed the social

11. Robert Lowie, ca. 1930. BANC PIC 1980.003:7—fALB, Courtesy of The Bancroft Library, University of California, Berkeley.

company of the graduate students. Cora found him "the most understanding, non-hortatory kind of elder," unlike "Papa Kroeber," who "could be pretty mean if he wanted to and very strict."[7] Also, Kroeber controlled the purse strings of the department. By contrast, Cora viewed Lowie as a more avuncular figure and a preferable mentor to Kroeber, who had "a paternalistic attitude that, for personal reasons, I objected to. There was a psychological problem there so that I didn't much like being bossed around by a father figure, whereas I was very drawn by a permissive uncle figure."[8]

Over time, Cora's relationship with Kroeber became one of mutual respect and friendship. He certainly admired her work, considered her PhD orals "brilliant," and, upon his retirement from Berkeley in the 1940s, tried to recruit her into the department. And, according to his wife, Theodora Kroeber, Cora was one of a small set of women whom Kroeber considered "warm friend[s]."[9] In 1929, however, based on her need to forge an identity as an independent woman—independent of traditional family life—one can understand Cora's slight antipathy toward the paternalistic and authoritarian Kroeber and her preference for Lowie. She had, after all, only recently freed herself from familial obligations to her mother and had selected Berkeley over Columbia so as to avoid Boas's paternalism, especially his paternalism toward women.

That spring semester Cora jumped right into the graduate anthropology program, taking the second semester of Lowie's seminar on theory, Kroeber's seminar on pre-Columbian Mexico, Frederick Teggart's seminar on social institutions, and an independent research course. In a late-January letter home she wrote, "I did a piece of work for Kroeber's seminar which was duly appreciated so I feel very joyous about that, though Lowie's seminar [on theory] still leaves me with a feeling of being a total ignoramus."[10] In addition, Cora read avidly because the program required competence in the classical four subfields of anthropology—archaeology, physical anthropology, linguistics, and cultural anthropology—but the requirements far exceeded what the teaching staff could offer. Cora had positive memories, as she put it, of having to "bone up for oneself": "I think that it placed the responsibility on the graduate student who," she reported in later years, "was accepted immediately as a serious intellectual and capable of sailing along without having his hand held every minute.... [T]he fact that you were put on your own and you had to find your own way was, I think, very good training and also it boosted one's ego.... The coddling hadn't yet set in that now exists, it seems to me, in graduate training."[11]

Cora's letters home indicate that she flourished in this atmosphere. As early as January 20, 1929, she wrote about "the joy of living" and "my permanent state of bubbling over about my work and life in general." She also reported that she was enjoying the other graduate students, who were "a most cordial and helpful lot . . . [but none] promising material for a playmate as yet, except possibly one Dorothy Demetracopoulou, a Greek girl."[12] In later years Cora would remember her cohort of graduate students as "a very pleasant group . . . for whom I formed deep affections and loyalties, which have lasted all my life."[13] In addition to Dorothy Demetracopoulou (Lee), it included such notable figures as Julian Steward, Ralph Beals, Isabel Kelly, Theodore McCown, Laura Thompson, and Carl Vogelin.

Cora's seminar with Kroeber introduced her to the Mayas, and for a brief period she became interested in becoming a Mayan specialist but was advised by Kroeber that, if this interest were to persist, she "had best go to Harvard," where the major Mayan experts were. Meanwhile, she began making plans for summer fieldwork, having quickly learned that "the field was clearly the objective of any anthropologist."[14] She applied to Harvard to participate in Alfred V. Kidder's summer archaeology excavation of an abandoned New Mexican pueblo. Kidder, an eminent Harvard archaeologist, had recently published *An Introduction to the Study of Southwestern Archaeology* (1924), the first major synthesis of archaeological work in that part of the United States and something to which Cora had been exposed. However, she knew that Kidder generally did not accept women on his excavations because their presence was believed "to complicate" field expeditions, so she also began seeking alternatives.

By early March Cora had talked with both Kroeber and Lowie about doing summer fieldwork somewhere and reported in a letter home, "They have suggested turning me loose on the Wintu Indians of Northern California."[15] Kroeber's personal mandate, after coming to California, was to map the diverse indigenous languages and cultures of the region, just as Boas and his graduate students had been doing for other regions of North America. The objective was to retrieve as much information about different Native American tribes as possible while there were still native speakers and practitioners of their various cultures, despite the devastating impact of Euro-American settlers. By 1929 Kroeber had published his fairly exhaustive *Handbook of the Indians of California* (1925), but there were still areas that had not been covered, and he believed that there were Indians living north of Redding—in an area now submerged by Shasta Dam—who should be linguistically related to the Patwin and Wintun Penutian speakers of the Sacramento Valley. In addition, Kroeber suggested that Dorothy

Demetracopoulou, who was in her second year at Berkeley and specializing in linguistics, accompany Cora. By late March Cora had acquired, for one hundred dollars, a seven-passenger 1923 Willys-Knight for the two of them to drive into the wilds of northern California for this first foray into fieldwork.

Before the summer arrived, however, Cora had her first experience with a Native American informant, a Tolowa woman whose tribe was from northwestern California but who was in domestic service in nearby Oakland. Lowie had learned about her and had sent Cora to meet with her. Cora, in a series of interviews, gleaned enough information from Agnes Mattz, a full-blood Tolowa of forty-five, to publish an article several years later in the *American Anthropologist* about such topics as Tolowa girls' puberty rites, boys' education, marriage, social ranks, wealth and property, the position of women, and shamanism.[16]

In preparation for fieldwork among the Wintu, Cora read Kroeber's *Handbook of California Indians* and a small handful of existent ethnographies about California Indians. Lowie taught her some phonetics and how to transcribe an unwritten language. But when she went to Kroeber for advice in ethnographic field methods, she received the following response: "He looked thoroughly perplexed and, after stroking his beard and gazing out of the window for a few minutes, his face brightened and he said, 'Be sure you have a good supply of pencils and note books.' Seeing that this somehow did not allay the anxieties that every field trip seems to engender, he thought again and then said, 'Well, most Indians keep packs of nasty curs. They rush out barking but they are all cowards, so if you just pick up a stick and threaten them, they'll run.'"[17] That was the extent of fieldwork preparation that she and Dorothy received. "Armed with this advice, an enviable innocence and a great sense of adventure, Dorothy and I set out on our first fieldtrip."[18] They would spend three and a half months tracking down and working with Wintu informants in the Mount Shasta and Trinity Alps area of northern California.

Fieldwork among the Wintu

In early May Cora and Dorothy set off in their used car, which they named "Beastie," north from Berkeley to Redding, California—the major town just south of Mount Shasta, which marks the boundary between California and Oregon. Unlike today, there was no direct route to Redding, so they drove along the coast and then crossed over hill and dale into the Sacramento River Valley, where it became very hot. In a letter to her mother, Cora wrote,

> Beastie behaved incomparably. It kept a 40 mile pace without a quiver for what must have been 200 miles on end. Toward evening that pace brought us within view of snow covered mountains, Shasta and Lassen in particular. By supper time we were in Redding which is on the Sacramento River but pretty well out of the valley.
>
> That same night we drove out to a gas station some 10 miles farther on where we had heard the Wintuns had a dance lodge and where they were in the habit of congregating. That first evening I made my first Injun friend. Now some 36 hours later I am the bosom companion of all of them within a radius of fifteen miles.

And, in her ironic voice, Cora added, "Don't you regret that I never exerted all this social charm in the drawing room?"[19]

That first night Cora and Dorothy slept in a field behind the gas station. The next morning they returned to Redding to see the Indian commissioner, presumably to get permission to do fieldwork in this area. Then they headed north to the junction of the McCloud and Pit Rivers, where there was another gas station and a small cabin that they were able to rent from a German couple, the Bayhas, who managed the gas station. They were quickly adopted by the Bayhas, with whom Cora spoke German, and in the same letter home Cora reported, "They are treating us royally, particularly in the food line."

From this base, Cora and Dorothy were able to find numerous Wintu who would serve as informants, describing their language, culture, and society from the period that preceded Anglo-American dominance. Dorothy was able to work for the rest of the summer, recording the Wintu language and collecting Wintu myths, with one Wintu individual who lived close by. Cora had to forage farther afield in Beastie, but she, too, located an array of interesting and willing informants. In a letter home she explained that she spent about six hours a day with informants and another two to three hours writing up her field notes, adding, "I wish I could convince you [her mother] how really respectable and secure my existence is—no matter how much fun it would be to make up lovely adventures."[20] Mattie was clearly worried about her daughter's first foray into the wilds of northern California.

On May 18, 1929, Cora sent her first report to "Professor Kroeber":

So far I have collected what seems like a fairly complete account of such matters as marriage regulations and procedures, puberty ceremonies, food tabus, shamanism, etc. Myths, calendar system as it was, and other esoteric information, are coming more slowly. . . .

[W]e are paying informants $2.00 a day or $.25 an hour apparently to their perfect satisfaction. . . .

For the moment I am struggling with kinship terms, and am using basket designs as a form of relaxation. Miss Demetracopoulou has been of great assistance to me in recording native terms. Also as a commissary department she has been a great success since we feel as though we had been living on the fat of the land, yet she has just told me that we are not spending more than a dollar a day a piece.

All in all I am enjoying my work enormously and I hope that the results will prove satisfactory.[21]

Midway through the summer, Cora and Dorothy returned briefly to Berkeley to confer with Kroeber and to request more funds for their fieldwork. Cora also consulted with a UC Berkeley psychology professor who provided her with some emotional instability tests to administer to four shamans whom she had come to know and to a control group of nonshamans.[22] Early in her fieldwork Cora had witnessed Wintu shamans going into altered states of consciousness after frenetic dancing and singing, and she was intrigued by their capacities to become possessed by spirits and to go into trance and unconscious states either for traditional curing ceremonies or as part of their new Pentecostal faith and practices. Holy Rollers and members of other Pentecostal movements had moved into the region and had begun converting many of the Wintu. In a letter home, Cora wrote, "Just now I am on the trail of the psychology of shamanism, and since they themselves suggested the similarities between shamanistic trances, etc., and those which they received in their Pentecostal faith, we accompanied them last night to Redding to observe Holy Rollers in action."[23]

In another letter home Cora reported, "One old woman, who is the head doctor [shaman] of the crowd, has almost literally taken me to her bosom, calls me grandchild lustily. In fact, I hope I have lured her into doctoring the rheumatism of a neighbor and permitting us to see her in a 'trench' as my interpreter calls it. They are rather suspicious of white people on such occasions and we feel highly honored."[24] That summer Cora seems to have quickly established rapport with a set of Wintu informants. She discovered that despite her natural reserve and detachment, she could be a successful fieldworker.

The shamans whom Cora met and observed that summer, together with others whom she learned about from informants, all had personality characteristics that the Wintu recognized as unusual. But instead of being considered crazy, they were viewed as having special access to spirits that gave them powers to cure others. The Wintu considered becoming a shaman hard work. As one of Cora's informants put it, "Doctors [shamans] have to starve themselves. They have a hard time. I don't see why they want to be doctors." Another young man had "shamanistic seizures" and was taken "by concerned white people of the vicinity" to an insane asylum at Napa (Napa State Hospital), where he was diagnosed by Western-trained physicians as an "epileptic psychotic." However, when he returned home, no stigma was attached to him by the Wintu, and he became "a doctor," the new terminology that the Wintu had begun using for their traditional curers.[25]

All in all, this first summer with the Wintu was enormously successful. Not only was it an adventure for these two budding anthropologists, but Cora and Dorothy had cut their teeth as ethnographers. And they had successfully collected a lot of linguistic and ethnographic material, which, supplemented by more fieldwork among the Wintu the subsequent summer, led to two lengthy joint publications on Wintu mythology and, for Cora, a more general ethnographic monograph about the Wintu.[26] Furthermore, and perhaps most significantly, Cora had begun to identify an important theoretical orientation for herself—that is, studying the psychological characteristics of seemingly aberrant individuals and their fit within society. Cora had personally witnessed, during this first fieldwork expedition, the significant relationship of culture to personality that she would explore in greater depth in the late 1930s as a member of the new interdisciplinary field of inquiry known as "culture and personality."

From Student to Professional Anthropologist

Cora was now on her way to becoming a professional anthropologist. Various aspects of her childhood and youth had coalesced to move her in this direction: her early encounters with different cultures and languages; her personal identity as a "curious observer" of humankind; and her experiences as an outsider in her own society that helped give her perspective on both her own culture and that of others. Furthermore, growing up with a seriously problematic brother and having to come to terms with her own stigmatized sexual orientation probably contributed to her special interest in combining the study of other cultures with a psychological focus on the individual and that person's fit within society.

During the next three years, Cora would complete all the requirements for a PhD in anthropology, do more fieldwork and publish a variety of papers and monographs, make new friends, and explore parts of California and Hawaii—all topics addressed below. And Dorothy Demetracopoulou—better known as Dorothy Lee, the author of *Freedom and Culture* (1959)—would become a special friend with whom she shared an apartment in Berkeley for the academic year following their joint fieldwork. In addition, during this period Cora's relationship with her mother improved immensely.

PhD Requirements and the Intellectual Climate of the Era

In addition to demonstrating fluency in reading French and German, anthropology graduate students at Berkeley had to pass a five-day series of written qualifying examinations that covered all the subfields of anthropology. This was followed by an oral qualifying exam with five or six examiners, half of whom were from other departments, such as geography, law, or economics. In addition, of course, there was a PhD dissertation and dissertation defense. Whereas in most contemporary anthropology programs, the dissertation is based on original ethnographic, archaeological, or biological field data, during this period at UC Berkeley the dissertation was usually a library research endeavor used to demonstrate a student's effective handling of the cross-cultural literature with respect to a particular topic. Fieldwork, as already noted, was central to the enterprise of becoming an anthropologist, but students were expected to do it, and to publish an ethnographic monograph, *before* undertaking the dissertation.[27] After her first summer of fieldwork with the Wintu, Cora was well on her way to fulfilling this particular requirement.

The combined focus on (a) contributing to the ethnographic record through original fieldwork and (b) doing a library research dissertation using already published ethnographic or archaeological materials represented a continuation of the academic tradition established by Boas at Columbia and experienced there by Alfred Kroeber and Robert Lowie. As Cora reported much later, in the 1960s,

> [Kroeber and Lowie] saw the recording of the rapidly disappearing American Indian tribal life as both a primary duty and the basic training device of a young anthropologist. We were all expected to go out and do an ethnographic monograph. The pattern of such monographs [was] phrased in terms of [Clark] Wissler's universal patterns of culture which really amounted to little more than a series of chapter headings: Material culture, kinship and social life, the life cycle, and religion. Here Leslie Spier, who was a frequent but intermittent member of the faculty, insistently drilled us on the observing [of] behavior and artifacts in minute and objective detail. He stressed using indigenous terms and categories, of knowing what native speakers meant when they use a word like "xxx" for house. It was a precursor of what is now known as ethno-science, although it was then seen only as good field technique and had not yet been elaborated, complicated, and possibly desiccated, into what is the "new" . . . ethno-science.[28]

Cora and her fellow graduate students at Berkeley belonged to the second generation of Boasians, who were being taught to do what she later called—perhaps a bit too harshly—"unthinking, non-problem-oriented ethnography." The principal issue they were grappling with, as she put it, was "historical reconstruction, born of the Boasian rebellion against the *a priori* history fashioned by British and German cultural evolutionists. . . . Comparisons were [also] much on our minds."[29] The orientation was, accordingly, more about tracing the spread of cultural "traits"—specific practices and artifacts—through time and identifying "culture areas" based on these trait lists than it was about understanding how particular cultures were structured or the roles that individual practitioners played in a given culture. Although such noted anthropologists as A. R. Radcliffe-Brown and Bronislaw Malinowski—both leaders in developing theories about how societies were structured and functioned as integrated systems—visited Berkeley for brief periods during Cora's graduate-student days, their different versions of functionalism seem to have had little impact on the intellectual orientation of the department.

Ralph Beals, one of Cora's fellow graduate students, has corroborated her memories of this period at Berkeley, also noting the strong focus on historical reconstruction, the distribution of cultural traits, and questions of cultural diffusion versus independent invention. In his memoir, Beals also alludes to Cora: "We [graduate students] talked unabashedly about what *culture* did and did not do without shame for our apparent reification [using "culture" as if it were an actor rather than the ideas, practices, and inventions of groups of people]. Culture we used as a shorthand and we knew very well that only human beings really acted. And a little later if we were in danger of forgetting, Homer Barnett, Dorothy Demetracopoulou, Cora Du Bois, and George Devereaux were there to insist that we were wasting our time studying anything else but individuals."[30]

Nonetheless, Cora's early interest in the psychology of shamans and the relationship of individual personalities to culture made her something of an anomaly in this intellectual context. Although Devereaux, who had a strong psychoanalytic orientation, would surely have shared some of her interests, he was several years behind her in the anthropology program and, consequently, is not someone whom she mentions as a member of her cohort. And although Kroeber had himself undergone a brief analysis in New York City and had even practiced some pychoanalysis in San Francisco, he rarely brought these interests to bear on his teaching of anthropology. His interests were in identifying both specific and broad processes of cultural growth and change that he preferred to view as "superorganic" or "superindividual" phenomena—that is, processes that could be analyzed without reference to individuals. Kroeber strongly preferred such historical, superorganic explanations of cultural processes to ones that focused on individuals and that introduced psychological factors into sociocultural analyses.[31]

While a psychological orientation was *not* part of the intellectual climate in anthropology during her years at Berkeley, in later years Cora would note that other new ideas were "in the air."[32] For example, it was during this period that Kroeber began his famous trait survey of California ethnography with the assistance of the Polish statistician Stanislaw Klimak. Klimak was someone from whom Cora also learned statistical methods that may have contributed to her later formulation of "modal personality" (see chapter 5). In addition, Kroeber and Carl Sauer, a professor of geography, taught a joint seminar on an early version of cultural ecology, a research area that Julian Steward, one of Cora's fellow graduate students, would develop throughout his career. Kroeber also taught a seminar on comparative law with Max Radin, a professor of jurisprudence in the law school, which foreshadowed later work in comparative law.

Max Radin's brother, Paul Radin—"an urbane, peripatetic and informal teacher"—was also, according to Cora, "very much part of our graduate group on the Berkeley campus during the depression."[33] In fact, he may have been the most compatible member of the group for Cora because of his focus on the individual and his use of personal documents in his anthropological research and publications. Radin had completed a PhD in anthropology at Columbia but, unable to find a position during the Depression, he worked part-time for the Works Projects Administration (WPA) in San Francisco and spent his spare time in the Tin Bin on the Berkeley campus, occasionally teaching a course. Just before Cora's arrival at Berkeley, Radin had published *Crashing Thunder: The Autobiography of a Winnebago Indian* (1926), as well as his seminal book, *Primitive Man as Philosopher* (1927). "[W]e were all exposed to his insistence on the uniqueness of the human experience and the emphasis on the role of the thinker and the skeptic in non-literate societies," she reported.[34] Radin would, therefore, have represented the antithesis of Kroeber with respect to thinking about culture in relationship to individuals.

So, by the end of Cora's first semester and summer at Berkeley, she had demonstrated her proficiency in French and German and had undertaken her first fieldwork. The second full year was focused on studying for the written and oral qualifying exams to come and preparing her Wintu materials for publication. It was a period of intense study, mixed with an active social life with fellow anthropologists, which was marred only somewhat by the October 29, 1929, stock market crash and the beginning of the Great Depression. Cora's economic independence was affected, but her inheritance from her father, fortunately, was not decimated. In fact, with her "vast income of $1,800 a year" she was able to help some of her fellow students with their college registration fees of twenty-five dollars. As she reported in later life, many students had to work at other jobs, including trafficking in illegal alcohol (bootlegging), in order to pursue their graduate work. The Depression, she said, engendered a sense of mutual responsibility.[35] Its effects at first appeared to Cora, at least, to be less severe in California than in the East, where her mother and stepfather resided. In a fall 1930 letter to them, she wrote, "You in the east seem very much more concerned by the general business than we are out here on the coast. It is possibly the difference between an industrial as opposed to an agricultural area. It may also be that we move in a circle which is comparatively less affected by business conditions."[36] Two years later, however, Cora had become better aware of the effects of the Depression and reported that she had voted "a straight socialist ticket" in the historic 1932 presidential elections.[37]

Despite the Depression, in letters home (sent every week or two) Cora talked about trips into San Francisco for shopping, dinner, and the theater, weekend trips to nearby Marin County to hike on Mount Tamalpais and to explore Stinson Beach, and other weekend trips to Carmel, where a Berkeley friend had a family home. Robert Lowie was frequently mentioned as taking small groups of students out to dinner in San Francisco. So, by the spring of 1930, Cora was referring to herself and Dorothy as "the life of the department"—the two women who helped Kroeber and Lowie entertain a constant flow of visitors. Some of the entertaining was quite elegant and required evening dress. For example, for one dinner party at the Kroebers' home Cora reported that she wore a long black gown that her mother had sent her for such occasions, and she described the evening as having "the proper amount of dancing, conversation, and wine."[38] Prohibition seems not to have stopped the flow of liquor among anthropologists, although "bathtub gin" was occasionally mentioned.

In these wonderfully descriptive accounts of life in Berkeley what is most striking is the warmth that Cora regularly expressed toward her mother, whom she now addressed as "Dearest Marmy" or "My own darling Marmy." Distance, combined with an increased sense of independence and a clear direction toward a career, seems to have helped Cora move past her deep ambivalence toward her mother. Reciprocally, Mattie seems to have accepted her daughter's path toward a professional career and to have tried to be helpful by sending her regular shipments of clothes, household goods, and even darned stockings. Richard, Cora's stepfather, made prints of her photographic negatives from her Wintu fieldwork—something he would also do for her during her two-year period of research in Alor, Indonesia, in the late 1930s. And of great importance, he and Mattie also oversaw her financial investments and sent her periodic reports. At Cora's strenuous urging, Mattie and Richard crossed the country and joined her in Berkeley for Christmas 1929, the conclusion of her first full year there. She was now ready to show them her new home and to introduce them to her new friends.

Cora's journal shows, nonetheless, that she was still struggling with how to balance her need for independence, and some degree of isolation, with friendship and intimate ties with others. In January 1929, after just arriving in Berkeley, she wrote,

I have always admired self-sufficiency and a certain proud isolation of the individual. Isolation is of course inevitable, particularly for a complexly organized person, but what I admire is a certain glad sure acceptance of this loneliness, not the craven evasions so common. Friendship, family relationships and even, or maybe especially marriage, are so frequently compromises of the individual with his sense of aloneness. Friendship, it seems to me, should rest on a community of taste, a joy in companionship, not on a fear of loneliness. . . . I must learn to be totally detached and yet not inhuman. I must continue to experience passion, friendship, and family ties, but only in their positive aspects. I must guard against all negative feelings of dependence and yet be careful to give no offense. It is a strength which must be kept more secretly hidden than any weakness.[39]

By May of the following year, while back doing fieldwork among the Wintu, Cora made an important new distinction about herself and personal relationships: "It would be desirable to attain *perspective* without *detachment*," she wrote in her diary. "Perspective lends true value to experience and gives its possessor poise; while detachment is a protective device which rapidly makes life cold and freezes its owner."[40] Her inclinations toward detachment seemed to decrease as her first year at Berkeley progressed and as she became socially active and comfortable within the Department of Anthropology.

In addition to her growing departmental friendships, Cora also sought out other women, outside of anthropology, who shared her professional goals, recreational interests, and also her sexual orientation. She made three such close friends during her first year in Berkeley, whom, with herself, she referred to as "the quartet." These were the friends with whom she spent weekends hiking in Marin County or exploring Carmel and other parts of the San Francisco Bay Area. One of these women was Emily Huntington, a young professor of economics at UC Berkeley who came from the socially prestigious and wealthy Huntington family. She was eight years older than Cora, had a doctorate in economics from Radcliffe, and had begun teaching at Berkeley in 1928. Huntington remained at Berkeley throughout her career, specializing in social welfare issues. She also played a significant role in opening the UC Berkeley Faculty Club to women. The official University of California memoriam for Huntington, following her death in 1982, described her as "a person of pleasant demeanor: erect in carriage, in dress soignée, articulate but not loquacious, in glance somewhat reserved though neither aloof nor unfriendly"—very much the kind of person Cora liked and admired.[41] Many years later, in the summer of 1948 when Cora returned to Berkeley to teach in the Summer School, she lived in the Faculty Club while Jeanne Taylor, Cora's long-term partner who had accompanied her to Berkeley, stayed in the Huntington home.

The second member of the quartet was Dorothy Williams, a Berkeley law student who would practice in San Francisco and become Emily Huntington's long-term partner in life. She is described in the Huntington memoriam as Huntington's "long-time friend" and "a lawyer of great intelligence and wit. Together they [Huntington and Williams] contributed much to the social milieu of their campus friends, with splendid parties marked by serious discussion in a hospitable environment." Ironically, however, despite recognizing Huntington's long-term and probable lesbian relationship with Williams, the same memoriam noted that women of Huntington's generation "who aspired to professional careers frequently did not expect to marry."[42]

The third member of the quartet was Eleanor "Nell" Barnes, a psychiatric social worker at the Letterman Army Medical Center in San Francisco, which at the time was the U.S. Army's largest general hospital and the first one to hire women. Dorothy Williams and Nell had known one another as students at Wellesley College. And it was Nell who, in the summer of 1930, introduced Cora to Abram Kardiner, a New York psychoanalyst with whom Cora would later collaborate as part of the culture and personality movement. Kardiner was spending the summer in Carmel attending to a patient. During Cora's third year in Berkeley, she would begin to share a house with Nell, and in 1935 Nell would move with her to the East Coast.

Nell also inspired some of Cora's poetry writing during her Berkeley days. Below are two of her poems from that period:

TO N.B.
Spring brings acacias
Nauseatingly sweet,
Japonica and iris
With dancing feet.

You bring misty thought
Deliriously mad,
Noli me tangere,
And beauty where I walk.

TO N.B.
My dear, your pardon.
If for the moment

I err in considering you lightly;
For the moment, I say,
You are a beautiful adventure,
A gay interlude,
An island of delight,
In too much humanity.[43]

Nell seems, indeed, to have been "a gay interlude" for Cora, not a lasting love relationship. Cora's life as an anthropologist and then as an OSS officer during World War II, took her away on new adventures and to new parts of the world. Nell, by contrast, seems to have settled permanently in New York City, where she pursued a career in social work and counseling, becoming head of the Counseling Service of the New York State Society for Mental Health.

Cora, in her letters home, sometimes referred to another "quartet"—one that consisted of Dorothy Demetracopoulou, Robert Lowie, Paul Radin, and herself. "We are an inseparable quartet in the Tin Bin," she wrote. Lowie and Radin had been close friends as young men growing up in New York City and, according to Cora, had had "a delightful relationship."[44] And, as two bachelors, they probably enjoyed spending time with these two younger, engaging women graduate students. Both men even began consulting Cora about their own manuscripts, something that pleased her immensely. In one letter home, written on New Year's Eve 1931, Cora mentioned that the Tin Bin was empty of people except for herself and Radin, who was "still jobless but charming" and liked to talk. With wry humor, she added, "I am his only victim."[45]

While the relationships with Lowie and Radin were both academic *and* social, the relationship with Alfred Kroeber was strictly academic, except for occasional dinner parties at his home. Kroeber was the person whom Cora had to keep impressed if she were going to receive funds for fieldwork, fellowship support, and support in getting work published. Given this more formal relationship, whenever Kroeber praised her written work, Cora was elated. "I am doubly pleased since he is chary with praise," she wrote home in September 1929 after Kroeber had read and lauded "Wintu Myths," the manuscript she had written with Dorothy Demetracopoulou.[46] Before leaving on sabbatical that spring, Kroeber arranged to have it published by the *University of California Publications in Archaeology and Ethnology*. At the time, few journals of anthropology existed, and publication was largely financed institutionally in monographic series.[47]

In the spring of 1930, while Kroeber was away, Cora audited a course in abnormal psychology, served as a teaching assistant for Loeb's course in primitive religion, and began to draft her Wintu monograph. That spring she was also invited to join the Phi Sigma Pi National Honor Fraternity but considered it "an empty honor, except when filling out application blanks for jobs."[48] And she and Lowie worked out a schedule for taking her qualifying exams, writing a thesis, and defending it that would enable her to receive the PhD in September 1932. In addition, in May she returned for a month to the Wintu to collect more data for her monograph.

When Kroeber returned to Berkeley in June, Cora reported that she had a long talk with him "about life in general. He neither urged nor discouraged my going ahead rapidly with my Ph.D. He said that since there was no financial pressure and I was enjoying my work and getting things published, he saw no reason to hurry, unless I definitely pined for a position. He said that the more I had published, the better the job I could step into."[49] That turned out to have been an overly optimistic assessment by Kroeber of the job market, especially for women.

By late June Cora was ready for a break from her intense work and social life in Berkeley. She boarded the ss *Maui* and set sail from San Francisco for Honolulu, writing in her diary, "I am still oppressed by a year and a half of constant human company."[50] She needed a period of aloneness and resuscitation that anonymous ship travel provided. Why Hawaii? Probably because it was easily accessible from San Francisco and provided a new geographic and cultural terrain to explore that was located farther west in the Pacific. Margaret Mead's *Coming of Age in Samoa* (1928), which had recently been published to great public acclaim and which Cora had read and liked, may have also sparked an interest in exploring some of the Pacific islands. In a 1929 letter home Cora wrote, " I have just been reading Margaret Mead's *Coming of Age in Samoa*. It is an excellent book of its sort. You might enjoy reading it. . . . It is the kind of anthropological analysis I should like to be able to make."[51]

Cora's six-week trip to the islands of Oahu and Maui was resuscitating. She explored both islands and waxed poetic about their beauty, their tropical plants, and their wonderful mixture of peoples. On board ship she made friends with a mother and daughter who lived in Honolulu and who introduced her to other local residents. She also met a variety of anthropologists, who showed her through the Bishop Museum and took her to various archaeological sites on Oahu. And she attended, and was asked to speak at, her first meeting of the American Anthropological Association, which happened to occur while she was there. The trip—a mixture of recreation and professional activity—would inspire her to return to Honolulu to teach for a semester in the 1950s.

Completing the PhD

In the fall of 1930 Cora taught several sections of Introduction to Anthropology while working to complete the requirements for her PhD in anthropology. In a letter home she wrote,

> Today should have been an epoch making event in my career. It was my first day of teaching—college students at that; but instead I surprised myself by being very calm and collected and by talking fluently and effortlessly. I have 3 sections of some 15 to 18 students, twice a week. . . . I also surprised myself by talking fluently and at length in Kroeber's seminar, even to the point of successfully disagreeing with him. Do you suppose I am growing up at last? Or do you suppose that I adapt slowly and therefore it takes me a year and a half to become sufficiently accustomed to my environment to gain assurance?[52]

For those of us who knew her as an eminent and formidable Harvard professor, it is hard to imagine Cora Du Bois being nervous about teaching, let alone about speaking up in a graduate seminar. But she, too, had to build self-confidence as a young woman.

During that semester, Cora and Dorothy began working on their second lengthy Wintu mythology paper, which Cora sent to Ruth Benedict for consideration in the *Journal of American Folklore*, which Benedict edited. In a letter to Benedict, Cora wrote,

> Miss Demetracopoulou and myself are sending the *JAFL* under separate cover a somewhat lengthy study of Wintu mythology. In fact the length of the accompanying texts, if not the study proper, has discouraged us

from submitting it to the University of California press which already has a collection of Wintu tales in its printing office. . . .

I am anxious to return east in the not too distant future and renew my acquaintance with you. I feel distinctly indebted to you for my interest in Anthropology, and that is no small obligation.[53]

Benedict responded quickly and positively, writing, "Congratulations on your Wintu paper. I hardly got to my party last night because I was so genuinely interested in it—and that is positively abnormal with me."[54] The manuscript was accepted and published in 1932.

In August 1931 Cora passed her five-day written predissertation qualifying exams "creditably," according to Kroeber, and then took her orals in September, although they left her feeling anxious. In a letter home she wrote,

I waited to write you until I could tell you that my orals were successfully over. I thot [*sic*] that I would have the world by the tail. Actually I'm afraid I haven't. Even the relief of being thru with them doesn't buoy me much after the fiasco I made of them. I couldn't seem to agree with anyone. For three full hours I wrangled with all six members of the committee in turn. The only modicum of cheer which I can squeeze from the ordeal is that I must have remarkably original ideas. Of course I passed, but my laurels are moth-eaten. I "lit out" before I saw Kroeber. I was feeling too low to face him. Isabel [Kelly] called me up to say that Kroeber didn't seem ill disposed—so I am making the most of that grain of comfort.[55]

Kroeber and the other faculty were, apparently, satisfied with Cora's performance, and in October Kroeber offered her a $1,000 fellowship for the next academic year, substantially more than she earned as a graduate student teaching assistant.

Following these exams, Cora concentrated on completing her Wintu monograph and undertaking the research and writing of her PhD dissertation. What is most interesting about her Wintu ethnography is its psychological orientation, which she made evident at the very start. "The present account," she wrote, "lays stress upon behavior and attitudes of mind; this, however, has not affected the presentation of material in traditional ethnographic form. Artifacts employed are merely tools of behavior. For that reason, descriptions of them are relegated to a separate section which is mainly for purposes of reference." Then she asserted, significantly, that "culture types" are just "compilations or averages to which the individual only partly conforms and which have no existence in reality" and that, accordingly, she would attempt "to distort as little as possible the personal and anecdotal nature of the material as it was procured in the field."[56] Du Bois was making an important theoretical point about what constituted a "culture"—it was made up of a diverse set of individuals whose variability was generally not recognized or presented in standard ethnographies of the time. Furthermore, she indicated that she intended to present some of that variability by using personal documentation—that is, accounts of individual Wintu and how they themselves talked about their society and cultural practices. In this respect, Du Bois was way ahead of her time. With a few exceptions, the use of informants' voices did not enter anthropological writings until the postmodernist period of the 1980s.

Cora did indeed use personal documentation whenever possible in her ethnographic account of the Wintu, especially with respect to shamanism, which, she asserted, was "one of the most vital aspects of Wintu culture still extant." And she concluded the ethnography with the argument that because the Wintu had resided in small, informally organized villages, "[p] ersonalities are more important than social forms."[57] Individual shamans could, she argued, shape society.

Du Bois's focus on the individual in culture was very much counter to Kroeber's perspective at the time and that of the Anthropology Department in general. Nonetheless, Kroeber praised the ethnography and helped Cora get it published in the *University of California Publications in American Archaeology and Ethnology*. In a letter home, Cora reported, "Kroeber said my ethnography was a very good piece of work—which, coming from him, gave me the sensation of licking the cream off of the top of the bottle of milk."[58]

Cora considered her dissertation, by contrast, "a very dull and tedious library job" on a topic that Lowie had suggested.[59] It was entitled "Girls' Adolescence Observances in North America." Women's first menstrual rites were something that had been observed and written about but not systematically examined, so Cora scoured and synthesized the Native American literature. "Puberty and menstrual customs," she wrote, "would seem to lend themselves particularly to an investigation of what is cultural and what is psychologically fundamental in human behavior since they center about a definite physiological condition."[60] At the time, however, there was not enough cultural, psychological, or physiological information about menstruation for her to do very much with the data. In reflecting back on her thesis, she noted that she found lots of other practices associated with girls' puberty rites—such as boys' adolescence rites, vision quests, and certain child-rearing practices—but no order beyond that of culture areas. "The best formulation of my insights occurred a few years later in Kroeber's concept of 'stimulus diffusion' (I may say without acknowledgement—but then, ideas are in the air and a young professional is often proprietary about the obvious)."[61] Here she was alluding to the notion that ideas, such as menstrual pollution, can diffuse from one culture to another without all the concomitant practices. Rather, what such new ideas do is stimulate inventions that fit the new culture.

Cora's final PhD oral exams were, by contrast, a lively and satisfying affair. The night before them Lowie took Cora, Paul Radin, and a third person into San Francisco for dinner, dancing, and a movie "to cheer me before my exams. . . . It was not too hilarious, but Robert is so nice about things and so enthusiastic about his parties that it is impossible not to enjoy oneself."[62] The next afternoon, on October 6, 1932—just twenty days before her twenty-ninth birthday—Cora met in a Tin Bin seminar room with Kroeber, Lowie, and three other UC Berkeley professors—Ronald L. Olson, a recently appointed anthropologist; Edward C. Tolman, a prominent psychologist; and Olga Louise Bridgman, an MD and psychologist—for several hours of conversation about her thesis and related matters. Cora's gleeful letter home following the exam says it all:

I am pleased to report with my usual modesty that I passed with flying colors. Of course the committee was inexplicably amiable and gave me much occasion to hold forth to my heart's content without having to answer shot-gun factual questions. They all said very nice things to me after the ordeal. In fact Lowie said that the exams had only one drawback—that members of 2 other departments, who are rather critical, were not there to witness the performance. You see—I am a shameless boaster—but if one can't boast to one's family, it is a pretty sad affair.[63]

Two different sets of graduate student friends feted Cora that night, and the next, with dinner parties. And soon thereafter Kroeber would write, in a December 1932 letter of recommendation for Cora, "Miss Du Bois is a young woman of superb cultural background, with genuine flair for theoretical problems, which is combined with interests in empirical research. Her Ph.D. examination was unquestionably one of the most brilliant I have ever attended and aroused the admiration of the non-anthropologists of the Committee. I should not hesitate in grading her 'A.'"[64]

Postdoc Years

Cora's outstanding conclusion to her graduate school years and receipt of the PhD in the fall of 1932 did not, however, lead to a job. For the next three years she marked time at Berkeley—usefully, by doing more field-work and publishing—while trying to find a teaching position or get a postdoctoral fellowship that would enable her to pursue her interests in anthropology and psychology. Not only was it the Depression, when jobs were scarce, but what jobs there were in anthropology usually went to men, who were considered to be in greater need because they were "the heads" of households. Furthermore, although anthropology as a profession had seemed welcoming to women, it was not welcoming with regard to professional positions. Because of the prominence of women like Ruth Benedict and Margaret Mead, we tend to think of anthropology as a field in which women achieved parity with men of their same era, but this is not the case.[65]

Benedict had been unusual in ultimately getting a full-time, permanent position at Columbia in the 1930s. Despite being the senior member of the department, however, when Boas retired in 1937, she was passed over for chairing the department and Ralph Linton was brought in from the outside to serve as chair. Mead had a secure position at the New York Museum of Natural History but was never awarded a professorship at Barnard, Columbia, or elsewhere. The one exception was Gladys Reichard, another Boas student, who, as mentioned in chapter 2, was appointed to the newly created position in anthropology at Barnard in 1921.

Only a few women of Du Bois's age cohort achieved academic professorships. For the most part, during the first half of the twentieth century, women anthropologists with PhDs were relegated to untenured lecturer and research positions or to positions outside of academe. For example, the Peabody Museum of Archaeology and Ethnology at Harvard had begun hiring women fieldworkers as early as the 1880s, but none of them ever achieved a professorship. (In fact, it was not until much later—when Du Bois was appointed the Zemurray-Stone Professor of Anthropology in 1954—that Harvard acquired its first tenured woman professor.) The Bureau of American Ethnology in Washington DC was treating women in a manner comparable to museums and academic programs. They hired women as fieldworkers but then refused to allow them to become members of the Anthropology Society of Washington.[66] Furthermore, because anthropology was a relatively new and small field, teaching positions were particularly scarce. Consequently, many young female anthropologists built careers around a series of temporary fellowships or positions in government institutes, or, like Charlotte Gower, simply disappeared from anthropology. Gower had been the first woman to receive a PhD in anthropology from the University of Chicago, in 1928, after which she had a brief faculty appointment at the University of Wisconsin, where, after six years, she was not retained and disappeared from all anthropology records.[67]

If one examines Du Bois's age cohort—that is, those American women anthropologists who were born during the first decade of the twentieth century and who received their PhDs in the late 1920s and 1930s—only *one* woman other than Du Bois had a successful academic career—however surprising this may sound.[68] That was Frederica de Laguna (PhD 1933, Columbia University), who had an appointment at Bryn Mawr College for most of her career. Cora's friend Dorothy Demetracopoulou Lee received her degree just ahead of Cora and had a one-year appointment at the University of Washington. Marriage took her east, where she had a brief appointment at Sarah Lawrence College and a longer one at Vassar. However, she chose to leave Vassar when she was widowed and had four children to support, taking a variety of short-term positions that were presumably more lucrative.[69] Neither of the other two female members of Cora's immediate UC Berkeley cohort—Laura Thompson and Isabel Kelly—ever had permanent academic appointments. Both women had unstable professional careers based on a variety of research grants and appointments and, in the case of Thompson, as an itinerant teacher. Kelly spent most of her career in Mexico working for various international institutions. As in the other sciences, women anthropologists of this period were marginalized.[70] In fact, Julian Steward's biographer, Virginia Kerns, has suggested that Steward's concept of a patrilineal band was a suitable metaphor for the profession.[71]

More Fieldwork

In later life, Cora described a conversation that she had with Kroeber soon after completing her PhD orals:

> There I was. I had finished my degree, and there was no job, and Kroeber said, "Well, you'll become a research assistant. We'll give you $600.00 for the year for your expenses and you go out [and he paused] and what would you like to do?" And I said, "Well, I'm really quite bored with the salvage ethnography [historical reconstruction of disappearing Native American societies]. How about [investigating] this Ghost Dance movement that is reputed to exist in some of these revivalist cults that [have emerged] in California and adjacent areas of Nevada and Oregon?" He said, "All right, fine."[72]

So Cora spent the next several years tracking evidence of the 1870 Ghost Dance religion, a revivalist cult that spread from the Northern Paiutes of California to other groups of Indians in California, Nevada, and Oregon. In response to the intrusive (and to them, destructive) Euro-American culture during the mid- to late nineteenth century, followers of the Ghost Dance religion believed that their dead would return and that peaceful and prosperous conditions would be reestablished if they performed the rituals of the Ghost Dance. Although this research project also fell into the category of historical reconstruction, it gave Cora entrée to numerous Indian communities in northern California, southern Oregon, and parts of Nevada and provided her with more opportunities to further her study of the psychology of shamanism.

During periods when she was not traveling, Cora visited several different psychiatric clinics in San Francisco to learn more about Western diagnoses of psychoses. She wanted to learn about the kinds of personality types that were considered abnormal by Western physicians and to compare them with Native American concepts of normal and abnormal behavior. In a January 1934 letter home, she wrote, "You mustn't mind if my vocabulary shows the influence of psychiatry for the next few months. I'm really not hipped—but I am attending Dr. Herman Adler's [UC professor of psychiatry] psychiatric clinics in the U.C. hospital in order to see mental patients in the flesh. It is all part and parcel of my desire to acquire some sort of orientation and technique for getting at shamans in field work."[73] Cora was moving into uncharted territory. There was, as yet, no recognized body of work that today we would call "psychological anthropology." Rather, there were just some preliminary ideas about how anthropologists might make use of developments in the fields of psychology and psychiatry (see chapter 4).

Cora's work on the 1870 Ghost Dance and other revivalist cults resulted in two publications: a short monograph entitled *The Feather Cult of the Middle Columbia* (1938) and a book-length monograph, *The 1870 Ghost Dance* (1939), that has recently been republished. In both works she used personal documents, such as life histories, to try to communicate the motivations underlying individual and group conversions to one messianic religion or another and to document how specific individuals became prophets and helped to spread particular belief systems and practices. What they all had in common—the Ghost Dance and the Feather, Shaker, and Smohalla Cults—Cora concluded, was an effort to regain some authority, in Native terms, first to resist the impact of Euro-Americans and then to make inevitable adjustments to the dominant society.[74] Cora's main scholarly contribution was twofold: the historical reconstruction of these movements and her psychological insights into them.

Trials and Tribulations

Cora made this period of more or less unemployment a productive one. Still, it became financially and emotionally trying as the years went by. Financial discussions in her letters home became more frequent, as well as expressions of frustration with Kroeber, from whom financial support was always uncertain. Kroeber, of course, had other not yet fully employed graduates whose financial support he was trying to juggle during these Depression years, when his university resources had been reduced.

In a May 1933 letter home, Cora wrote,

The $2,000 which I am hoarding in Postal Savings in Berkeley should see me thru a couple of years if I am careful. And of course there is always the possibility of getting a job, tho God only knows from whence that will be forth coming. If my present one [research associate] exists next year, and if Kroeber doesn't give it to me I am going to be pretty damn mad. It may not amount to more than fifty a month with the cut which the university has received from the legislature, but that means food and rent in Berkeley.[75]

By February 1934 she was sounding more distressed but also more philosophical about the state of the economy and the nation:

In these days when the lid is chattering on top of the cauldron and threatens to blow off completely almost any time, it is well to have access to detailed news—"history in the making" as you would say. Politically and economically I can't see anything ahead but a large dark fog bank. I am adjusting myself psychologically to living in a period of uncertainty and unrest which is more than temporary as far as a human life span is concerned. The old philosophy of stability and free will is pretty much of an anachronism for the future. I don't think it needs to affect one's happiness very much. It is simply a difference in outlook. The individual usually manages to get, or not to get, satisfaction out of almost any social order.[76]

The Depression also affected publication of Du Bois's dissertation. In a letter home she mentioned that she would like to have it published as a monograph associated with the American Anthropological Association, but this required outside financing of some $1,000. Cora hoped to approach Elsie Clews Parsons, "the standard angel for that series," if and when she had an opportunity to meet with her in New York City, where Parsons lived.[77] Parsons, an independently wealthy woman with a PhD in sociology from Columbia, was a patron to many anthropologists during her lifetime as well as an accomplished ethnographer herself. But Cora's dissertation was never published, probably because it lost its import to her when she moved into her next phase of research.

In July 1933 Ruth Benedict, with whom Cora continued to correspond during her years at Berkeley, offered her some research funds ($500) from Columbia to expand her work, during the next academic year, on revivalist cults beyond California and immediate parts of Nevada and Oregon. Cora hoped that she could use her UC research stipend ($600 annually) for half the year and the Columbia funds for the other half.[78] But in August of that same year, in a letter home, she wrote, "I have spent the last 4 or 5 days fencing with Kroeber—and lost as usual. He refuses to release me and in the bargain is trying to use me as a cat's paw to get money out of Ruth [Benedict] for his own schemes. . . . By the time I am thru with this department I shall have had a course in devious polity which will fit me for political life."[79]

Apparently, Kroeber had told Cora that he would not release her from her UC research position so that she could use the Columbia funds for a portion of the next year and that she could not have both stipends simultaneously. He indicated, however, that he would try to procure the funds from Benedict for some other research project for the department. Cora had to diplomatically explain all of this to Benedict, both thanking her for her generous offer and describing the complexities of the situation with Kroeber and the UC Department of Anthropology, while also alerting her to Kroeber's intentions.[80] In old age, Du Bois would characterize Kroeber as "a great and good man" who "during his maturity [was] financially tight, administratively timid and devious, and toward his students often high handed to the point of being authoritarian."[81]

Despite this setback, life in the Department of Anthropology continued to be engaging. In 1933 Cora and some of the other graduate students prepared a Festschrift for Robert Lowie's fiftieth birthday. And later that year, to the delight of everyone, Lowie became engaged. "Robert Lowie," Cora wrote home, "after a half century of bachelorhood has gotten himself a lady friend. . . . He has already lost pounds and become positively sprightly! Of course everyone is pleased as punch in large part because the lady is so nice."[82] Lowie married Luella Cole, who would also become a friend of Cora's and with whom she would collaborate in the editing of a book of Lowie's papers following his death in 1957.[83]

In between fieldwork trips and trips into San Francisco to observe patients in psychiatric clinics, Cora wrote numerous letters of inquiry for teaching positions and applied for a variety of postdoctoral fellowships.

Kroeber and Lowie, as well as Benedict, wrote supporting letters for her. The Social Science Research Council, which did not award her a full fellowship, did give her an $800 grant-in-aid that allowed her to do four months of fieldwork in Oregon. In a May 1934 letter to Benedict, thanking her for her letters of support, Cora wrote, "For next year, that is 1935–1936, I am cherishing the pious hope of securing a National Research fellowship. The plan is to have six months at Boston Psychopathic [Hospital] under C. Macfie Campbell [the medical director] and six months in the field on a group of [Great] Basin shamans—case histories, concepts of the normal, range of personality types subsumed under shamanism and that sort of thing. . . . I feel that I am an excellent example of what Dr. Johnson called the triumph of hope over experience."[84]

During this period Cora also helped Lowie prepare a Festschrift for Kroeber, *Essays in Anthropology in Honor of Alfred Louis Kroeber* (1936), for which she contributed a paper entitled "The Wealth Concept as an Integrative Factor in Tolowa-Tututni Culture." Her paper was a psychocultural analysis of how the value placed on wealth in this Native American society gave it the appearance of social cohesion—a feature that was, however, only a veneer under which lay deep-seated interpersonal conflicts.

Finally, in April 1935, all the hard work during this period of postdoctoral semiemployment paid off. While Cora was in Ukiah (northern California) doing fieldwork, she received a telegram from the Department of Anthropology informing her that she had been awarded a one-year National Research Council fellowship for her proposal entitled "Personality Types in Shamanism." She wrote home with great excitement: "A short but exuberant scrawl to announce that I am a National Research Fellow! Hot dickity! Honorarium $1620. To begin probably around September. Location not yet absolutely determined. There seems to be some question about Boston Psychopathic. Have written [Edward] Sapir at Yale who is to be my mentor for this coming year."[85]

Cora's years at Berkeley would soon come to a close, and she would set off on a new set of adventures that would lead to her pioneering work in culture and personality.

CHAPTER 4

Culture and Personality

The culture and personality field in its first two decades, roughly 1918 to 1939, was arguably one of the most exciting intellectual explorations launched by American social science in the 20th century.

—Robert A. LeVine

Once again, in the fall of 1935, Cora Du Bois crossed the continent on a quest—this time to acquire tools that might help her better understand the relationship of the individual to culture. She knew there was more momentum on the East Coast than in the West with respect to exploring psychology and psychiatry to this end. But she could not have imagined how central she was to become to that "movement"—the coalescence, in the 1930s, of ideas and of leading figures in what has become known as "culture and personality" in anthropology.

Cora would have preferred to remain in California but had come to realize that on the West Coast "they had hardly heard of Freud. In general, at that time I think the West Coast lagged about ten years behind the East Coast, in new fashions and fads," she later reported. "And certainly New York was a hotbed of psychoanalysis, Freudian and pseudo-Freudian and post Freudian psychologizing, so it was perfectly clear that I should have to come east to get some training, and I was offered, much to my astonishment, . . . a National Research Council [fellowship]."[1]

Cora's receipt of this National Research Council (NRC) fellowship was significant in at least two respects. It was an honor in a year when only two

NRC fellowships were awarded to anthropologists, but it also signified recognition of a new interdisciplinary orientation in American social science research. The NRC had been organized in 1916 by the National Academy of Sciences to address scientific and technical needs during World War I. By 1929 a Division of Psychology and Anthropology had been established within the NRC, although both disciplines were considered natural sciences at the time—psychology because of its experimental character and anthropology because of its physical (biological) anthropology branch. Some psychologists and anthropologists were eager to broaden the NRC's research areas by encouraging collaboration between more *clinically oriented* psychologists and *cultural* anthropologists—in particular, to explore interrelationships between cultural factors and individual personality formation. In 1934 the eminent anthropological linguist Edward Sapir was selected to chair the Division on Psychology and Anthropology of the NRC because of his commitment to this kind of interdisciplinary research.[2] It was Sapir, then, who chaired the division in 1935 when Cora was awarded her fellowship. And, not surprisingly, Sapir was named as her NRC mentor for the year, the person who would oversee her postdoctoral training and research in psychology and psychiatry and her proposed fieldwork.

The proposal Cora had written for the NRC was entitled "Personality Types in Shamanism." As mentioned in chapter 3, she had suggested spending six months getting intensive clinical experience at the Boston Psychopathic Hospital and then another six months with a Great Basin or Plateau Indian group. She wanted to study a functioning society with a sufficiently large population that there would be at least six to ten shamans whom she could examine for individual differences in personality and in shamanistic practices. She would collect in-depth case histories for each shaman, which would be matched by case studies collected from a control group of nonshamans. Her proposal concluded with this summary statement: "[This proposal] seems of real importance [1] because it may reveal to anthropologists some of *the dynamisms of culture which are rooted in the individual*; [2] because it tests—in terms of specific field work—the suggestive concept of configurations of culture recently postulated by Ruth Benedict; and [3] because, for the psychiatrist, it may throw light on the part culture plays in the concept of abnormality and the different ways in which divergent cultures meet the problem of the aberrant individual."[3]

Here Cora was making reference to Ruth Benedict's just-published book, *Patterns of Culture* (1934), in which Benedict had suggested that there was a close correspondence between the predominant cultural values and practices in any given society and its patterns of personality—that is, culture is personality writ large. Cora, while a great admirer of Benedict, nonetheless stressed in her NRC application the importance of studying *individuals* and *individual variability*, not just broad configurations, or patterns, of behavior as Benedict had done.

A Prelude to the 1930s Culture and Personality "Movement"

In order to situate Cora Du Bois's contributions to the culture and personality movement of the 1930s, it is necessary to provide a brief summary of the critical events leading up to her work. A suitable place to begin is the historic meeting, in 1909, of Franz Boas and Sigmund Freud at Clark University. Freud had been invited to give a series of lectures on "The Origin and Development of Psychoanalysis" to celebrate the university's twentieth anniversary. This was his first opportunity to present, in person, his theory of personality and psychoanalysis to an American audience. Boas—whose first academic appointment in the United States had been in the Department of Psychology at Clark University—had also been invited to give a lecture during Freud's visit. His lecture was entitled "Psychological Problems in Anthropology." This was a meeting, therefore, of two major intellectual figures that nicely symbolizes the cross-fertilization that was to develop between their two emerging fields of inquiry—psychiatry and anthropology. Soon thereafter Boas would publish *The Mind of Primitive Man* (1911) and Freud would publish a number of papers and books, such as *Totem and Taboo* (1913), that made use of anthropological information and generated much interest—and controversy—among anthropologists.

From the start of his work in anthropology—which grew out of a scientific expedition to the Arctic when he spent a year (1883–84) with the Inuit on Baffin Island—Boas was interested in psychological issues as well as ethnographic ones. Following that expedition, he apprenticed himself to the Royal Ethnographic Museum in Berlin, at which time he argued that "the goal of ethnology was to study ethnological and anthropological phenomena in their historical development and geographical distribution, *and* in their physiological and *psychological* foundation."[4] In his 1909 Clark University lecture, Boas laid out many of the issues that would become pertinent to the culture and personality movement of the 1920s and 1930s and to today's branch of anthropology known as psychological anthropology. He argued for the psychic unity of mankind in terms of "mental endowment," but he also spoke of "the probability of variations in the types of mental characteristics" from culture to culture. Such variations, he suggested, would arise from "the habitual reactions of the society to which the individual in question belongs." Boas also expressed an interest in the "emotional value" of beliefs and actions, and he hypothesized that beliefs learned early in life "by unconscious imitation" would be the most resistant to change. And he laid out a research agenda into human cognition, which was to determine "the fundamental categories" in which phenomena are classified by humans in different cultures, together with their attributes and meanings.[5]

Over his many years of teaching, Boas would also cultivate in some of his students an interest in questions of culture and psyche. Cora had benefited from this intergenerational process at Barnard in her undergraduate coursework with Ruth Benedict, although at UC Berkeley, as we have seen, the situation was quite different. All three of Cora's principal teachers in different places—Benedict, Kroeber, and Lowie—were Boas students, but each had taken a somewhat different path in the new discipline of American anthropology. Joining this list would be Edward Sapir, another Boas student, who was about to become Cora's NRC advisor.

Early in their careers Kroeber and Sapir had had a public debate over the relevance of studying individuals with respect to culture. In 1917 Kroeber had published in the *American Anthropologist* his now-classic paper "The Superorganic," in which he laid out his theory that cultural processes operate independently of individuals—they are, to use his words, "super" organic or "super" individual.[6] His intent was largely to try to distance anthropology from the pernicious effects of nineteenth-century social Darwinism and nineteenth- and twentieth-century racial theories that argued that some social groups were superior to others. By treating "the growth of civilization" as cultural invention sui generis, issues of race and heredity could be eliminated. "The attempt today," he wrote, "to treat society as organic, to understand civilization as heredity, is as essentially narrow minded as the alleged mediaeval inclination to withdraw man from the realm of nature and from the ken of the scientist because he is believed to possess an immortal soul." Kroeber took the argument even further by saying that "civilization is not mental action itself; it is carried by men, without being in them" and that civilization "begins only where the individual ends." Accordingly, he tried to rule out the relevance of individuals and "psychic activities" to anthropology and the analysis of culture.[7]

Sapir responded in the next issue of the *American Anthropologist* with "Do We Need a 'Superorganic?,'" in which he objected to Kroeber's "complete elimination of the peculiar influence of individuals on the course of history" and to Kroeber's interpretation of social phenomena as built "out of the organic, but . . . not entirely resolvable into it, hence it implies the presence of an unknown principle which transcends the organic"—some mysterious force.[8] Clearly there was no lack of disagreement within the anthropology community. This was Sapir's first public statement about the relevance of the individual to cultural analysis and one that he would go on to refine during his lifetime. Despite this public debate, Sapir and Kroeber had a cordial relationship, as evidenced in their work together on languages and in their ongoing written correspondence.[9] By the 1920s Sapir had formed two even-closer relationships that were germane to the development of his ideas about the individual and culture. These were his intimate friendships with Ruth Benedict and Margaret Mead, with whom he shared poetry and debated issues of culture and personality.

In 1931 Sapir was invited to join Yale University as the Sterling Professor of Linguistics, to help build an interdisciplinary program within the Social Sciences Division of the Graduate School and to offer a seminar entitled "The Impact of Culture on Personality." The latter was described in the 1931–32 Yale catalogue as "a seminar course on the meaning of culture, its psychological relevance for personality, its value relativity, and the problem of reconciling personality variations and cultural variations."[10] Initially, this was a showcase seminar that was sponsored by the Rockefeller Foundation and that Sapir taught with the assistance of the eminent New York psychiatrist Harry Stack Sullivan, whose focus was more upon individuals' networks of relationships than upon intrapsychic phenomena. The course, therefore, marked culture and personality as a legitimate field of interest within the academy.

In the years between the 1917 Kroeber-Sapir debate and the 1931 establishment of Sapir's landmark course at Yale, there were a variety of activities and publications that anticipated the emerging field of culture and personality. Three publications were of particular import—Margaret Mead's *Coming of Age in Samoa* (1928), Bronislaw Malinowski's *Sex and Repression in Savage Society* (1927), and his *The Sexual Lives of Savages in Northwestern Melanesia* (1929). All were based on original fieldwork in non-Western societies, and they addressed one or more psychological questions. The fact that these books' publication dates are so close together is *not*, I think, a coincidence. Rather, it reflects the coalescence of people and of ideas in a new, unfolding field.

Mead, with Boas's encouragement, went to Samoa to examine the relationship between a particular developmental stage—adolescence—and culture, asking the question, "Are the disturbances which vex our [American] adolescents due to the nature of adolescence itself or to the civilization?"[11] She studied fifty girls in three small Samoan villages and found that, unlike in the United States, adolescence was not an emotionally difficult period of life for them. Despite some controversy about Mead's research in subsequent years, this book's clear contribution to culture and personality was its cross-cultural examination of a Western psychological assumption about a particular stage of life, one that had been characterized in the West as a period filled with tension, emotional conflict, and rebellion.[12] Mead's study provided evidence for the impact of culture on human development, and it quickly became a bestseller in the United States, where, with the changing sexual mores of the 1920s, there was a market for "the scientific study of sexuality, adolescence, and the exotic."[13] But there was also an increasing appetite for cultural relativism—for evidence that culture outweighed biological inheritance with respect to race and other issues.

By contrast with Mead, Malinowski's roots in anthropology were very different, although they bore some similarity to those of Boas. Born and educated in Poland, Malinowski first attained an advanced degree in mathematics and the physical sciences before pursuing anthropology. (Boas, who was born and educated in Germany, also studied the physical sciences before discovering anthropology.) As a sickly youth, Malinowski read widely and discovered such works as James Frazer's *The Golden Bough: A Study in Magic and Religion* (1890). This and other such works inspired him to go to England, where he was able to study with the British ethnologist C. G. Seligman and others at the London School of Economics. In 1914, just before the outbreak of World War I, Malinowski traveled to New Guinea and northwestern Melanesia on his first fieldwork expedition. As a Pole in British territory when the war started, he was given the choice of remaining where he was or being incarcerated. He chose the former and had an intensive period of fieldwork (1915–18) in the Trobriand Islands that resulted in a series of significant ethnographic publications.

Malinowski's contributions to the nascent field of culture and personality are at least twofold. First, he tried to integrate emerging cultural and psychological theories by suggesting that social and cultural institutions serve human needs, which are both biological (e.g., the need for food) *and* psychological (e.g., the need for beliefs and rituals to ward off fear) in origin. Very simply put, he urged anthropologists to examine sociocultural institutions in order to determine how they functioned to satisfy the needs of individuals in a particular setting, and in this way he linked the individual to culture.

Second, and perhaps most famously, in *Sex and Repression in Savage Society* Malinowski questioned the universality of Freud's concept of the Oedipus complex. He argued that the Trobrianders had a very different family and kinship system from the Western European one on which Freud had based his theory. Unlike the patrilineal, patriarchal Western family, the Trobrianders were matrilineal and traced descent through women, with sons inheriting from their mothers' brothers rather than from their fathers. Thus the relationship of potential antagonism for a boy, Malinowski argued, was with his maternal uncle, *not* his father. While there have been many efforts over the years by some psychoanalysts and anthropologists to refute Malinowski, his contribution to the emerging field of culture and personality at the time was, like Mead's, to question the universality of a psychological assumption about human behavior with carefully collected ethnographic data from a non-Western society.

The capstone to this period, which led up to Du Bois's receipt of an

NRC fellowship to study personality psychology and psychiatry, was the 1934 publication of Ruth Benedict's *Patterns of Culture*. Whereas Kroeber wanted to write individuals *out* of the analysis of culture and Sapir wanted to put them back *in*, Benedict managed to *blend* the two together in what has become known as the "configurational" approach to culture and personality. Benedict saw the small, nonliterate societies that anthropologists were studying at the time as culturally patterned, integrated wholes, and she used "personality type" labels—taken from psychiatry and Nietzsche's studies of Greek tragedy—as a way of expressing their *ethos*, or dominant configurations as manifested in beliefs, rituals, and other practices. Accordingly, the three societies discussed in Benedict's book—the Dobuans of Melanesia, the Zunis and other Pueblos of the American Southwest, and the Kwakiutls of the Northwest Coast—were labeled, respectively, "Paranoid," "Apollonian," and "Dionysian."

These labels, which have been criticized for oversimplifying and essentializing cultures, have proved to be a distraction from what Benedict was trying to do. She was using personality types to evoke a sense of the dominant configurations of a culture that, she thought, made it distinctive and different from other cultures. As she put it, "A culture, like an individual, is more or less a consistent pattern of thought and action."[14] She used individual personality as a model for depicting cultures, taking the analogy a step further by suggesting that cultures had patterned histories similar to the patterns of development of an individual personality. Accordingly, she wrote, "[W]e can understand [a culture] only by understanding first the emotional and intellectual mainsprings of that society."[15] Underlying this analogy between culture and personality was Benedict's belief in human plasticity and the capacity of societies, once established, to mold individuals to fit their distinctive cultural configurations. As she put it,

> The vast proportion of all individuals who are born into any society always and whatever the idiosyncrasies of its institutions, assume, as we have seen, the behaviour dictated by that society. . . . Most people are shaped to the form of their culture because of the enormous malleability of their original endowment. They are plastic to the moulding force of the society into which they are born. It does not matter whether, with the Northwest Coast, it requires delusions of self-reference, *or*

with our own civilization the amassing of possessions. In any case the great mass of individuals take quite readily the form that is presented to them.[16]

In Benedict's configurational theory, culture and personality were iso-morphic—that is, they closely corresponded with one another. It must be noted, however, that Benedict recognized that, in any given society, a minority of individuals would *not* fit the dominant configurations and would be perceived as deviant. And she devoted the final part of her book to addressing such "misfits" in American society, as well as in small, non-literate societies, and she argued for a greater tolerance of diversity in all societies.

Newspaper reviews lavished praise on the book, and even Kroeber, in his professional review of it for the *American Anthropologist*, was reason-ably positive. Calling it a "work for the intelligent non-anthropologist," he wrote, "The basic concept is that of culture occurring in certain pat-terns which determine its fabric and are of influence on the lives led by all individuals under a culture. These patterns make up the character or distinctive quality of each culture; its 'genius,' to use an old phrase aptly reused by Dr. Boas in the preface [to the book]. . . . Very considerably, the book is propaganda for the anthropological attitude."[17]

What Kroeber meant by "propaganda for the anthropological attitude" was American anthropology's commitment to cultural relativism. Benedict had supplied the American public with yet another readable book—like Mead's *Coming of Age in Samoa* and her soon-to-be published *Sex and Temperament in Three Primitive Societies* (1935)—that emphasized the role of culture over heredity in determining how individuals think, feel, and behave. It is important to note, however, that Benedict's configurational approach to assessing the relationship of culture to personality was an intuitive one that did not lay out a methodology for assessing culture and personality. Nor did it address *explanations* for cross-cultural differences.

There was, as yet, no explanatory model for examining the relationship of culture to personality in this emerging field of inquiry. Rather, there were a lot of different ideas about personality formation that were emerg-ing from different branches of psychology and psychiatry that intrigued anthropologists interested in how culture and personality affected each other. And there were increasing numbers of anthropological field studies from non-Western societies that challenged many of these psychological ideas and intrigued some of the field's practitioners. The time was ripe for the emergence of culture and personality as an interdisciplinary field of inquiry. The question was, where would all of these intellectual explorations lead? And, of particular interest to us, how would Cora Du Bois become part of them?

The Harvard Psychological Clinic and the Boston Psychopathic Hospital

Cora would spend the first six months of her 1935–36 NRC fellowship year in Cambridge and Boston, Massachusetts, working with Henry A. Murray at the Harvard Psychological Clinic and making observations at the Boston Psychopathic Hospital. First, however, she stopped in New York City to make contacts with a variety of psychiatrists, psychoanalysts, and anthropologists. In late September she wrote a lengthy letter to Kroeber, whom she now addressed as "Dear Kroeber" rather than "Professor Kroeber," to report on her activities. By then she had had visits with Edward Sapir at Yale, who suggested that she go see his friend and psychiatric colleague Harry Stack Sullivan. "Sullivan," Cora reported of the meeting, "spent about two hours reviewing the psychiatrists on the east coast, their biases and their interrelationships. It proved to be a helpful preliminary orientation in practical matters." From there Cora visited about a dozen analysts and reported to Kroeber,

> Of the people I've seen Karen Horney and A. Kardiner stand out in my mind. They are both Freudian but have a grasp of cultural factors, have themselves struggled with them and realize the significance that anthropological data may have for them. There is enough common ground with them to permit an interchange in discussions—which isn't always the case, God wot. On the whole, however, I feel that the analysts are far less rigid in their point of view than they were a few years ago when [Freud's] Totem and Taboo was sacred and [Géza] Roheim was its commentator.

(Cora's more fully developed views of Freud's *Totem and Taboo* are presented below.)

Cora also visited Franz Boas, Ruth Benedict, and Margaret Mead. "The two latter are full of enthusiasm and amiability," she reported in the same letter to Kroeber. "Benedict has casually suggested field work [for me] in Melanesia on the relationship of the sexes, with feminine masochism as the psychological emphasis. This is a direct outgrowth of a paper by [psychoanalyst Karen] Horney." Then Cora added, "I am anxious to make this an opportunity for field work outside of North America."[18]

In addition, in her letter Cora told Kroeber that "the consensus of opinion" in the East was that six months of observations at the Boston Psychopathic Hospital would be enough for her to spend on psychotic material and diagnostic psychiatry. (Kroeber had urged her to spend a full year immersing herself in this world and had included his view on this topic in his letter of recommendation for her to the National Research Council.) Kroeber had also warned her that the people whom she would be meeting in the culture and personality field would recommend that she herself "get analyzed," and she reported that they were indeed doing this but were not insistent. In later life Cora would recall that analysis "was urged upon me because [the experience of analysis oneself as a part of training was] at that time fashionable at Yale. John Dollard [Yale psychologist] and Edward Sapir were urging it; that's where I first met the Whitings, John and Bea Whiting [later to become her anthropology colleagues at Harvard]. This was the fashion at that time. But I refused. I felt that my own orientation was sufficiently fragile that I didn't dare risk it. I spoke with Margaret Mead about it one time and she supported me, saying, 'Don't do it if you don't feel like it.'"[19] Cora never did go through any kind of psychoanalysis. Her reference to having a "fragile orientation" was probably a veiled allusion to her sexual orientation and to her disinclination to have to explore it with analysts who pathologized homosexuality.

Cora concluded her letter to Kroeber with, "I'm writing Robert [Lowie] in the near future and shall tell him all the chit chat about personalities which he will probably pass on to you. I still feel a nostalgia for the many charms of Berkeley but fortunately there isn't much time for that sort of self indulgence. Please give my love to Theodora and the children."[20] Cora would continue to correspond with both Kroeber and Lowie during much of their lifetimes, with the letters to "Papa Kroeber" being somewhat more formal than the ones to "Uncle Robert." In the absence of entries to her journal and letters home during this busy year, her correspondence with Kroeber and Lowie provides invaluable insights into her thoughts and activities.[21]

From New York City, Cora went to Cambridge, Massachusetts, to look for housing and to begin her work with Henry A. Murray at the Harvard Psychology Clinic as well as at the Boston Psychopathic Hospital. People at Berkeley had recommended this combination of activities, and presumably Edward Sapir, her NRC mentor, concurred.

The Harvard Psychological Clinic

In 1935, when Cora arrived in Cambridge, the Harvard Psychology Clinic, which had been founded in 1927, was a somewhat maverick operation. Founded by Morton Prince, a physician who specialized in neurology and abnormal psychology, the clinic provided a base for Prince's efforts to establish clinical psychology as an academic discipline. In 1928 he hired Murray as an assistant. Murray, like Prince, was a physician, but with a PhD in biochemistry. He had become interested in psychogenic factors while working with medical patients and had had lengthy conversations with Carl Jung in Switzerland. Murray would become director of the clinic in 1937, but his appointment at Harvard remained a problem for some years. Not only did he not have a degree in psychology, but his position was "complicated by the fact that he stood at the fringe of a discipline that was itself at the fringe of acceptance."[22]

So the work that Cora proposed to do lay at the fringes of two disciplines—psychologically oriented *anthropology*, on the one hand, and clinical and abnormal *psychology*, on the other. She would be working with Murray, who would soon become renowned as a personality theorist and would, later in life, collaborate with Clyde Kluckhohn, an anthropologist at Harvard who also had interests in the emerging field of culture and personality.[23] And Murray and Kluckhohn would both become founding members of Harvard's interdisciplinary Department of Social Relations, established in 1945, to which Cora would have an appointment when she came to Harvard in 1954. But I am getting ahead of the story.

The First Six Months

For six intense months Cora, who was about to turn thirty-two, divided her time between the Harvard Psychological Clinic and the Boston Psychopathic Hospital. She also attended seminars sponsored by the Boston Psychoanalytic Society. She found Harry Murray "enormously cordial" and "a marvelous impresario" who brought together all kinds of people. He immediately invited Cora to join his various research seminars and daily luncheon groups at "his shop," his clinic on Plympton Street. As she explained to Kroeber, "There is a weekly seminar in which reports of the last 2 years of work are read by those who gave the tests [to the subjects of study]. They (reports) are to form part of an 800-page volume which is to appear next year. There is also a weekly round table at which each [member] of the group reports in turn on any outside work being done."[24] The reference here is to Murray's landmark publication *Explorations in Personality: A Clinical and Experimental Study of Fifty Men of College Age* (1938), published in collaboration with the "Workers at the Harvard Psychological Clinic."

At the Harvard Psychological Clinic, Cora immediately had entrée to a dynamic set of psychologists, psychiatrists, and a few anthropologists, all of whom were collaborating with Murray in his endeavor to develop a theory of personality by studying, in depth, fifty-one young men of college age, some of whom were Harvard students and others "from the ranks of the unemployed."[25] Over a period of two and a half years these men were given a series of interviews, "free-association hours," and a battery of new experimental tests and questionnaires in an effort to assess both their overt behavior and their unconscious fantasies and thoughts, with the goal of codifying major factors that contributed to personality formation. From this project Murray developed a theory of motivation based on human "needs" or "drives"—biologically based primary needs (e.g., food, water, sex, avoidance of pain) and secondary or psychogenic needs (e.g., achievement, dominance, affiliation, nurturance).

Murray had twenty-seven collaborators in this endeavor, many of whom became well-known psychologists, psychiatrists, and psychoanalysts and included such notable figures as R. Nevitt Sanford (coauthor of *The Authoritarian Personality*, 1950), Robert W. White (*The Abnormal Personality*,

1964), and Erik Erikson (the prolific author of such works as *Childhood and Society*, 1950; *Young Man Luther*, 1958; and *Identity: Youth and Crisis*, 1968). The latter two men would become Cora's colleagues at Harvard. Cora recalled, with some amusement, that at the time Erikson "was still so involved in rigorous Freudianism that he referred to Freud as 'the master,' and if any criticism was leveled, he flushed with indignation."[26]

Cora and Walter Dyk, a postdoctoral student in anthropology from Yale and a student of Sapir, also became collaborators. Murray invited them to help give Thematic Apperception Tests (TATs)—a projective test that he was developing—to a series of students. In his book, Murray described TATs as a procedure "to stimulate literary creativity and thereby evoke fantasies that reveal covert and unconscious complexes."[27] Cora wrote in a letter to Kroeber, "We are supposed to present them [the students] with 20 carefully selected pictures for which they must compose a story. The twenty stories are then analyzed and the 'personality themes' of the subject is written up. It gives you a very good idea of their general approach here." And she added, "Murray is eclectic—quite avowedly—and is attempting to reconcile the 'manifest psychology' of trait tests with the 'latent psychology' of psychoanalysis. In other words—they have developed elaborate tests for psychoanalytic interpretations."[28] At Murray's clinic, Cora had firsthand experience with TATs, as well as with Rorschach and other projective tests, some of which she would make use of in her subsequent culture and personality research in Indonesia.

Cora spent four mornings a week—from 9:00 a.m. to 1:00 p.m.—at the Boston Psychopathic Hospital, where she was admitted as a full-time staff person and was allowed to make ward rounds and to attend staff conferences. As she reported this experience later in life, "I had entrée to what was then the Boston Psychopathic Hospital. Again, this tremendous hospitality of just saying, 'Here's a white coat. Go where you want.' I think it was the damned foolest thing I ever heard, to let me into the closed wards . . . and to talk to anybody. There were one or two somewhat tense episodes in my ineptitudes. . . . I worked like a dog for six months and got to the point where every time I got on top of a new psychiatric disease, I would develop it for a few weeks."[29]

Initially, Cora found work with doctors and patients at the Boston

Psychopathic Hospital perplexing. Both Kroeber and Lowie tried to reassure her. Kroeber, who had had some experience with psychoanalysis, wrote,

> I hope you will not be disconcerted by the psychiatrists' approach to clinical material being concrete and casual. That is inevitable for a professional, even if he is interested in theory. It may be quite a time before you begin to see anything emerging out of the chaos of individual facts. . . . You have just got to have so much experience with material before theorizing is worth anything. A lot of the shaking down in the interpretations will occur after you have got away from the experience. This year is the only one you are likely to have in which you will get this exposure. I am confident you will be glad the rest of your life you have had it, even if it seems puzzling now. For the same reason I hope that you will be able to keep on with clinical studies the whole year rather than chop off in February.[30]

Kroeber had clearly become very supportive of Cora's ambitions in the culture and personality field. In fact, in his letter of recommendation for her NRC fellowship, he had written, "The Psychiatry-Ethnology combination impresses me as of fundamental importance in the progress of the next decade or two. With all the talk about personality and culture, we have as yet, apart from a genius like Sapir . . . almost nothing in the way of actual workers with genuine double-barreled training."[31]

In another exchange with Kroeber, Cora mentioned that she had begun to attend a seminar at the Boston Psychoanalytic Society "which promises to be highly illuminating from a theoretical point of view. Either the stuff [at the hospital] so far is way over my head or it is just naturally confused. I suppose I shan't be happy until I can reduce psychoanalysis to a lovely little diagram. As Kaufman said last night, all 'scientists' are obsessional neurotics. Yours for bigger and better obsessions [!]"[32] Kroeber responded, saying, "That about obsessions is rather good because it is partly true. A doctor cannot have them and that is why he normally does not become a scientist. Meanwhile I hope you continue to get abundant exposure to doctors and especially to patients."[33] Cora had clearly reawakened Kroeber's interests in psychiatry.

Lowie also wrote to Cora to reassure her about her work at the Boston

Psychopathic Hospital, saying, "Kroeber tells me that you are somewhat perplexed by the observations you are making in the clinic. However, both Kroeber and Cy [Lowie's wife] agree that you need not worry about this. The main point now is for you to see as many cases in the flesh as possible. *Ultimately you will be able to bring some order into the chaos.*"

Lowie's letter (from Berkeley) continued in a more lighthearted vein. He expressed pleasure at Cora's having been "hospitably received in the effete east" and expressed amusement at her "account of contacts with Margaret Mead"—someone about whose work he had grave doubts. In fact, he went on to say that Mead's most recent book, *Sex and Temperament in Three Primitive Societies* (1935), was "incredibly bad; in fact I was in a towering rage about it"—so much so that he had written a long diatribe to a colleague, with a copy to Boas, "with the result that I am now probably the black sheep in the higher circles of New York anthropological society."[34] Lowie objected to Mead's broad generalizations about men's and women's subjective attitudes in the three different New Guinean societies that she had studied, without providing the reader with "the most rigorous demonstration . . . upon what basis of observation this amazing picture rests."[35]

Both Kroeber and Lowie, in their letters, asked Cora whether she was seeing anything of the Harvard anthropologists, to which she replied, "only Kluckhohn." It was probably at Harry Murray's lunches and seminars that Cora and Clyde Kluckhohn became acquainted with one another, and their lives would intersect in interesting ways in years to come.

Meanwhile, during this busy six-month period in Cambridge and Boston, Cora began planning for the following year, when she would once again be unemployed unless some unexpected job came along. She began drafting research proposals with the hope that she would be funded to do some kind of fieldwork within the emerging field of culture and personality, preferably outside of the United States. As early as October, she asked Kroeber if he had "any succulent projects for next year's field work" up his sleeve. "I'd like to have several [projects] to mull over and pop on the proper people at the proper time. I'm so wound up in immediacies I find it difficult to be planful about next year."[36]

However, by November Cora had become "planful" and had sent both Kroeber and Lowie copies of two research proposals for their feedback.

One, as she put it, was the "good old one on shamanism." The other was a proposal entitled "Sex Differences in Relation to Cultural Determinants," the development of an idea "originally suggested by Benedict and eagerly seconded by the analyst [Karen] Horney whose paper on Feminine Masochism suggested certain definite lines of inquiry for ethnologists . . . Horney is willing to lend moral support from an analytic end, but I should very much like both yours and Lowie's reaction to it from the anthropological angle. I've grown pretty dependent on the comments you both make in such matters."[37]

The latter proposal would build on Mead's recent ethnographic work on sex and gender in New Guinea by addressing issues that psychoanalyst Horney had recently raised in an article entitled "The Problem of Feminine Masochism." Horney questioned the Freudian theory that women were universally masochistic in their attitudes toward sex and reproduction because of the trauma of discovering they lacked a penis, and she called for a cross-cultural examination of this theoretical assumption in Western psychoanalysis. She even laid out a research agenda for anthropologists on "observable masochistic attitudes"—such as inhibitions on the expression of anger and aggression, a self-concept of weakness and helplessness, an emotional dependence on the other sex—in order to determine whether they were, in fact, exhibited more frequently by women than men and, if so, under what cultural conditions. Accordingly, Cora proposed a systematic examination of childbirth, early education, menstruation, marriage, the economic role of the sexes, and "prestige values" for each sex in order to assess men's and women's "aggressive and passive expressions and outlets" and their "realms of dependency on one another."[38] This was, indeed, an ambitious research agenda that was a harbinger of the work she would ultimately do in Indonesia.

Kroeber responded to Cora's two proposals, saying, "I like your sex study plan, although I think the last two unnumbered topics [about dependency and passive and aggressive outlets] bear expansion. It is probably also wise to suggest being sent to Melanesia, because the exotic and expensive sometimes has the best chance of being [financially] supported." With regard to Mead, he wrote, "Mead's theory of course has something in it, but as a whole it strikes me as more of an effective device to sell than a hypothesis for which a serious demonstration can be made. I have a good deal of faith in that young woman's intuitions—I think their value is under-estimated—but am . . . greatly concerned over her philosophizing."[39]

Both Kroeber and Lowie disliked Mead's popularizing inclinations and had doubts about publications that did not contain substantial amounts of ethnographic data. Their critiques of Mead's work would influence how Cora handled her as-yet-unplanned research in Indonesia. And, in response to Cora's sex differences proposal, Lowie encouraged her to consider doing the project somewhere in Africa rather than in Melanesia, so as to distance herself from Mead's work.[40]

Kroeber, in his response, suggested that she could, if necessary, do the same kind of project less expensively among Native Americans. Then he suggested another theoretically important possibility:

Also there occurs to me a third possibility; the study of personality as such among some primitive group irrespective of sex, shamanism, or any other specialization. This problem as I see it involves *how far personalities differ, in what, and if possible, due to what*. Inasmuch as nothing worth while has been done that I know of in this line, it might be a little difficult to shake the problem down to specificity the first time. But sooner or later a beginning will have to be made, and a good beginning would be of pretty fundamental importance even if it were only a beginning. My own interest, and I think yours, is really rather in *the normal variability of personality* than it is in extreme or special forms. I am inclined to think that Sapir's interest would lie the same way, although he may be more aware of the difficulties of making an entirely new beginning via field studies. I think it might be worth while thinking the idea over and suggesting it to him. I have got in mind not a mere classification into more or less accepted types, *but an empirical examination* from the ground up.[41]

This suggestion played to the heart of Cora's interests in culture and personality—to understand individual variability within a particular socio-cultural system. Kroeber was trying to redirect that interest away from more aberrant populations, such as shamans, to the more "normal" distribution of persons. As it happened, this would become sound advice for Cora's ultimate culture and personality research project. Interestingly, in the course of these communications with Du Bois about issues in culture and personality, Kroeber seems to have begun to reconsider the relationship of individuals to culture.

By the time this contemplation of future research projects was playing out, Cora had completed the first six months of her fellowship year. She had had an intense exposure to abnormal psychology (through clinicians and patients at the Boston Psychopathic Hospital) and to personality theory (with Murray and his collaborators at the Harvard Psychology Clinic). While pondering whether to continue with these activities or begin her own fieldwork, as outlined in her NRC proposal, an unexpected invitation altered her plans.

The Kardiner–Du Bois Seminar and the Development of a Theoretical Model in Culture and Personality

In January 1936 Cora wrote home excitedly, saying, "What do you suppose has happened! K (i.e., Dr. [Abram] Kardiner—psychoanalyst—N.Y.C.) wrote asking me to collaborate with him in a seminar at the N.Y. Psychoanalytic Society! I got in touch immediately with Sapir, who to my great surprise, said he thought it would be quite alright under the terms of my fellowship. That means I should move down to New York by the middle of March."[42] Before accepting the offer from Kardiner, Cora consulted not only with Sapir but also with Lowie and Kroeber. As she explained in a letter to Kroeber, Kardiner was a New York analyst "of very good standing who has developed an interest in 'sociology.' (He really means anthropology.) He is pretty green on the subject of culture but he is intelligent, comes around slowly and is anxious to have an entrée to that sort of material."[43] Kardiner's invitation came at a time when, as Cora put it, she "was ready for greener pastures," plus it would make her the local cultural expert in a seminar for psychiatrists in training and psychiatric social workers. Lowie and Kroeber concurred that it sounded like a good opportunity for her.

Once again, however, Kroeber reiterated his conviction that Cora should continue with some clinical work. "Perhaps you have had an excess of shattered or deteriorated psychotic cases," he wrote, "and could arrange to have less grave material put at your disposal."[44] Cora assured him that she planned to continue clinical work, which, in fact, she would undertake at the New York University outpatient clinic and in children's wards at Bellevue Hospital. Unbeknownst to Kroeber, she had already begun to formulate her perspectives on psychiatry in drafts of a paper to be discussed below.

"Of course—there are always curls and spirals," she explained in her letter to Kroeber. "The particular spiral is that Kardiner and Zilboorg hate the sight of each other and Zilboorg is a possible (but very tentative) source for [research] funds. . . . Letters are very poor mediums for discussing this sort of thing. Besides, you should really be able to size up the various prima-donnas involved!" And in her ironic voice, Cora added, "I'm learning more about personality from handling my elders and betters than from the clinics."[45] Gregory Zilboorg was a New York psychoanalyst who had such famous clients as George Gershwin and Lillian Hellman and who had access to private research funds. He was proposing to undertake a cross-cultural study of suicide, and Sapir had recommended Cora to him as a potential fieldworker for it. She must, at some point during the year, have begun preparation for such a project because her 1935-36 papers, archived at Harvard, include notes, a bibliography, and a rough manuscript entitled "Suicide as an Index of Cultural Values."[46]

So, in March, Cora moved to New York City, where she and her Berkeley friend, Nell Barnes, shared an apartment. (Nell, who had accompanied Cora when she moved east, had already moved to New York City and was working there as a psychiatric social worker.) From New York City, Cora was able to take the train on Thursdays to Yale and attend Sapir's graduate seminar on the impact of culture on personality. But most of her time was focused on preparing for the joint seminar with Kardiner that she would begin teaching in April 1936.

The Kardiner–Du Bois Seminar

This seminar, which became a series of seminars for young psychiatrists with interests in culture, led to the formulation of a significant theoretical model for understanding the relationship of culture to personality. For the first two years, Abram Kardiner and Cora Du Bois jointly taught the seminars. In 1937, when Du Bois received funding to do fieldwork to test out the model they had developed, the anthropologist Ralph Linton—who had recently been appointed chair of the Department of Anthropology at Columbia to replace Franz Boas—took over her role. Initially, at least, the seminars should have been called the "Kardiner–Du Bois seminars." Later they might well have been called the "Kardiner–Du Bois–Linton seminars." Ironically, however, Du Bois's name has evaporated and they have become known in the anthropological literature as the "Kardiner-Linton seminars." Perhaps because Linton wrote the foreword and two of the ethnological reports contained in Kardiner's groundbreaking book, *The Individual and His Society: The Psychodynamics of Primitive Social Organization* (1939), he gained prominence over Du Bois. Nonetheless, it is another example of the androcentric tendencies existent within anthropology at the time that has not been corrected in most of the pertinent literature.

In the first Kardiner–Du Bois seminar, in the spring of 1936, Cora began by explaining to psychiatrists in training, who were immersed in Freudian theory, "why the greater part of Freudian sociology was unacceptable to the students of society."[47] In older age she described it more bluntly: "Well, the seminar began very simply in my destroying Freud's *Totem and Taboo* (1913), saying, 'This is nonsense.'"[48] In *Totem and Taboo*, Freud's first sustained foray into the domain of culture, he tried to identify causal processes in cultural evolution. He theorized that Homo sapiens' original social organization was a patriarchal band in which a patriarch held exclusive sexual privileges over his sisters and daughters. At some unspecified moment, his sexually deprived sons plotted their father's murder, killed him, and ate him. Overcome with guilt, they henceforth repressed their desire to have sexual relations with their mothers, sisters, or daughters. In addition, in expiation of their murderous deed and cannibalistic orgy, they created the myth of the totem—the animal symbol of their father—that thereafter became taboo as a food except on ritual occasions. Accordingly, the primal patricide gave rise to the Oedipus complex, nuclear family incest taboos, group exogamy, totemism, and other features of "primitive" societies. Freud's thesis was, in every respect, anathema to Boasian anthropologists, who had rejected this kind of evolutionary speculation. Hence Du Bois's immediate critique of it in the seminar.

What Cora probably did was to give a careful analysis of *Totem and Taboo* along the lines of a lecture that she had delivered to the Boston Psychopathic Hospital staff before leaving Cambridge, which was published in 1937 as "Some Anthropological Perspectives on Psychoanalysis."

First, she pointed out that Freud had accepted the fallacious nineteenth-century biological analogy that early anthropologists had used to organize societies as if they had evolved from the simple to the complex, which held that contemporary nonliterate societies represented the primitive heritage of Western society. Second, she indicated that Freud had made another fallacious analogy between the evolution of societies, on the one hand, and the developmental sequences of the individual, on the other. What he asserted was that the developmental sequence of the individual "recapitulated" cultural development—and that the psychology of children and neurotics was akin to that of primitive peoples. Cora then asked a rhetorical question: "Do primitive people represent earlier phases of psycho-cultural adjustment?" She proceeded to address the question by raising a series of problems about which, she said, "every person who discusses psychology and anthropology must be clear." These were: "(1) The fallacy of generalizing about non-literate groups as though they were homogeneous; (2) The assumption that non-literates are archaic; (3) The dangers involved in discussing material out of context; (4) The confusion centering about the term primitive; and (5) The use of the term primitive psychology for both the individual behavior of unliterate persons and the presumed psychological significance of institutions."[49]

Cora then cited examples of how Freud, in *Totem and Taboo*, had equated animism with narcissism, totemism with the Oedipus phase, and so on. In *Totem and Taboo*, she said, "psychoanalytic terms are attached to problematic cultural entities and the coincidence of the two have no demonstrable basis in reality."[50] Clearly, Cora had developed an unambiguous and pithy voice. And in her 1937 publication, she elaborated on each of the above problems—something that she probably had had to do repeatedly in the course of the seminar.

With enough psychology and psychiatry under her belt, it was Cora's task to teach Kardiner and other seminar participants about the immense cross-cultural variability in institutions, childcare practices, rituals, and beliefs that, in turn, challenged their Western-based psychodynamic theories. She, and other guest speakers, did this by presenting ethnographic descriptions of a variety of non-Western cultures so that seminar participants could appreciate cultural variability and might begin to identify key institutions in different societies that could be formative in the development of individual personality. In an April 1936 letter to Lowie, she wrote enthusiastically about the seminar and her role in it:

I'm so pleased about the seminar at the Psychoanalytic Society that I have to write and tell you all about it. . . . There is a group of about sixteen younger analysts who are keen and awake and give me a grindstone to sharpen on. I was enthralled last night to discover that they would sit thru 2 solid hours of Trobriand social organization without protest. There is to be another session on the Trobriands, two on the Kwakiutl, one on the Zuni for which I've called in Ruth Bunzel, one on American negroes by John Dollard, one on the Navaho in which [Walter] Dyk's autobiographies will be used and then one or two final sessions to which Benedict, Horney, [Erich] Fromm and others will be invited.

[Sandor] Rado, who is director of research [at the Psychoanalytic Society], was present the other evening. He seems to be one of the great moguls in the group. When he made a fine long winded speech on the desirability of studying the Indians because he had seen a few in the southwest last summer, I got up and cheered. Only by the exercise of great self-discipline did I refrain from simultaneously holding out an upturned palm. However when he began delivering himself of theories on the origin of culture and taking sly but good-natured swats at anthropologists, I rose to the defense of our noble profession. . . . The point is that there is much missionary work to be done [and] that it may be well worth the doing.[51]

Cora found the spring of 1936 immensely stimulating. The combination of the joint seminar with Kardiner, trips to Yale to attend Sapir's seminar, plus invitations from Harry Murray to return to Harvard to speak at his psychology clinic on two different occasions must have been exhilarating. "With Sapir I'm finally establishing a better rapport," she wrote to Lowie. "The regular attendance of his seminars had helped in that respect. He, very amiably, invited Benedict and me up for lunch and a sociological meeting last week and has invited me frequently to join the staff luncheons after the Thursday seminars."[52] Cora was now in the center of the culture and personality movement.

During this period Cora also became Lowie's sounding board for several of the chapters he was preparing for his new book, *The History of*

Ethnological Theory (1937). For example, in response to the draft chapter on French sociology, she wrote, "It seems to me that you might have brought out even *more* forcefully that Durkheim relies essentially upon psychology although verbally rejecting it. After all—the distinction between sacred and profane depends essentially on a psychological condition." And with regard to Lowie's handling of Lévy-Bruhl in the same chapter, Cora wrote, "I'm not so sure that I should be as dispassionate about L-B,—largely for reasons not his fault. Only I do think he has had a nefarious influence on non-anthropologists, particularly on psychiatrists—with his 'pre-logical' pish posh. More than almost anyone else but Freud & Co., he [Lévy-Bruhl] has been responsible for the slovenly equation of primitive and pathological which I am fighting tooth and nail [with psychoanalysts]."[53] Cora was not shy about expressing her opinions to Lowie regarding his manuscript.

Finally, Cora both praised the book and chided Lowie for not doing more with the contemporary work in culture and personality. "The book ends with a slam bang," she wrote. "Really, you have no idea how much I enjoy your way with words. The smooth restrained yet devastatingly scholarly criticisms. It does my heart good." However, she was critical of "the section on psychology" where "you . . . limit yourself to comments on the more pedestrian aspects of 'scientific' psychology but I don't feel that you have even touched the more searching, if less sound, attempts being made in the realm of what might be subsumed under Sapir's rubric of the impact of personality on culture, and vice versa—the sort of more intimate relationship which Mead at her rare best is getting at."[54] Cora did not mince words with her graduate mentor, and Lowie, in the preface to his book, thanked her, together with A. L. Kroeber, for "their comments."[55]

Nonetheless, despite all her stimulating activities, Cora was becoming increasingly anxious about employment for the following academic year. But by late June she was able to write joyfully to Kroeber and Lowie to tell them that their joint efforts had not been in vain and that she was "now among the employed." She had been offered a one-year instructorship at Hunter College that would enable her to remain in New York City, continue her clinical work, and do another joint seminar with Kardiner.

To Lowie, she wrote, "I thank you, Herr Professor, again and most warmly. It appears that both [Ruth] Bunzel and Hortense Powdermaker were being considered for the job too. You and Kroeber must have done some pretty hard pushing a) to get me in over local competitors and b) to have them raise the ante on the salary."[56] Her salary would be $2,000 for teaching two different courses in two different locations—a total of fifteen hours of teaching each week.

In the letter to Kroeber she remarked, "[Kardiner] wants to continue cultural presentations next spring and is planning a book. Since the analysts are coming to realize more and more the inadequacies of the libido theory and their ignorance of ego development, they are turning to culture for elucidation. . . . I have pious hopes that a certain limited contribution to anthropology may be made along these lines, although no one has yet posited the necessary questions—for which sharp and unequivocal answers can be found."[57]

Accordingly, in the spring of 1937 the Kardiner–Du Bois seminar, in association with the New York Psychoanalytic Society, was repeated. Again Cora made some ethnographic presentations and invited others—Benedict, Bunzel, Sapir, and so on—to make presentations in their areas of expertise. (Mead was absent from the list because she was away doing research in Bali at the time.) As Cora remembered it in later life, "Kardiner wanted to know who the anthropologists [of the day] were and this was a convenient way for me to invite [some of] the leading anthropologists. They were very gracious and they came."[58] And with further comparative analyses of ethnographic data and dialogue with anthropologists, Kardiner began to develop his concept of "basic personality structure" and, most significantly, an explanatory model for how culture and personality might be interconnected that would inspire a major research project by Cora Du Bois.

Kardiner's Theoretical Model

First, it is important to note that in the course of the seminar with Du Bois, Kardiner came to appreciate the diversity of sociocultural systems and their implications with respect to individual personality development. He acknowledged this in the introduction to *The Individual and His Society: The Psychodynamics of Primitive Social Organization* (1939) when he wrote, "The individual cannot be studied without the institutions in which he lives, and institutions cannot be understood except as the creations of man. Whether the starting point is the individual or the institution, one must end by knowing both."[59] This was an important step away from the biological determinism of Freud's libido theory and an important recognition that culture had an impact on the psychological formation of individuals.

How did Kardiner integrate current theories of culture and personality? He did this in two ways—by inventing the concept of "basic personality structure" and by dividing "culture" into two different parts (discussed below) that were *integrated* by personality. Kardiner defined "basic personality structure" as "the effective adaptive tools of the individual which are *common* to every individual in the society."[60] In other words, members of a given group or society would, he hypothesized, share certain ways of perceiving and thinking about the world and thereby share ways of acting in and upon it. This is what Kardiner meant by shared "adaptive tools," or what today we might call "cognitive schemas."[61] He was *not* asserting that all members of a society had the same personality but that they would have similar "adaptive processes" that produced a recognizable "basic personality structure."

For any given society, Kardiner theorized, a basic personality structure evolved in response to individuals experiencing common cultural practices as they grew up. Some practices, he hypothesized, were more fundamental to the shaping of an individual than others. He called these "primary institutions" and argued that they helped to produce shared habits of mind and behavior. Primary institutions included a society's subsistence system—the procuring, sharing, and preparation of food—and a society's family and kinship system—the way in which people handled marriage, reproduction, and the nurturing and socializing of children. Primary institutions, according to Kardiner, served the basic needs and drives (e.g., food, sex, nurturance) of a community of individuals.

"Secondary institutions," by contrast, were generated from the basic personality structure of a community and served other kinds of needs and drives. Here he located theories of disease and healing practices, religious beliefs and ritual practices, myths, folktales, and so on—what he called the more "expressive" institutions of a society. It is important to note the causal chain here: the secondary cultural institutions developed in response to the shared individual personality structures that, in turn, had developed in response to the primary cultural institutions. The pressures of a particular sociocultural system, Kardiner theorized, would not only create adaptive strategies in the individual but also create conditions of repression, anxiety, and conflict. Because not all needs, drives, and impulses would be adequately satisfied, individuals in any sociocultural system would experience some degree of frustration, anxiety, and conflict that would produce behaviors in need of control, redirection, or alternative sources of satisfaction. Secondary institutions served such "socially created" needs.[62]

With this theoretical model—which will be illustrated with ethnographic data collected by Du Bois in the Dutch East Indies (chapter 5)—Kardiner managed to integrate selected aspects of psychoanalysis and cultural anthropology, making personality both a *product* of culture and a *determinant* of culture. (It was a model adopted by the Institute of Human Relations at Yale and continued, in a slightly modified form, by Beatrice and John Whiting at Harvard and now by many of their students.)[63] It is important to note, however, that Kardiner emphasized that personality resided in the individual, *not* in the culture as a whole. He objected to tendencies by some psychoanalysts and anthropologists to characterize a whole society using terms drawn from psychopathology or from literary and mythological sources. "No culture is predominantly 'paranoid,'" he wrote. "To lose track of the sharp differentiation between individual and group, and of the fact that society is not an individual, is to abandon the chance for any precision in studying reciprocal relations empirically."[64] Without mentioning Benedict and Mead by name, he was clearly critiquing this aspect of their work.

In his seminar at Yale, which Cora was attending, Edward Sapir was asserting very much the same kind of thing about the individual with respect to culture and society. Sapir, however, was more outspoken in his attack on Benedict and Mead. He is reported to have said, "This is what Mead and Benedict do—they confuse the individual psychology of all members of a society with the 'as-if' psychology of a few. I use the term 'as-if psychology' to describe the process of projection of personal values by the individual to evaluate cultural pattern, [so that a cultural standard of conduct is seen as if it represented the expression of a personality. This is a metaphorical identification,] not to be interpreted literally."[65]

Cora, after attending the Sapir seminar for some months, indicated in a letter to Kroeber a preference for Sapir's approach over that of Benedict and Mead. She wrote, "My feeling is that Sapir comes nearer to seeing things in his stress on [the individual in] personality and culture than does the Columbia group with its translation of cultural data into the lingo of another field."[66] A concern with the individual *in* culture had, of course, motivated much of Du Bois's thinking and written work since her first years in graduate school.

The Next Step: Fieldwork

By the end of the second (1937) Kardiner–Du Bois seminar, Kardiner agreed with Cora that they had "talked ourselves out" and that "only field work could test the procedure."[67] The seminar had been a good exercise in trying to identify both institutionalized and informal factors that had the most formative effect on personality development in a given society, but they had been using ethnographic data that had been collected for other purposes. As Cora put it in her preface to *The People of Alor* (1944), "Were individuals predominantly what we might suppose them to be from the institutions under which they lived, the childhood conditioning they received, the values they shared, the goals for which they strove?"[68] New fieldwork was going to be required.

With Kardiner's blessings, Cora set about selecting a site for research and trying to garner financial assistance. As she reported it later in life, "We both agreed that to go to a place where there was some well-known malady, such as memetic compulsions, it would be better. [I]t's always easier to study pathology than it is normalcy. . . . That was what we looked for first, and we found these memetic compulsions in Siberia and in Malaysia [e.g., "Arctic hysteria" and "Latah," respectively]. I said, 'That's all very well, but look, suppose nothing comes of this problem [being able to find a suitable psychopathology to study]? I still want to [produce] some ethnography for people who are not known ethnographically.'"[69] Cora decided, however, that Siberia was not her "dish of tea," so she began looking for unstudied sites in Indonesia and Malaysia. After consulting two Indonesian specialists—Raymond Kennedy at Yale and J. P. B. de Josselin de Jong at Leiden—she selected Alor, a remote island at the eastern edge of the Indonesian Archipelago. Funding for the eighteen-to-twenty-four-month research project would be provided in part by Kardiner and in part by Social Science Council research funds to which Ruth Benedict had access and that she made available for the project. The joint "grant," which totaled $4,400, was handled by Columbia University.[70]

Once again, in the fall of 1937, Cora would set off on a new set of adventures—this time to do her own culture and personality research on a remote island where the Pacific meets the Indian Ocean. A new and significant chapter in her life was about to begin.

CHAPTER 5

A Pioneer in Culture and Personality Research

Du Bois has tackled a very difficult and a very significant problem seriously and courageously. . . . We are only at the beginning of research on the cultural conditioning of personality and all studies of this type are necessarily of a pioneer character. This one is particularly important because of its thoroughness and because of its exploratory nature.
—Hortense Powdermaker

Each stage of Cora Du Bois's life was marked by a significant voyage—by sea or by train. This time was no exception. For her pioneering fieldwork in culture and personality, she would spend several months on ships, working her way eastward to the island of Alor, which then lay in the Netherlands East Indies (today's Indonesia), midway between Java in the west and New Guinea in the east. She thought of this expedition as her first *real* fieldwork because she would be studying an existent society rather than doing historical reconstruction with severely disrupted Native American groups in the United States. In Alor she would work in a small illiterate society that had never before been studied and whose language was unknown.

By her calculations, Du Bois had sufficient funding for about two years of travel and fieldwork. However, when her Berkeley friend Paul Radin heard about all the different research techniques that she planned to use, he estimated she would need at least five years.[1] In addition to doing ethnographic research, Du Bois planned to use a variety of psychological tests and to gather a set of autobiographies. She would have to be expeditious, but then she was a careful planner and an experienced fieldworker. At the time, two years of sustained fieldwork was considered a substantial period and was considerably longer than Margaret Mead, for example, had spent in any one society until her fieldwork in Bali.[2]

Fieldwork Preparations

Needless to say, careful preparations were required for such an expedition to a remote part of the world, where supplies of food, clothing, household equipment, and medications would be unavailable and where everything had to be brought in by boat. Du Bois sought advice from Margaret Mead, who at the time was in Bali doing research with her husband, Gregory Bateson. Mead and Bateson had considerable experience in New Guinea as well as in Bali, which was also a part of the Netherlands East Indies. Mead responded to Du Bois's inquiries with an eleven-page, single-spaced (with no margins) letter full of information, suggestions, and directives.[3] First, in her take-charge fashion, Mead advised Du Bois *against* working in a Dutch colonial region because of language issues (one needed to know both Dutch and Malay, the lingua franca of the area), high expenses, and poor Dutch ethnology.

After a rather negative two-page preamble, Mead wrote, "[F]rom now on, I shall assume that you are going just where you now plan and answer your questions from that point of view." And she proceeded to offer Du Bois detailed advice about travel plans and supplies that were unavailable in the East Indies and should be acquired in the United States and instructions about how to pack them. "I suggest that you get some kind of uniform boxes," Mead wrote, "and pack them full. You will also need a strong box for your notes, and get it after you have decided what kind of paper and note books you are going to use. . . . Get good padlocks." Perhaps Mead's most valuable piece of advice, however, was to bring a supply of medications that could be used to treat villagers. "I don't know how you feel about doing medical work," Mead wrote, "but it is undoubtedly one of the most fool proof ways of getting to know a community quickly and keeping au courant with what goes on." Mead also offered to send Du Bois a conversation book in Dutch, English, and Malay and invited her to come stay with them in Bali for a while "to work up your Malay with our Madé, who is a seasoned linguistic informant."[4]

More significantly, however, Mead concluded her letter with a different and contradictory invitation—to come do research with her and Bateson in Bali rather than in Alor: "[T]wo years is a very long time to be on one's own, Cora, always speaking an unfamiliar language even to servants and stray government officials." In Bali, Mead suggested, Du Bois could have her own village in which to work and her own secretaries—"it works amazingly well"—and she would have colleagues and could become part of the Mead-Bateson collaborative research team.[5] Mead had greatly underestimated Du Bois's linguistic capacities as well as her independence and commitment to her own research project. Cora responded cordially and agreed to stop in Bali to visit Mead and Bateson for several days on her way, by local ship, to Alor.

Meanwhile, Cora made use of Mead's practical advice and packed twenty-two tin cases and wooden chests full of things that she would need in Alor, which included some medications, with more to be acquired in the East Indies. She also packed a list of medical instructions in English and Malay for the principal diseases she would be seeing and trying to treat, such as malaria, tropical ulcers, fungus, dysentery, and yaws (a tropical infection of the skin). And she had made up some official stationery with the heading

Professor Dr. Cora Du Bois
Ethnological Mission
Columbia University
New York City

To her mother, she sent a sample of the letterhead stationery, saying, "Dearest Mammy, Doesn't that knock your eye out. It does mine, to such an extent I don't believe I'll dare use it except among friends."[6] Cora would learn, however, that in colonial regions such as the Dutch East Indies—and many years later, in postcolonial India—official stationery and business cards were a necessity.

During these fieldwork preparations, Cora wrote to Robert Lowie, saying, "It is all so exciting and improbable I have to pinch myself from time to time. . . . I hope 'I do you both [Lowie and Kroeber] proud' on this coming venture. It is, after all, the only opportunity that students have of repaying the multitudinous obligations they incur. That is both sentimental and infantile, I fear, but I do feel pretty much that way."[7] Cora was clearly excited about her first major fieldwork expedition outside of the United States.

The Voyage to Alor

On September 25, 1937, Cora's mother and stepfather saw her off in New York City as she set sail on the RMS *Veendam*, a Holland-American passenger liner bound for the The Hague, Netherlands, her first stop on her long voyage to the island of Alor. This was still an era of travel by ship, with no jet airliners to hasten the voyage from one side of the world to the other. On board ship, Cora found that most of the passengers and crew were Dutch so that she could practice speaking Dutch, which she had been studying over the summer. Fortunately, she had the advantage of already knowing German. In her first letter home, written on board ship, Cora thanked her parents "a million times for all the presents and help and love you have given me. It is a very reassuring anchor to windward and one which I rely on no end."[8] Richard Bicknell, Cora's stepfather, had become her legal executor who would handle her finances while she was away. In addition, he would process all her photographs from Alor. Both he and Gregory Bateson, who was doing extensive photographic work in Bali, had advised her about what equipment to take and how to store it safely.

Upon arrival in The Hague, Cora was greeted by two of her Du Bois relatives—Aunt Susy, who lived there, and Uncle Georges, who had come from Frankfurt to see her. He was the uncle with whose family she had lived in Frankfurt for several months when she was eighteen. In Holland she particularly wanted to meet with de Josselin de Jong, the professor of anthropology at Leiden University who had given her advice about a suitable research site in the Netherlands East Indies. De Josselin de Jong, she wrote, "took me in tow. Everyday, all day, for 2 weeks he primed me with information both practical and scientific. He even took me to Amsterdam to supervise the purchase of a camp bed and mosquito net and such other equipment as he thought should be gotten in Europe."[9] And he helped Cora get official backing from the Dutch government for her research expedition. Finally, de Josselin de Jong introduced Cora to one of his graduate students, Martha Margaretha Nicolspeyer, and suggested that

Nicolspeyer come do her PhD dissertation research under Cora's supervision once she was settled in Alor. Cora agreed to this plan.

Then it was another month's sea voyage to Java, with a variety of stops along the way. When Du Bois reached Sabang, Sumatra, she felt that she was finally having her "first taste of the Indies" and that she could begin using her "abortive Malay" that she had been studying on board ship.[10] She was also able to do a little sightseeing during stops in Colombo (in what was then Ceylon and is now Sri Lanka) and Singapore and reported in a letter home, "I haven't been so excited by pure sightseeing and superficial travel since my first adult impressions of Europe. I rather thought it was a faculty I had lost and it is gratifying to rediscover it, again."[11] Colombo would be a place that she would return to during World War II when she served in Ceylon in the Office of Strategic Services (OSS).

On November 18 Cora arrived in Batavia (today's Jakarta, Indonesia), the capital of the Netherlands East Indies on the island of Java, where she spent a week paying formal calls to Dutch officials, garnering more information about Alor, and acquiring additional equipment. "My residual shopping—which was considerable—was all done for me and the government even presented me—gratis—with 4 cases of medical equipment to carry me over my 2 years of free 'clinics' in Alor. Standard Oil saw to ordering very swank zinc cases which they use on their field jaunts. This last courtesy I scooped because I knew Doc Normland and the man who got me the cases works under Doc. Good old politics! Their ramifications are legion."[12]

In Batavia Cora also met a "Mrs. Holt"—Claire Holt, who was at that time a reporter for the *New York World* and who was studying Javanese dance and helping to document it.[13] She and Cora would become lifelong friends, and they would both serve in the OSS during World War II. It was Claire who took Cora around the city and introduced her to Javanese dance. Then, because there was no boat heading out to Alor for another two weeks, Cora did some traveling around Java, escorted by "a beautifully trained" Javanese young man, who would also accompany her to Alor. In a letter home, she reported that she loved Middle Java and found the people "exquisite," adding, "one feels so incredibly gross by comparison."[14]

The next stop on Du Bois's six-hundred-mile journey from Java to Alor was the island of Bali to visit Mead and Bateson, as promised, for "3 frantic days having as much as possible crammed down me."[15] It was both an interesting and a trying visit for her that would have a permanent effect on her relationship with Mead. Mead "had just assumed I would jump at the opportunity of working with her and went ahead on that assumption. As a result I found an extra room built on their house (or at least 1 of their 3 houses) and found that furniture had been gotten for me and a practical program of work laid out. . . . She is undoubtedly the most insatiably cannibalistic person I have ever encountered. I have the feeling that she just goes around grabbing up everything and everyone."[16] Two strong-willed and talented women anthropologists had come into conflict.

Cora had to be adamant with Mead, forcefully asserting that she intended to proceed on to Alor, where she would undertake her own fieldwork. Mead, however, was resentful and wrote a scathing letter to Ruth Benedict about Cora's lack of appreciation of her efforts.[17] Nonetheless, Cora had a pleasant time being shown around Bali "from north to south," taken to several dance and music performances, and introduced to some of Mead and Bateson's collaborators. She particularly liked Bateson, whom she described as "a sweet lamb—very polite, very loyal but I felt not beyond considerable irritation."[18] From Bali it took another eleven days to get to Alor by a boat "coyly called the Valentyne." The length of time was not so much due to distance as to having "to chase our own tail around all the Lesser Sundas [a small set of islands located to the north of Alor, between Sulawesi and New Guinea] in order not to miss [picking up or delivering] one pig, one water buffalo or one bag of rice. Toward the end I was the only passenger which meant I had a swell time with an unusually nice batch of officers. I left them feeling once more as tho I were leaving a house & lot which I owned."[19]

The Island of Alor

Finally, on January 6, 1938—after more than three months of travel—Du Bois arrived at Kalabahi, the island of Alor's only port town. In a letter to her Berkeley friends Jane and Julian Steward, she wrote,

> I found there 9 Europeans—all officials—as pompous as they are insignificant. The ranking official—a controleur—fortunately was married so I could stay in their home. What I had hoped would be

two or three weeks at most on the coast lengthened into five. I had to make exploratory jaunts into the mountains to find a village. However Holland was expecting an heir and all officials were ordered to stand by the ear phones so that they might shoot off their firecrackers the minute of the Happy Event (the Dutch euphemism—not mine). One day jaunts—there and back—revealed nothing worth having. To add to my distress—a new batch of officials had just come in—were at dagger points with each other and knew no more about the island than I. Finally I insisted upon sallying forth unchaperoned with the radjah [a local Dutch-appointed official]—who is a duck if ever I saw one. Our first jaunt out and I found exactly what I wanted—got a piece of ground and staked out a house. Two days later a craftsman was sent up to start the house. In 3 weeks reports came thru that it was nearing completion so I went up with the controleur, the doctor, the radjah and 28 coolies worth of luggage—only to discover that the house was barely underway. I was so enraged that I became positively fluent in Malay.[20]

Cora's intent from the beginning had been to find a reasonably remote mountain village in which to do research that was away from coastal Dutch influences. The Dutch had divided Alor, an island fifty miles long and thirty miles wide, into four "radjahships," each with an appointed official (the radjah), for the purpose of collecting taxes and handling litigation among the island's diverse cultural and language groups. The village—actually, a cluster of five villages—that she selected was named Atimelang and was situated in a mountainous region above the island's northwest coast. She found it attractive because its elevation at two thousand feet, in an old volcanic crater, made for a moderate climate, and it had a year-round source of water. Furthermore, it was located six hours up into the mountains by horseback from Kalabahi—well away from Dutch officials.

The radjah, who had accompanied Cora by horseback on her first trip to Atimelang, was reluctant to let her reside there because the villagers had been involved, twenty years earlier, in the murder of his uncle, the former radjah. But she somehow succeeded in convincing him and his underling, the "kapitan," that this was where she wanted to be, and the kapitan ultimately agreed to vouch for her safety.[21] Clearly, Du Bois—a strange American woman anthropologist—was persuasive, and the radjah would have an unusual person residing in his district for the next eighteen to twenty months.

In 1938 Atimelang had a population of about 180 inhabitants, with another 300 people living in several nearby villages in the same valley. One might wonder what their response was to the arrival of this strange woman. Once her house was completed, Cora gave a large feast, which included the cooking and sharing of a goat and an all-night dance. This, she had learned, was the way the Alorese celebrated any special event, including housewarmings, and it immediately helped to establish her status in the community. When the villagers asked her what her lineage was, she explained that she came from America. "In Abui this name means 'your' Merica and became a gracious gesture of hospitality to the chief. He then called the house 'her' Merica (Hamerica). My nation and their lineage concepts were all satisfactorily blended, unfortunately through sheer misunderstanding."[22]

Initially Cora relied on the skills of Ali, the young Javanese man who had accompanied her to Alor and who was fluent in Malay, which was spoken by a handful of villagers. The Alorese perceived him as "a gentle-man of wealth and prestige."[23] For six months, before returning to Java, Ali devoted himself to managing Cora's new household, including the hiring and training of a local Alorese staff. Meanwhile, Cora established a daily "clinic" and began treating people for infections, ulcers, and so on, which helped her to establish some degree of rapport and to begin to learn the local language, which had never before been studied and had no written form. She called it Abui, the word the villagers used to designate themselves as opposed to coastal people.

As Cora wrote in the preface to *The People of Alor* (1944), "Daily I bathed infections, dispensed quinine or castor oil or aspirin, and gradually even the women and children were sufficiently used to my touch to forgive me the size of my body, the whiteness of my skin, and the blue eyes, which looked so frighteningly blind to them. That my nose was long and sharp was, however, to the very end of my stay, a never-ending source of merriment." And she concluded her introductory reflections with these words: "It is therefore to those friends in Alor, to their shrewd but toler-ant acceptance of my peculiarities and to their vigorous engrossment in their own affairs that any contributions which this volume may make to an understanding of the varieties of human character are primarily due."[24]

Establishing Rapport in Atimelang

Cora moved to Atimelang on February 16, 1938. Her house—a four-room structure with a large verandah, plus separate cooking and bathing facilities—looked out on one of the village plazas and a cluster of split bamboo and thatch-roofed houses. This provided her with a close-up view of numerous village activities. On two sides of the house there were cornfields, and in back there was an area adequate for her to grow fruits and vegetables and to keep chickens. Cora did not import foods but relied on what she and her staff could either grow or acquire from her neighbors. Other than eating eggs and an occasional chicken, she became a semivegetarian like the villagers, who consumed meat only on feast days, except for the wild rats that they caught and grubs that they collected. (Cora, too, would sample rats and grubs during her stay in Atimelang.) "The house," she wrote to her parents, "is a gem except that all the neighborhood *will* sit on the path to the John [outhouse] and that the thatch rains chicken lice and droppings of all sorts. Fortunately, the 'staff' is thoroughly aroused over the latter issue and we all busily flit, Lysol or smoke the floor and walls—each according to his particular prejudice in the matter."[25]

Cora discovered that the setting of Atimelang was generally healthful. The temperature ranged from seventy to eighty degrees Fahrenheit, with 75–100 percent humidity. "There are no mosquitoes," she wrote. "Such cases of malaria as have appeared in the clinic were contracted on the coast. There are yaws and bad tropical ulcers, but they are scarcely contagious. For the yaws of course there is nothing I can do, but the ulcers clear up remarkably rapidly with a little cleansing and salve. Of dysentery I haven't seen a single case [although she would]."[26]

Within a month of being settled in her house, Cora had become established as "a great medicine man" as she put it, with some irony, in a letter to her parents:

My fame rests on having gotten Johans' [one of her staff] wife over a bad fever, on the good Dutch Boorzalf for wounds and having nursed Fantan's [one of her Malay-Abui interpreters] sister back to health after divination revealed she would die. (I thot too for a while—tho she had nothing more severe than a bad attack of flu). The chief of a village I never even heard of sent a messenger to ask for medicine for himself. This reputation may be a bit of a handicap yet—especially since you can never get any symptoms out of people beyond that they feel sick and maybe that they are feverish. Aspirin, castor oil and oatmeal plus some orange juice combined with their own sturdy constitutions are surefire cures on most ailments. The local medicine men don't seem to resent me. On the contrary—I attend their sessions—send them patients when a little mental work seems in order and they in turn attend my clinic. In fact I have since discovered that one of the most noted seers here was one of my first and most regular clinic patients—for 2 bad tropical ulcers which fortunately cured up rapidly. As far as I can judge I have been pretty thoroughly accepted as a "safe" person.[27]

Cora was quickly accepted into village life in Atimelang, and now her work began. Rather than summarizing for the reader some of the results of her ethnographic and psychological research in Alor, I shall present her work more or less the way it developed. Cora's long, descriptive letters to family and colleagues, together with detailed field notes and journal entries, make this possible and help to illustrate the actual *process* of ethnographic research and discovery.

The First Stage of Fieldwork

The first six months of fieldwork constitute a critical stage for an anthropologist. In addition to trying to establish rapport with members of a new society, it is a period when one works through the "culture shock"—a term Cora Du Bois is credited with inventing later in life when she was working with the State Department—that one is likely to have while immersing oneself in an unfamiliar society.[28] It is a time when everything is dramatically new and different, and one must cope with not knowing the rules for behavior and, potentially, with having little or no facility in the language. But it is also a time of intense learning as one becomes acclimated to a new way of life. For Cora, this period was eased by the presence of Ali, who supervised her household, and by the success of her medical clinic, which gave her an immediate role and status in the community.

12. Cora Du Bois sitting at a typewriter, Alor, Netherlands East Indies, 1939. © President and Fellows of Harvard College, Peabody Museum of Archaeology and Ethnology PM#972-29-70/10856.1.3.1, digital file #98560168.

Cora's journal entries and letters from this period indicate great enthusiasm about her fieldwork in Alor, pleasure in her new home, and relief in finding the climate comfortable and reasonably free of disease. As she wrote repeatedly to family and friends, "There is about as much relationship between field work here and in the States as between flying and walking. Here I positively have to protect myself against ethnology in order to have any time to take notes and work on language."[29] And "this business of being plumped into the middle of a vigorous culture—sink or swim—still amazes me by the richness of the experience."[30]

Cora was enmeshed in a live culture rather than having to elicit people's memories of a precontact culture in the United States. Such culture shock as there was probably lay in two areas: One was Cora's initial aesthetic response to the Alorese. Unlike the slender and graceful Javanese and Balinese, with whom she had just become acquainted and whom Westerners have tended to romanticize, Cora at first found the short, stocky Alorese, with their "black teeth and red squirts of betel juice," physically unattractive. In physical type they were more Melanesian than Malay. But within a month she had "quite forgotten" her initial response and "now think them lambs of God."[31] Second, Cora immediately became aware of a high degree of quarrelling among the Alorese. She found herself in a noisy and seemingly belligerent society where village life was filled with the sounds of men's and women's public arguments, children's temper tantrums, and frequent all-night feasts and dances with much beating of gongs.

During the first week of having established her daily clinic, Cora was made aware of the seriousness of some of these disputes. A woman arrived one morning with a badly infected thumb. "As I cleaned and bandaged a wound which looked like a jagged cut penetrating to the bone, Kolmau was telling loudly some tale, obviously of a resented wrong."[32] It was not until later, when she could confer with her interpreter, that Cora learned the wound had resulted from a confrontation between two women—Kolmau, a first wife, and a woman whom her husband was planning to take as a second wife. In a scrimmage between the two women, the "second wife" had bitten Kolmau's thumb to the bone. The feud between the two women would continue for another year.

Cora began the more formal part of her ethnographic research by mapping the complex of five villages in which she lived and, with the help of local Alorese assistants, taking a census, collecting genealogies, and trying to learn and record the language. Three weeks after her arrival in Atimelang, in a letter to Ruth Benedict, Cora wrote, "[T]hings are going swimmingly. . . . Stuff comes in faster than I can get it down and I am still in an omnivorous frame of mind. As a result I feel pleasantly harassed by all there is to be done and definitely annoyed when the day ends or my head begins swimming about in a wash of Malay and Abui."[33] And she reported, with some glee, that the same afternoon, while recording a genealogy, she had made great strides in figuring out the Alorese kinship system. "And who wouldn't burble when you can get a whole kinship system in an afternoon with an informant who immediately grasped kinship diagrams. It makes me squirm when I ponder the genealogies and the hours spent on the same chore in California or Oregon." With regard to her special research focus, she added, "Psychologically of course I can do nothing yet except observations on behavior, a few dreams in texts and jottings which suggest themselves from the language."[34]

With respect to language learning, Cora reported to Benedict, "Just now I'm communicating with those who don't know Malay (and that means most of the population) with a few words strung together and gestures which are positively acrobatic. However, everyone is taking my education seriously in hand, including the children."[35] By the end of six months of fieldwork, Cora wrote to Alfred Kroeber about her language facilities: "Despite the harrowing Dutch and Malay preambles, my enthusiasm for Abui is undiminished. The enthusiasm, you understand, has no relationship to fluency. In fact it seems rather an inverse ratio. In Dutch and Malay for which I have no great enthusiasm, I seem to have acquired far more facility in a few months than I have in Abui. However, the pleasures of figuring out grammatic structure are undeniable. . . . I have a terrific yearning to do a really good linguistic analysis—at least just once in my life."[36]

Cora's handwritten notebooks, in which she kept records of her daily observations, include a dictionary with thousands of Abui words and notebooks filled with careful recordings of Abui sentences together with line-by-line English translations. In the same letter to Kroeber, Cora reported that Abui appeared to be a Melanesian language. This, she said, was de Josselin de Jong's best inference based on the samples of transliterated Abui that she had sent him to analyze. This also led Cora to tell Kroeber about the "hopelessly entangled historical background" of Alor:

On the "Melanesian" substructure are Javanese gongs and metal hourglass drums and parallels in scraps of sky lore [myths]; the coast is probably under Celebes influence—maybe even influences from the Molucca radjahship of Ternate and Tidore [two of the Lesser Sundas], and coastal influences have been seeping up into even my remote mountain crater for a long time; the eastern part of the island is in constant touch with Portuguese Timor. Although the Dutch have made themselves felt here for only twenty years (providentially putting an end to head-hunting) the Portuguese must have had considerable and indirect influence for 3 centuries. Maize—the staple if not ceremonial food—they certainly introduced, along with tobacco—perhaps. Sheep and goats maybe. The occasional carabao [water buffalo] is probably old Javanese via Timor. Oddly enough the horse is still absent except for some 100 (maybe) imported from Timor for local Dutch and Native officials.[37]

It was Kroeber, the cultural historian, to whom Cora reported her efforts to piece together the complex merging of so many different cultural influences on this seemingly remote island.

Within the first six months of her fieldwork, Cora had been absorbed into village life. "Now I am free to climb into [villagers'] houses at any time," she wrote to Kroeber. "[V]ery few of the children still go into a tail spin when I approach, my special lady friends and I embrace when we meet on the trail, my gentlemen friends and I have a whole series of jokes—largely gesture still since my Abui is so lame."[38] She found that she could comfortably take photographs of the Alorese, who would carry on with their chores rather than posing for the camera. (Cora regularly sent rolls of film to her stepfather, who developed and printed them, sending her copies to share with the Alorese.) And in a remarkable letter to her parents, Cora summarized her early fieldwork experience in the following manner:

> So time flits by—between delight over a new prefix and drooling over rare [beef] tenderloin memories. I suppose I should try to make it all seem esoteric and adventurous because that is what it is supposed to be, but really it's just another job—much pleasanter than most and very relaxing to the spirits. I wouldn't swap it for anything—but it's not high adventure or romance or anything like that. I shall return to the States with several more square yards of experience and even perhaps an added stratum of depth and what more can a squirrel ask of existence?[39]

One might assume that this rather philosophical portrait of fieldwork in a remote part of the world, living with former headhunters, was primarily an effort to reassure her parents that life in Alor was safe, even mundane. But there is another message of some significance here. Du Bois was disinclined to romanticize her fieldwork among the Alorese, however stimulating she found it to be. Rather, she remained focused on her research goals, which required basic ethnography *and* the collection of extensive psychological data. She had neither the time nor the inclination to romanticize her activities and the people among whom she was living. Years later she would be criticized by some for her seemingly "negative" portrait of the Alorese and for not having been "more sympathetic" to them.[40] Cora's numerous boxes of carefully kept field notes—both in longhand and in typewritten form—together with her journals and extensive photographic collection, attest to the care and thoroughness with which she approached this research project and the people who collaborated with her. Furthermore, it has been demonstrated that ethnographers who employ a variety of research techniques, as Cora did, are less inclined to be "romantically biased" than others and are more likely to report negative as well as positive personality traits in their subjects.[41]

Ethnographic Insights

By the end of six months, Cora had become a successful participant observer—the principal research technique used by cultural anthropologists—and had acquired a good grasp of the principles underlying Alorese social structure, or what in Kardiner's theoretical model (chapter 4) were called "primary institutions." And she had also learned a fair amount about Alorese cultural beliefs and practices—the "secondary institutions" in Kardiner's model.

In Cora's case, participant observation meant that, among other things, she was expected to participate in the Alorese wealth/prestige system. From an Atimelang villager's perspective, Du Bois was a woman of wealth and status—someone who could have a house built, sponsor a housewarming feast, and set up a medical clinic. Accordingly, she was expected to participate in the local wealth system, even though this was principally the domain of men. As she explained to Benedict, "I find myself in a 'wealth' culture where I am an object for exploitation but also where I must hold up mine own end of giving—a pig here, a goat there along with all the other small-fry gifts like soap, tobacco, salt, nails and so on."[42] What she meant by a "wealth culture" was that the villagers had special goods, other than the food they grew, that constituted currencies and were used for accumulating wealth and acquiring social prestige. Cora had not anticipated such costs in planning her research budget and was relieved when Benedict found her an additional few hundred dollars.[43]

The underlying base of the Alorese economy, Cora learned, was horticulture—the small-scale growing of corn, rice, beans, and other vegetables in the rainy season and cassava, taro, and other tuber crops in the dry season. A large variety of tropical fruits—oranges, mangoes, papayas, breadfruit, jackfruit, and bananas—were also grown. It was a subsistence economy, with only some surplus rice produced for ceremonial occasions. Villagers also raised pigs, goats, and chickens, but these were for ceremonial purposes, not for regular consumption. Pigs, in particular, were part of the prestige economy and belonged to men.

Every individual, whether male or female, owned fields that were given to them as children or inherited later in life. On the average, a married couple tended to have six fields on which to grow their food, although the actual range was from one to eighteen per nuclear family. Inequities existed both in the number of fields owned and in their size and fertility, but such inequities were never mentioned by people and seemed to have no bearing on their prestige rating.[44] Gardening in all fields, whether owned by men or women, was principally the domain of women, and women owned and had distribution rights to all the produce.

Because adult women were the principal food producers—although they expected some help from men in the clearing and planting of fields—adult men were largely freed to participate in the wealth/prestige system that was built on three different currencies—pigs, gongs (prized musical instruments), and metal kettledrums called "mokos" (bronze vessels of Javanese origin). Alorese men spent much of the day negotiating for, trading, borrowing, and lending these goods, which were used to arrange marriages, build ceremonial houses, and pay for an innumerable long series of death feasts. Men, Cora learned, had to become expert accountants. "The bookkeeping involved in these elaborate and long-drawn-out transactions [of borrowing and repaying debts] must be carried in people's heads," she wrote. "There is no system of writing, not even a system of tallies, to keep track of their complexity. One man who gave such a [death] feast summarized the transactions in connection with that ceremony alone. He had fifty-seven creditors and debtors involving two hundred items to remember, certainly no mean intellectual feat."[45]

Early in her fieldwork Cora described, in a letter to Abram Kardiner, this sexual division of labor:

Men's chief preoccupation is sitting on the gong house verandah playing gongs on feast days or talking about wealth manipulations, planning feasts, etc. If the spirit moves them they may assist the women in shelling beans or husking corn for the dry season. However, the bulk of the work, and perhaps more important still, the responsibility of the gardens and food rests with the women. What with weaving the necessary baskets for storing food, they are busy most of the time—in direct contrast to the men. But the interesting thing is that men know how to do most of the women's tasks except basket making. The men are really concerned over cultural things, in the narrower sense of the word, and women with subsistence. . . . And men are caught all their lives in debts which cannot be liquidated—a long series of bride payments and death obligations. But in all these feasts it is the women who are depended upon to furnish the real labor involved in the preparation of food. . . . For instance the local chief is giving a death feast for his father in law who has been dead some 20 years. He is concerned with divination, and organizing things but it is his female relatives and his wife's female relatives who have been working for the feast for the last ten days.[46]

Cora went on to describe to Kardiner how girls and boys were socialized into these different roles and to add that she anticipated finding "a pretty sharp sex dichotomy in character formation."

In another early letter, to her Berkeley friends Julian and Jane Steward, Cora described the kinship system—often the foundation of social structure in small-scale societies—that she was discovering: "I have dug up the darndest kinship grouping yet encountered called the Male House and the Female House. To the Male House belong all the descendants of one's great uncles—paternal & maternal. To the Female House belong all the descendants of one's great aunts—paternal & maternal. These Houses are the basic functioning groups for the endless death feasts involving terrific expense which go on for a generation after a man's death. I found myself absolutely stymied in understanding local tie ups [kinship ties] until I began getting genealogies which explained these Houses."[47]

Cora was witnessing kinship in action while also eliciting genealogies and transcribing Abui—no mean feat. To her parents, she wrote, "I now have 3 mammoth genealogies—about 800 names covering 6 generations and they dovetail nicely in spots—which spots are carefully blue penciled. This has led to my discovering a very odd sort of kinship grouping which so far as I know is unique. It has aroused all my antiquarian, stamp collecting instincts—or more accurately—predilections."[48]

Cora learned that, although her Alorese villages were in some respects patrilineal (descent traced through males), in other respects they were bilateral (descent traced equally through both one's mother and father). Accordingly, each village had a ceremonial house for each of its patrilineages, but it also had male and female houses that incorporated people whose kinship ties were traced through both male and female kin, with the mother's brother being a particularly significant relationship. Du Bois described households as mostly nuclear in structure—mothers, fathers, and children living together—but her household census indicates that there was everything from single-mother–child households to extended households with two couples, widowed mothers or mothers-in-law, and children residing together.[49] As a society, the Alorese had a flexible family structure and were neither strictly patrilineal in structure nor strictly patriarchal in their gender system.

Women, at the time of marriage, usually moved to their husband's village, but their own kinsmen were not far away. Furthermore, as previously mentioned, women owned land and controlled the food that they produced, which gave them a source of power over their husbands, who needed the produce for ceremonial purposes as well as for daily consumption. In fact, Du Bois argued—anticipating some of the discussions by feminist anthropologists in the 1970s and 1980s—Alorese women's work gave them real power and status, even though men's financial work was more culturally valued.[50] Women were not afraid to act assertively—even quite aggressively—in public with their husbands. For example, Cora reported to Kardiner the following incident:

> Again, the woman took the initiative in overt aggression. In the middle of the dance place she began to hit and berate her husband. He was angry but also embarrassed and sheepish. He simply warded off her blows until she spat at him and then he gave her a push which sat her down pretty emphatically. . . . When a row of this sort is going on, it is the woman who talks and complains to all who will listen. The men

simply stand by, interestedly enough, but saying nothing. The female audience usually says little but nods sympathetically with the woman's tale. Of course all the children cluster around and listen to such tales of woe. There is no attempt to keep anything from them.[51]

In addition, if a woman was not happy in a marriage, she could leave. "Divorce is easy and usually a woman takes the initiative," Cora wrote to Kardiner. "This is simply a matter of returning to live in her father's or brother's house. If after waiting a while it becomes evident that this is not just one of the usual marital spats, and that she really does want a divorce, then the [husband's] father sets about the negotiations which must equalize the bride payments with the return [of] gifts given by the [bride's] father."[52] Marriages were, in fact, quite brittle, with individual men and women experiencing, on the average, two divorces during their lifetime. Some individuals had had up to six divorces.[53]

Early in her fieldwork, Du Bois was fortunate to witness both "a long series of negotiations in bride purchase" and a burial that "set in motion a most complicated series of reciprocal feasts." These were processes, she would discover, that were central to the Alorese social system. She described the latter one to Benedict:

A death starts a whole series of feasts going in which, so far as I now see, the Maternal House has to bear the brunt—not only of the feasts but for paying a series of mokos (the bronze hour-glass drums used as wealth here) to the Male House. The Male House does the burying & all the payments are putatively for the cloth used in making the corpse bundle. I had the good fortune to be in on a death & am now trying to trace the complicated negotiations which may go on for a generation. Also a death is just another excuse for the men to beat gongs. For two successive nights—from dark until dawn, this has gone on unceasingly. Fortunately the gongs are really lovely and they get rhythms very much worth listening to.[54]

Cora would gradually learn that the wealth/prestige system was closely linked with marriage negotiations and burials. A young man entered the system when trying to acquire a wife—through a series of bride price and dowry negotiations—and he remained in the system throughout his life as he contributed to ongoing series of burials and death feasts. People were believed to have two souls. One at the time of death—if it were not a violent death—would go to a village "down below." The second would loiter about the village as a potentially malignant force, causing illness and other troubles, and these souls needed to be ameliorated by a series of expensive feasts. Such feasts not only served to placate the dead but provided opportunities for men to pressure their creditors, display wealth, and enhance their prestige. Many pigs would be sacrificed and their meat distributed, a prerogative of men, while women would provide baskets of rice, fruits, and vegetables that they would distribute.

The Alorese believed in a variety of supernatural agents—from those that left a person's body at the time of death to ones that inhabited corners of villages and fields and were capable of both good and evil influences. In addition, it was believed that each person inherited or acquired, through nonpossessional visions, a "personal familiar" or guardian spirit. Each village also had a guardian spirit that needed to receive a sacrifice every year or two. Divination by seers was used to determine the source of illness and other bad omens, and the sacrifice of pigs and offerings of rice constituted the principal source of worship. Alorese "religion" was not a well-integrated ideology but rather a set of ceremonial occasions that brought people together for all-night feasting and dancing. Feeding, according to Cora, was "the chief cultural tool for symbolizing social euphoria and for placating supernatural beings."[55]

The Second Stage of Fieldwork

By the end of her first six months of fieldwork, Cora reported to Benedict, "Of course the cream skimming is pretty well finished after these 6 months and as a result there are dullish days. Probably by the time Miss Nicolspeyer [de Josselin de Jong's graduate student] from Leyden gets here (middle of October), I'll be ready for some company—however problematic." And then she described with great enthusiasm what "a good tussle with linguistics" she was having and what "a pity" it was that she had "missed the fun of linguistics all these years. Besides it must be such a satisfaction to be a linguist," she asserted. "At least in the field. The job is so nicely defined, not too easy and yet definitely capable of solution"—very different from the exploratory nature of research on the relationship between culture and personality that she was undertaking.[56]

As Du Bois moved into the second stage of fieldwork in Alor—for what would become another twelve months—her research became increasingly focused on gathering psychological materials that could be used to test Kardiner's theory and thereby contribute to the field of culture and personality. In the same letter to Benedict, she wrote, "I am amused to discover that practically every 'theoretic' reason for coming to Alor is not valid. Latah, amok, possessional shamanism are all absent."[57] In other words, there was no institutionalized psychopathology for her to explore culturally. She would have to heed Kroeber's advice about exploring "the normal variability of personality" rather than its extreme forms.

The one specialized role available to Du Bois for psychological examination was that of the seer, or the traditional diviners and curers in Alorese society. She found herself comparing them with the Native American shamans whom she had witnessed early in her graduate student years. To Robert Lowie, she wrote,

My zest for local phenomena is waning a bit, as I expected it would once the exotic wore off, but a dose of radio dispatches [anticipating World War II] throws me into new enthusiasm into the subject of seers and their dreams. Or maybe these guys are shamans. I can't be very sure. On occasion, especially if they are "feeding" their altars, they will speak with altered voices and are presumably "possessed" of their familiars [guardian spirit]. However there is no pretense of trance. When they work at extracting disease objects they certainly do not act or imply that they are in a "supernatural" state, although they do claim that their familiars perch on their shoulders the while. Massage is the usual type of extraction but sucking with mouth or drinking tube also occurs and even the good Plateau [Indians] "sweeping" with a feather duster of leaves. Seers are paid for cures—but very little and will cure relatives for nothing. This is one area which the preoccupation with wealth has failed to invade. The most distinguished of the lot is coming daily to the house with his nightly batch of dreams which may run as high as 15 to a night. . . . On the whole the pickings are rich both as far as his personal psychology goes & for general village gossip. As you see I am gradually shifting from straight ethnography to the avowed psychology I was sent to get.[58]

The exotic stage of research may have worn off, but this excerpt from Cora's letter to Lowie makes it clear that she had moved on to some of the more psychological aspects of her research project. (By this time, Cora's command of Abui was adequate to work most of the time without the assistance of a Malay-speaking interpreter.) In addition, she indicates that she was grappling with another psychological issue—whether or not Alorese seers utilized trance and possession such as she had witnessed among California Wintu shamans when she was a graduate student. In her short visit to Bali, Cora had learned that possession trance was common there. By contrast, she would learn that the Alorese considered "losing one's normal personality" dangerous and distrusted trance states and the use of any intoxicants. Furthermore, they associated spirit possession with insanity and premature death.[59]

Perhaps Cora's most interesting correspondence during this period, however, was with Kroeber, with whom she discussed some of the difficulties she was having in trying to relate social institutions to psychological factors among the Alorese. For example, she wrote, "From a purely institutional point of view loyalties are scattered from hell to breakfast. Add to this a pattern of rapid fluid emotional expression—often of the most violently aggressive sort—and you can imagine how befuddled I am when I see a hundred odd men and women shouting and scampering about at a ceremony. To add to my confusion they frequently play at anger with perfectly straight faces—everyone but the poor ethnologist understanding from connotation that its [sic] all a joke. I still have to ask all too often is so-and-so really angry, ashamed, afraid."[60]

Kroeber responded to Cora's letter, saying, "I have been thinking and conversing a good deal about psychology and anthropology during the past year, in fact my present seminar deals just with this. I must say that I still feel about as groping as you describe yourself." Cora, it seems, had helped to renew Kroeber's interests in psychological issues. And Kroeber continued,

For my part I should feel that if you came back with an account of the culture which did full justice to all of the affects [kinds of emotions]

with which the culture is charged, you would have accomplished all that anyone could legitimately be expected to do. . . . You should not feel defeated at not having been able to build a bridge [between psychology and cultural anthropology]: no one else has yet built one. If your people have no amok [uncontrollable disruptive or destructive behavior]—well that means simply that you get no chance to inquire into one sensational peculiarity. However, the problem of amok research is essentially one of clinical individual psychology in the study of which the psychologist must take cognizance of culture.

You will no doubt bring back a mass of material on dreams, personalities, children's play, and the like which will be of interest to certain psychologists as well as to certain anthropologists, and this will be to the good. But I do hope that you are not worrying too much about not bringing back a systematic construct: it probably does not exist.[61]

Despite these reassuring words from Kroeber, one of the most preeminent anthropologists of the day, the dialogue continued. Cora took umbrage with Kroeber's emphasis on "affect" and responded as follows:

As for the affect of a culture—or [Gregory] Bateson's ethos—that is again another abstraction and impressionistic sort of thing-just a little more sketchy than the type descriptions of cultures which ethnologists use [*sic*] to bring back. If reports on customs are difficult to establish—that is if the true norms are often hard to ascertain, how much more difficult it is to ascertain the "norm" of affects. These are legitimate fields of descriptive work in the area of both cultures and individuals but like all descriptions the approach is preliminary and static. The real problems as I see them are in that very vague question—"Why do human beings behave as they do?"—in Berkeley or in Atimelang. In other words not *what* is something, but how does something work. But that isn't a correct antithesis—since one has to know what one is dealing with before one can begin to ponder on how it works. Ethnology and psychology are still so unsatisfactory in the descriptive entities that it is perhaps premature to posit dynamic inquiries. One thing is sure, I shant come back a flag-waving psychologizing ethnographer, but on the other hand what slight orientation in psychology I've had, has made a world of difference in not only what I see but in *searching for the meaning of the behavior* I observe to the individual indulging in it.[62]

As a pioneer in culture and personality research, Cora Du Bois was coming to realize how difficult it was going to be to make generalizations about the relationship of Alorese cultural practices to individual personality, let alone to understand what motivated the kinds of behavior she was seeing. These are issues with which, more than seventy years later, psychological anthropologists and cross-cultural psychologists are still grappling. However, in the process of describing her ideas to Kroeber, she identified what has become one of the major foci of contemporary research—to understand how behavior can have different cultural meanings for people in different societies or different subgroups of the same society. Furthermore, as we shall see below, Cora did not disregard affect in Alor. What she opposed were efforts to characterize a whole society as having a particular affective orientation or ethos, which she considered not unlike Benedict's use of personality terms for characterizing societies—something, as she told Kroeber, she had come to see as "a very fallacious formulation."[63]

For the remainder of her stay on Alor, Cora deepened her ethnographic understanding of village life and interpersonal relationships while collecting a massive amount of psychological material—the largest set of such data ever to be collected, at that time, from one small non-Western society. These included in-depth observations of childrearing and child development; autobiographies elicited from four men and four women, each averaging more than fifteen hours of interview time; Porteus Maze tests (problem-solving intelligence tests) administered to fifty-four men and women; word association tests given to thirty-six women and men; children's drawings collected from fifty-five girls and boys; and finally, Rorschach (inkblot) projection tests administered to thirty-seven men and women. She would return to the United States with a wealth of data to be analyzed by her, Kardiner, and other specialists.

In October 1938—Cora's ninth month in the field—Martha Margaretha Nicolspeyer arrived from the Netherlands. Other than a brief visit by some Swiss botanists, this was Cora's first European visitor in Atimelang. Unfortunately, from Cora's perspective, it was not a particularly successful "experiment." "Miss Nicolspeyer," she reported to Kroeber, had "a very hard time adjusting to the differences between Atimelang and an unusually snug conservative Dutch home" and her "interest in field work has proved to be wholly theoretical. Her days are spent exclusively on the verandah with an acceptable interpreter and informant. There is here fortunately a 'genealogical genius' so I have set her to work on the structure and functions of a single lineage. Her training in kinship structure seems good so she is willing to and capable of wrestling with the maddeningly practical functioning of a theoretically complex kin structure."[64] Nicolspeyer's stay in Atimelang lasted only three and a half months, but it sufficed for her to write a dissertation and attain a PhD. In the foreword to her dissertation she thanked Cora Du Bois for her friendship and for making her fieldwork in Alor "an unforgettable period of my life."[65] And although Nicolspeyer did not practice anthropology professionally, she and Cora continued to have cordial communications with one another.

For both financial and security reasons—due to the buildup to the Second World War—Cora concluded her fieldwork in Alor in June 1939 and returned to the United States by ship. To Lowie, she wrote about her ambivalence about leaving: "Don't take this [damaged] paper to heart. It does not reflect my mood. If it did, it should be a bright rose. You see—going home is at hand. Yet being myself—I am torn two ways on every issue. Getting back seems swell but I'll miss my Atimelang and Atimelangers. And that is an expression of real devotion after this day. What an one it has been!" Cora went on to describe a hurricane that had hit their part of the island that day, knocking down people's houses and devastating their fields. The women, who had been out working in their fields when the hurricane struck, had been retrieved and were gathered, with their children in their arms, near Cora's more sturdily built house.

> I've been pretty touched at the way the women have all come scudding to me and sit in the lee of the wall which forms the foundation of my house. There is something terribly pathetic about their confidence in me—largely I suppose because they have no confidence in anything or anyone here. Thereby hangs a long story which links up

with a messianic cult. They believe that sky-beings can come down to earth & when they do, disease & death will end. They have been trying their best to make a sky-being (Something Good as they call it in their language) out of me.[66]

Cora alludes here to two important matters: first, the general mistrust—to be explored below—that characterized Atimelang villagers' lives; and, second, villagers' efforts to transform her into some kind of savior. The success of Cora's medical clinic had undoubtedly contributed to the appellation "sky-being" or "Good Being" (*nala kang* in Abui). As she reported it to Lowie, "A few lucky treatments when I came and a low death rate for a few months almost convinced them. It was ages before I caught on and of course have been combating the idea ever since."[67] What is remarkable, however, is that to this day Alorese villagers still talk about Cora Du Bois as a *nala kang*. She has attained a kind of cult status among the descendants of the people she knew in Atimelang in the 1930s, and even though they have been informed that she is deceased, they continue to speak about her returning one day.[68]

The Psychocultural Synthesis

In September 1939, a full two years after sailing from New York City, Cora Du Bois returned home with, as she put it in a letter to Jane and Julian Steward, "no pat psycho-social picture" of Atimelang villagers. "There is a hell of a lot of material and I'm still too embroiled in it to see it clearly."[69] Fortunately, just before leaving Alor, Cora had received a cable from Sarah Lawrence College offering her a part-time teaching position in anthropology for the 1939–40 academic year. This would provide her a small income and a base in New York City, where she could begin to analyze her research data and make a series of presentations to the psychoanalytic seminar that Kardiner now ran, together with anthropologist Ralph Linton, at Columbia University.

The focus of Du Bois's first presentation to the seminar would be Alorese economics, and an unfortunate rivalry with Margaret Mead would ensue. Mead, who had recently returned from Bali, was giving a lecture at Vassar on the same day and, as indicated in a letter she wrote to Ruth Benedict, was miffed that "[n]one of the 'enemy' came to hear [her] . . .

[and] that 'everybody, just everybody' went to hear Cora Du Bois lecture in a dull manner for two hours, elaborating on minor details of land tenure, pig raising, and what people ate. 'It's incredible to take up the time of grown up people listening to stuff that one ought to be able to summarize in the first five minutes.'"[70] Clearly, Mead was still angry with Cora for not accepting her invitation to work in Bali and did not like the competition for colleagues' attention.

Although Cora may not have been ready to write a psychocultural synthesis of Alorese society upon arriving home, she did return having made a variety of important inferences about the relationship of culture to personality in Atimelang. One of the most poignant of these was captured in her reference above to women huddling near her house during the hurricane because they had "no confidence in anything or anyone here." She had learned that mistrust tended to characterize interpersonal relationships in Atimelang. From the start of her fieldwork, Cora had witnessed numerous arguments and fights among people and had observed that lying and thievery were commonplace. And by the end of her fieldwork she had concluded that, despite individual variability, mistrust was deeply rooted in Alorese personality structure. So a major question for her analysis became, why? What in Alorese primary institutions—to use Kardiner's theoretical model—might produce such behavior?

Cora had a partial answer to this from her initial observations of the sexual division of labor in Atimelang and surrounding villages. Women did most of the gardening, which took them away from home for long hours during the day, especially during the wet season, when there was extensive weeding to be done. In some societies, when women do agricultural work, they take their infants with them to the fields in order to be able to nurse them during the day. However, this was not the practice in Atimelang. Rather, after a short period of seclusion (four to six days) with a newborn, mothers returned to their fields, leaving infants and young children in the care of others—older siblings, fathers, or an occasional grandparent. Cross-culturally, mother surrogacy is a widespread practice, but it can leave nursing infants without a suitable source of food for extended periods of time.[71] And in Atimelang, Cora found, the quality of care by others was highly variable and inconsistent. For example, in one of the autobiographies that she collected, an adult woman recalled, as follows, her frustrations with being the caretaker of a younger sister:

On the way [to the fields] Maliema cried a lot, so I put her down and slapped her. Then I talked nicely to her, and we went on when she was quiet. . . . When Maliema was a little older, she would cry to go to the fields with me. If I was not angry with her, I would take her along to dig sweet potatoes. I would give her the big ones and keep the small ones. . . . [I was angry] because she was always crying. She cried to go places; she cried to be fed. I hit her on the head with my knuckles and then I would feed her. *She cried because she was hungry.*[72]

And below is another excerpt from one of the autobiographies, this time from a male informant:

Once mother and I were living in a field house near our gardens. She told me to carry Senmani [younger brother] while she worked. At noon he was hungry and wanted to nurse. I gave him food but he only vomited it. He cried and cried and wouldn't stop. I cried too. Finally I went and told mother to come and nurse him but she wouldn't. So I took Senmani, laid him down on a mat in the house and ran off to Folafeng. There from the ridge I shouted, "Mother, your child lies in the house. If you want to care for it good. If you don't want to, that is also good. I am going to Atimelang to play."[73]

These two accounts of sibling childcare are striking in that they were unsolicited. They just emerged as part of these individuals' memories of their own childhoods—the frustration and resentment they experienced as caretakers of younger siblings. And they are consistent with Du Bois's observations of early childcare. In the absence of stable extended households, or some alternative form of cooperative childcare, older children were not supervised in childcare and were not very reliable caretakers. Their fathers were usually preoccupied with financial transactions, and there was no regular presence of grandmothers or other extended kin to help out.

In *The People of Alor*, Du Bois makes it clear that infants were not deliberately mistreated or rejected. In fact, they were carried about in shawls by a variety of people during the day, and they slept next to their mothers at night, thus receiving much tactile comfort. Furthermore, both toilet training and attitudes toward sex were casual. For example, caretakers would massage infants' genitals to soothe them. But the experience of hunger and frustration was a reality for most infants, who expressed their frustration by rejecting the premasticated foods (including rat) that they were offered and, instead, tried to suckle at the breasts of men and sibling caretakers. And, in the autobiographies that Cora collected, hunger was a common theme, not because food was scarce but because of these early childhood experiences with irregular feedings.

Hunger and frustration turned to rage when, as toddlers, young children tried unsuccessfully to follow their mothers to fields. "Rages are so consistent, so widespread, and of such long duration among young children," Cora wrote, "that they were one of my first and most striking observations."[74] These emotional outbursts, usually instigated by the departure of a child's mother for her gardens, lasted anywhere from a few minutes to as many as twenty minutes. The child, who was now walking, would begin to follow her mother to the fields and be rebuffed; hence the emotional outburst. Clearly, young children were sufficiently attached to their mothers as sources of food and comfort that they did not want to be left behind. But mothers did leave their toddlers behind during the day under the casual supervision of older children, fathers, and aged adults, with no one in charge of feeding them. Toddlers had to entertain themselves and learn to scrounge and beg for food. As Cora astutely noted, "[A]fter the child learns to walk, his frustrations with respect to hunger are increased, and simultaneously he loses the constant handling and support he had during the first stage of life in the carrying shawl."[75]

In Alor, the sexual division of labor, combined with no reliable caretaking system for infants and young children while mothers were gardening, produced both hunger and expressions of frustration and anger in children. These circumstances, Du Bois and Kardiner would argue in *The People of Alor*, produced in children deep feelings of insecurity and distrust of others that characterized their adult personalities. As Cora reported in her last letter to Lowie before leaving Alor, "All this belief set-up [about sky-beings] goes back I am sure to the basic fear & distrust in which they live. . . . I was struck recently on asking my interpreter if there was anyone he would trust with property and he couldn't name anyone. And since property has a definite—even *conscious*—linkage with food & sex gratifications, you can imagine how deeply their insecurity roots. No wonder they phantasy supernatural beings & grasp at any straw to create one."[76]

Alorese adults, as Cora had discovered, were emotionally brittle and easily provoked into anger, which affected the stability of marriages despite the complicated financial transactions that underlay that institution. From a young age, therefore, children experienced not only food deprivation and inconsistent care but also the emotional outbursts of adults—the frequent verbal disputes, and occasional physical fights, that Du Bois had witnessed when she first arrived in Atimelang. They also experienced shifting households and personnel as mothers retreated to their own kin when angry with their husbands, or when mothers built temporary sleeping huts near one or another of their fields in order to guard it from thefts at night, or when fathers were traveling as part of their financial negotiations. The autobiographies that Cora collected are filled with informants' memories of these comings and goings of mothers, fathers, siblings, and other relatives. Mobility of residence, Cora suggested, also contributed to a child's sense of instability and insecurity.[77]

Kardiner's assessments of Alorese personality characteristics were based on his analyses of each of the eight autobiographies that Du Bois had collected, as well as on the ethnographic material and psychological insights that she presented to his psychoanalytic seminar.[78] The Rorschach tests, Porteus Maze tests, and children's drawings were analyzed "blind" by experts who were not privy to Du Bois's cultural materials nor to the discussions of the seminar. They would, then, provide independent evidence for the possible corroboration of Kardiner's assessments. In a February 1940 letter to Benedict, who was away from Columbia at the time, Cora described what was happening:

> [T]he crux of matters [is] whether individual data support Kardiner's analysis from institutions. The Rorshachs seem to be giving him full confirmation. Only that is still tentative. Oberholzer and I are still working at them and O. is gratifyingly cautious. If the individual stuff really confirms K's analysis I'm going to be permanently pie-eyed. It will be just too damned good to be true. I may have unwittingly selected data to skew K's analysis (which coincides too consistently with my

impressions), but I can't have tampered with the Rorschachs. Oberholzer, without really knowing the other implications, is as excited as I am. He knows nothing about the culture except what is necessary to explain the responses. He views it as a triumph for Rorschachs and I for the whole business of interpreting from sociology to psychology. Exciting, isn't it?[79]

Emil Oberholzer, a New York psychiatrist who had helped Hermann Rorschach develop the Rorschach test—a projective test using a set of black and white, and colored, inkblots that people were asked to describe—agreed to analyze the set of Rorschachs that Cora had administered to thirty-seven male and female Alorese adults. Strikingly, Oberholzer identified many of the same personality characteristics that have already been discussed. On the basis of the Rorschach tests only, he wrote,

> [T]he Alorese are suspicious and distrustful; they are so not only toward everything that is unknown and new to them, such as foreigners, for instance, but also among themselves. No one will trust another . . . they are fearful [and] this fearfulness is something that is part and parcel of their natural and normal emotional disposition. . . . [There is] a lack of mastery of affect. They are not only easily upset and frightened, easily startled . . . but also they easily fly into a passion. There must be emotional outbursts and tempers, anger and rage, sometimes resulting in violent actions.[80]

Cora's use of Rorschachs with a nonliterate group was, at the time, highly experimental, but these analyses of projective materials were in remarkable agreement with her and Kardiner's insights into Alorese personality structure. It is also of interest that Oberholzer, who had been hesitant to try to score Rorschachs for a non-Western society, became convinced that "the test could be applied cross-culturally."[81]

The children's drawings that Cora had collected were also analyzed by an outside expert and provided yet further validation. Mrs. Schmidl-Waehner, an Austrian artist with psychoanalytic training, noted in the drawings "a feeling of aloneness," adding, "they look like children who have good abilities but are apart from each other . . . there is never unity" and "their relationships are poverty-stricken, as evinced by the fact that each figure is lost among others."[82]

The Porteus Maze tests—a nonverbal intelligence test developed by the psychologist Stanley Porteus, who had successfully administered them to Australian aborigines—were analyzed "blind" by Porteus, and they demonstrated a strong sex difference. Porteus wrote in a letter to Cora, "I am surprised at the high level of the men's performance . . . an average IQ of 97. Such a high average would seem to indicate that the Maze is comparatively independent of schooling." Women's scores, however, were much lower, averaging "an approximate intelligence quotient of 67."[83] Clearly, environmental factors had to have affected this measure of IQ. The thirty-point disparity between men's and women's test scores, Cora suggested, may have been related to men's financial transactions and to the complex mental records that they, unlike most women, had to keep. In other words, men may have developed a cognitive ability that helped their performance on this particular test.

Initially, during the first stage of her fieldwork, Cora had expected to find major differences in men's and women's "characters," as she put it. While there were some subtle differences in men's and women's Rorschach responses and some quantifiable differences in the objects that girls and boys chose to draw, sex differences were negligible in the word association tests that Cora administered. Despite the clear sexual division of labor, Cora learned that individual men and women were respected for excelling at cross-gender skills. Some women, for example, were good at finance and debate and were referred to admiringly as "men-women," and some men who possessed "female" aptitudes for gardening, cooking, and basket making were called "women-men." "In these cross-references from one sex to the other," Cora noted most interestingly, "there are none of the derogatory connotations that go with our [American] phrases of mannish woman or womanish man."[84] Accordingly, her "tentative conclusion" was that similarities in Alorese "modal personality" outweighed sex differences—"that a sex-based dichotomy is not so pronounced as cultural theory indicates."[85]

Nonetheless, Atimelang boys and girls were socialized into very different gender roles—boys more casually so than girls. Once children were old enough to forage for food by themselves, boys tended to roam in groups, hunting and cooking rats, sometimes growing their own sweet potatoes, but most often pilfering vegetables and fruits from other people's gardens. By contrast, girls by the age of nine or ten began to accompany their mothers to the fields, where they became helpers and where they also had more direct access to food. "Because boys must search for their food," Cora wrote, "they learn incidentally a great deal about the society in which they live. Girls, on the other hand, are deliberately trained in the food quest and the role they must play as providers."[86] Also, by late adolescence, boys tended to break away from their hunting and pilfering play groups and attach themselves to adult men in order to learn more about the world of finance and to begin to accumulate wealth for a bride price—a necessary step toward marriage.

Cora emphasized, however, that both girls and boys experienced "inconsistency in adult behavior toward them" and learned "to assert themselves by running off, by seeking the protection of other kin, and by vigorous and often violent resistance"—themes that emerged in all the autobiographies that she had collected.[87] As a consequence, both sexes shared aspects of a *modal personality*, the term she preferred to Kardiner's "basic personality." It was a more statistical concept that recognized individual variability in the psychological makeup of members of any given sociocultural group and that tried to prevent any attempt "to reduce individuals to a level of uniformity"—one of Cora's bêtes noires ever since her graduate student days.[88]

Cora Du Bois had set out to test Kardiner's theoretical model, which posited that there were "primary institutions"—such as subsistence patterns, family organization, and childrearing practices—that would have a direct effect on a society's "basic personality structure," which would, in turn, have an effect on the society's "secondary institutions"—such as folklore, art, and religious practices and beliefs. Her ethnographic and psychological data lent significant support to this model. To briefly summarize this argument: Because of the sexual division of labor in Alor (a primary institution), with women doing most of the gardening and not taking their infants and young children to the fields with them, children experienced hunger, frustration, and irregular caretaking. These early experiences produced interpersonal insecurity and distrust in children and a degree of emotional instability (aspects of basic personality structure) that made marriage, for example, a fragile institution. Feelings of distrust among the Alorese were then projected onto the supernatural world, which was believed to be inhabited mostly by unreliable spirits—harbingers of ill health, hunger, and death that had to be placated by regular sacrifices of food (secondary institutions).

Writing, Teaching, and Readjustment

For three years (1939–41), following her return to the United States, Du Bois would teach at Sarah Lawrence College, present some of her Alorese materials to the Kardiner-Linton seminar at Columbia, and draft *The People of Alor: A Social-Psychological Study of an East Indian Island* (1944), a book that would permanently establish her reputation within American anthropology. It was a monumental piece of work and singular in the degree to which it was a collaborative enterprise that used a multiplicity of research techniques. As Hortense Powdermaker wrote in her review of the book for the *American Anthropologist*, "Du Bois has tackled a very difficult and a very significant problem seriously and courageously. . . . We are only at the beginning of research on the cultural conditioning of personality and all studies of this type are necessarily of a pioneer character. This one is particularly important because of its thoroughness and because of its exploratory nature."[89] As an exploratory piece of work, the book has inspired controversy as well as accolades, but it is uniformly considered a classic case study in early culture and personality research. More than sixty-five years later, it is still cited and discussed by scholars interested in the cross-cultural study of socialization and personality development.[90]

Although Du Bois would complete a draft of her book by the fall of 1941, it was not actually published until 1944. (By that time, ironically, she had returned to Southeast Asia as a member of the Office of Strategic Services during World War II and did not get to see the finished product, nor read the reviews, until the end of the war.) Because it was a collaborative project that included chapters by Kardiner and Oberholzer, it took time to get the different parts of the manuscript together in a form that could be presented to prospective publishers. In a letter to her parents during this period, Cora wrote, "I'm going out to Westport with Kardiner to wrastle [*sic*] over the Book."[91] Working with Kardiner was not always an easy process.[92]

What Cora's personal life was like upon her return from two years away is unclear. There are no journal entries or personal letters for these years, although her letters to Benedict and Lowie contain interesting reflections on teaching at Sarah Lawrence and on friendship. To Benedict, Cora described her first impressions of Sarah Lawrence: "[It] is a civilized institution. That's pleasant. By civilized I seem to mean polite and flexible. Students are a bit below par and handled on a case work basis. So far it doesn't bother me, probably because this time I had no illusions. [The reference here is to her earlier, unsatisfactory teaching experience at Hunter College.] What a nuisance illusions are. If I extracted anything personal from the tough-minded Alorese, it was a sense of how zestful existence can be without them."[93]

In fact, Cora's teaching at Sarah Lawrence seems to have gone very well. She was given a three-year contract that, in 1942, was extended for another three years. And in 1941 she was one of the invited speakers at the college's thirteenth annual commencement. One of her Sarah Lawrence students whom I was able to interview, Sonia Hodsen (class of 1942), remembers Cora as "one of the best professors she ever had"—someone who was "very knowledgeable, with a razor-sharp mind," who was "unique in her great range of interests and intellect," and "who tried to connect with the students' interests."[94] Years later, furthermore, Cora remained interested in Sonia's art career.

Despite her successes with teaching, presentations to the Kardiner-Linton seminar, and writing, Cora revealed a somewhat morose side of herself in a 1941 letter to Lowie. Ostensibly, it was a response to a recent publication by Lowie, "Reflections on Goldenweiser's 'Recent Trends in American Anthropology.'" She wrote, "Your 'reflections' seem to me a recognition of the essential uniqueness and 'apartness' of all human beings. . . . *If* you are only now recognizing it emotionally [rather than intellectually], under the stimulus of Goldenweiser's querulous and posthumous article, you seem to me singularly fortunate in having avoided so long a conclusion most of us have forced upon us earlier in life." Then Cora continued in a more personal and somewhat disturbed manner:

This is all very pious and solemn in tone. Please forgive that tone. It is my mood these days. I have been grappling for some time with the business of friends becoming enemies and enemies becoming friends, and, more importantly, with the quality, flux and instability in all mature relationships. Stable relationships and loyal solicitude seem to me relevant only to infantile and familial patterns. Since that is the period in life when most of us form our expectancies of existence, it is usually shocking and disillusioning to find that expectancies do not correlate with fact. Emotionally, I am convinced, the problem is not in recognizing the facts, but in eliminating the elements of shock and disillusionment. All this sounds cynical. It's not. I have never before felt so well prepared to offer friends genuine understanding and support as now, when I no longer expect or demand unswerving understanding and support from them.

This is getting to be a confession of faith (or unfaith—whichever you wish) and high time to stop.[95]

Reading between the lines, it would seem that Cora's special friendship with Nell Barnes had not survived her two-year absence and that other friendships were in flux. In addition, there were anthropology colleagues, like Margaret Mead, who resented the attention Cora was receiving upon her return from Alor. At that time anthropology was a small profession, and everyone knew what everyone else was doing with respect to field-work and publications. There was only one major journal that everyone read, and professional meetings were small and intimate. There may have been some colleagues who resented the special opportunity that Cora had received to do culture and personality fieldwork in the Dutch East Indies. In addition, as she would explain to me nearly thirty years later, when I returned from my first two-year period of fieldwork in India, there is "return culture shock." It is the shock of seeing one's own culture through a new lens after an intense period of fieldwork in a radically different culture to which one has become acclimated, and significant readjustment may be required.

Cora was in a period of transition and, I suspect, emotional readjustment—both personally and professionally—as she completed a major five-year period of intense research and writing and was uncertain of her future. She captured some of these ambivalent emotions in the following poem that she wrote during this time.

Something is coming to an end
And nothing else has started.
(I talk like this to myself
When I'm quite sure no one else could listen.
Too much singing to let anyone listen.)
Now it's half way, not anywhere
Except talking to myself and wonderment.
I read about Daniel Boone
And wonder about Horace Gregory in the New Yorker.[96]
I even pour a drink and light a Kool.
All the while work lies on the desk
For months getting sooty
But something is coming to an end
Nothing else has started.
It's like a train trip, or a boat.
Only months long.
You hang between two worlds
The one ending slowly
And the one which won't really begin.
But it isn't death, this thing
It is the between times when something is growing
Not leaving anywhere
Not coming anywhere
Just being—but being alive;
Knowing you will be ready and sure
No matter what comes
Maybe two inches taller for it
Not dead, not living
Just being,
Coming into being
For what's becoming[97]

CHAPTER 6

World War II and the OSS

[B]y virtue of her high ability, professional knowledge, force-ful leadership and devotion to duty, [Cora Du Bois] contributed in a determining degree to the success of 18 major clandestine military operations directed against the enemy. . . . [That she is] the only woman to whom a position of similar responsibility has been entrusted by the OSS is a clear indication of the high quality and value of her work.

—Excerpts from 1946 Exceptional Civilian Award and support-ing documents

The new stage of life that Cora Du Bois anticipated in her poem "Something Is Coming to an End, and Nothing Else Has Started" arrived abruptly with the December 7, 1941, bombing of Pearl Harbor by the Japanese. This event triggered both the entrance of the United States into World War II and the implementation of the country's first international intelligence system—the Office of Strategic Services (OSS). The groundwork for developing such a system had already begun. President Franklin Delano Roosevelt and his staff had been closely monitoring developments in Europe as Nazi Germany's aggressive movements expanded. With the fall of France on May 10, 1940, and Britain's increased susceptibility to attack, FDR sent his friend Major General William J. Donovan—a highly decorated World War I officer—to England to do some reconnaissance work. Donovan became a kind of roving ambassador for the president, making subsequent trips to England, the Balkans, Albania, Greece, Turkey, and Egypt, where he met with heads of state and high-level military and intelligence officers in an effort to evaluate the war situation and to keep the president informed. On June 10, 1941, Donovan sent Roosevelt the following message: "Although we are facing imminent peril, we are lacking an effective service for analyzing, comprehending, and appraising such information as we might obtain (or in some cases have obtained), relative to the intention of political enemies. . . . Even if we participate to no greater extent than we do now, it is essential that we set up a central enemy intelligence organization."[1] By the next month—July 1941—Roosevelt had appointed Donovan as coordinator of information and had asked him to begin forming an office of American intelligence "that would prove equal to the Nazi challenge."[2]

"Wild Bill" Donovan, as he was known to friends, was a prominent lawyer in New York and a veteran of national politics as well as a highly decorated World War I officer. A Republican, he had served as assistant attorney general under President Calvin Coolidge and was a formidable character—a mover and doer who had friends in high places, both nationally and internationally. Donovan and Roosevelt had met as law students at Columbia University and, despite their different political affiliations, liked and trusted one another. After Pearl Harbor, Donovan rapidly built a powerful intelligence agency, pulling in a mixture of business executives, corporate lawyers, left-wing intellectuals, artists, and university scholars—the first of whom to be tapped were Ivy League professors.[3] For help recruiting people in the last category, he called on James Baxter, the president of Williams College, and William Langer, an eminent Harvard historian. Both men, who were registered Republicans, helped Donovan locate suitable scholars for intelligence work in Europe and in the Pacific.[4]

The tentacles of the Baxter-Langer recruiting effort rapidly reached out to numerous prominent and less prominent academics. In early June 1942 Cora received a telephone call from Charles Remer, a University of Michigan economist and East Asian specialist, asking her to report to Washington DC within forty-eight hours. (Remer had recently interviewed her in New York City about possible intelligence work.) En route to Washington by train, she scribbled the following note to her parents on Pennsylvania Railroad stationery: "Surprise! Surprise! On my way to Washington for a month's job, at least, in Special Information Division of Coordinator of Information office. Was a 48 hour call—don't yet know what I am to do, where I'll be officed & still less where I'll live. I'll let you know all as soon as possible."[5] Cora Du Bois—not yet a prominent academic but a person with recent experience in the Dutch East Indies and a founding member of the East Indies Institute of America, Inc. (an interdisciplinary organization established in 1941 to promote the study of Southeast Asian history and cultures)—had been drawn into the war effort. And she would become one of the highest-ranking women in the OSS and the only one to head an overseas branch office. Like Donovan, she would prove to be formidable.

The Research and Analysis Branch of the OSS

On June 13, 1942, shortly after Du Bois was called to Washington, the Coordinator of Information Office (COI) was officially renamed the Office of Strategic Services, and William Langer was put in charge of its first official branch—the Research and Analysis Branch (R&A). According to most accounts, the R&A became the heart and soul of the OSS.[6] It was this branch that collected and analyzed all overt and covert materials for the planning of subversive operations that would be carried out by other branches of the OSS. "Langer's staff was the first to demonstrate what scholarship could accomplish for an intelligence agency. R. and A.'s adaptation of the techniques of academic study to the requirements of shadow warfare and the sale of this product to American leaders was a vital element in the development of a regular, central, intelligence system in the United States."[7] It has been estimated that there were about two thousand R&A personnel, with approximately three-quarters of them in Washington DC and another quarter in overseas offices, but the actual number may have been much larger.[8] We know that the branch included many already well established scholars, such as Langer himself, and many others who would become famous after the war—Edwin O. Reischauer (ambassador to Japan in the 1960s and director of the Harvard-Yenching Institute), John King Fairbank (one of the leading historians of China and a Harvard professor), Arthur M. Schlesinger Jr. (Pulitzer Prize–winning historian and special assistant to President John F. Kennedy), and Walt W. Rostow (economist and political analyst who served as special assistant for national security to President Lyndon B. Johnson), just to name a few.

It was, in part, a training ground for future statesmen. As one historian of the OSS has described it,

> The branch resembled a star-studded college faculty. A peek into the R&A offices might reveal a heated discussion between historian Sherman Kent and political scientist Evron Kirkpatrick. A committee meeting of the Economics Division might find Charles Hitch, Emile Despres, Charles Kindelberger, and Richard Ruggles sitting side by side. In other rooms, classicist Norman O. Brown could be writing a report on Greek politics, historian John King Fairbank studying an aspect of Chinese foreign policy, philosopher Herbert Marcuse analyzing German social structure, or anthropologist Cora Du Bois pondering the problem of European colonialism in Asia.[9]

Du Bois was one of the few women to be invited into this august group. Most women who joined the OSS held clerical jobs and spent the war years behind desks and filing cabinets in Washington. Unlike Cora, they never went overseas or had administrative positions. Rather, they were the "*invisible apron strings* of an organization which touched every theater of the war."[10] There were, however, a handful of women, like Cora, who had regional and linguistic expertise that made them valuable for research work as well as for an occasional spy operation.[11]

Du Bois was initially recruited as an "area expert," something that she dismissed in later years when interviewed about this period of her life. In her often self-denigrating way, she reported, "Yes, we were picked, one presumed, [because of our] area knowledge. Now I had no general Southeast Asia area knowledge, I can assure you. I barely knew Indonesia. My work at Alor certainly did not give me any broad or deep picture of the total heterogeneous Indonesian situation, and I had not been to Thailand and Indochina. I didn't know Burma. I didn't know anything, but we all became labeled as experts, which was most erroneous in most cases. But we learned as we went along."[12]

The Washington DC Years

It is not clear what Du Bois's assignment was when she was first called to Washington. All work for the OSS had to be kept secret, and only in recent years have most R&A reports become declassified.[13] When she returned to academe, Cora rarely spoke about her work in the OSS, and she kept no journals from that period of her life. Furthermore, the personal mail of OSS officers was censored so as to prevent the disclosure of sensitive information. What we do know, however, is that Cora was quickly promoted into the position of chief of the Indonesia Section and acting chief of the Political Sub-Division under Charles Remer, who headed the East Asian Division of the R&A. In her first letter home from Washington, Cora wrote, "Everyone I ever knew or heard of is here and it seems to me I have already run into most of them."[14]

Initially Cora stayed with her friends from Berkeley, Jane and Julian Steward, who were living in Washington, where Julian was employed with the Bureau of American Ethnology and was editing a six-volume work on South American Indians.[15] Then she moved to a hotel that was closer to her office, but she was not immediately committed to a full-time position in Washington. Instead, as she reported to her mother, "I am trying to see if a part-time job in the OSS is available in the New York branch and, if I stay, I shall ask for $3,800 [yearly salary] since that seems to be what most of my anthropological age-mates are getting down there."[16] With a part-time position in New York City, Cora could have continued teaching at Sarah Lawrence and could have offered a course that had been scheduled for her to teach at Columbia. However, by the end of the summer it was clear that the OSS wanted to keep her in Washington and offer her an administrative-cum-research position, which she accepted. The lure of doing critical research for the war effort and rubbing elbows with eminent figures in Washington must have outweighed the attraction of teaching primarily at Sara Lawrence, which at that time was a low-ranking institution. Furthermore, Cora was single and ready for new adventures. Like many other academics, she requested and was granted a leave of absence from Sarah Lawrence College in order to join the war effort in a full-time capacity.

In thinking about this decision many years later, Cora reported that she had felt "very patriotic during World War II, very idealistic, very 'gung-ho.'"[17] And, of course, she was not alone. After the bombing of Pearl Harbor the American populace, which had been in an isolationist mood following the First World War, had quickly changed perspective and had become galvanized behind the war effort. Along with the general public, most academics supported American involvement in the Second World War. Illustrative of this fact was an abrupt change of attitude by the "father" of American anthropology, Franz Boas. Although he had opposed the Nazis, until the Japanese attack on Pearl Harbor he had publicly opposed U.S. entry into the war in Europe, as he had during the First World War. After Pearl Harbor, however, Boas "either joined or contributed to virtually every organization dedicated to anti-Nazi activity in the United States . . . [and he] frequently used the podium to attack anti-Semitism, pseudoscientific race theory and the suppression of free thought."[18]

Meanwhile, some members of Cora's UC Berkeley graduate student cohort, such as Julian Steward and Ralph Beals, organized discussions at the 1941 annual meeting of the American Anthropological Association (AAA) about how anthropologists might support the war effort. And the AAA passed the following resolution in 1941: "Be it resolved that the American Anthropological Association places itself and its resources and the specialized skills of its members at the disposal of the country for the successful prosecution of the war."[19] It has been estimated that a vast majority of anthropologists were engaged in some kind of war-related work during World War II—as soldiers, officers, research analysts, linguists, propagandists, and spies.[20] This is in striking contrast with today, when the ethics of anthropologists working with the military in Iraq and Afghanistan has been hotly debated by members of the American Anthropological Association, resulting in the appointment in 2007 of a special committee—the AAA Commission on the Engagement of Anthropology with U.S. Security and Intelligence Communities (CEAUSSIC)—to review the pertinent ethical issues.[21]

Du Bois's patriotism and idealism were characteristic of the times and of OSS personnel, many of whom had received their undergraduate or graduate education during the Depression years, which had made an indelible impression on them. Accordingly, they were sympathetic to the social idealism that underlay FDR's New Deal and that came to pervade the OSS. "A sampling of thousands of intelligence analyses produced by the OSS Research Branch reveals certain recurrent terms: democratic, progressive, social reform. These words were more than clichés to the young academicians who used them. They represented the hope, shared by their colleagues behind the lines, for the triumph of universal democracy and the progress of the common men of all nations."[22] And these ideals, as we shall see, put many American intelligence officers in Asia and other parts of the world into ideological conflict with their British, French, and Dutch counterparts who were committed to maintaining their colonial empires.

In retrospect, Cora also remembered her years with the OSS as "terribly exciting," reporting,

> One felt one was really doing something important, even though one wasn't quite sure what that was. The personnel of the Office of Strategic Services was, of course, an enormously stimulating one. Almost everybody that one ever wanted to know was there, but the actual assignments seemed pretty indefinite and what you did yourself, whether it had any influence or anyone paying any attention to it, one was never quite sure. This is certainly the way I spent the first year and a half in Washington [before going to Asia], slowly building up a small staff, occupying myself with biographical information largely on persons both Western and Asian, who might be good informants for further information for searching out details, and then finally a paper, which was the last I wrote, on Japanese prisoners of war in Indonesia.[23]

In addition to building up a staff and biographical information, we know of Du Bois's involvement in two specific R&A projects during this period in Washington DC. One she mentioned—probably inappropriately—in a 1942 letter home:

> I suppose I may as well break down and tell you about my job. There really isn't any reason for the hoop-la. It is compiling confidential navy sailing directions for the NEI [Netherlands East Indies]. Specifically it means drawing together all the economic, social, population, geographic, fortification etc. etc. dope on which we can lay our hands—often from secret Dutch, English and American Intelligence files. It is a stupendous job, but for better or worse it is beginning to end—at least my part of it. When I go back on the [regular R&A] job it will no longer be a full-time-all-the-time preoccupation and there will be a few spare hours to apply my notorious organizational aptitude [to other endeavors].[24]

Cora's reference to her "notorious organizational aptitude" was undoubtedly written with some degree of irony. However, she must have been discovering that she had an aptitude for administration as well as for research. Clearly, others in the OSS had noted this and had quickly put her in charge of the Indonesia section of the R&A. Even Cora had, with some amusement, acknowledged her organizational and administrative skills when leaving Alor in 1939. In her last letter home before her departure, she had written,

Meanwhile only 3 more days in Atimelang. My packing is about done. That is symptomatic I'm afraid. But it is beautifully planned. There are 14 cases, or tins & all, so packed that at each place en route I can say, "Number so and so thru to number so and so goes on," or "Can be stored on the wharf—the rest goes with me." Since I have 3 lay-overs before N. Y., I consider this the major achievement of these 2 years. First thing you know, I'll be organizing explorer's expeditions. Have discovered a positive administrative ability in myself. Wouldn't Richard [Cora's stepfather] like to employ some of my spare time between Sarah Lawrence and writing up Alor data to administer Isolantite [Richard's manufacturing company]? It would give him a bit of rest and certainly be revolutionary for Isolantite. Don't forget—I've also become a demon boss in the last 2 years. Ask my Atimelangers.[25]

Instead of being applied to her stepfather's company, however, Cora's emerging administrative skills were tapped by the OSS.

In the 1970s, when recalling this period of her life that had had to remain secret, Cora mentioned one other R&A assignment that she had undertaken while in Washington DC:

The first assignment was to find out what we knew about New Guinea. We had to write up secret hydrographic documents of the shorelines of New Guinea at various strategic points. We had access to the Office of Naval Intelligence's files. I've never seen anything so barren! Newspaper clippings, once in awhile, and copies of British Intelligence. Everything was so clearly dated and incidental that they were of no use.

So then the job was to collect people all over the country who had, in some fashion or another, some contact [with New Guinea]. . . .

Missionaries, or whoever they might be, who had been along these particular stretches of the New Guinea shore where counter-attacks to invasion were expected. And this is where I learned a profound distrust for [some] anthropological observations.

Anthropologists who had worked in New Guinea, Du Bois asserted, had learned nothing practical about the shorelines of that island. They were too involved with their "reconstructions of primitive life and they saw nothing around them. Whereas you'd get a 'nanny' from England who had taken care of a little boy on a beach, or in one of the settlements, and she knew exactly where the waterline started, and the tides, and if there was a road."[26]

In her work with the OSS, Cora also acquired a new regard for the knowledge and skills of all kinds of people: "As I went on in this 'skullduggery' of OSS and ran into lawyers and New York bankers and Washington liquor dealers, all kinds of people, I realized how profoundly intelligent people in the real world were. In my stupidity I had assumed that intelligence was a central preserve of the academicians. I learned a great deal during those years, which I brought with me when I returned to the 'groves' and to that extent I became very skeptical of a lot of theory-spinning that goes on in the academic world, especially in the social sciences."[27]

Shortly before joining the OSS, however, Cora had completed the manuscript for *The People of Alor*—a major contribution to anthropological ethnography and theory—and was trying to get it published. In September 1942, more than a year after she joined the OSS, the University of Minnesota Press accepted the book. An informal appraisal of it by Ruth Benedict had probably helped. In a September 22, 1942, letter to the press, Benedict wrote, "[*The People of Alor*] is an important and pioneering contribution to the study of personality in an alien culture. It supplies more material, and more significantly presented material, than any other book so far published. It is a first class contribution to anthropology and psychology."[28] A few days later Cora wrote to Benedict, thanking her for "her pretty elegant letter" and reporting, "It must have turned the trick because I have just heard airmail that the Minnesota Press has accepted the effusion."[29] Nonetheless, it took another year of negotiations with the press and with her two psychiatric collaborators—Abram Kardiner and

Emil Oberholzer—to get the job completed. In correspondence with her mother, Cora referred to it as the "Big Book," which—at 654 pages—it certainly was.

During this busy period in Washington, Du Bois somehow managed to be active in two of her professional organizations. She was secretary for the American Ethnological Society, which was founded in 1842 and was the oldest anthropological organization in the United States. And, as already mentioned, she was a founding member of the East Indies Institute of America and served—along with Ralph Linton, Margaret Mead, Claire Holt, and others—as one of its directors. Interestingly, however, Du Bois did not join the Society for Applied Anthropology, which was founded during the war by idealists interested in social change and the application of anthropological tools to effect such change. According to at least one analyst, the society became "*the* wartime anthropological society devoted to the practicalities of applying anthropological methods and theories to the problems of the war."[30] Cora, however, always considered her role as an OSS research analyst and administrator distinct from her role as an ethnographer and research scholar. Nonetheless, as we shall see, her wartime experiences had a major impact on her subsequent academic research and on issues of anthropological ethics that she would have to address both as an academic researcher and as president of the American Anthropological Association.

From Washington DC to Ceylon

After a year and a half of writing confidential reports in Washington and having no idea what became of them, Cora requested a transfer to the Southeast Asia Command (SEAC) in India, where she would be closer to the center of action. She was first offered a post in London but turned it down "firmly and promptly." In a letter to her mother, she wrote,

> They'll have to think of something better than that. As long as we [OSS] stay out from under the military I can still afford to be picky and choosy. I'll settle for nothing less than the Far East, or Australia at a minimum. The job was really silly, too. A Dutch translator in a British intelligence office. I'd still be on the OSS pay roll, but I don't see why they have to send Americans to England to translate Dutch when England must

be alive with Hollanders. I suspect the gent in England (whom I met here some months ago) was just trying to increase his staff without his budget. I told the OSS so, too.[31]

Du Bois must have been persuasive, because by February 1944 she was on her way to India and Ceylon, where the SEAC was being relocated under the direction of Admiral Lord Louis Mountbatten, the British supreme commander for military forces and intelligence in South and Southeast Asia. She sent her parents a hasty note, saying, "Some frantic last days and now en route. The air priorities were dished [out] at the last moment. I am not free to be more detailed."[32]

Cora was sent to Wilmington, California, adjacent to the Port of Los Angeles, where she boarded a one-time luxury liner, the SS *Mariposa*, together with hundreds of male GIs en route to Asia and a handful of other women. The group of women included eight other OSS personnel, one of whom would become a special friend of Cora's—Julia McWilliams, who later became the celebrated French chef and TV personality Julia Child. The nine women all shared one cabin with three sets of triple-decked bunks, one bathtub, one sink, and one toilet. In a letter to her parents from on board ship, Cora described this experience:

> Curiouser and Curiouser, as Alice in Wonderland said. This trip has no more relation to any other, or to anything I had anticipated, than to the man in the moon. We are an island of civilian and G.I. females in the welter of a troop ship packed like the proverbial sardines. Our course is a source of endless speculations as we squat on the decks finding what comfort we may from the Mae Wests (life preservers) which we carry constantly with us. Meals are two a day, but ample and good. Nine of us are stacked 3 deep in what was once a luxury cabin. Fortunately the 9 are an amiable and amusing lot, congenial and considerate. Ventilation, and eventually heat, will be our chief discomforts. Dirt fortunately bothers me less than it does some of my more fastidious companions. I have not yet found cold salt water and no laundry an insuperable obstacle to well being.
>
> The day's schedule is: up at 8:30—breakfast at 9:30; then lounging on deck, reading, studying Dutch and conversing until 5:30; dinner at

6:45; two hours of lounging and then to bed which is always a long and hilarious process infinitely complicated by the facts of excess baggage and congestion. I was somewhat put out by the military aspects of this super Cook's tour until I relaxed enough to accept the whole business as an interesting experience which has come the way of very few women. I regret only that security regulations forbid a really detailed account of the new impressions as they crowd in. I am afraid that by the time they can be told, too many of them will be forgotten or overlaid by what is to follow.[33]

The trip to Bombay [now Mumbai], India, from San Francisco took a month, including a one-day stop in Australia for supplies and a destroyer escort to cross the Indian Ocean, where a Japanese task force had been sighted. In later life Cora would describe it as "adventurous." She recalled that they sighted an enemy submarine once, but nothing happened "except a few drills and some sleeping on deck at night with one's tote bag and wondering what was going to happen." She also remembered the crowded cabin that she and eight other women shared:

> It was a mad place. The bathtub was always full of laundry, and Julia Child was in that group, and she is a lovely mad woman, you know, when she gets sportive. Every now and then, she couldn't stand the disorder, though she was one of the main constructors of the disorder, and everything would be taken from the fo'castle, [to] wherever [space] was available, she'd make a great heap in the middle of the floor. The only floor space we had would be just littered with our debris, and then we had to sort it out, straighten things out.[34]

It was also Julia Child who, in an effort to reduce wolf whistles from the men aboard ship, spread a rumor that these women were missionaries.[35]

The Southeast Asia Command (SEAC)

From Bombay, Cora traveled by train to New Delhi, where the OSS headquarters were located, only to discover that they were being shifted to Ceylon (today's Sri Lanka). Mountbatten had decided to move to a more remote and comfortable location in the hills of Ceylon near the town of Kandy. As Cora reported later in life,

Most of the people had already left for Ceylon. I was sent with about 4 or 5 civilian and military personnel to transport, I think, [about] 11 cases of classified material over which a guard had to stand the whole time, and we were to go by train across the southern end of India, [and] take the ferry over to Ceylon from there. I can assure you it was a madhouse. And it was very hot and a very long drawn train trip, on not the most comfortable or sanitary trains imaginable in India at that time. Anyhow . . . finally [we] got to Colombo [a port town] and then found that that was only a temporary way station. We were due up in Kandy in the hills, where Mountbatten had established his headquarters.[36]

Cora's small entourage was taken by jeep up into the hills, through lush green jungles and coconut tree and tea plantations to Kandy, the ancient highland capital of Ceylon that lies at an elevation of 1,250 feet. The women were housed in the old colonial Queen's Hotel in the center of Kandy, opposite the famed Temple of the Tooth, whereas the men lived in bamboo huts on the military detachment property. Each day the women had to be transported by truck to a tea plantation where headquarters were located and where Mountbatten had elegant quarters and was attended by a well-groomed staff that chauffeured him and others by limousine to various offices scattered around the tropical gardens of the plantation.[37]

The Establishment of the OSS/SEAC

In Ceylon Du Bois joined a complex military and intelligence organization that was part of the outcome of a secret meeting in Quebec City in August 1943, held between the British, U.S., and Canadian governments. Each head of state—Winston Churchill, Franklin D. Roosevelt, and William Lyon Mackenzie King—was in attendance. It was here that the Allies began planning the invasion of France, agreed to share nuclear technology, and decided to expand operations in Southeast Asia with the establishment of a new overall Allied command center. Until then, Southeast Asia had been recognized as primarily a British military responsibility, the southwest Pacific an American one, and China that of the Chinese national government headed by Marshal Chiang Kai-shek. U.S. interests in the area had been focused on the long supply route that stretched from Calcutta (Kolkata), India, into Nationalist China through the jungles and mountains of Assam (northeast India) and northern Burma. With the establishment of SEAC under a new theater commander, Admiral Mountbatten, and with an integrated Anglo-American staff, the Allies hoped to improve the China/Burma/India war effort. General Donovan seized the moment and concluded a tentative agreement with Mountbatten to permit OSS intelligence operations to continue, and even to expand, as part of SEAC.[38]

In November 1943 Donovan traveled to New Delhi to finalize this agreement, which became a battle among different interest groups—British and American military officers and British and American intelligence personnel.[39] General Joseph Warren Stilwell, the American theater commander, and navy commander Milton E. Miles, who was forging an intelligence operation with the Chinese, did not want to see the OSS, an American operation, come under British political domination. Stilwell and Miles believed that the risk of increased British dominance over intelligence outweighed the advantages of expanded operations. Donovan, however, managed to achieve a compromise that gave the OSS the right "to gather strategic intelligence independently, through its own agents, everywhere in the Theater that U.S. interests required, regardless of whether or not such intelligence was required or requested by SEAC."[40] The United States, accordingly, acquired a check on British intelligence and, in return, gave Mountbatten a token force of specialized American troops for guerrilla activities—OSS saboteurs, guerrilla fighters, underwater swimmers, and morale subversion experts—along with R&A personnel.

Du Bois's Position

It was into this complex situation that Cora Du Bois moved when she arrived in Kandy in April 1944. In January 1944 Dr. Charles Burton Fahs—an East Asian expert from Columbia University and the chief of the India Section of R&A in Washington—had written to Colonel Richard Heppner to say, "As you know from cables, I have agreed to send Cora Du Bois out for R&A work in SEAC. This is a severe loss to us, but I hope the move may be justified by work she will be able to do in her field. I would appreciate as full an explanation as possible as to the jobs open to her."[41] It is not clear how Heppner, the young man Donovan had put in charge of overseeing the implementation of the newly created OSS/SEAC, responded. Soon after Cora and some of the other women assigned to

OSS/SEAC had arrived in Kandy, however, Heppner wrote to Major Carl O. Hoffman in Washington to say, "I don't know whether your reference to the group of six refers to *the girls* or the six paratroopers who just arrived. In any event, I am very happy to report that all the girls are doing an excellent job, and are a credit to the mission. The paratroopers look like very tough men, and I'm sure Mansfield is pleased with them."[42]

Of the six "girls" sent to Kandy, Du Bois was the most senior in terms of age, education, and professional experience. Julia McWilliams (later Child), a Smith College graduate who was sent to Kandy as head of Registry (record keeping), was thirty-one. Too tall to enlist in the Army WACS or the Navy WAVES, she had worked as a clerical assistant to Donovan in Washington before being sent to Ceylon. Jeanne Taylor, also thirty-one, was a young New York City artist who enlisted in the OSS and joined Paul Cushing Child as an assistant in the Visual Presentation Branch for the War Room in Kandy. Child headed that branch of the OSS and, after the war, married Julia. By contrast, Cora arrived as a forty-year-old top research analyst and by the following month (May 1944) had been made acting chief of R&A for OSS/SEAC. On May 22 Fahs sent Cora a long letter, stamped "SECRET" at the top and bottom of each page. It said,

> Welcome as Acting Chief of R&A in SEAC. If you keep on in the style of your first letters, I am sure the outpost will be a success.
>
> When you left we were somewhat pessimistic of opportunities in SEAC. In the first place MU SO SI, and OG [various branches of OSS] all show signs of real activity out your way. This should mean lots of operational geographic and cartographic work for R&A. If this work for OSS is well done, you are likely in turn to have plenty of opportunities for important work for the Theater Command. . . .
>
> Secondly, but perhaps most important, I think you have real intelligence possibilities. We are counting on you to develop liaison with both the Dutch and the British and to help SI [Secret Intelligence] keep on the most profitable lines. There is now at least a fair possibility that we will have an outpost in the Southwest Pacific. When we do, intelligence from SEAC will be very important. . . . Moreover, much intelligence moves from Australia to India rather than to Washington. Keep your eyes open and give us any tips you get.

It is hard to tell from here how you will want to divide your staff between Kandy and Delhi. There is considerable difference of opinion here as to the degree to which British intelligence will remain concentrated in Delhi. We just don't know. Consequently, we shall assign personnel to you at Kandy and leave [them] to your reallocation as seems essential.[43]

Fahs's letter to Cora also contained many more suggestions about how to coordinate with other branches of the China/Burma/India war theater and how to share OSS senior analysts and Japanese-language personnel, especially with the Delhi office, which did not close down completely when Mountbatten moved to Ceylon. Cora had to coordinate R&A operations in Kandy (Detachment 404) with those remaining in Delhi (Detachment 303) and Calcutta (Detachment 505).

In a June 1944 letter home, Cora reported, "The work at least goes well enough—although far from fast enough for my tastes. I am the only female 'executive' here and I am continually impressed at how nice the gents are about it. In fact in this month's report to the home office I was the only one commended by name. It was a gesture, of course, but a very amiable one."[44] In reality, Cora's promotion to acting chief of R&A, with the presumption that she might become chief, was *not* a smooth one. There were considerable gender politics involved.

William Langer, director of R&A in Washington, preferred to fill the position with a man. He wrote to Colonel Heppner, extolling a Lieutenant Junior Grade Edward Rhetts, whom he described as

tall, attractive-looking and energetic. . . . He is in no sense a Far Eastern expert, but on the other hand he is a fellow of excellent character and a good deal of personal charm. . . . [T]his at once raises the question of Cora Du Bois' status. No one could have a higher opinion of Cora than I have and I am delighted to learn that she has been carrying on so ably as acting chief of R&A. She has much greater regional experience and professional competence than has Rhetts. There could be no comparison between them on this score. On the other hand, *it seems to me that a man could function better than a woman as chief of R&A* and that Rhetts, as a naval officer, could be particularly effective.[45]

13. Cora Du Bois at her desk, OSS headquarters, Ceylon, ca. 1944. Cora Alice Du Bois Papers (SPEC.COLL.ETHG.D852c), Tozzer Library, Harvard College Library, Harvard University.

Despite Rhetts's young age (thirty-three or thirty-four) and lack of regional or professional experience, Langer deemed him preferable to Cora to become chief of R&A operations in Ceylon.

Fahs wrote directly to Cora about Rhetts, saying, "You must already know that the possibility of Lt. Rhetts' being appointed R&A Chief for SEAC has been considered. We do not wish to dictate such an appointment from here, however, and are leaving his position and functions to be determined by you and Col. Heppner with this background in mind. I am much less concerned as to how the official titles are divided up than I am that you and Lt. Rhetts should work together in such a manner as to make the strongest possible team for R&A in the theater." And Fahs added, "Despite your recommendation that we recruit a regionalist for the headship of R&A in SEAC, I see no solution along that line. I have no hope of being able to recruit a more competent expert than yourself."[46]

Cora, cognizant of Langer's preference for a man but also of Fahs's recognition of her regional expertise, was clearly put in a difficult situation. Somehow she was supposed "to work things out." Langer, however, left the final decision up to Heppner, the young attorney from General Donovan's law firm whom Donovan had sent to oversee the new OSS arrangements in Asia. Initially Heppner did not take well to Cora. In an undated interview, he described her as "an exceedingly brilliant woman; personally my relations [with her] were of the best. However, she is tactless and sharp and sometimes very overbearing, and I think you have the usual problem of Army officers being placed under a woman's command which causes trouble."[47] In an interview that I had in 2007 with one of Heppner's OSS/SEAC colleagues, Lieutenant Guy Martin, Martin dismissed Heppner's remark as coming from someone with limited experience with highly educated and articulate women. "Cora," Martin said, "was a quintessential intellectual; Heppner was not."[48] Martin, like Heppner, had been a young lawyer from Donovan's law firm whom Donovan had sent to Southeast Asia to help coordinate activities there.

Despite these initial impressions, by early July 1944 Heppner wrote to Langer to say that Cora was doing "a splendid job" and "let's leave the position open for a period of time following Rhetts' arrival and after a period of observation, make a permanent appointment to the job."[49] By September Cora was still serving as acting chief, and Heppner had written to Langer to say that "Cora is doing a truly excellent job, and has made herself an indispensable member of our staff. . . . [She] takes part in all meetings of the Operations Committee and no operation is even contemplated until a full briefing has been furnished us by R&A. Without this service, I do not see how we could operate."[50] Accordingly, Cora became the only woman to meet regularly with the supreme commander, Lord Admiral Mountbatten. According to Elizabeth P. McIntosh, a former OSS officer and a historian of women in the OSS, "Mountbatten—to everyone's amazement—sought Cora's advice. It was an honor," McIntosh told me in a 2007 interview, "that he would come to see her. Cora had access to [Mountbatten] that others did not."[51]

Ultimately, Cora Du Bois's intelligence, competence, and integrity outweighed the sexism of the day, and she was able to gain the respect and loyalty of a hard-working staff (both military and civilian) in the collection

14. Cora Du Bois with Lord Mountbatten (*left*), OSS headquarters, Ceylon, ca. 1944. Cora Alice Du Bois Papers (SPEC.COLL.ETHG.D852c), Tozzer Library, Harvard College Library, Harvard University.

and dissemination of intelligence. Rhetts was assigned elsewhere and Cora was made chief, but not for another year and not until there had been further gender-related correspondence between Washington and Ceylon. Cora was generally philosophical about all of this and recognized the historical peculiarity of her position as a woman in this otherwise man's world. And she was determined not to allow gender issues to interfere with doing a competent job. In a December 1944 letter to her parents she wrote,

> I'd like to tell you boastfully of what goes [on] here. For a woman in a G.I. world I've done very well. And people have been very generous about the sex-liability. I'm not being funny about that. It is very real. But I've tried not to embarrass them for their generosity. Harry the Chief calls me General Patton. There is truth in it and I am undoubtedly my mother's daughter. But the world is full of mediations and pacifism. If

I can come out of my corner fighting, I may move someone a few feet in the direction I consider right. I am considered opinionated but I think and believe a few opinions (judiciously founded) are important in this foggy world. I suffer from the opprobrium of not feeling confused about my job.[52]

And so Cora Du Bois, a woman, became a major player in OSS/SEAC.

OSS/SEAC Purposes and Operations

The purpose of OSS/SEAC was to provide detailed intelligence for Burma, Malaya, Thailand, Indochina, the Andaman Islands, Sumatra, and Indonesia—for all parts of the Southeast Asian war theater where anti-Japanese military operations were being contemplated. This required recruiting, training, and equipping native agents as well as American and British ones and placing them behind enemy lines. These agents would gather intelligence—such as the specific locations of Japanese ships, troops, and industrial plants—and forward it to Kandy, where it was analyzed by OSS/SEAC officers and used for Allied military operations. Getting agents behind enemy lines for these purposes required detailed knowledge of access points that could be penetrated by motorboats, small planes, and underwater swimmers. OSS/SEAC also developed new types of equipment, organized resistance groups among native peoples, developed and used propaganda, and effected counterespionage measures.[53]

There were over 120 such operations during Du Bois's tenure in Kandy.[54] The principal operations involved establishing bases in reasonably accessible parts of enemy territory: for example, a sea base on the Arakan coast of western Burma, a clandestine air base on the Burma-Thai border, a jungle air base in the highlands of Malaya, and sea bases in the Malacca Straits, the southwest coast of Sumatra, and the Gulf of Siam near the Thai-Indochina border.[55] The largest single operation, to be discussed below, was the penetration of Thailand. OSS also set up a weather-reporting service throughout the area and a radio communications system between points in India, Ceylon, and Burma that was used for administrative purposes as well as to broadcast "black" radio programs (subservice propaganda) into enemy territory. "At one time 47 circuits were feeding intelligence into headquarters at Kandy . . . and an average of 40 students per month—speaking 7 different languages—were trained in cryptography."[56] Approximately 215 native agents—Chinese, Burmese, Thais, Malays, Indonesians, and Karens (an ethnic group in the former Burma)—were trained in Kandy for clandestine operations.

Cora's job, as head of R&A, was to build up a staff of area experts, research assistants, cartographers, geographers, economists, and other specialists who could provide as much background information as possible for the planning of such intelligence operations. She and her staff prepared special reports, provided "an unexcelled map service," and, according to Colonel Heppner, "in a real sense became the 'brain' of the organization [OSS/SEAC]." And, as Heppner further reported, "a party which had the benefit of all [that] the training experts knew of the area into which they were to go, from the organization of the Japanese secret police to the rig of native sailing craft, had greater assurance and were in a better position to report accurate intelligence than a party which wandered out, like the bear that went over the mountain, to see what it could see."[57]

Du Bois's Communications with Washington

Cora Du Bois was not only a mature forty-year-old when she took over command of the R&A Branch of OSS/SEAC, but she was an experienced anthropologist and world traveler, with in-depth experience in the Dutch East Indies. In addition, she had been honing her writing skills since childhood. Her belief in clear, precise prose would become invaluable for the interminable communications required of her—telegrams, weekly letters, memos, and monthly reports. In fact, this "lean, handsome woman with a habit of peering quizzically over her glasses as she discussed operations with her staff," as she was described by McIntosh, also became known for her "acerbic cables" to her Washington bosses.[58]

After her initial three months as acting chief of R&A, for example, Du Bois wrote the following trenchant and lengthy memo to Fahs, her immediate boss in Washington:

There is no use mincing words about a situation of which you must be fully aware. R&A in SEAC is understaffed in comparison to the operational branches here, particularly SI [Secret Intelligence] and MO [Morale Operations]. I cannot meet the present requests and find

I must constantly turn R&A work over to personnel in other branches who show a modicum of competency in that direction. This is no way in which to educate operational people to the importance of what we have to contribute, or to set high standards of work. However, when the alternative is a question of men going into operations without intelligence—however incomplete—there is no choice. I think you will agree with that.

This brings me to the Washington attitude concerning this theatre. The main point of confusion is between our operations as a clandestine organization and the military strategy which will defeat the Japanese. It is unlikely that a death blow will be dealt from Ceylon. No real blow may ever be dealt, for all I know. However, we now *are* operating actively as a clandestine group as you must know if you read the Monthly Progress Reports sent the General [Donovan]. In addition we operate as OSS and not simply as a recruiting agency and pay roll service to other groups. On the score of integrated OSS operations I would wager that we here are more vigorous than any other outpost (no matter how ham-strung R&A happens to be.)

It may not be amiss to repeat that we are now operating, or are about to operate in Thailand, Malaya, Sumatra and southern Indo-China; that we have had directives from Washington concerning operations in these areas; and that we, as the largest American group in this theatre, have in a sense a very heavy responsibility to American foreign policy.

It may also be an impertinence to tell you that this area is the largest unexploited colonial region of the Far East and therefore, a potential bone of contention in the future. It may seem dramatic to say this, but I am convinced that the U.S. position in the next Pacific war will be greatly influenced by the present effectiveness of OSS in this theatre. It is necessary to say this because most people are apt to overlook this theatre and to ignore our role in it. In the rest of the Far East our responsibilities are shared and our action is diffused by its collaborative character. Here responsibilities cannot be muffed by us without serious repercussions. But responsibilities cannot be met effectively by an undermanned group of juniors who come dribbling out at the last minute.

In this connection I deeply appreciate the flow of material you have sent our way. That it is arriving often too late for use is not your fault except as the R&A branch is not aggressive enough in its request for air freight. The same lack of aggression seems to characterize its shipment of personnel. Secretaries and visiting firemen get out here in two weeks. Valuable and badly needed research men are permitted to beat their way out here in two to three months time. These arrangements are not within your jurisdiction, but you have every right and duty to insist on your needs to those who service you.

If there is a note of asperity in this letter, it is because I write from a deep sense of conviction which is shared by my associates out here.

Believe me, I am not crabbing so much as I am trying to convince you that a casual attitude toward the SEAC theatre is a serious misjudgment of the long range situation.[59]

What is striking about this memo is not only Du Bois's directness and forcefulness with respect to her R&A staffing needs but her perspicacity with regard to the future. She was, in no uncertain terms, trying to call Washington's attention to the significance of this region to U.S. interests in a post–World War II era. Ultimately, she would be dismayed at how those relations would unfold.

Other of Cora's communications with Washington were short and pithy, as in this one sent directly to General Donovan: "For your private information, General Donovan, on 14 January 1945, after a day of consultation the Supremo [Mountbatten] was strongly and unreservedly in favor of having *all* OSS south of the Hump attached to SEAC, designated OSS/SEAC, and with headquarters at Kandy. At that time he had not yet seen General Sultan [Stilwell's replacement], but he was reported to be in a mood *to tell* General Sultan and *not consult* him."[60]

Du Bois, along with other American OSS and military officers stationed in Asia, was sensitive to relations with the British, whose colonial interests they did not share. So in this cryptic message to Donovan, Cora alludes to Mountbatten's inclination to make decisions without first consulting his American counterpart (General Sultan). Furthermore, the memo indicates that Mountbatten wanted to close down the OSS offices in New Delhi and Calcutta, something the Americans were opposed to because these offices enabled the United States to keep an eye on nationalist movements in India and on British intelligence on the mainland.[61]

Cora, at times, could be outrageously funny in her reports to Washington. On March 28, 1945, for example, she included the following item in her report to Fahs. It was entitled "Materials Procured from Thailand," and it read, "7. Sample of 'Local Toilet Tissue,' specifically requested by MD. This tissue is only used by the elite. It is a rare specimen and the last of the species. The sandpapering has worn off. Handle with care! It is very brittle."[62]

At other times Cora combined irony and humor in her memos to Washington, as in the following Outpost Letter, dated May 21, 1945, regarding communiqués from Washington:

1. Reluctant Entry into Debate
The Outpost Letter [from Washington] argument seems to us to divide into three camps:
A. "Give Us News" School
What about the Situation Reports, the Work in Progress Reports, all the individual memos and just plain Uncle Sugar postal service? Then there is always the Pouch.
B. "Oh! The Pain of it all" School
See Mr. Freud on Super-egos.
C. "Let's not be Frivolous" School
Chacun à son goût.
Summary of Kandy's opinion:
We like to get Outpost Letters; the variety we write is painless to us. We are not convinced they are vital, but they are pleasant. *Plea for Clemency*: Don't, repeat don't, in an access of piety ask us to write a ponderous Weekly Situation Report confined to our own round dozen professional souls. *Compromise*: Why not have the Outpost Letter from Washington consist of summarizing statements such as the one on JANIS [one of the Southeast Asian operations]? They need not be weekly. The more immediate and smaller items can be handled by memos.[63]

Here Cora seems to be arguing that Washington should keep up its end of communications. At their end, under her leadership, R&A produced a prodigious number of significant reports and memoranda: some 223 from Kandy, 123 from New Delhi, and 30 from Rangoon, Burma.[64] In the process, she established a reputation for writing crisp, focused, sometimes amusing, and sometimes trenchant prose. And that prose was long remembered by some of her OSS colleagues. For example, in *Cloak & Gown: Scholars in the Secret War, 1939-1961*, Yale historian Robin W. Winks reports that his colleague George May—a leading scholar of French literature at Yale—credited Cora Du Bois with helping him to write "crisp prose."[65] May, who was born in France, had enlisted in the U.S. Army after the fall of France and had served in the OSS, where he met Cora.

Associates in Work and Play

Service in the OSS/SEAC provided Cora with an intensely interesting set of associates for both work and play. As Guy Martin recounted it to me while sitting in his Georgetown parlor, Cora was "an intellectual who was interested in everything; she was not narrow and could talk about anything. . . . [Furthermore,] she was not politically ambitious like Dillon Ripley, who was on the make 100 percent of the time. . . . And she did not engage in administrative politics. . . . It was an exciting opportunity for her as a woman."[66] The reference above is to S. Dillon Ripley, the renowned ornithologist who became head of the Smithsonian Institution for two decades (1964-84). Ripley was one of the many interesting persons who served with Du Bois in Ceylon.

Three previously mentioned people—Julia McWilliams (Child), Paul Child, and Jeanne Taylor—were of considerable significance to Cora. Ironically, Paul was initially attracted to Jeanne, who assisted him in the War Room and whom he found "very genteel and intellectual, a good painter and art school graduate," whereas he described Julia as somewhat "hysterical" and "slightly afraid of sex," although "*extremely* likable and pleasant to be around."[67] Paul, like Cora, was a decade older than these two young women and reasonably urbane in his tastes for women, wine, and food. Furthermore, he was seeking a new serious relationship to replace a lover who had died several months before he joined the OSS, so he wrote to his twin brother about the various possibilities in Kandy.[68] And Julia, who at six feet two towered over Paul, was not his initial choice. By the end of the war, however, it was Julia whom Paul would marry and inspire to become interested in food and cooking, whereas Jeanne would become Cora's lifelong partner. However complex these interpersonal machinations in Kandy may have been, they resulted in this particular foursome becoming good friends for the remainder of their lives.

Julia towered over all the other women as well as many of the men. One of the exceptions was anthropologist Gregory Bateson, who was somewhat taller than Julia and extremely thin. According to Julia, "He always looked like his pants were falling off because they hung low on his hips."[69] Julia first got to know Bateson aboard ship, on the way to India, where they studied Chinese together, and she found him immensely interesting. Cora, of course, already knew Bateson from her visit, in 1937, to Bali, where he and Margaret Mead were doing research. Bateson, who was British, had joined the OSS after being turned down by the British armed services. He served mostly in the Morale Operations Branch, helping to produce and disseminate "black" propaganda (false information used to vilify, embarrass, or misrepresent the enemy). In Kandy he helped operate a radio station that tried to undermine Japanese propaganda in Burma and Thailand. "We listened to the enemy's nonsense and we professed to be a Japanese official station. Everyday we simply *exaggerated* what the enemy was telling people."[70]

Bateson also served as an R&A analyst under Du Bois and participated in at least one clandestine operation, behind enemy lines, in an effort to rescue several Indonesian OSS agents. Cora considered him a member of her "reliable inner core with whom you can talk about most things and who are always ready to respond to each other's inner tedium."[71] In addition, as anthropologists they shared a special interest in local cultural practices. "Last night," Cora wrote to her parents, "Gregory and I invited five or 6 well beloved friends to a dance put on by a local dance troop—in a temple."[72]

Julia's height was something that Cora also noted in letters home, always referring to her as "Tall Julia." In one such letter, Cora recounted an amusing episode of Julia with a young elephant:

Then one day his little toto [elephant friend] visited us, "only two years old"—and obviously domestic-bred. Tall Julia loves elephants and they love her with an affinity only out-sized beings can have. She fed Toto sour-balls. Toto, being very young, prefers sour-balls to humans but never-the-less followed Tall Julia down a concrete path, sheltered from the rain by a thatch roof, through a G.I. guarded gate, and finally squeezed through a mere man-sized door. Inside Julia's office his pink, prehensile trunk lollopped across the desk asking for another sour-ball. Who could resist? We all melted as fast as the sour-balls. Of such is life made here. (Not counting business).[73]

Others among the cast of characters who made up Cora's work and social environment were anthropologists David Mandelbaum (PhD Yale, 1936) and Weston La Barre (PhD Yale, 1937). Initially Captain Mandelbaum oversaw intelligence in the New Delhi office and served as deputy chief to Du Bois. He was also the intelligence officer attached to a field unit of Detachment 101 that, with the help of Kachin resistance fighters, successfully infiltrated Burma behind enemy lines.[74] After reaching Rangoon, Mandelbaum became the head intelligence officer there and was in charge of getting out reports about Japanese activities in Burma. In a July 1945 letter to Robert Lowie, her UC Berkeley mentor and friend, Cora wrote, "Dave is still here—i.e. this Theatre. He is in Rangoon doing a very good job. I shall hate to see him leave but feel that he too [like Bateson] is approaching the time when he should get home."[75] Following the war, Mandelbaum became an India specialist and had a long and distinguished career in anthropology at UC Berkeley.

Just when Lieutenant Junior Grade La Barre joined the navy and began to do intelligence work for OSS/SEAC is not clear. Earlier in the war he had been hired by the War Relocation Authority as a community analyst for one of the relocation camps for Japanese Americans and Japanese foreign nationals.[76] By January 1944, however, he was in Burma and sending Du Bois intelligence reports on such topics as the status of roads and railroads along the northern Tenasserim coast, Burmese attitudes toward the British, and suggestions for Karen agents who were being sent into Burma.[77] Cora seems to have been impressed by his work because in March 1945 she sent a letter to her boss Fahs in Washington, asking him to keep an eye on La Barre during a leave he was about to take. She was concerned that, following his leave, the navy might deploy him elsewhere. "I strongly urge you to keep track of Lieut. La Barre when he returns," Cora wrote, "and see if we are in a position to make him an interesting offer. I have found him productive, ingenuous, and imaginative in his work and very much wish to retain his services."[78] After the war La Barre returned to his career in anthropology and a professorship at Duke University.[79]

Finally, there was Lieutenant Commander Edmond Taylor, who would take over command of the Kandy detachment when Colonel Heppner was sent to China. He was a journalist and writer who became close friends with Cora. Before joining the OSS, he had covered the early part of the war in Europe and had published *The Strategy of Terror: Europe's Inner Front* (1940). After the war he would publish *The Fall of the Dynasties: The Collapse of the Old Order, 1905–1922* (1963) and *Richer by Asia* (1966). One can imagine the rich conversations—probably over drinks late at night—these two would have had about the fall of Europe and the growing importance of Asia. In his memoir, *Awakening from History* (1969), Taylor acknowledged Du Bois as one of several anthropologists who had had an impact on his thinking about culture.[80]

Long workdays for Cora were lightened by such conversations and by the liveliness of such colleagues as Julia McWilliams (Child), who liked to joke and play and "retained her sense of humor throughout her tour."[81] Julia also organized parties. For example, Jeanne Taylor arrived in Kandy on Christmas Eve 1944, and Julia was in charge of the festivities. Jeanne recorded the following event in an unpublished, undated memoir:

> I followed Julia as she swept down the broad stairway [of the Queen's Hotel] into the great open lobby, waving and greeting everyone with her boisterous enthusiasm. I followed breathlessly, wondering how I WAS GOING TO SURVIVE A PARTY AFTER MY LONG, arduous flight. . . . In the dark we drove two or three miles out into the countryside. . . . Finally past a rather flimsy open gate, up a small hill, Jack stopped the jeep in front of a tiny, palm-thatched building—one of several others like it that were all lighted up—people drifting here and there. An air of festivity seemed to be everywhere. "There she is!" someone shouted as we walked into the Registry room. "The hostess has arrived!" . . . Julia had used the last of her paper clip supply from Washington to decorate the Registry with loops and swags of them hung from the rafters, some interspersed with frangipani flowers picked from some of the trees on the Detachment. . . . "Would you like a drink?" I heard a deep British voice asking. . . . "My name's Bateson," he said, "Gregory Bateson."[82]

This was Jeanne's introduction to the social life in Kandy, where men outnumbered women by about thirty to one and where, twice a week, movies and dances were held at the American officers' club.[83] On Sundays there were picnics, golf, tennis, and swimming outings and, according to Julia Child, there were also occasional weekend escapes to the city of Colombo.[84]

Cora's letters home do not mention these kinds of activities, but she did entertain her mother and stepfather with descriptions of "horse trading"—that is, clothes swapping—and of liquor rations. Cloth was rationed, so in order to have some sense of variety, women began swapping what they had. Cora, for instance, described in detail her three-way swap of two pairs of pajamas that she did not like. "Of course all this takes finesse," Cora wrote. "You must arrive with garments and flowers just when gals are dressing for the evening, are sick of their own clothes and receptive to flowers. We are all becoming very astute in these matters—and very good natured." "The 'jungle ration' (liquor) this month," Cora continued, "would both shock and amuse you. A bottle of Cypriot Brandy, a bottle of Palestinian Cherry Brandy (so called) and 1 bottle of white and one bottle of red Capetown wine. I am willing to wager that before the week is out a party will have been given in which the punch bowl will consist of all four in equal parts plus coconut milk and ice from a spot, surely out of bounds."

Cora went on to mention that her "age and status" tended to put her in a "dean of women" role with respect to the other women in Kandy. "This has so appalled me that I have over-reacted to the point where I am hardly civil to anything in skirts. . . . The favorite joke at the moment is the tale of the Camp Commandant (new, I need hardly say) who entered my office a few days ago and said pleadingly 'Miss De Boys—you're dean of the women around here, aren't you?' Ad and Nelson, who share my office, guffawed so that he was put right even before my tantrum broke."[85]

In another letter Cora reassured her parents that although her work was intense, she did take time off now and then. "I take leave. A day here and a day there and if I felt like it, even a week (I've had one of those in the last 17 months). Besides, I get a business trip about once every 3 months [to New Delhi & Calcutta], which helps a lot. I am fat and more energetic than most people like. . . . I enjoy the work more than any I have ever set the hand to. It seems so worth doing and that compensates for any amount of small harassments or pressures."[86] Then Cora went on to describe a six-day adventure that she and "the most ill assorted personalities you ever saw" had had as they explored some of the highland jungles of Ceylon, looking for wild elephants, Veddahs (indigenous inhabitants), and ancient Buddhist ruins.

The Free Thailand Movement

Throughout her tenure with the OSS/SEAC, Du Bois never ceased her efforts to get Washington to pay more attention to South and Southeast Asia—not because she thought the war would be won there but because she recognized how strategic this part of the world would be after the war. She also recognized the currents of anticolonialism and nationalism that the war had fostered. In an August 1944 memo to Washington she wrote,

> The Japanese, by breaking up the European colonial system, seem to be advancing the cause of nationalism in Southeast Asia. They have injected a new confidence in the natives and it will be next to impossible for them to go back to their old way of life. The British, French, and Dutch have no positive program to offer these people, who witnessed the defeat of the European colonialists at the hands of the Japanese. The United States has a backlog of prestige over here now, but the generalities in our foreign policy must be made specific or we will soon lose this prestige.[87]

In a number of her memos and reports, Cora chastised those in Washington for their lack of vision. For example, in a 1945 memo entitled "Random Jottings," she included the following items:

> 3. Chauvinism
>
> I am interested [in] how exclusively European minded the Executive Committee meetings [in Washington] are. I suppose it is determined by the personnel composing it. It is my old cry, of course. Why do we expend the bulk of our energy on a small peninsula in which avowedly our future influence is secondary, when war came to us from the Pacific and there is a vast continent and the bulk of the world's population in

which influence is potentially a major one? From R&A, at least, one ought to expect a *world's* eye view.

4. Just polemics on my part—but I can't resist at times.[88]

In yet another letter to Washington Du Bois wrote, "Sometimes we [OSS/SEAC] wonder just how long range your long range is? Southern Asia contains almost a quarter of the world's population and an extremely dynamic quarter at that. We can't expect the China-Japan wallas to be excited about our area. We should appreciate, however, an effort to understand and follow our situation."[89] At times Cora did not hesitate to be blunt, and such letters contributed to her reputation for "acerbic" prose. But she had been trying for more than a year to get Washington's attention to longer-range goals in Southeast Asia, especially to the potential significance of Thailand.

Thailand was the region's only independent country—one that had not been colonized by the British, French, or Dutch but that had come under Japanese occupation in 1941. The Japanese had used Thailand as a base for attacking and defeating British forces in Malaya and Burma, and in January 1942 the Thai government, in a conciliatory gesture toward Japan, had declared war on the British and Americans. This had outraged the British. The young Thai ambassador in Washington DC, Seni Pramoj, had not agreed with his country's declaration, however, and had made his position clear to the U.S. State Department. He had then proceeded to begin to organize a Free Thai movement that consisted of students from Thailand who, at the time, were residing in either the United States or Britain.

There were, accordingly, different forces at work to bring Thailand to the attention of the U.S. government during the war. Domestically there was Seni and his band of "warriors" who were looking for American support and guerrilla training. In Asia there was Cora Du Bois, who, in concert with her former nemesis, Colonel Heppner, kept the pressure on Washington. Thailand, they recognized, was not only the crossroads for Japanese troops traveling overland between Burma, Malaya, Indochina, and China, but it was also the spawning ground for organized resistance against the Japanese. Furthermore, both Cora and Heppner were concerned that their British allies, in an effort to maintain their colonial empire after the war, would try to bring Thailand under Britain's sphere of influence.

Heppner, for example, wrote directly to General Donovan on October 4, 1944, to report, "It would appear that the strategy of the British, Dutch, and French is to win back and control Southeast Asia, making the fullest use of American resources, but foreclosing the Americans from any voice in policy matters. . . . In our own sphere [OSS/SEAC], the British have united, and are pretty much shoulder to shoulder against us."[90]

On October 9 Heppner, sounding more and more like Du Bois, wrote a more pungent letter to Donovan:

> To my mind, R&A, Washington has badly miscalculated on the importance of Southeast Asia as a field for its operations, especially in connection with the post-war period. . . . All of our reports have stressed the tug of war now going on in Thailand and Indo-China with our Allies, and it is recognized by all that OSS is deeply involved. . . .
>
> Recently, Miss Du Bois sent in a request for one Thai language man to be attached to her R&A group [which was denied].
>
> [Colonel] John Coughlin is turning over to us all of his Thais [from the Free Thai movement] because of the inadvisability of using them from China. A direct message recently received from Ruth [code name for a high-ranking Thai official] inside Thailand states that all land routes out of Thailand are so carefully guarded by the Japanese through a system of informers that very few Siamese or Chinese trying to leave or enter the country by land escape death or capture. General Stilwell himself is interested in our methods for penetrating Thailand, and gave me the green light when he was here last month.
>
> If R&A [Washington] does not wish to staff its SEAC branch adequately . . . we can get along without their aid. I will be very disappointed, of course, because I am a great believer in R&A and in the value of the tasks which it can perform. However, *when the final report on the activities of this theater is written, I shall certainly point out how this great opportunity was lost, and especially comment on its effect on post-war problems.*[91]

For the previous six months Du Bois had been trying to get Washington's approval for the OSS/SEAC, and specifically Detachment 404 in Kandy, to become actively engaged in Thailand. In June 1944, for example, she had critiqued a memorandum, entitled "American Policy in Asia," that suggested the United States should limit its involvement with SEAC to northern Burma and should not participate in British-proposed campaigns aimed at Malaya and Sumatra because they would align the United States with a doomed imperialism and "place us in opposition to the rise of nationalism in Asia." On the contrary, Du Bois had argued, only by being involved would the United States be in a position to help determine the area's postwar future. "Americans should participate, but their involvement should be based on a clear national policy."[92] Also, in June 1944 Du Bois had sent Heppner a memo in which she argued that Thailand, in particular, was of strategic importance, that Detachment 404 had not acted decisively because of British malaise and its focus on Singapore, and that there should be a special committee appointed to plan and push through OSS operations aimed at Thailand.[93] And in July 1944 Cora had sent Washington a twelve-page proposal, drafted by Army Specialist Dwight Bulkley—the son of a prewar missionary to Thailand and an OSS political analyst—entitled "Documentary Objectives for Political Intelligence from Thailand."[94]

While the U.S. State Department was considering policies for Southeast Asia, the British were parachuting agents into Thailand. In September 1944, Detachment 404 in Kandy, without informing their British allies, sent in two Thai agents, one of whom succeeded in making contact with Pridi Banomyong (Pradit). Pridi, a highly regarded Thai politician who had opposed his government's accession to Japan, had built up an underground resistance movement and had succeeded in getting his opponent, Premier Phibun, to resign. By December Pridi had responded positively to a message from Donovan indicating his willingness to collaborate with the OSS. From then on events in Thailand happened rapidly. The U.S. State Department formulated a policy paper in early January 1945. Later that month the OSS entered Thailand "officially," and by May 1945 it had established a nationwide intelligence network. Finally, on June 16, 1945, Donovan received Joint Chiefs of Staff support for arming and helping to train the Thai underground. Later that month significant supplies were dropped by plane into Thailand, and an American guerrilla trainer and a Thai radioman were successfully parachuted in.[95]

When interviewed in her late seventies, Cora remembered the OSS operation in Thailand as their most successful one in Southeast Asia. As she reported it,

> In Thailand . . . we had put in something like 15 or 16 Thais, who were students in the States and were willing to undertake dangerous underground missions, with radios and all the rest, and they didn't show up for almost a year. We heard nothing from them and were really in fairly deep despair. Then, shortly before Christmas that year [1944], we were contacted from Bangkok, and a certain percentage of those 15 or 16 showed up. We knew they were there, and they were safe, and that they were being protected by the Free Thai Movement. After that, we had the most remarkable communication system with the free Thais who were, of course, underground and unknown as such, to the Japanese. They would have a conference daily with the Japanese in headquarters, and the Thais would walk around a block or two to the house where our agent and his radio communications existed, and it would come to us in a matter of a few hours. So we were constantly in touch with what was happening in Thailand with the Japanese.[96]

The End of the War

Thai resistance efforts, along with many other OSS/SEAC efforts in the region, came to an abrupt stop with Japan's surrender on August 15, 1945, following the dropping of atomic bombs on two Japanese cities—Hiroshima and Nagasaki—on August 6 and 9, respectively. By August 22 Du Bois had disbursed most of her R&A staff, which had numbered fifty-two persons before some were transferred to China toward the end of the war. Most of her remaining staff were sent to Singapore, Bangkok, Saigon, and Batavia [Indonesia] to collect postwar political and economic information for the U.S. State Department. They were sent off with the following message from her: "You will be judged, quite correctly, as representatives of the United States. Your behavior both professionally and personally will be under constant scrutiny and criticism both by Europeans and Asiatics. I have not the slightest question concerning the integrity and good breeding of any members of the R&A group. I hope that you will make felt your influence and example."[97]

On September 20, 1945, Du Bois received the following praise from her immediate Washington boss—K. E. Wells, chief, Southern Asia Section of the OSS—who wrote, "This evening Dickason and I shall attend the King's Birthday reception at the Siamese Legation [in Washington]. We are following Seni Pramoj's movements and British-Siamese peace negotiations with interest. Our government has evidently acted with almost unprecedented vigor in this connection, thanks in large part to you and your team."[98] And in 1949 the Thai government would recognize Du Bois's efforts on the country's behalf during the war and award her the Order of the Crown of Thailand, third class, and the Santimala (Peace) Medal—honors reserved for individuals who have contributed outstanding service to the Kingdom of Thailand.

Du Bois's Return to Washington DC

In a September 2, 1945, letter home, Cora described the planning that had gone on for a "premature peace," the false alarms, the uncertainties of her organization's future, and her concerns about her staff and friends who were being sent home on twenty-four-hour notice. Mixed into this "distraught atmosphere," she wrote, were the innumerable V-J celebrations—"five nights of Kandy's most splendid processions (really a superbly oriental, splendous spectacle)." "It seems scarcely possible," she continued, "that a month could see so many changes. The shattering business of the atomic bomb; Russia's entry into the war and her treaty with China; the complexities of a Japanese surrender; the job of getting to our American POWs and pulling them back to safety before peace arrangements were really settled—all these important things in the midst of innumerable local shifts and changes has been a pretty bewildering experience."[99] With respect to herself, she added, she expected to return to the United States by October or November at the earliest, February (1946) at the latest.

In fact, Cora left Kandy on September 15, having been called to Washington for a two-week OSS conference. She appointed Lieutenant W. L. Barnette Jr. to serve as acting chief of R&A in her absence. However, in a Mission Letter dated September 18, 1945, that Barnette distributed to the remaining staff in Kandy, he indicated his strong suspicion that Cora would not be returning:

15. Cora Du Bois receiving the Exceptional Civilian Service Award, Washington DC, 1946. Cora Alice Du Bois Papers (SPEC.COLL.ETHG.D852c), Tozzer Library, Harvard College Library, Harvard University.

Well, the big news is Cora's departure. She will report to Washington pronto (by air) on a TD, but it is highly improbable that she will be back. Obviously we are all a little desolate about this. It seems so patently the beginning of the end. We are counting on her to dig up lots of hot dope on certain postwar plans that will be of interest to a good many of us. And, when we get them, I'll pass them on to you. . . . This means that one Barnette, after first walking briefly in Guy Martin's shoes as Executive Officer, will be acting for the Chief. Sometimes this, frankly, gives me the shakes. I have no illusions about being able to do the job as magnificently as Cora did, but I shall try to continue on the lines that she has laid down.[100]

The war was over, and it was unclear what would happen to the OSS and its many personnel. Cora was on a mission to find out. She reached Washington DC at 6:00 a.m. on a Saturday after "a long and hideous plane trip, in bucket seats," with a brief landing in Gander, Newfoundland, for a midnight snack, where she was presented with a mimeographed sheet informing her that a couple of her colleagues had been killed in Indochina. In Washington she went to her office, where she could not raise anyone. "I couldn't even get into my own office that I still had rights to, until someone recognized me and said it was all right and I was let through the security guard. I spent most of that day trying to reach people and find out what had happened."[101]

What had happened was that on September 20, 1945, while Du Bois was en route from Ceylon to Washington, President Harry Truman had signed Executive Order 9621, dissolving the OSS. Accordingly, a momentous and often exhilarating period of Cora's life came to an abrupt end. Her service to the country would be recognized the following year when, on May 6, 1946, she was awarded the Exceptional Civilian Award, the highest award granted by the secretary of the army to army civilian personnel. Now, however, she had important decisions to make about her immediate future.

CHAPTER 7

Disillusionment in the Cold War Era

I have served for the last five years in a sensitive agency of our government. I know how demoralizing suspicions and repeated questioning of motives, thoughts and actions can be and I also know that the nation is ill served when such demoralization attacks its employees. Whereas such scrutiny may be justified in sensitive agencies of the government, it seems unpardonable in academic institutions, one of whose important functions is to foster the spirit of free and fearless inquiry.
—Cora Du Bois

The Second World War was followed almost immediately by the Cold War—the term that has come to characterize the geopolitical tensions that quickly emerged between the Soviet Union and the United States and other Western powers. Although the USSR had been an ally in the fight against the Axis powers in Europe, severe differences in political ideologies and in attitudes about how a postwar world might be configured soon undermined that alliance. Besides, in the United States, seeds of anti-Soviet distrust dated back to the 1917 Bolshevik Revolution in Russia and the establishment of a communist state that wanted to compete with the capitalist West for global supremacy. It did not take long, therefore, for relations between Moscow and Washington to deteriorate and for political and economic competition to flourish in a postwar era of anti-colonialism and the emergence of new political states. This competition, however, existed in a significantly new and dangerous context—that of nuclear weapons. It was these tensions, as they played out internationally and domestically, that provided the backdrop for the next stage of Cora Du Bois's life.

At the close of the war, Du Bois had imagined herself remaining in Asia "to see this show through," as she put it in a letter to her UC Berkeley friend and graduate student mentor Robert Lowie. "I have been too invested emotionally in the whole matter to want to pull out before the end," she wrote.[1] Cora had not anticipated a sudden callback to Washington, only to learn that the OSS had been dissolved while she was en route from Kandy, Ceylon, headquarters of the OSS/SEAC. She had, however, begun to contemplate a return to civilian life, which she mentioned in a September 2, 1945, letter to her parents. Having explained that she would probably have some temporary employment in Washington upon her return to the United States, Cora wrote,

> Of course I shall be on the alert for a job—not a very opportune time for job hunting, but must be done. Like many people out here, I have found it difficult to think coherently and practically about the return to "civilian" life. Now that it is to be contemplated within a measurable span of time, the sense of readjustment hangs heavy but there is no information with which to think planfully.
>
> Should an attractive government job turn up, I would not wrinkle the nose—at being Assistant Secretary of State for instance! Academic life and anthropology have lost much of their vitality for me. More than anything these days I want to be a useful citizen. I have at long last and by circuitous routes become a "socialized" being.[2]

The war had provided Cora with an extraordinary opportunity to work closely with a team of men and women to try to defeat the Japanese in Southeast Asia. It is in this sense, I suspect, that she used the term "socialized being" in this letter to her parents. She had lived and worked in close contact, and under intense pressure, with an interesting assortment of civilians and military personnel who had come to respect her intellect and leadership. To return to the classroom to teach anthropology at Sarah Lawrence College, which had kept her position available, could not possibly hold the same allure. "I have been one of those fortunate persons for whom the war has provided inflated opportunities," she had written to Lowie just before the end of the war.³ Furthermore, Cora had emerged from the war committed to the ideals that she had so ably articulated in memos to Washington, and she hoped to see Washington work constructively with new nations in South and Southeast Asia as they emerged from a colonial past and acquired independence. Her political idealism and patriotism remained intact.

From the OSS to the State Department 

By June 1945, before the conclusion of the war in Asia, General Donovan (director of the OSS) and William Langer (chief of the Research and Analysis Branch of the OSS) had begun to consider what should happen to intelligence operations in a postwar era. In a June 11, 1945, memo to Donovan, Langer wrote, "I remember well that from the very inception of the branch [R&A] it was your idea, as it was mine, that ultimately our highly qualified professional staff should be brought into the work of peacemaking. The discussions of the past year have led many of us to the further conviction that some research organization like the R&A Branch should continue into peacetime and should supply the interested government agencies with continuous analysis of foreign situations as they develop."⁴

Langer continued his lengthy memo to Donovan saying, "[T]he uncertainty as to the future is gnawing at the very vitals of the branch." He was worried about his R&A personnel, who were being pressured to return to their university posts or being offered more secure positions in other government agencies. "I am having very serious difficulty in holding a well-rounded staff together. . . . [T]he R&A field staffs have during the past year become more and more important to our operations, so that now I would be tempted to describe them as furnishing our very lifeblood." Langer also made reference to a six-month-old pending agreement with the State Department to recognize and use R&A personnel, but he was skeptical about this working because, as he put it, "They [R&A] do the basic studies which underlie a great many [State Department] decisions without having any opportunity to participate in any discussions. I am convinced that this is not only the most unprofitable use of some of the best talent we have in the country, but I am also convinced that it is a demoralizing situation."⁵

From the start, Donovan had had the goal of making his clandestine intelligence operation a permanent part of the U.S. government, and he waged a yearlong battle (1944–45) for survival that took on aspects of a crusade.[6] With the death of President Franklin Delano Roosevelt in April 1945, however, Donovan lost his principal ally. In addition, in running his own version of "shadow warfare," Donovan had made his share of both civilian and military enemies, one of the most powerful of whom was J. Edgar Hoover, director of the Federal Bureau of Investigation (FBI). Hoover did his best—including spying on Donovan and spreading vicious rumors about him—to prevent any chance that President Harry S. Truman might keep him on.[7] Truman, who succeeded Roosevelt, did not have the same close and trusting relationship with Donovan, plus he needed to be responsive to the American public's desire to return to a postwar state of normalcy. Accordingly, Truman tried to demobilize wartime agencies as quickly as possible, with the OSS being one of the first to go.

Although Donovan lost the immediate battle for OSS immortality, he won the fight in the end. In 1947 Truman would create the Central Intelligence Agency (CIA) very much along the lines that Donovan had proposed, and Donovan's R&A chief, William Langer, would hold a major post in the agency until 1961, when he returned to Harvard.[8] Meanwhile, however, Truman's Executive Order 9621 allowed for many OSS functions, as well as some of its personnel, to be absorbed into the State and War Departments. In particular, R&A, which was renamed the Interim Research Intelligence Service and initially headed by U.S. Army colonel Alfred McCormack, was assigned to the State Department. This turbulent situation is what Cora faced when she returned to Washington from the OSS/SEAC headquarters in Ceylon in September 1945.

By early October Cora had begun to assess the situation and wrote to her staff in Ceylon describing the transitional process that was underway in Washington:

> R&A's relations with State are being discussed between Dr. Langer and Colonel McCormack (now Mr. McCormack). This shift is only until 31 December. Meanwhile War Department will continue to pay our personnel until the long and troublesome shift to State can be effected. Dr. Langer, without any concurrence as yet from State, but with some

agreement from McCormack, thinks in terms of some 500 from R&A in Washington with perhaps some 30 outpost people (for both IBT [Indo-Burma Theater] and China) who would consist of 1 or 2 observers in each key place. . . . I must stress again that this is only one-sided and preliminary thinking. . . . Col. McCormack is an outstanding New York Lawyer. All who know him agree in their high regard for his intelligence, his vigor, and his record of cutting through red tape.[9]

By early December Cora had decided that she must remain in Washington and not return to Ceylon as she had originally planned. She wrote her staff accordingly:

Now I have decided to stay on. The factor leading to this decision was the need to get the area of our choice strongly established on the home front. If we can get up a sufficiently impregnable staff and sufficiently infallible files, we can then withstand any of the organizational buffets. If we are well established, the IBT [Indo-Burma Theater] staff's home berth and future field chances will be more nearly assured. If we gain the confidence of the Foreign Service personnel who are responsible for policy and for action, we shall be nearer to having our points of view heard and implemented. Lastly, the emphasis which our work now bears requires close and constant cultivation of the Washington scene.[10]

Clearly Du Bois had become as determined as Langer to preserve R&A's research strengths and its potential for influencing State Department decisions. And she was not alone in recognizing the value of the interdisciplinary, team-style regional research that had evolved in the OSS during the war. Regional programs—or what became known as language-based area study programs (e.g., Russian Studies)—would shape university research for at least two decades following World War II. As McGeorge Bundy, former president of the Ford Foundation—a major funding source for graduate area study programs—observed in 1964, "The first great center of area studies in the United States was not located in any university, but in Washington . . . in the Office of Strategic Services. In very large measure the area study programs developed in American universities in the years after the war were manned, directed, or stimulated by graduates of the OSS—a remarkable institution, half cops-and-robbers and half faculty meeting."[11]

Meanwhile, by the end of 1945 remnants of the Research and Analysis Branch of the OSS became part of the State Department, and later some would evolve into a unit of the CIA. This, as several historians of the OSS have pointed out, did not occur through conspiracy and deception but rather because R&A was not very threatening to government agencies and because it represented a new system of intelligence research that some government leaders found useful.[12] R&A "survived in one form or another because it brought to intelligence activity academics of such quality that once government leaders became accustomed to their services, they were unwilling to forgo them."[13] And this kind of collaboration between individual scholars and universities, on the one hand, and government agencies, on the other, continued without rancor until the Vietnam War, when such relationships became not only controversial but, in some cases, explosive.[14] That war set off a wave of soul-searching, anguish, and ethical debates among American academics that has never fully abated.[15]

The State Department Years

Before the close of 1945 Du Bois was appointed to the State Department as chief of the South East Asian Branch, housed under the Division of Research for the Far East and part of the new Office of Intelligence—the entity that replaced the Interim Research Intelligence Service. Her responsibilities were to build a staff of Southeast Asian experts and to oversee research on the political, economic, and social problems of Southeast Asia. Although much of Du Bois's government work during this Cold War era remained secret, she gave a number of public lectures, participated in a variety of professional organizations, and published a short but visionary book, *Social Forces in Southeast Asia* (1949)—all of which give us some insights into her thinking during her State Department years.

Domestic Life

Cora took over an apartment to rent in Washington DC from her UC Berkeley friends Julian and Jane Steward. By November 1945 her OSS colleague Jeanne Taylor had moved in with her.[16] Jeanne, along with Paul Child and Julia McWilliams (Child), had been transferred from Ceylon to China

16. Cora Du Bois relaxing with a cigarette, 1948. Cora Alice Du Bois Papers (SPEC.COLL. ETHG.D852c), Tozzer Library, Harvard College Library, Harvard University.

toward the end of the war, so Cora had not seen her for several months. When Jeanne returned to Washington, she too was assigned to the State Department, in the Presentation Branch, doing the same kind of work that she had been doing in Ceylon for the OSS—creating graphic designs, illustrations, posters, charts, and graphs for internal use.

Jeanne was an artist—a painter and graphic artist—who had grown up in an upper-middle-class family in St. Paul, Minnesota, where she had studied fine arts at the St. Paul School of Art. Subsequently she moved to New York City, where she joined the Art Students League, an art school founded in 1875 by local artists for the purpose of training new artists. During the Depression Jeanne returned to Minnesota and worked for the Federal Arts Project, supervising the Index of American Design and producing lithographs of historic import.[17] When World War II broke out, Jeanne applied to the OSS in Washington DC. She was accepted and assigned to the Presentation Branch, where she worked with Paul Child. When Paul was transferred to Ceylon, he requested that Jeanne be sent there as well to assist him in the Map Room at OSS/SEAC headquarters.

As an artist, Jeanne had a strong visual orientation to the world that complemented Cora's prowess with words. In many respects, she represented Cora's more humanistic side—the side that motivated her to write poetry and to admire authors of good fiction. Jeanne was also ten years younger than Cora and a more gentle person who helped to balance Cora's more forceful persona. Jeanne had soft brown wavy hair and large brown eyes—very unlike Cora's intense blue ones. In a poem that Cora wrote during their first year together, entitled "To J.T.," she described Jeanne's eyes as "dark" and "sorrowful."[18] In that poem Jeanne was also depicted as "generous," "tender," and "giving." The relationship worked, and Jeanne would become Cora's intimate companion for the rest of her life, outliving Cora by only one year.

With Jeanne, Cora began to establish an active social life in Washington. Writing to her parents in early 1946, she said, "As for socializing—it has never been so heavy. I seem to know more people in Washington than I have in any community in which I have lived."[19] By May she wrote, "New and old friends keep cropping up to be wined and dined."[20] Cora also reported that Jeanne's mother had come to visit them from St. Paul for a weekend. And two weeks later Jeanne's father arrived, "driving a

17. Jeanne Taylor as a girl. Personal acquisition from Taylor's niece, Lisa Schlingerman.

red Chevrolet convertible" to give to his daughter.[21] That convertible would enable them to take occasional trips out of the city, which provided Cora some necessary respite from the intensity of her work in the State Department.

For more solitary recreation, Cora gardened. "The inherited garden [that came with the Stewards' apartment] is full of herbs most of which I don't recognize," she wrote to her parents. "I've planted radishes, chard, cabbages and tomatoes. There are roses on either side [of the] fence and lush honeysuckle on the back fence. The birds twitter all over the place morning and evening."[22] Gardening was something that Cora had enjoyed when living in Berkeley as a graduate student, and it would remain a pleasing avocation for her during the remainder of her life—especially as she established her own homes in Georgetown and later in Cambridge, Massachusetts.

By the summer of 1946, however, Cora was ready to escape for a time from Washington, and she and Jeanne began planning a trip in the red convertible. "I need to be reduced to a dot in a landscape instead of feeling I am Mrs. Atlas," she wrote to her parents.[23] Initially Cora and Jeanne considered a trip to the West, with its big, open landscapes, but instead they drove to Maine to visit their OSS friends Julia McWilliams and Paul Child, who were using a cabin there that belonged to Paul's brother.[24] Paul had recently been let go by the State Department and was in between jobs. He and Julia would marry in September 1946, and Julia's father, like Jeanne's, would give them an automobile as a gift—a large Buick that Paul described as "a steel-blue wonder-chariot."[25] The Buick would accompany Paul and Julia to France when, in 1948, Paul was hired by the U.S. Foreign Service and assigned to the U.S. Information Agency in Paris.

Cora and Jeanne visited the Childs in Paris once they were settled there. In fact, Julia, in her memoir *My Life in France* (2006), devotes several pages to describing in detail the foursome's night out on the town. It began with dinner at the five-star restaurant Tour d'Argent and ended at 5:00 a.m. at Les Halles, Paris's central food market. In between dinner and dawn, they visited a cabaret in the Place du Tertre, the colorful square near Montmartre's Basilica of the Sacré Coeur. They "strolled along the terrace in front of Sacré-Coeur to stare down at the city. Paris was serene and quiet in the moonlight, and seemed to stretch away to infinity."[26] Then they visited two nightclubs in the Left Bank, and at 3:00 a.m. when the second night-club closed, they moved on to Les Halles. "It was cold and dark, but the vast marketplace was beautiful under splotches of yellow electric light," Julia wrote. "As dawn lightened the edges of the sky, we found ourselves at Au Pied de Cochon for a traditional bowl of onion soup, glasses of red wine, and cups of coffee. At five-fifteen, we straggled home."[27]

From a rustic cabin in Maine to a sophisticated night out in Paris, Cora and Jeanne would remain in close contact with Paul and Julia Child. And by the 1960s both couples would be residents of Cambridge, Massachu-setts, where Cora was a Harvard professor and where Julia began her television series, *The French Chef*.

Meanwhile, however, Cora was settling into life at the State Depart-ment and waiting for her job to become secure. "The bureaucracy moves slowly," she wrote to her parents. "I hope to know whether I am in or out by July [1946] sometime."[28] Cora remained "in" and began searching for a house to buy. By January 1947 she had found one in Georgetown and wrote to her stepfather, Richard, with a business proposition. She hoped that he might be able to lend her the down payment ($12,000 on a purchase price of $22,750) at 3 percent instead of the going rate of 4.5 percent. "I grant I am buying at inflated prices," she wrote, "*but* a $12,000 investment can *always* be recovered in terms of location, Georgetown chi-chi, etc." She described the house and her finances in detail and attached a floor plan of the three-story brick house at 1662 Thirty-Fourth Street NW. Jeanne Taylor, she explained, was prepared "to stand half of current [operating] expenses. As long as I have my present job—on which I expect soon a raise of about $1,000—the house would be well within my means. It would mean room to entertain, have guests and generally realize a fantasy of many years standing, even though it is in Washington instead of Berkeley." Cora concluded her letter by saying, "I'm as excited as a school girl—*but* please don't feel you have to be sold a bill of goods. I can swing the job in any case, or I should not have entered into it."[29]

Richard, who had taken care of Cora's finances for many years—including her two years in Indonesia and then her years in Cey-lon—responded that he did not have available cash and would have to sell securities at a loss in order to lend her money. So Cora proceeded on her own, and by late April she and Jeanne moved into what would be their home for the next seven and a half years. Following their move, in a letter to her mother Cora wrote, "I've decided for the sake of looks to repaint the living room. Tomorrow night I convene in 1662–34th St. with knowledge-able friends and a painter to discuss colors and arrangements. Also curtain material has been ordered and a curtain maker enlisted. But aside from that I've had very little time and energy to plan the multifarious details."[30] Cora and Jeanne's domestic life together was now well established.

In the same letter to her mother Cora mentioned that she had been in correspondence with Uncle Georges, one of her father's younger broth-ers, with whom she had lived in Frankfurt for several months when she was eighteen. Georges was now retired in Switzerland, and at his request, Cora was sending forty dollars a month to her uncle Philippe's widow and son, who lived in Holland.

> Uncle Georges seems to have been strapped by the war and asked for help. It seems little enough to do for Uncle Georges who has always helped everyone so generously and for anyone who is caught in the grinding poverty and starvation of Europe. I also send monthly food packages to de Josselin de Jong, Mabs Nicolspeyer [Dutch Indonesia colleagues] and Joy Du Bois in Holland. I've sent all sorts of clothes packages too. Now it is possible to help a person or two in the Indies who have written me. I feel so guilty about our American fat and our greediness and our callousness that all this seems little enough to do.[31]

Cora had begun to assume some of her uncle Georges's familial respon-sibilities, and she was greatly saddened by news of his death in June 1947. Informing her mother of Georges's demise, Cora wrote, "I feel more upset even than I should have anticipated. For me it seems so much the end of an era—as tho' Europe, which I had long since repudiated, were now really no part of my accessible heritage any more."[32]

Professional Life

Working at the State Department was a very different experience from that in Ceylon, where Cora was central to all OSS/SEAC operations and where a small group of men and women lived and worked together in close proximity. By contrast, the State Department had become a large bureau-cracy during the war, expanding from some nine hundred employees in

1939 to thirty-two hundred in 1945.[33] These personnel included former OSS researchers like Cora who were often considered interlopers by other State Department staff. To further complicate matters, State Department employees were dispersed among seventeen different buildings until George Marshall, who became secretary of state in 1947, ordered them to be consolidated—at which point they moved into a building that had recently been vacated by the War Department when it moved to the Pentagon.[34] During Cora's tenure, the turnover of a string of different secretaries of state—Edward Stettinius Jr. (1944-45), James Byrnes (1945-47), George Marshall (1947-49), and Dean Acheson (1949-53)—added to the department's state of disarray. Fortunately, Acheson, who had served as undersecretary of state from 1945 to 1949, provided some continuity during this immediate postwar period.

There were, however, more serious impediments to Cora's dream of seeing the United States take a constructive role with respect to the postwar emergence of new nations in South and Southeast Asia. In remarks that she delivered to a State Department conference in 1949, she bluntly named what she saw as the two closely related difficulties with U.S. policies in the region—*indifference* and *commitments elsewhere*. "The persons interested in the Far East are termed 'specialists,'" she wrote,

> while every 5th person in the US has no hesitancy about speaking authoritatively about Europe. He may even do it in fluent French or German. It is not astonishing, therefore, that [in] both our war and peace strategies our concern has been primarily for Europe. It is, undoubtedly, both practically and emotionally an area requiring urgent and vigorous effort. If, however, we are not to go on waiting for crises to develop before we become aware of them, it will be necessary to act like the USSR [more strategically] on a global basis. *In respect to Southeast Asia we are on the fringes of crisis.*[35]

These potent remarks were delivered at a meeting of the Jessup Commission that Secretary of State Dean Acheson had organized, ostensibly to review the administration's Asian policies. He asked his friend Philip Jessup—a distinguished international lawyer, Columbia University law professor, and ambassador at large—to chair the commission, prepare a report outlining a viable policy for Asia, and then embark on an inspection tour of Asia. Cora was correct in her assessment of the administration's Eurocentrism. The Jessup Commission was formed *not* because the administration had a sudden interest in formulating an Asian policy but rather because it needed to blunt the attacks it came under when, in 1949, the communists won China's civil war and founded the People's Republic of China. Truman and Acheson had been caught off guard and needed to take some kind of action.[36]

In an in-depth biography of Acheson and review of the Cold War, Robert L. Beisner confirms Du Bois's remarks about the Truman administration's Eurocentric orientation. He writes, "President Truman never knew or learned much about Asia. Not a page in two volumes of his memoirs treats a series of important 1949 events—arguments over Formosa, the founding of the People's Republic of China (PRC), or the festering controversy over recognizing Mao's government."[37] And in an overall favorable assessment of Acheson's tenure as secretary of state, Beisner notes, "Acheson's tendency to see Asia as a blank sheet suggests how little connection he had to any non-Europeans, and a few of his remarks about Asians make one wonder if he had donned a pith helmet to make them. . . . Acheson traveled to Europe eleven times as secretary of state but never made an Asian landfall."[38]

These observations were not intended to devalue the many significant accomplishments of the Truman administration, with its focus on rebuilding Europe and containing Soviet expansion. Following the war, as Cora noted, Western Europe was understandably "an area requiring urgent and vigorous effort." The economies of Britain, France, Italy, the Netherlands, and West Germany were in shambles, and those nations were not in a position to protect Europe from Soviet incursions. As Truman and Acheson learned, "the British were now out of the business of world management," and the United States would need to assume leadership.[39] And leadership came in such noteworthy forms as the Truman Doctrine of 1947, which provided economic and military aid to Greece and Turkey in order to prevent their falling into the Soviet sphere of influence; the European Recovery Program of 1947–1951 (the Marshall Plan); and the North Atlantic Treaty Organization (NATO), founded in 1949 as an intergovernmental military alliance that remains in existence today. The result, however, was that the anticolonial sentiments that had been engendered among Americans during World War II were set aside as the administration buttressed the European nations that still had interests in preserving their colonial empires in Asia. Ironically, it took a communist victory in China to get U.S. attention somewhat refocused.

All the while, Du Bois was overseeing the collection of information from different parts of Southeast Asia, where numerous independence movements were underway. As she told the Jessup Commission, "[T]he revolution in progress in Southeast Asia is not coeval with US-USSR tensions. It is a revolution of certainly 50 years duration. It has affected, more or less acutely, all functions of the cultural life of these disparate peoples. Yet it is a revolution which has not always been disorderly; nor is all disorder necessarily revolutionary. *For the US to interpret the Southeast Asian scene solely in terms of our own preoccupations with anti-Communism is to run the risk of seriously misunderstanding the forces at work and of alienating the leadership of that area.*"[40] Cora was trying to refute an overly simplistic Cold War perspective on Asia.

"The revolution in Southeast Asia," Du Bois went on to say in her presentation to the Jessup Commission, "can be subsumed under three major blanket terms: nationalism in political thinking, socialism in economic aspirations, and humanitarianism in societal programs. . . . That these major trends are Western European in origin gives the US a tremendous psychological advantage in dealing with Southeast Asian leaders. However, it would be a mistake to expect no mutations in the course of transplanting these ideas." Furthermore, she cautioned, "[N]ationalism is the major preoccupation but is still phrased to a large extent as anti-imperialism."[41]

For nearly five years Du Bois had been trying to educate State Department officials, as well as the more general public, about South and Southeast Asia and the postwar status of this part of the world. Her lectures always began with a discussion of the ancient, diverse, and rich history of this region; its linguistic, ethnic, and cultural diversity; and the effects of different phases of Western colonialism that had produced "a dual economy—the European colonial system as it coexisted with the persisting and functioning native system."[42] Then she would move to examining the current forces that were reshaping the region. For example, in a series of lectures that she delivered at Smith College in 1947 and that were published two years later as *Social Forces in Southeast Asia* (1949),

Du Bois wrote, "In this south Asian region as a whole and its interior area of Southeast Asia a new world is shaping itself out of its own indigenous traditions stimulated by the expansive energies of Hindu, Islamic, Chinese, and European cultures. There is probably no other area of the world so richly endowed with diverse cultural strains and so prepared to view the world tolerantly."[43]

Du Bois wanted Americans to have an appreciation of this region's past as well as some understanding of the postwar forces of change that were underway. World War II, she explained, had accentuated nationalist sentiments already existent and peoples' determination to achieve independence. Furthermore, these societies had been given the hope of self-determination by the 1941 Atlantic Charter—a British and U.S. agreement that included reference to the rights of all people to self-determination—and by the formation of the United Nations in 1945. "To Southeast Asians news of these two pledges were heard over short-wave radio sets at the risk of reprisal [to the listeners]. Promises concerning the autonomy of dependent peoples were accepted with deep trust and literalism," Cora wrote.[44] The peoples of what would become India, Pakistan, Sri Lanka, Burma (Myanmar), Malaysia, Thailand, Laos, Cambodia, Vietnam, and Indonesia had witnessed the defeat by the Japanese of their colonial conquerors and, Cora predicted, European prestige and power would never be regained.[45] "The US is now heir to whatever is left of western influence in the area. It behooves us to approach this region with more knowledge than is generally current in the US on the Far East and even more importantly to use our new powers with judicious and constructive wisdom," she wrote in a 1949 speech to the Strategic Intelligence School of the Intelligence Division of the U.S. Army.[46]

In such speeches Du Bois would then outline what she saw as some of the crucial forces of change underway: rapid population growth and its many implications, such as the danger of famines; the need for educational resources to cope with questions of a growing agricultural population that was largely illiterate and that required technological improvements; the lack of skilled labor; and the emergence of labor unions. The latter had, in part, "introduced that most potent of all European ideals, the dignity of the individual—an idea so profound, so delicate, so human, that our own time and tradition is still struggling to implement it."[47] In public lectures she also touched carefully on what she called "political readjustments" as different parts of South and Southeast Asia asserted their independence. For example, in her 1947 Smith College lectures, Du Bois wrote,

> This adjustment is coming either with good grace as in Burma, grudgingly and legalistically as in Indonesia, or accompanied by bitter fighting as in Indochina. At the moment nationalism in Southeast Asia is not only a positive political conviction; it is also a symbol of the deep emotional rejection of metropolitan Europeans as a superior caste. Both the people and their leaders are united in at least the negative determination not to accept their old masters on the old terms. The more grudging the metropolitan adjustment, the more intense will be the hostility engendered against Europeans. In long range terms Great Britain seems to be taking the most constructive role. The hatred which the French show of arms is creating in Indochina endangers not only France's economic and political future in the area, but in addition is fostering all the negative and destructive aspects of relations between Southeast Asians and Europeans. In a wider frame it weakens all relationships between the democracies and the so-called dependent peoples of the world. For a limited period of time the Southeast Asian moderates will recognize the need for support and will be willing to turn to the metropolitan countries for it. If they find there not genuine appreciation of their aspirations, they will either be discredited in the eyes of their own people or may turn elsewhere for the assistance they avowedly need.[48]

This was a stern warning to an American audience that the United States needed to build constructive relations with this part of the world by investing in education and technological development, *not* by coming to the aid of European colonists such as the French. In the preface to the second edition (1959) of the book based upon these lectures, Du Bois wrote even more forthrightly about the French:

> In 1947 the self-defeating obduracy of the French in Indo-China was not generally apparent. It has taken [the 1954 defeat of the French in the battle of] Dien Bien Phu, American intervention, and North Africa to make the handwriting on the wall clear to all, including the French. Yet

the untenability of the French position was already apparent to those who followed events in detail and with dispassion. That this was not more baldly stated in the lectures presented here was a function of my employment at the time in the Department of State and the restrictions on plain speaking such a position entails.[49]

In the paper that Du Bois presented to the Jessup Commission, she also warned of the Indochina situation and the need to work with "leaders who (like all politicians) will be under local pressures we can only vaguely understand and may not sympathize with." She also alluded to the moral leadership that the United States had had in the region when Allied troops arrived in September 1945. "The streets of Saigon and Batavia," she wrote, "were plastered with slogans from Jefferson, from Lincoln, from the Declaration of Independence, from the Constitution." But U.S. commitments to Europe and antagonism with the USSR had begun to undermine that moral leadership, she asserted. "Whether or not we as individuals prize our traditional morality or have been won over to *real politik* is not relevant sociologically. What is relevant is, to the extent that the US temporizes with its own principles, it is abandoning an instrument of great political force in Southeast Asia."[50]

Of course, Cora Du Bois was not some kind of lone visionary and moralist. There were others who shared her opinions and who also tried, unsuccessfully, to influence U.S. policies in Southeast Asia. Most notably, George F. Kennan, the Soviet specialist who is often considered one of the architects of the U.S. containment policy against the USSR, advised Acheson against "guaranteeing [to support] the French in an undertaking which neither they nor we, nor both of us together can win."[51] Du Bois's clear and principled voice, however, deserves to be recovered and preserved, and it is useful to consider why she and other such "specialists" chose to leave the State Department during this era.[52]

By 1950 the United States had poured a half-billion dollars into France's war in Indochina. As Beisner puts it in his biography of Acheson, by "indirectly financing the French national budget, Washington in effect held a mortgage on Indochina."[53] By 1952 the United States was supplying military assistance as well as covering some 40 percent of the total French expenditures in Indochina.[54] After their defeat at Dien Bien Phu in 1954, the French finally pulled out, but the United States persisted in providing military and economic aid to the part of French Indochina that became South Vietnam. By then the United States was engaged in the Korean War, and anticommunist fears were a potent political force domestically. When Dwight D. Eisenhower became president in 1953, he helped to articulate what became known as the "domino theory"—that if Indochina fell under communist dominance, the rest of Southeast Asia would go very quickly, like a row of dominoes. The Cold War had, effectively, come to Southeast Asia. President John F. Kennedy, who succeeded Eisenhower in 1961, accepted this theory and enhanced U.S. involvement in the region.

Given what we know of Du Bois's insights and advice—let alone that of many other government specialists and advisors—leading up to the American war in Vietnam (1955–75), Robert S. McNamara's remarks below are particularly ironic and offensive. McNamara, who served as secretary of defense from 1960 to 1968 and who oversaw the expansion of the war in Vietnam under Presidents Kennedy and Johnson, had the temerity to write in his 1995 mea culpa publication, *In Retrospect: The Tragedy and Lessons of Vietnam*, "None of this [the falling dominoes theory in Southeast Asia] made me anything close to an East Asian expert, however. I had never visited Indochina, nor did I understand or appreciate its history, language, culture, or values. The same must be said, to varying degrees, about President Kennedy, Secretary of State Dean Rusk, National Security Adviser McGeorge Bundy, military adviser Maxwell Taylor, and many others. When it came to Vietnam we found ourselves setting policy for a region that was terra incognita. *Worse, our government lacked experts for us to consult to compensate for our ignorance.*"[55] Cora Du Bois's voice is but one tiny, courageous footnote to this tragic series of events.

In this context it is interesting to note that, in 1953, an American official in Saigon sent the following telegram to the secretary of state: "Have had steady stream of American political, military, economic and social service experts visiting Indochina. Need to take new look at problems and find new or improved solutions. Suggest useful to have visit from someone like *Miss Cora Dubois* [sic], author of *Social Forces in Southeast Asia* (1949)—She could appraise our MSH projects and policies and France and Vietnam relations, policies, and activities with standards and methods of cultural anthropology."[56] Not only was Du Bois not invited for this assignment but, ironically, she was deemed "unsuitable" because she was perceived to be a general social scientist, *not* a cultural anthropologist.[57]

The Red Scare

Early in the Cold War a flood of anticommunist paranoia—exacerbated by reports of Soviet spy activity in North America, tensions with the Soviet Union abroad, and economic anxieties at home—struck the American public. And the flames of this paranoiac fire were fanned by the opposition to the Truman administration in the Congressional elections of 1946. The Republican Party, assisted by a coalition that included the Catholic Church, the FBI, and private entrepreneurs, worked to inflame public fear and suspicion, and there was a sweeping Republican victory. Ten days after President Truman addressed the new Republican-dominated Congress in March 1947, he lay out what would become known as the Truman Doctrine. As an inducement to resistant conservatives to join his efforts to stop the spread of communism abroad, he proposed the creation at home of a security and loyalty program to identify and remove any communists from the federal government (Executive Order 9835). Accordingly, Truman could no longer be accused of being soft on communism. "Those who had criticized the administration 'for not standing up to the Russians,' James Reston [a Pulitzer Prize-winning *New York Times* journalist] claimed, now had to stand behind Truman."[58] It was a shrewd political move, but one that would have devastating effects domestically.

Just three weeks after Truman's announcement of the "Federal Employee Loyalty Program," Cora wrote to her mother as follows:

> In Washington, as elsewhere, the red-smear is flourishing and the witch-hunt resembles the 1920's. The nasty smell of fear pervades the streets. In a very small way it must be like Germany in 1934 or Russia in 1947. Despite complaints, I still feel that the next decade is decisive and if you are a citizen this is the time to hold the fort. Northwestern and UCLA recently offered me academic jobs which I refused. Wise or unwise, right or wrong, I cannot *feel* other than the necessity to give the government all I have got,—tho I may be kicked out tomorrow as a luxury or as new dealer.[59]

The loyalty program required all government servants to sign loyalty oaths, and it authorized background investigations into anyone suspected of being disloyal to the country or of being a security risk. The former concern (disloyalty) targeted persons who had ever had any association with communism, the Communist Party, or other subversive organizations—the so-called Blacklist, or the Attorney General's List of Subversive Organizations. People were targeted who had simply associated with such persons or organizations or who had expressed opinions that could be interpreted as being sympathetic to communism. The latter issue (security risk) targeted gays and lesbians because it was assumed that they could be blackmailed.[60] J. Edgar Hoover and the FBI had a field day with their investigations.

Executive Order 9835 mandated that each executive branch of government would have its own loyalty and security investigatory boards, with a hierarchy of appeal boards. For example, in the State Department, Secretary Acheson could reverse decisions of his own boards, but a higher board could overturn his decisions. "Under Acheson, only about fifty employees were rousted from the state department and fewer than twenty dismissed outright, none for disloyalty. But morale began to plummet in the foreign service."[61] In addition, the FBI began to conduct its own loyalty inquiries of federal employees. By January 1952 there had been some eighteen thousand FBI investigations; by 1958 the number had expanded to some twenty-seven thousand. Furthermore, during this period of little more than a decade (1947–58) the bureau ran name checks on some 4.5 million U.S. citizens.[62] The results of these FBI investigations and name checks were shared, as shall be seen below, with certain State Department officials and leaked to members of Congress such as Senator Joseph McCarthy.

A witch hunt was, indeed, underway, and Cora's partner, Jeanne Taylor, was one of the early casualties. In an illuminating letter to her family dated April 27, 1947, Jeanne tried to explain what had happened—why she had been forced to resign from the State Department. I quote from her letter at some length:

The Department of State has at last made up its somewhat cumbersome mind about me. Last Wednesday I was given the "privilege" of resigning. This "privilege" was given me because I had been so frank

and honest in the two interviews with the Security Division [about having voted for a communist when she was a young artist in New York
City]. . . . I want you to get some sort of idea of the procedures which
the government has used, and is using, and that these procedures are
becoming tighter and tighter—so that by now with the recent Executive
Order—government employees are told how to think, and must *always*
have thought that way—or be branded Communists.

I believe that Communists, Fascists or any persons advocating the
overthrow of the government by force or violence should not be allowed
to work for the government. If I were a Communist—I ought most
certainly to be fired from the government.

But you see—what is not taken into consideration *ever* in this whole
matter is the human being—and the fact that, as a human being, one
grows—develops through adolescent periods of rebellion against family, against society—and then gradually one begins to compare more
maturely the values which, in adolescence, were all haywire and out
of proportion. I feel so strongly that these experiences are *valuable*
and necessary—and that they add to the total personality. If—at the
age of 19 or 20—I had become a rabid vegetarian—or a Catholic—or
a Buchmanite [a member of a controversial Protestant evangelical
movement]—or whatever—it would have represented the same kind
of phase as the particular one I happened to go through.

The fact that—during this youthful period of rebellion—I committed
the unpardonable sin of voting for a Communist—makes me now (a
more mature and more thoughtful person) a dangerous and disloyal
one in the eyes of the government. . . .

I was presented with no charges—therefore had no opportunity to
answer any—nor could I present witnesses to attest to my character.
The inescapable conclusion is to see the similarity between this procedure and those used in Nazi Germany or in Soviet Russia. And you
must understand that I am only one of thousands in all of government
(hundreds in the State Department) who have been fired in exactly the
same fashion.[63]

Jeanne was not allowed to take notes during the several "hearings"
that led to her forced resignation. When queried by her, her panel of

interrogators could not explain why this was the case but just asserted it was policy. Jeanne tried to explain to them that it was important to her to have a record of why she was being dismissed because, as she put it, "I'm going to have to explain this to my family—who are rather conservative Republicans in Minnesota. I don't want to misinform them." She was simply told that she could make corrections on the official transcript of the meeting but could *not* have a copy of it. In other words, she could have no documentation of why she was being asked to resign.

Cora knew of Jeanne's youthful political action, which had not prevented her from serving in the OSS during the war but which now required her resignation from the State Department. Jeanne's leftish leanings had been referenced in a six-page typed letter—printed in caps so as to simulate an official cable—that one of Cora's research analysts in Ceylon had sent to her in January 1945 just before leaving on a dangerous mission.

MY DEAR CORA:

THOUGH SAILING TIME IS YET A FEW DAYS REMOVED . . . YOU, UNHAPPY WOMAN, PROMPTED LARGELY BY YOUR OMNIVOROUS APPETITE FOR FACTS ON PEOPLE . . . HAVE COME TO KNOW CALHOUN (1944–1945 CIRCA). . . . SINCE YOU ARE MY BOSS YOU DO DESERVE A STATE OF THE NATION REPORT OF SORTS. . . . [Lieutenant Junior Grade John D. Calhoun then informed Cora of his upcoming expedition with seven men to go behind enemy lines, after which he switched to his love life and a recommendation that Cora had once made.] YOU OFFERED A SERIES OF SUGGESTIONS. . . . INDEED I AM STILL AMUSED BY THE ONE THAT SUGGESTED CATCHING A FEW NIGHTS SLEEP WITH SOME YOUNG THING. . . . YOU KNEW IT WOULD TAKE A BLAST TO DRIVE ME OUT OF MY MASOCHISTIC MOOD. . . . [But Calhoun reported that he had not cared for any of "these young ladies of yours" until he played tennis with] THIS GIRL TAYLOR. SHE COULD PLAY GOOD TENNIS. . . . MOREOVER SHE COULD TALK, AND SHE SAID THINGS AND HAD DONE THINGS THAT INTERESTED ME. . . . *JEANNE IS AS FAR LEFT OF CENTER AS I, AND WHILE I DO NOT KNOW IF SHE HAS EVER PICKETED THE BETHLEHEM STEEL CORP. OR MOUTHED AND CLUBBED IT OUT*

OH, INCIDENTLY I DO NOT THINK I HAVE *SNOWBALL'S* CHANCE IN HADES OF RECIPROCAL FEELINGS FROM JEANNE IN ALL THIS BUSINESS . . . [but he asked for Cora's help—"talk to her and con her for me"].

GOODBYE CORA. I AM YOUR IRKSOME COLLEAGUE AND MOST GOOD FRIEND.

Jack

TRINCOMALEE, CEYLON[64]

It is difficult to know how much of this letter was written in jest by a male friend who understood Cora's feelings for Jeanne and how much it was a serious missive sent by a young man about to undertake a dangerous mission from which he might not return. He and Cora seem to have had intimate conversations, over bottles of Scotch, during which they discussed life and death, love and war. In addition to humor and intimacy, what the letter makes clear is that Jeanne's OSS friends and colleagues knew of her youthful political activities.

One year after Jeanne's dismissal, on May 19, 1948, J. Edgar Hoover authorized "a full field investigation" of "Cora Alice Du Bois"—an investigation that would continue into the 1960s.[65] Several different factors seem to have triggered this investigation. (1) In the State Department's own loyalty investigation of Du Bois, they had learned from the House Un-American Activities Committee (HUAAC) that, in 1940, she had signed an open letter and petition to the president of Brazil on behalf of Luís Carlos Prestes, honorary chairman of the National Liberties Alliance of Brazil and an opponent of Brazil's then dictator, Getúlio Vargas. (2) Jeanne Taylor had used Cora as a personal reference in her review by the State Department, so Cora was tainted by association with "an undesirable employee." Furthermore, Jeanne was known to reside in the same house as Cora. And (3) in January 1948 Cora had accepted a nomination to the Board of Directors of the American Council of the Institute of Pacific Relations, a tainted organization from the FBI's perspective because it had members who had been accused of being communists or communist sympathizers. (These suspects' names are blacked out in Du Bois's FBI file.) Although the FBI, in its initial report, indicated that the State Department's own investigation of Cora "was favorable concerning her loyalty" and "indicated she was a person who merited employment in the State Dept.," the bureau proceeded with its own full investigation.[66]

A full investigation meant that the FBI had as many as seven agents at a time making inquiries about Du Bois's beliefs and activities in every part of the country in which she had ever lived or worked. They tried to track down and interview her various landlords and neighbors in New York City, Berkeley, Boston, and Washington DC. They pursued friends and colleagues at every educational institution at which she had ever studied or been employed—Barnard, Columbia, UC Berkeley, Harvard, Hunter College, and Sarah Lawrence—and examined her PhD dissertation and various UC Berkeley publications. They interviewed other State Department officers. In addition, in a letter to Samuel D. Boykin, acting director of the Office of Controls in the State Department, J. Edgar Hoover directed him "to institute appropriate investigation at Alor, Netherlands East Indies, and Kandy, Ceylon, to determine if the employee adheres to the doctrines of the Communist Party or is a member of any organization declared by the Attorney General to be within the purview of Executive Order #9835."[67] The State Department was expected to do Hoover's bidding in foreign investigations. Thus Cora Du Bois, who had already been through an internal State Department review with regard to her loyalty, was now being more fully reviewed by the FBI in collusion with another branch of the State Department.

In its recorded "interrogatory" of Du Bois, the FBI focused on two of the above three issues. Below, I present much of the interview verbatim:

> *Q.* "Are you, or have you been, a member of, affilate [*sic*] with, or in sympathetic association with the Council of Pan American Democracy, 100 Fifth Avenue, New York, New York?"
>
> No. I never heard of the organization before. I have never been interested in Latin American affairs.
>
> *Q.* "Has your name been used by this organization with, or without, your permission? If so, please state fully."
>
> To my knowledge my name has never been used either with or without my knowledge by the Council of Pan American Democracy.

Q. "Have you ever signed a Communist sponsored petition?"

To my knowledge no. However, in searching my memory I recall that the only petition I have ever signed which might have political implications involved the following situation.

[Cora then explained how, when in 1939–42 she commuted by train to Sarah Lawrence College in Bronxville, New York, she would occasionally meet and chat with another member of the Sarah Lawrence staff (name blacked out). That person had asked her to sign a petition on behalf of Prestes, who had been arrested by Vargas.] Both names were vaguely familiar to me as associated with Brazil but I had no further knowledge of the personalities. To the best of my memory I asked who Vargas and Prestes were. Again, to the best of my memory, [name blacked out] said that Prestes was a liberal intellectual; that Vargas was a Fascist dictator; that intellectuals should take a stand on the matter and would I sign the petition. I believe that he held out a green sheet of paper and I know that I hastily signed it with a pen I had in hand while working on my class notes. . . .

Q. "Have you ever subscribed to, or made literary and financial contributions to, the New Masses or the Daily Worker?"

I have never subscribed to, made literary or financial contributions to the Daily Worker. I doubt that I have ever bought more than 5 issues on the newsstands. It always impressed me as a tedious, slanted and doctrinaire paper which controverted the best traditions of American journalism. . . .

Q. "Are you acquainted with one [name blacked out, but clearly a reference to Jeanne Taylor]."

Yes.

[Much that follows is blacked out but presumably was about how Cora had met Jeanne in the OSS in Ceylon. Then she explained how they had become reacquainted in Washington after the war and decided to share an apartment, and then a house, together. Cora also explained why Jeanne had been asked to resign from the Presentation Division of the State Department and that she was aware of Jeanne's "intention to vote the Communist ticket" in the early 1930s when she first came of voting age. Cora concluded this response as follows:]

My association with [name blacked out] convinces me that she is not a Communist and never has been a Communist and that she lacks real political interests or knowledge in either domestic or foreign affairs and finally that the evidence leading to her forced resignation were actions of an idealistic but immature person trying to assert her personal independence. I was convinced that a personal injustice had been done. On hearsay from [name blacked out] via her Division Chief, I gather that [name blacked out] had the same conviction. Since no charges were preferred and she was permitted to resign, it appeared likely that [name blacked out] was generally considered merely technically caught in a set of regulations.

The FBI interrogation continued with questions about two other persons whom Cora had known and whose names are blacked out. One was clearly Jane Foster, an OSS colleague, an Indonesian specialist, and as Cora put it, "the first American woman into Indonesia after the reoccupation [by the Allies]." She was also an "unreconstructed rebel" from a wealthy San Francisco family who had joined the Communist Party in 1939.[68]

The interrogation concluded with:

Sworn to by Cora DuBois [*sic*]
this 17th day of November, 1948,
at Washington DC.
/s/ [name blacked out] Notary Public
Washington DC.[69]

J. Edgar Hoover had a variety of motivations for investigating and harassing someone like Cora Du Bois for a dozen years. That she had signed a petition, along with hundreds of other notable persons—such as anthropologists Ruth Benedict, Franz Boas, and A. F. Montagu; psychologist Otto Klineberg; poet Robinson Jeffers; musician Horace Grenell; and Utah Supreme Court justice James A. Wolfe—was just a ruse. However, the petition was likely a personal affront to Hoover, who considered himself in charge of keeping Latin America free of communism. In fact, Latin America had been Hoover's international fiefdom during the war, a region of the world in which Donovan was not allowed to operate.[70] Furthermore, as we have seen, Hoover viewed Donovan as a competitor in the world of intelligence gathering. Thus the presence in the State Department of people like Cora—former OSS intelligence officers—might have rankled Hoover. And as an anthropologist, she belonged to a suspect organization—the American Anthropological Association—that the FBI was monitoring because of its liberal positions on issues of race and its support of Native Americans and other minorities.[71] As David Price has convincingly argued in his book *Threatening Anthropology: McCarthyism and the FBI's Surveillance of Activist Anthropologists*, loyalty hearings and FBI surveillance were used collaboratively to try to quell activism for issues of social justice during the Cold War. "As an analyst who recognized both the power and justice of anticolonialist movements in the postwar world, Du Bois attracted the scrutiny of Hoover's FBI."[72] And finally, Cora was a lesbian.

The Cold War witch hunt in Washington was not exclusively focused on purging the federal government of communists and communist sympathizers. The "Red Scare" also became a "Lavender Scare"—the title of David K. Johnson's 2004 book about the persecution of gays and lesbians during this same period. In fact, under Acheson there were more homosexuals—some four hundred—"fired or harried into resignation" from the State Department than suspected "reds," and none were found to have assisted the USSR. "Acheson's own language could take on the tinge of this assault on the sexually heterodox when he defended his associates as 'clean-living' and the department as a 'good, clean loyal outfit.' He glumly went along when Styles Bridges [a New Hampshire Republican senator] badgered him in a hearing to include 'perversion' as a 'security risk.'"[73]

During the New Deal era and the Second World War, there had been an influx of people into Washington DC. New opportunities had opened up for both men and women—Du Bois being an example—and many gays and lesbians had begun to live more openly. However, the flood of anticommunist paranoia was accompanied by a fear of the sexually "different," and the 1947 loyalty program opened the door to many kinds of persecution. "The vehemence of the State Department's antigay campaign can hardly be overstated," writes Johnson as he documents all the steps taken to eliminate "the homosexual problem."[74] Potential homosexuality, accordingly, became an excuse for J. Edgar Hoover's operation to monitor government employees' living arrangements and sexual orientation, using techniques that included illegal wiretapping and breaking into homes and offices without warrants.[75] Hoover—who himself cohabited and vacationed with FBI assistant director Clyde Tolson for nearly fifty years—used his knowledge of others' sexual proclivities as a source of blackmail.[76]

The released segments of Du Bois's FBI files make it clear that agents were monitoring her living arrangements. They frequently mention her "single status" and "residence with [name blacked out]." It is clearly Jeanne Taylor who is mentioned. And it is Jeanne Taylor who is asked about in one FBI interview after another with Cora's neighbors, friends, and colleagues. In the released FBI files there is no overt mention of homosexuality; however, one wonders what the nineteen pages withheld from the files might reveal. It seems likely that the FBI was trying to document Cora's sexual orientation for purposes of blackmail or manipulation. And probably Cora suspected this kind of surveillance because when she took a brief leave of absence from the State Department to teach summer school at UC Berkeley in 1948, she arranged to live in the Faculty House while Jeanne lived with Berkeley friends.

The FBI documents that have been released for this first of several "full investigations," with only one exception, strongly attest to Du Bois's loyalty and patriotism, her invaluable service to the government, her "thoroughly straightforward and truthful person[hood]," and "her honesty and outspokenness." The one exception was someone interviewed from Hunter College, where Cora had been an instructor in 1936–37, who "was of the opinion that DUBOIS was a communist, although she had no tangible proof."[77] With regard to Du Bois's membership in the Institute of Pacific Relations, her boss at the State Department testified that he had advised her to remain in the organization, despite accusations of communist membership, since it was "the only professional, competent Far East Association and it was more or less part of his job and [that of] members of his staff to join [it]."[78] In the 1948 investigation the FBI did not turn up anything to use against Du Bois except, perhaps, her relationship with Jeanne Taylor.

When a second full investigation was authorized in 1953, for reasons that will be explained below, the testaments on Du Bois's behalf were even more powerful. A number of Cora's former colleagues from the Division of Research for the Far East in the State Department were interviewed and described her "as one of the foremost cultural anthropologists in the world" and a person who "is both loyal to the U.S. and in no way constitutes a security risk." Another testified that Du Bois "was very hostile toward Communism." Yet another described Du Bois as "a highly distinguished scholar, most capable and on the opinionated side. He stated that the latter was a desirable thing for her to possess in the position which she held in the Department of State . . . that she believes in self-determination on the part of all peoples and that this appears to be her ideological make-up . . . that she believes that independence must be granted to all subjugated people and that independence will be obtained sooner or later." This interviewee concluded his testimony, "MISS DU BOIS thinks clearly and quickly and is very articulate." Finally, another State Department colleague, who was asked about Cora's relationship with Jeanne Taylor (although her name was blacked out) and who was aware of Jeanne's resignation from the State Department, asserted that "MISS DU BOIS had the far stronger mind of the two individuals, and that most certainly there could have been no influence exerted upon MISS DU BOIS by [name blacked out] but that the influence would be very much so in the opposite directions."79

A portrait of a loyal, highly competent, intelligent, and forceful persona emerges from these documents. Again, however, the FBI was able to find two counter voices. One such person voluntarily appeared at FBI headquarters and stated that when she worked for "the Far-East Southern Areas Branch of the State Department" she believed it was "infested with persons she believed were Communists or pro-Communists. She advised this branch was headed by Dr. CORA DU BOIS. . . . [H]er suspicions of some of those in the branch were aroused when she found them staunch supporters of HO CHI MINH a Moscow trained Communist who organized and heads the Viet Minh Movement, a nationalistic group opposed to colonial rule."80 The second counter voice was Northwestern University political science professor Kenneth Colegrove, who testified about the Institute of Pacific Relations before the Subcommittee to Investigate the Administration of the Internal Security Act and Other Internal Security Laws of the Committee on the Judiciary, U.S. Senate. In the course of his testimony, he referred to Du Bois's briefing on Southeast Asia to a 1949 State Department roundtable discussion on American policy toward China

18. Portrait of Cora Du Bois, ca. 1950. Cora Alice Du Bois Papers (SPEC.COLL.ETHG. D852c), Tozzer Library, Harvard College Library, Harvard University.

(the Jessup Commission) and asserted that she "was very sympathetic toward the Communists." He then presented the committee with portions of Cora's briefing that, as reported earlier, was intended to inform State Department officials that the revolutions underway in Southeast Asia were nationalistic in origin and should not be interpreted "solely in terms of [U.S.] preoccupations with anti-Communism."[81] Accordingly, this part of Colegrove's testimony to the Senate Judiciary Committee became part of Du Bois's FBI file.

Under conditions of national hysteria and a witch hunt, Cora Du Bois's insights into and convictions about the contemporary situation in Southeast Asia could, as seen above, be misinterpreted and used against her. Senator Joseph McCarthy, who by early 1950 had become the leader of this witch hunt in Congress, particularly targeted the State Department. In his infamous February 9, 1950, speech to the Republican Women's Club of Wheeling, West Virginia, McCarthy attacked the State Department, saying that it was infested with communists and that he had in his hands a list of 205 people known to the secretary of state as being members of the Communist Party who were, nonetheless, still working for and shaping policy in the State Department.[82] And Du Bois was, according to State Department records contained in her FBI file, number sixty on McCarthy's list.[83]

Moving On

On March 25, 1948, Cora wrote to Robert Lowie as follows:

> So much happens so fast in this racket that it seems impossible to keep my friends posted. At the moment I am more than a little distressed by the stench of fear which pervades the bureaucracy. If it were a decent honest fear of the world as it is shaping itself, I would welcome it. Instead it is the nasty crawling fear born of blackmail and bullying in a red-smear era. All I can say for it, is that it is excellent experience and I wish that I had been an aware citizen in the 1920's. I would now have some perspective. At the moment, I don't. In any case honest convictions must be held no matter if hands are chopped. I so deplore the ease with which we adopt the tactics of our enemies.[84]

At this stage of things in Washington Cora was prepared to persevere.

Besides, it would have been out of character for her to buckle under to tactics of intimidation. Yet as the year progressed and more and more of her colleagues in the Far East Branch of the State Department were being investigated and purged, her morale must have plummeted along with that of others.[85] As Du Bois recalled this period many years later, in a 1981 letter to anthropologist George Foster, who had inquired about her experience with the World Health Organization (WHO), "[The] State Department was under considerable pressure from the McCarran-McCarthy communist infiltration hysteria. Although I personally was only lightly brushed, colleagues and staff were under fairly harsh pressure. After some four to five years of this I found my cool (such as it was) dissolving and felt a change was indicated. As I did not wish to resign under pressure of continuing and time-consuming loyalty investigations of my Southeast Asia research and analysis, I applied for a year's leave of absence to take the WHO job."[86]

Yet it was not just the red smear that was demoralizing. It was also, as Langer had predicted when some of his former OSS research analysts were first absorbed into the State Department, a demoralizing situation because one felt so ineffectual in a large bureaucracy where one's expertise was largely ignored and where, as Cora put it, "the permanent foreign service staff were not at all receptive to this gang of people that had been wished on to the Department."[87] In a 1978 interview, Cora recalled that difficult time:

> During this period of 1948–49 I saw that we were futile, or I was futile, and that we had nothing to contribute, except we did contribute a little to our policy in Indonesia. We foresaw very clearly what was going to happen in Vietnam, and tried to warn but we met this constant resistance because the policy was being formed out of reports from Paris and London, and other places, and we couldn't get into that.
>
> I found that this young group that I had aggregated [about thirty-five] were people who had some academic training but most of their training had been with the army language and area program. They had learned languages and they wanted desperately to work on this. So, I recruited a fair number of these; but not exclusively, others also. I found them getting more and more frustrated, more hysterical at their frustrations, and I remember saying to two or three of them, "Look,

you've lost your judgment on this whole thing. Get the hell out of here and back to academic life. You can't stand this, it's destroying you." Then I woke up one morning and said, "It's destroying me, too!"[88]

In many respects 1948–49 was a pivotal year for Cora. At a personal level, she lost a special friend and inspiration, Ruth Benedict. Benedict died of a heart attack on September 17, 1948, two days after returning home from a fatiguing series of UNESCO lectures in Europe. She was sixty-one years old and had just been promoted to full professor at Columbia that May—the first woman so honored in the Faculty of Arts and Sciences.[89] Cora was one of the persons who spoke at her memorial, making reference to Benedict's "rare personal qualities"—her "integrity," her "unstinting generosity toward the infinitely varied persons who sought her advice," and "her rare sensitivity in matters both of the intellect and of the feelings." "Her personality was subtle, complex, encysted," Cora continued, "and in later years highly dedicated. Her personality was one in which malice and aggression were singularly unvoiced; it was one in which dispute was an intolerable derogation not only of the self but of others. Achievement was a means of self-expression, and not a weapon of self-assertion. She gave, and commanded for others, compassion—which is not a fashionable emotion but one we cannot yet afford to outlive."[90]

These remarks eloquently captured some of Benedict's remarkable characteristics. But they also alluded, in only a slightly veiled fashion, to the unpleasant politics that Benedict had endured at Columbia in the years following Boas's retirement when Ralph Linton had been selected from the outside, over Benedict, to chair the Department of Anthropology. At the time Benedict was the senior member of the department and acting chair. There was, accordingly, some degree of mutual tension between Benedict and Linton. For Linton, however, interpersonal tension seems to have become outright hostility. Following Benedict's death, for example, he would pull out a Melanesian charm bag and boast that he had used it to help kill her.[91] And on the night of Benedict's memorial, he had the effrontery to turn to Cora and say, "You know as well as I that she was a witch. A devil. We both know enough of the world to know that witches are real! She hated men, look what she did to her students! She destroyed them by feeding on them. She tried to kill me too—But I've won out. She's dead but I'm still alive."[92] Furthermore, in his remarks to the FBI when they were investigating Benedict, Linton described her as "'being on the fringe'—clarifying that in using this phrase he meant to characterize her as being almost fanatical but not intentionally a fellow traveler of Communist or other radical organizations."[93] Linton was perhaps the better candidate for "witchhood."

During this same year, Alfred Kroeber—now retired from the anthropology program that he had built and chaired for many years at UC Berkeley—was teaching at Columbia and had occasional visits with Cora in New York City and Washington DC. He knew that Lowie, who had taken over chairing the department, was getting ready to retire and that they would need to recruit someone to replace him. Cora was already on an informal list that had been compiled and that also included their former student Julian Steward.[94] After visits with Cora and conversations with others about her, Kroeber wrote, in November 1948, to the department to strongly recommend that they pursue Cora:

> I have seen Cora Du Bois several times lately and feel reasonably confident that she is about ripe to drop from the State Department tree at the opportunity.
>
> If Berkeley could offer her a full professorship beginning next year, my guess is that she would not only accept it but would do so with preference.
>
> She would be quite a prize for an institution having an Asiatic areal program or institute, or for one slanting its Anthropology that way with Foundation aid, and quite possibly she is due to be asked by some such. Once so established at a high salary she could hardly be asked to transfer to California for less.
>
> She is everywhere respected as the ablest woman in Anthropology, as wholly sound, and a stable personality.[95]

Soon thereafter the UC Berkeley Department of Anthropology began the administrative process of making Du Bois an offer, which resulted in a trip to Washington DC in December 1949 by President Sproul to visit her and to offer her a full tenured professorship. "President Sproul came in for a chat today," Cora wrote Lowie.

I answered his inquiries as to my intentions with as much frankness as my continuing indecisions on these issues permit. He assured me that he would return and write a definite offer. . . . In any event, I have definitely committed myself to a year with the World Health Organization as anthropological consultant. I go (on a leave of absence from my present job) to Geneva in March, will stay there about a month and then set out to look over technical teams in the Far and Middle East. . . . I am still indecisive about my future. . . . [I]f I accept California it will mean a resignation, not a leave of absence, when I leave here in March.[96]

That Cora could be indecisive about an offer from UC Berkeley—the place that she had always dreamed of working and living, with a home in the Berkeley hills[97]—is indicative of her deep-seated principles: *not* to cave in to malevolent forces and *not* to give up trying to influence State Department policy despite all the obstacles. But she had already accepted a leave of absence to spend a year with WHO "to heal myself of all of this [destructiveness] and see people who were doing good. (I was still in that mood and I thought really that they were doing good.)"[98] By February 20, 1950, however, Cora had made up her mind and accepted the offer from UC Berkeley, with the proviso that she begin her duties in the fall semester of 1951 so that she could spend a year (March 1950–April 1951) with the World Health Organization. She concluded her letter of acceptance to President Sproul as follows: "I need scarcely tell you that I return to the Berkeley campus deeply appreciative of the confidence you are placing in me and of the adjustments you have offered to make this return attractive in every way."[99] Cora Du Bois was, accordingly, the first woman to be offered a position in the Department of Anthropology at UC Berkeley.

The California Loyalty Oath Debacle

Du Bois's year away was not a particularly scintillating one. It began in Geneva, Switzerland, the headquarters for WHO, which had only recently been established under the United Nations but which built upon its predecessor, the Health Organization, an agency of the League of Nations. She was soon sent to parts of Asia—India, Thailand, Malaya, and Borneo—to examine WHO health programs as well as Rockefeller Foundation ones that had been established in the 1930s. The goal seems to have been to return to Geneva and advise them with the "$64 questions on social training and mental health programs for which there are only two bit answers. I'm afraid anthropology has been seriously oversold in that direction as in others," she reported to Lowie before her departure. "If all goes well, I shall be asked to break in a successor and suggest two or three additional anthropologists for regional office work."[100]

Cora quickly learned that social scientists were no more welcomed by the hierarchies of physicians abroad than they were by the hierarchies of State Department officials at home. In addition, she came to believe that "[t]he only group that had any real sense of the problem *as a human one*, were the nurses."[101] For example, as she reported to her anthropology colleague George Foster many years later, "My reception [in India] by Dr. Mani—an Indian military medic—was not cordial. I was left to make my own plans and schedules and I was more than a little perplexed as to what was expected of me."[102] These and other experiences reinforced Cora's ambivalence about applied anthropology.

More disturbing, though, was the news from home awaiting Cora when she returned to Geneva in September 1950. While she had been traveling in Asia, the Red Scare had descended upon the state of California and its university system. The University of California Board of Regents had amended a relatively mundane 1942 loyalty oath, which called for loyalty to the state, the nation, and their constitutions, with the following pledge: "Having taken the constitutional oath of office required of public officials of the State of California, I hereby formally acknowledge my acceptance of the position and salary named, and also state that I am not a member of the Communist Party or any other organization which advocates the overthrow of the Government by force or violence, and that I have no commitments in conflict with my responsibilities with respect to impartial scholarship and free pursuit of truth. I understand that the foregoing statement is a condition of my employment and a consideration of payment of my salary."[103]

To Cora, this signaled more of what she had already endured in Washington as an employee of the State Department. The loyalty oath had arrived for her to sign, along with her UC Berkeley contract, for the 1951–52 academic year. On September 27, 1950, Du Bois sent the following letter to President Sproul:

My dear President Sproul,

On my return from a prolonged trip to South Asia, I found waiting
for me the announcement of my appointment as professor of
Anthropology dated 21 July 1950. With it were the form for the
constitutional oath and the contract with the "Communist Party"
clause. In the same mail I found letters from friends enclosing
clippings from the New York Times on the deplorable difficulties
which the University is facing these days on the issue of signing
these contracts. I was particularly disturbed by news of the
action taken against the University of California by the American
Psychological Association.

To you, personally, I need scarcely reiterate my devotion to the
University of California and my interest in seeing it resume its
distinguished academic reputation. My loyalty to my country is
also unquestioned. It is based on a profound faith in the traditional
values expressed in its founding documents. I am deeply concerned
by attacks on those traditions from radicals of the extreme right
and extreme left. I recall my distress at the supine role of many
intellectuals when Germany was coming under the influence of the
Nazi Party. The miserable moral position of intellectuals in the USSR
is too well known to need comment. I should not like to be counted
among those who will justify any means for ends that may be
laudable. *However futile gestures against such means may sometimes be,
not to make them is the beginning of personal and social degradation. In
all conscience I cannot feel that I would be loyal to our country if I abet
the adoption of methods used by ideological systems antipathetic to those
of our democracy.*

I have served for the last five years in a sensitive agency of our
government. I know how demoralizing suspicions and repeated
questioning of motives, thoughts and actions can be and I also know
that the nation is ill served when such demoralization attacks its
employees. *Whereas such scrutiny may be justified in sensitive agencies
of the government, it seems unpardonable in academic institutions, one
of whose important functions is to foster the spirit of free and fearless
inquiry.* I would therefore have no hesitancy in signing the contract

were the first 2½ lines of the "communist clause" deleted. The statement would then read: "I have no commitments in conflict with my responsibilities with respect to impartial scholarships and free pursuit of truth . . . . ."

Therefore, before signing the papers sent me, may I ask you to forward a full statement of the facts in this complicated and unfortunate case? I realize the undesirable position in which my hesitancy places the Department of Anthropology and that my hesitancy is only a very trivial factor in the many more serious difficulties facing you as a result of decisions by the Board of Regents.

Please accept my personal regards and my apologies for adding to your burdens at this time.

Yours sincerely,

Cora Du Bois[104]

As one of her Berkeley friends who by chance saw the letter put it, "Your letter to Sproul is one of the most exquisitely vitriolic yet coldly polite pieces of prose it has ever been my good fortune to read."[105] For Cora, it was heartfelt and stood for principles that were no longer abstract. She had personally experienced attacks on her loyalty and vehemently believed, as she put it, that such scrutiny was "unpardonable in academic institutions, one of whose important functions is to foster the spirit of free and fearless inquiry."

President Sproul responded to Du Bois on October 31, 1950, asking her "to do nothing for the time being about the documents that you have received, and to await further word from me. In the meantime, I shall assume that you and I have a gentleman's agreement, if such a thing is possible between us, and that you will join the faculty of the University as previously agreed if a mutually satisfactory form of contract can be offered to you."[106] But Sproul was in the midst of a storm that, it seems, initially had his blessings and that would not settle down for some years.[107]

The regents' action had been taken in the spring of 1949 and had received little publicity until faculty discovered the amended oath appended to their contracts for the coming academic year. At that point a special meeting of the Faculty Senate was called, and a nationally recognized psychologist, Edmund Tolman, became the unofficial leader of the opposition. Despite organized opposition from the faculty, copies of contracts for the 1949–50 year were sent out with the newly amended loyalty oath attached, and many faculty refused to sign them. In February 1950 the regents passed a resolution that required faculty either to sign the new loyalty oath or be dismissed. Things had escalated to where academic freedom and tenure were now at issue.

By April 1950 the regents had approved a procedure for petition and review of the loyalty of faculty members who had not yet signed their contracts and loyalty oaths—a tactic very reminiscent of what the State Department was doing under Truman's Executive Order 9835. On July 18, 1950, Tolman wrote a long and powerful letter to President Sproul about this whole questionable process, to which he appended "a partial list of the men and women who address this message to you. You know them and their families well. Many are eminent scholars and scientists; all are loyal to the United States of America; all have served our country in or out of uniform; all share a deep love for their University; most have served it for years; some have dedicated their entire adult lives to that service."[108] Tolman went on to summarize what he viewed as the issues that defined "the year of turmoil" and "tragedy" in the hopes that Sproul would be able to negotiate a satisfactory outcome with the regents at their July meeting. But the regents held to their guns and insisted that reluctant faculty must either sign or get out. For them, the loyalty oath controversy had become an issue of discipline and obedience, whereas for Tolman, and some thirty other colleagues who would leave the university, it was a matter of upholding academic freedom and resisting what they considered totalitarian techniques being used in a democratic state.[109]

By the time Cora received her contract, with its appended loyalty oath, the controversy between the UC Board of Regents and faculty had become national news that was played out against the United States' entry into the Korean War. When Cora returned to the United States, she made a special trip to Berkeley to better assess the situation. She was deeply torn between her love of Berkeley and her dream job, on the one hand, and the principles that she had outlined in her letter to Sproul, on the other. As she had put it in a letter to UC Berkeley anthropologist Ted McCown, who had urged her to come join the fight, "There is a great difference in the position of faculty on the campus who have signed contracts under various pressures ranging from family responsibilities to the callousness that inevitably develops in a long quarrel of this sort and on the other hand the position of a person coming in fresh from the outside without such pressures. The argument of staying and fighting does not apply to the outsider since to join up and fight is the equivalent of giving yourself as a hostage before you even begin resisting."[110]

In Berkeley Cora talked personally with all the anthropologists and other faculty whom she knew, consulted with lawyers in San Francisco, and visited a variety of friends. "[I] talked around and couldn't decide. It was an important decision, I felt, in my life," she reminisced in later years. "I remember sitting, one of my last days there, in a little office under the eaves [in the Anthropology Department], making a list of pros and cons. 'How do I make up my mind?' And Lowie stepped in and said, 'Cora, have you decided?' And I said, 'Yes, I'm not coming.'"[111]

The Next Four Years

Cora returned to Washington and drafted a letter to President Sproul. She expressed regret that their "gentleman's agreement" had not been realized and that she had felt bound, so as not to further inconvenience the Department of Anthropology, to make a decision before the state supreme court had had a chance to review a faculty case that was working its way through the courts.[112] Accordingly, she explained, she could not accept an appointment at the university. In her three-page, single-spaced letter to Sproul, she reviewed her reasons for this regrettable decision, one of which is included verbatim below:

> Today no reasonable person can believe that oaths are an assurance of loyalty. The cause does not lie exclusively in subversive ideologies. When oaths are multiplied and loosely drafted, they can, and do, engender cynicism in even the most upright people who are forced by personal considerations to sign them. The function of an oath, with all of its important implications for the maintenance of our social and legal system, is thereby jeopardized. Instead of being an affirmation of personal integrity, the oath is being used increasingly as a device intended to provide legal sanctions against communists and suspected

communists. But many oaths, including the [new] California State Loyalty Oath, are so phrased that they can be used to serve against anyone holding certain kinds of opinions and joining types of organizations that are unpopular with a majority or even a powerful minority. The extension of such sanctions over a larger and larger portion of our population, even if not flagrantly abused, cannot fail to inhibit that free discussion and inquiry basic to the strength of our democracy. As I said to you in an earlier letter, I recognize the need for strict security controls in sensitive agencies of our government. But I believe also that the fundamental interests of our national security require us to guard jealously against the useless and unwarranted extension of such controls and their loose application. You will surely agree that we cannot scrutinize too carefully every method suggested to safeguard our internal security lest in the process we forge tools that willful men or even well-intentioned but short-sighted ones can use to intimidate their less powerful but equally loyal fellow citizens. Intimidation is an insidious disease. Like cancer it can develop undetected until it is too late to cure it. I feel sure that you join me in hoping that this disease will never gain headway among the California faculty despite the infection to which they are exposed.[113]

These concerns and insights continue to be as relevant today as they were in the early Cold War/McCarthy era. The question still exists: what security measures are compatible with a democratic state?

While Du Bois's decision was principled and courageous—she had no other job to return to—and her prose eloquent and powerful, these events had taken a toll on her psyche. Her journal entries from this period reflect deep pessimism about her self-worth and cynicism about a future in which "progress" and "development" became contemporary slogans "variously pious and impious."[114] Even her relationship with Jeanne was temporarily tainted. Cora viewed Jeanne and some of her friends as "unformulated and un-self-disciplined," whereas they considered her "rigid and hortatory," she reported. "In an era of such diverse and ill-resolved value systems," she wrote, "personal form, personal integrity, is constantly challenged. This is the dilemma of the so-called liberal and the essential problem of the American individualist in 1950."[115]

Fortunately, Du Bois was quickly offered another job in Washington, with the Institute of International Education (IIE)—a nonprofit organization that was established in 1919, in the aftermath of World War I, to foster greater understanding among nations by developing international exchanges of students and faculty. They hired her as director of research. At the time the institute was expecting a generous grant from the Ford Foundation that never materialized. But the Carnegie Foundation stepped in and helped support research that resulted in Cora's book *Foreign Students and Higher Education in the United States* (1956). While grateful for the employment, Cora developed a somewhat jaundiced view of "such institutions [that] are forced to adapt themselves to the demands of donors rather than cleaving to their own convictions or experience. The donors from government agencies and wealthy foundations were often staffed by ill-informed persons and guided by political considerations. In sum, it was my first exposure to the 'managerial revolution' that now flourishes in governmental regulatory agencies and in formerly independent universities and scholarly associations."[116]

From 1951 to 1954, Cora was essentially marking time, waiting for a suitable academic job to materialize. "At that point I knew that I was out of all of this kind of thing [government and institute work] and I put myself actively again on the market; let it be known indirectly, as one does, that one is looking for employment. Various offers came up but none of them were very palatable to me."[117]

Meanwhile, despite the fact that Du Bois was no longer a government employee, the FBI began another full investigation of her in June 1953 that would not cease until September 1960. Ostensibly they used Executive Order 10422, which prescribed loyalty investigations for United Nations employees, but by 1953 Cora's year with the World Health Organization was long past. What really triggered this new investigation was the arrival at FBI headquarters in Alexandria, Virginia, of a volunteer informant—a former State Department staff person—who reported that "Dr. DuBois [*sic*] had been offered a job at a university in California believed to be at Berkeley. [name blacked out] learned from [name blacked out], a State Department employee, that Dr. DuBois wrote to this university and said that she could not accept the position as she would be unwilling to sign a non-Communist affidavit. [name blacked out] had typed the letter for Dr.

DuBois." Accordingly, FBI agents were directed "to cover the employee's character, reputation, and associates as well as her loyalty. Office indices, credit and criminal, should also be checked concerning her relatives and the results incorporated in your report."[118]

By this time anticommunist hysteria in the United States had reached a peak, and for some the refusal to sign a university anticommunist loyalty oath was deemed a subversive act. Cora's friend Paul Child was also among those who would come under investigation. In April 1955 he received orders to return to Washington DC from France immediately, no reason given. Upon arrival, he learned that he was being investigated by the FBI as a "treasonous homosexual," and he underwent hours of excruciatingly painful interrogation.[119] Cora's words above, in her letter to President Sproul, are all too haunting: *You will surely agree that we cannot scrutinize too carefully every method suggested to safeguard our internal security lest in the process we forge tools that willful men or even well-intentioned but short-sighted ones can use to intimidate their less powerful but equally loyal fellow citizens. Intimidation is an insidious disease.*

The early Cold War period was a troubled one for the United States (both internationally and domestically) and for persons who were politically idealistic and were trying to have an effect on postwar American policies. Regrettably, Cora Du Bois's efforts triggered attacks on her own loyalty and integrity. It is not surprising that she and many other "specialists" would ultimately retreat from government service to academe—to "the Groves," as she liked to put it. But Cora had the courage *not* to return under what she considered tainted circumstances. As a result, at this time, her career was temporarily put on hold.

CHAPTER 8

Harvard, Crown of Roses or Thorns?

At Harvard, Cora Du Bois was a triple outsider.
—James Gibbs

Cora Du Bois had presence, which was commanding and also a bit adventuresome and humorous—a bit of Tallulah Bankhead-like presence but, of course, with academic standards and a firm code of honor.
—James Peacock

In early December 1953, Cora Du Bois received an extraordinary telephone call from Clyde Kluckhohn, a Harvard anthropology professor and one of the founders of the Department of Social Relations. He had heard through the grapevine that she was about to accept a position at Columbia, and he asked her to delay that decision because an offer might be coming from Harvard. Several decades later Cora reported this incident as follows:

> Various [academic] offers came up but none of them were very palatable to me: Minnesota, Columbia, so on. Finally, I decided to accept the Columbia professorship. It was not very nice or attractive and I hated New York [City]. The thought of living either in New York or commuting from outside was intolerable. At that point Clyde Kluckhohn heard that I was being offered Columbia and that I was being considered (which I did not know) for the Zemurray professorship at Harvard. And he said, "Hold on, until we can get in touch with you."

A day or two later [Wilbur Kitchener] Jordan, who was the president of Radcliffe, because this was a Radcliffe [funded] chair, met me in New York and offered me the job. Just like that! So, in twenty-four hours it was settled, whereas Columbia had been diddling around, bargaining, that sort of thing. So, naturally, I accepted it.[1]

In one respect Cora's memory of these events appears to be inaccurate. Before meeting with her, Jordan had sent her a letter, dated December 11, 1953, informing her that she had been nominated for the position. "It gives me great pleasure," Jordan wrote, "to tell you that a committee of the Harvard Faculty has nominated you as one of those who should be considered for the Zemurray Professorship at Harvard and Radcliffe. . . . It would give me the greatest possible pleasure to meet you and to talk with you about an appointment which is, I believe, one of the most distinguished within the gift of the Harvard Faculty."[2] Cora is quite right that, following her nomination, Harvard moved swiftly on her appointment after learning, via Kluckhohn, that she had another offer that she was about to accept. By December 22 Jordan had met with Cora in New York. In a letter dated December 24, McGeorge Bundy, dean of the Faculty of Arts and Sciences at Harvard, informed her that the president and fellows of Harvard had approved her appointment as the Samuel Zemurray Jr. and Doris Zemurray Stone Radcliffe Professor of Anthropology, "to serve *without limit of time* from July 1, 1954, at a salary to be fixed by the President of Radcliffe College."[3] A December 28 letter soon followed from President Jordan informing her of the salary ($11,000 a year) and that her appointment would begin on September 1, 1954. On December 30 Cora responded to Jordan as follows:

Dean Bundy's letter of December 24th was waiting for me on my arrival in Florida [where she was visiting her parents for Christmas]. I replied immediately and affirmatively. Your letter of December 28th reached me today. It was equally welcome. As I told you in New York, the possibility of an appointment at Harvard and Radcliffe is one that I view with enthusiasm and without any of the reservations associated with the other negotiations that were pending. Not the least of the pleasure involved is the cordiality and thoughtfulness that accompany the offer. I am also not insensitive to the honor and obligations entailed.[4]

A remarkable series of events had launched Du Bois into this next stage of life—her return not only to academe but to a prestigious chair at the most elite university in the country, where she would become the first woman ever to hold a full professorship *with tenure* in the School of Arts and Sciences.[5]

The Harvard-Radcliffe Zemurray Professorship

A brief history of the Samuel Zemurray Jr. and Doris Zemurray Stone Radcliffe Professorship at Harvard is requisite to understanding the special circumstances into which Cora was soon to be catapulted. Radcliffe College was founded in 1879 as an informal woman's annex to the all-male Harvard and was, indeed, known for many years as "the Harvard Annex." In 1894, with some degree of controversy, the annex was chartered by the Commonwealth of Massachusetts and named Radcliffe College, with a small set of its original women advocates constituting its administration. One of these advocates, Elizabeth Cary Agassiz, became its first president.[6] Although Radcliffe acquired a small set of administrators dedicated to women's higher education, along with a modest campus, it did not acquire its own faculty. Harvard professors taught Radcliffe classes, with a curriculum that had to be negotiated annually with Harvard's provost. Classrooms were sexually segregated, which meant that designated professors taught a course to men on the Harvard campus and then crossed over to the Radcliffe campus and taught it again. Even after joint instruction began in 1943—a wartime expedient when large numbers of men (faculty and students) had left to participate in World War II—examinations for men and women remained separate. Cora recalled that, in the beginning of her Harvard years, with respect to exams, "I would go to Harvard first, of course, and lay out the exams and get any questions about the exams that came up, and then I would walk over to the Radcliffe campus and do the same thing again for the Radcliffe girls."[7] It was not until 1963 that Radcliffe students, who were studying exclusively with Harvard faculty, began receiving Harvard diplomas that were signed by the presidents of both institutions. And it was in that same year (1962–63) that female graduate students were admitted to the Harvard Graduate School, rather than to Radcliffe, and were allowed to carry Harvard IDs rather than Radcliffe ones.

In September 1964 Nathan Pusey became the first Harvard president to attend Radcliffe's annual opening ceremonies. According to the *Harvard Crimson*, "Pusey spoke about the growth of the University, admitting that the definition of Radcliffe's place within it was still a little hazy to him."[8] That hazy relationship continued into the 1970s, when the two institutions began merging—a gradual process that was not completed until 1999.[9]

In 1943 Doris Zemurray Stone (Radcliffe '30) was serving on the Radcliffe Board of Trustees when her alma mater was able to negotiate an improved contractual relationship with Harvard. Instead of having to negotiate annually each individual course that Harvard would offer to Radcliffe students, "the University agreed formally to carry the responsibility for instruction at Radcliffe. . . . Now, in return for a certain percentage of our tuition, we are assured instruction of the same quality and extent as that given in the University."[10] In a letter explaining these improved arrangements to Samuel Zemurray (Doris's father), Bernice Brown Cronkhite, dean of the Radcliffe Graduate School, broached the possibility that Zemurray might be interested in establishing a professorship—designated for a distinguished *woman* scholar—who would teach both Radcliffe "girls" and Harvard men. "As evidence of this closer bond Harvard has told us that it would look favorably on the appointment of a woman professor. . . . This would be a unique appointment, the first of its kind."[11]

Wilbur Kitchener Jordan, who had assumed the presidency of Radcliffe in the fall of 1943 as the new agreement for temporary joint instruction with Harvard took effect, had decided to test the waters further by suggesting to Harvard's president, James Bryant Conant, the idea of a full professorship for a woman in the Faculty of Arts and Sciences at Harvard.[12] Conant was amenable as long as Radcliffe found the funds to endow such a position. Hence the letter of inquiry to Samuel Zemurray, the wealthy president of the United Fruit Company, after he had first been informally approached by his daughter Doris. The hope was that he would offer to endow this novel Harvard-Radcliffe professorship in memory of his son, Samuel Zemurray Jr., a graduate of the Harvard School of Business who had recently died in wartime action in North Africa, and to honor his daughter, a graduate of Radcliffe. Such a chair would symbolically conjoin the two institutions.

By May 1945 it became clear that Zemurray liked the idea, so Jordan began more serious negotiations with Conant. Two years later, in June 1947, a formal proposal for "The Radcliffe Professorship in the Faculty of Arts and Sciences of Harvard University" had been finalized. It stipulated the name of the professorship and its endowment ($250,000), which would be given to Radcliffe to hold and administer. The incumbent would be a woman scholar of full professorial rank. "Appointments to the professorship, whether visiting or permanent, would be made by Harvard University in accordance with wholly normal procedures governing appointments, with the understanding that Radcliffe may make suggestions through the proper channels and provided the final appointment be concurred in by the Council of Radcliffe College." And finally, the agreement noted, "Since it is understood that the person appointed to the Faculty would be chosen *not because she is a woman but because she is an outstanding authority in the field in question*, it is quite possible that no permanent appointment would be made for several years."[13]

By February 1947 Samuel Zemurray had agreed to all of the above provisions of the new professorship to be named in honor of his deceased son and his daughter, and he had agreed to endow it with a gift of five thousand shares of United Fruit Company stock, worth approximately $250,000 at that time.[14] Harvard and Radcliffe then released information about the new joint professorship, which became a headline—"Harvard Gets Woman Thanks to Radcliffe"—in the March 5, 1947, issue of the *Boston Herald*. History was being made, and soon thereafter a worldwide search for an outstanding woman scholar to join the all-male Harvard faculty was undertaken. Harvard's provost appointed a special committee of distinguished faculty to undertake the search and to make a recommendation. Its membership included representatives from twelve of the departments that constituted the School of Arts and Sciences, such as Bart J. Bok (astronomy), John H. Finley Jr. (classics), Edward S. Mason (economics), Paul J. Sachs (fine arts), Arthur M. Schlesinger (history), and Samuel A. Stouffer (social relations).

This august committee solicited nominations from all relevant Harvard departments, and an interesting variety of women candidates—which included anthropologists Ruth Benedict and Margaret Mead, as well as biologist Barbara McClintock—were considered. The Department of Psychology, however, chose not to nominate anyone, asserting, "There are no 'great women psychologists' say both our women correspondents. . . . Oh, the name of Ruth Benedict keeps coming up in our discussions, but she is an anthropologist."[15] Nonetheless, psychoanalyst Anna Freud became a finalist for the professorship, having been nominated by others than members of the Psychology Department. Cecilia H. Payne-Gaposchkin, a lecturer in astronomy at Harvard, was considered but ruled out because she would have been a within-house candidate. The final candidates for the new Zemurray chair were Helen Maud Cam, lecturer in history, Cambridge University; Anna Freud, training analyst and instructor, London Psychoanalytic Institute; and Joan V. Robinson, lecturer in economics, Cambridge University. It is perhaps noteworthy that none of these finalists was an American.

Helen Maud Cam's name was ultimately the one put forward by the Harvard provost and approved by all relevant parties at Harvard and Radcliffe. She was an eminent medieval historian at Cambridge and someone personally known to President Jordan, a historian of sixteenth- and seventeenth-century Britain. Cam accepted the position, and she made history at Harvard by becoming the first woman to hold a professorship in the Faculty of Arts and Sciences. Cam, who was sixty-three, was given a five-year appointment to inaugurate the new position and "to test the waters."[16] During her stay, Cam began to break down a few gender barriers at Harvard by being the first woman to attend morning services at Harvard's Memorial Church and by entering Lamont Library, an undergraduate library and reading room restricted to men.[17]

During Cam's fifth year at Harvard (1953–54), before she retired to England, the same search process for a second eminent woman scholar was put in place. This time the search committee was chaired by Katharine McBride, president of Bryn Mawr College, and included some of the same Harvard faculty as before. Arthur M. Schlesinger and Samuel A. Stouffer served again with such colleagues as William Y. Elliott (government), George Kistiakowsky (chemistry), and Francis M. Rogers (romance languages and literature). This search produced many more names than the first one, but by November 3, 1953, the committee had narrowed their selection down to six quite diverse women candidates: Cora Du Bois (anthropology, Institute for International Education), Anna Freud (psychoanalysis, London), Margaret Gilman (French, Bryn Mawr),

Susanne Langer (philosophy, Connecticut College), Maria Goeppert Mayer (physics, Chicago), and Virginia Rau (history, University of Lisbon). Du Bois's name was put forward by Stouffer, a leading empirical sociologist in the Department of Social Relations, with the unanimous backing of the other principal social relations faculty—anthropologist Clyde Kluckhohn, psychologists Gordon Allport and Henry Murray, and sociologist Talcott Parsons, all of whom were familiar with Cora's work.[18]

Before putting these six names forward, the committee had collected vitae, examined publications, and done background work on each candidate. For example, Professor Rogers contacted Donald Shank, executive vice president of the Institute of International Education and Du Bois's boss at the time, and reported,

> Donald Shank had only the highest praise for Miss Du Bois. He stated that she was one of the ablest women he had ever met. She is a researcher of the highest type and, from the Institute's point of view, she is particularly valuable inasmuch as she immediately sees the practical application of each problem. The Institute has been most satisfied with her work and Mr. Shank is sending me some samples of it which I shall forward to Professor Stouffer.
>
> Mr. Shank said that Miss Du Bois tends to resist social gatherings. He added that "she should not be wasted on undergraduates." Sam Stouffer and I agreed that these two reservations should be explored further. Sam is checking with contacts he has. I have to attend a meeting of the Institute of International Education Advisory Committee for Graduate students on October 29. Mr. Shank is subtly arranging for me to meet Miss Du Bois at that time.[19]

Meanwhile, President Jordan was doing his own research before personally visiting each candidate. On November 20, 1953, he sent a note to Stouffer, saying, "I have pulled Cora Dubois' [*sic*] books out of the Library and am going to settle down this week-end to do some work. The whole dossier on the lady is most impressive indeed and it seems to me that we must regard her as a very strong candidate."[20] He also contacted his friend Allen W. Dulles, the director of the CIA and a former OSS officer, about Cora. On December 10, 1953, however, Jordan received a telephone message from Stouffer informing him that Du Bois had another strong offer and that he should contact "Mr. Kluckhohn immediately about meeting her, etc."[21] The rest is history, as previously described. Cora Du Bois was offered, and accepted, the first tenured professorship for a woman in the Faculty of Arts and Sciences at Harvard.

In a process that Cora referred to as "the rituals reminiscent of the Mock Turtle and the Griffin dancing on the strand," she had to keep quiet about her new appointment, despite the fact that friends began to hear about it, until everything was finalized with the president and the Board of Fellows at Harvard.[22] Meanwhile, McGeorge Bundy, dean of Harvard, wrote to her recommending that her appointment be as "Professor of Anthropology," the title "we have ordinarily used for all member of your profession, omitting the special designation of 'physical,' 'social,' or 'cultural.'" "As you probably know," Bundy continued, "our anthropologists are to be found in at least three places: the Peabody Museum, the Department of Anthropology, and the Department of Social Relations. All three will be eager to have your company, and the choice will be up to you."[23] Although it was the Department of Social Relations that sponsored Cora's nomination, she was offered affiliations with both academic departments—social relations and anthropology—as well as with the museum, and she chose to affiliate with all three entities. She thus became professor of anthropology in two academic departments and an honorary curator at the Peabody Museum. It was the museum that housed the Department of Anthropology and that would provide Du Bois with her principal faculty office during her tenure at Harvard.

The First Year at Harvard

In May 1954 Cora was given a gala party—"with long skirts and black ties"—by her Washington friends to celebrate her Harvard appointment.[24] Then she and Jeanne Taylor took a cross-country trip to California for a conference. Following that, they backtracked to Boulder, Colorado, where Cora taught a two-week course on friendship in the Department of Psychology at the University of Colorado. Their next stop was Minneapolis–St. Paul to visit Jeanne's family, after which they returned to Washington to pack and move to Cambridge, Massachusetts. As was so often the case in Cora's life, a long voyage demarcated her movement from one stage of her career to another.

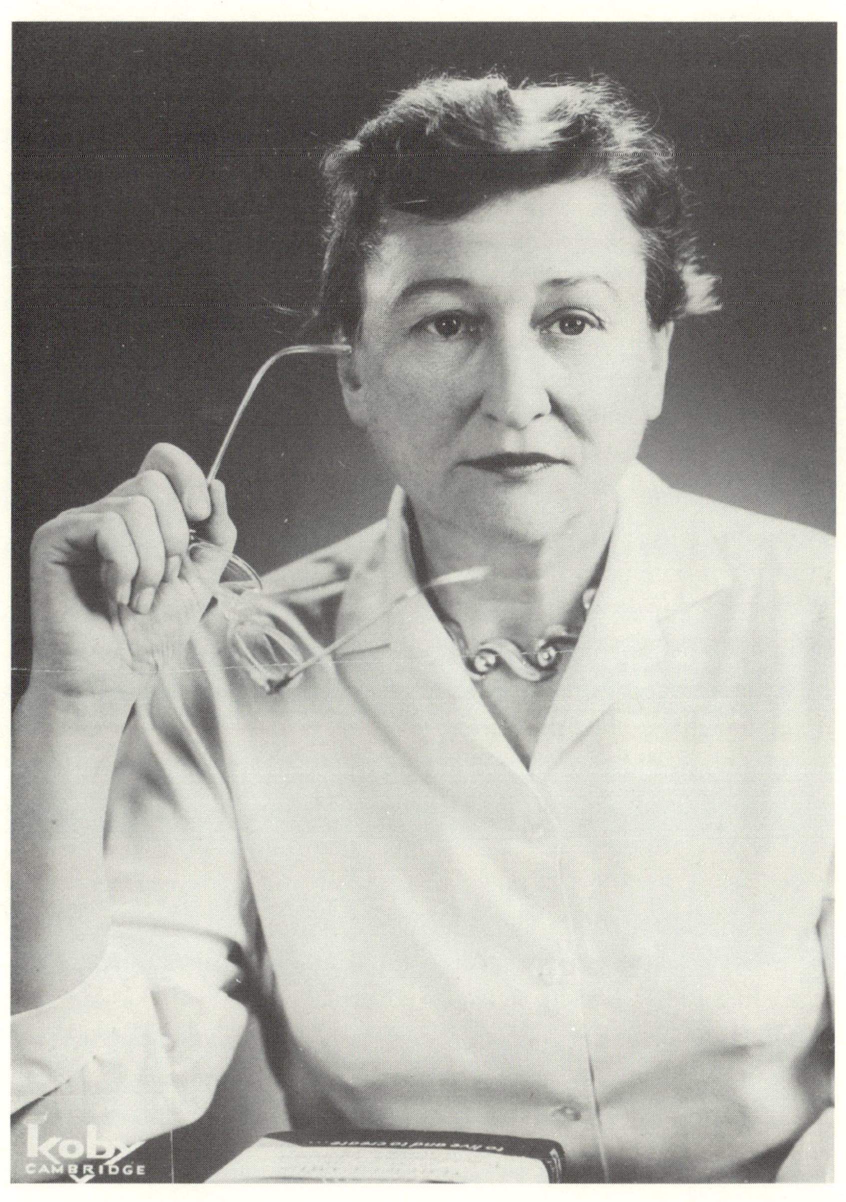

19. Portrait of Cora Du Bois, ca. 1957–58. Cora Alice Du Bois Papers (SPEC.COLL.ETHG. D852c), Tozzer Library, Harvard College Library, Harvard University.

In Cambridge, Cora and Jeanne would reside for the first semester in a house belonging to Clyde and Florence Kluckhohn. The Kluckhohns were spending the year at Stanford University's new Center for Advanced Study in the Behavioral Sciences and had offered their home to their new colleague. Regrettably, however, this meant that one of Cora's principal advocates—a person with many ties throughout the university—was not in residence during her first year to help inaugurate her into this highly patriarchal institution. Cora had taken in stride the sexism that she encountered during the war, but she had not experienced it in the departments of anthropology at Columbia and Berkeley, which were reasonably accustomed to women. And she had held her own as a woman in the State Department. Additionally, her full-time teaching had been at two women's colleges—Hunter and Sara Lawrence. So she was in for a novel experience when she joined this all-male university where, in 1954, she was the only woman professor.

Cora's memory of that first year is that she arrived "flattered and delighted" by the appointment and that she met "in the community, both the formal community and among old friends, the warmest kinds of relationships. And I think there was general curiosity about this new appointment, and I was invited out quite beyond my capacity to receive and profit from all of these kind invitations."[25] Cora did not feel marginalized at the start, despite student perceptions to the contrary.[26] She had, of course, been enthusiastically endorsed by members of the Department of Social Relations, but the faculty in that department—known as "Soc Rel"—were scattered all over campus and could not provide an intellectual home for her. Established in 1946, Soc Rel personified "the ebullient self-confidence of the postwar social sciences," bringing together the fields of sociology, psychology, and sociocultural anthropology, including Henry Murray's Center for Research in Personality, with which Cora had been affiliated as a National Research Council fellow in 1935.[27] But it would not be until 1965 that the imposing William James Hall was built to house this interdisciplinary department, at which time Cora was provided with a second office there. Unfortunately, her original advocates—Clyde Kluckhohn and Samuel Stouffer—had both died untimely deaths in 1960 and did not live to see this new stage of their interdisciplinary department.

The Peabody Museum of American Archaeology and Ethnology, which had been built in 1866, housed the Department of Anthropology. Through a gift from George Peabody, a wealthy banker and philanthropist, anthropology became the first of the social sciences to receive institutional support at Harvard. The museum is a large brick building that accommodates faculty and administrative offices, laboratories, classrooms, a library, and numerous storage rooms among its dramatic displays of archaeological and ethnological artifacts. The museum was where Cora's office was located, and thus it became her principal intellectual home. To get to Cora's office, in those days, required walking through a labyrinth of archaeological displays and winding one's way up to the fourth floor, where her large office was located at the back of the building. It was conveniently located near a medium-sized classroom that she frequently used for teaching, but otherwise it was quite isolated from other faculty offices. In order to smoke, Cora had to descend to the basement of the museum, where there was a "smoking room" that had been created in 1931 and that was the only space in the museum that allowed smoking. Furnished with comfortable leather-upholstered chairs, the smoking room contributed to the "male club" ambiance of the museum culture and, undoubtedly, was a space that Cora helped to integrate.

Cora Du Bois's arrival marked a dramatic change in what had essentially been a male club for nearly one hundred years.[28] Recalling this period many years later, she said, "Hooten may have been the man in the department least enthralled by the notion of having a full tenured professor on the staff who was a woman." (Earnest Hooten, an eminent physical anthropologist at Harvard, had died just months before Cora's arrival.) "But the others showed absolutely no discrimination or sense that this was no place for a woman."[29] What Cora had not yet had time to recognize were the subtle, and not-so-subtle, techniques that some anthropology faculty used to keep women at bay. For example, by putting all the required readings for a course in Lamont Library, which could be entered only by male students, some faculty effectively prevented female students from taking certain courses. When one Radcliffe undergraduate told her honors anthropology professor, Douglas Oliver, that she could not read one of the books he had assigned because it was available only in Lamont, Oliver retorted, "You mean we still have an area of sanctity left!"[30]

During her State Department years, Cora had done some teaching—a summer course at UC Berkeley, lectures for psychiatrists at the William Alanson White Foundation, and numerous lectures for the School of Foreign Service and the Institute for International Education. In fact, it was in lectures for the latter two institutions that she used the term "culture shock," which then became—erroneously, she said—attached to her name.[31] But Cora found the return to full-time teaching, after a dozen years away from academe, somewhat daunting. "I had to work like a dog," she reported in later years. "Both the Department of Anthropology and the Department of Social Relations offered me a roost in which to perch, and I divided my time, at their request, between teaching an undergraduate full course [in anthropology] and taking advisees, and teaching a seminar at Social Relations, also with advisees, theses and things of that sort coming my way. . . . I really didn't know what a load it could be, in that the courses are almost the minor part of the enterprise. It's all the other demands that are made on your time."[32]

During that first year Cora offered three courses: a course on India (Significant Aspects of Indian Social Organization) in the Department of Anthropology that was open to both undergraduate and graduate students; a yearlong graduate seminar on friendship in the Department of Social Relations; and the second half of the yearlong course Introduction to Anthropology: Ethnology and Social Anthropology, which was normally taught by Clyde Kluckhohn. So she had her hands full. It is noteworthy that she did not offer a course in psychological anthropology—the subfield in which *The People of Alor* had made her famous—but that she did offer a regional course on India and would offer a two-semester course on Southeast Asia the subsequent year. During her years with the OSS and the State Department, Cora's interests had shifted dramatically. The topic of friendship, however, had been an interest in her youth, an interest that was renewed during her employment at the Institute of International Education, where the subject of international and cross-cultural friendships had become a subject of discussion.[33] It was a topic that fit well into the interdisciplinary program of Soc Rel and would lead to major research projects for some of her first graduate students who were enrolled in the course.[34]

Introduction to Anthropology was the most challenging of the courses for Du Bois that first year. It was here that she faced an auditorium full of some three hundred to four hundred, mostly male, undergraduate students who had never before been lectured to by a woman. "I was appalled [by the numbers]," she would report later.[35] In fact, the students were accustomed to Kluckhohn, who, in an engaging manner, would stride back and forth before them in his cowboy boots. Cora, a somewhat austere and daunting woman who dressed in tailored suits, must have offered a strikingly different experience for these male undergraduates. Karl Heider (later the Carolina Distinguished Professor Emeritus of Anthropology, University of South Carolina) was enrolled in that course as an undergraduate and reported, "There were very high expectations from students for this new Zemurray woman professor, and many were disappointed."[36] (Heider, however, later became a fan and an advisee of Du Bois.) James Siegel (now professor emeritus of Anthropology and Asian Studies, Cornell University) was also enrolled in the course. He remembered little of Cora's lectures, which he blamed on his general lack of preparation for Harvard. However, he had a distinct memory of the remark that Cora wrote on the cover of his first midterm. "One of the questions," he reported, "was 'identify x book,' one she had assigned. I had read it, but I took her question literally, not having any idea of what was called for, and said, 'It has a yellow cover.' I am sure I answered the [other] questions with equal astuteness. She wrote [with her wry humor], 'This is superbly garbled.' She was right of course. I was grateful for the adjective."[37]

Two of Cora's graduate student teaching assistants in that course have their own distinct memories of it. James Lowell Gibbs Jr. (now the Martin Luther King Jr. Centennial Professor Emeritus of Anthropology at Stanford) was the head teaching fellow that semester and "thought Cora was superb, if a bit formal." He kept his lecture notes from that course for many years as a model for his own teaching. "Each lecture was exquisite," Gibbs said, adding that Cora's vocabulary was so extensive that he had to keep a separate sheet of new words in addition to his lecture notes. He also mentioned that Cora would write on the board, before class began, all the new anthropological terms that she would be introducing, along with her principal source material. She also integrated an excellent set of ethnographic films into the course. "The course became a model for my own teaching of Introduction to Anthropology [for which Gibbs won a teaching award at Stanford]," he said. "Being a woman, however, was part of the situation," Gibbs added.[38]

Laura Nader (now professor of anthropology at UC Berkeley) was also a teaching fellow for Cora that same semester and concurred with Gibbs about the quality of the course. She reported that the students were difficult. "Cora was the first woman to teach a big course in anthropology at Harvard. The students were expecting a 'flashy guy.' They were not ready to receive her, and Cora was aware of it. Once the students booed her, and Cora retorted, 'What's the matter? You can't take it!' The male students were hostile," Nader asserted.[39]

Cora, however, was critical of her own performance in the course and insisted on teaching it again the subsequent year. As she explained in a letter to Robert Lowie, "It is an excellent review for me and I am furious at not having done better with it this semester. Am going to keep with the darned thing until I feel I have it licked."[40]

Being a First Woman

Cora had, indeed, walked into a somewhat hostile environment, which is reflected in some of the gossip and joking that some former students remember from that period. There were jokes, such as, "It was better to have Du Bois, who only chews carpet tacks for breakfast, than Mead, who chews railroad spikes." The reference here, of course, is to Margaret Mead, another formidable woman anthropologist. The joke, however, used a piranha-type metaphor that suggested women were dangerous. More benignly, some male former anthropology students remembered Cora as much larger than she really was—five feet ten inches or more—with broad shoulders and a deep voice. While she did have a deep voice, which accompanied her upright posture and generally commanding presence, she was only about five feet six inches tall and did not have unusually broad shoulders. (Perhaps it was the tailored suits to which they were responding.) Sam Smith, a journalist who was a Harvard undergraduate during Cora's early years, has written about his days in "the dusty, dim recesses of the Peabody Museum" and of Cora Du Bois striding "into class in a trench coat as if just off a flying boat from the Pacific."[41] Clearly Cora's presence had added a colorful, if unsettling to some, new dimension to life in the Peabody Museum.

Another piece of gossip that some former students mentioned was that Du Bois had been foisted on the all-male anthropology faculty through the machinations of Doris Zemurray Stone. As a Radcliffe undergraduate, she had majored in anthropology, and in adult life she had taken up archaeology in Costa Rica, where she lived with her husband and children. Over the years she had periodic research affiliations with both Tulane's Middle American Research Institute and Harvard's Peabody Museum. There is, however, no evidence in the considerable documentation of the establishment of the chair and the selection process that Zemurray Stone had any voice in the matter. And Cora seems never to have met her. Such gossip was a signal that change was afoot—change that made some of the faculty and students uncomfortable. Regrettably, during Cora's first year, Kluckhohn was not present to help dispel such rumors.

In reference to Cora's experience that first year, Laura Nader—who, given Cora's resignation, became the first woman professor in the Department of Anthropology at UC Berkeley—said, "A first woman is never forgiven."[42] Nader, however, went directly to Berkeley from graduate school and entered the department as a young, not-yet-well-established woman anthropologist. By contrast, had Cora gone to Berkeley, she would have arrived as a senior member of the faculty, someone who had specifically been recruited to replace the eminent Robert Lowie, her graduate adviser and mentor. She would have known and been known by all the players and would *not* have been (as she was at Harvard) the lone woman on the entire UC Berkeley faculty. There were others—enough so that Berkeley had a Women's Faculty Club. By contrast, when Cora arrived at Harvard, the all-male Faculty Club required that she enter through a side door and take her meals in a separate dining room, thus preserving the all-male ambience of the main dining room. Cora, in time, would integrate the main dining room, becoming the first woman to eat there and thereby helping to break down some of the barriers to women at the university.[43]

Cora was not only "a first woman" in the Departments of Anthropology and Social Relations at Harvard, but a woman who had been recruited for a special professorship designated for a woman—potentially a double whammy. As James Gibbs noted, Cora was triply an outsider at Harvard:

she was a woman and a lesbian, and she had arrived after spending the past dozen years outside of the academy.[44] As the first African American graduate student in anthropology at Harvard, Gibbs could identify with being in the position of "an outsider."

Public vs. Private Life

Harvard and Radcliffe celebrated Du Bois's arrival by publicizing her appointment and by having two of her books republished by Harvard University Press. Both *Social Forces in Southeast Asia* (1959) and *The People of Alor* (1960) were brought out in new editions and with new prefaces. Writing the preface to the latter volume must have been painful for Cora. It was here that she communicated in print what she learned had happened to some of her Atimelang villagers during World War II. The Japanese had garrisoned the island of Alor and had sent troops crisscrossing it. In Atimelang they used Cora's former house, which the villagers had named "Hamerika," as a patrol station. In Cora's words,

> Word reached the Japanese command in Kalabahi that the village leaders of Atimelang were claiming that Hamerica would win the war. This could have been nothing but the most innocent fantasy to my friends in Atimelang since they had never even heard of the United States prior to my arrival. But to the Japanese, suffering from all the nervous apprehensions of any occupying power in a strange and therefore threatening environment, such talk could mean rebellion. . . . So the Japanese sent troops to arrest five of my friends in Atimelang. . . . In Kalabahi they were publicly decapitated as a warning to the populace.
>
> There is no end to the intricate chain of responsibility and guilt that the pursuit of even the most arcane social research involves. "No man is an island."[45]

The republication of these books not only helped to publicize Du Bois's appointment at Harvard, it also gave her the opportunity to acknowledge the unforeseen consequences of anthropological fieldwork.

Du Bois's formal responsibilities to Harvard were reasonably clear—she was a teacher, adviser, researcher, and departmental committee member. However, she found the less formal structure of Harvard somewhat puzzling. To Lowie, she wrote,

In general I am slowly acclimatizing not only to Cambridge and Harvard—but to academic life. As an administrative structure, the freedom and old-fashioned liberalism of Harvard entrances while it bewilders. The formality of Cambridge life is tolerable because there are so many breaches in its dikes and because of its traditional tolerance for eccentricity. . . . Talcott Parsons tells me that in about 10 years one catches on to the covert structure of Harvard. Others tell me that one is puzzled by Cambridge the first year, dislikes it heartily the second, and would never part with it the third. I await these developments with such patience as my impetuous nature permits.[46]

Du Bois's responsibilities to Radcliffe were less clear. Her close friends would tease her, calling her "Ropy" (Radcliffe's Only Professor).[47] By the end of her first year, President Jordan tried to engage her in committee work at Radcliffe by asking her to accept an appointment to the Scholarship Committee for a three-year term.[48] Cora politely declined, explaining that she would find it difficult to meet "both the Radcliffe and the two [Harvard] departmental requirements next year," in which she was expected "to assist with both graduate and undergraduate examinations, written and oral; theses and honors papers; admissions and fellowships." However, she acknowledged that she had "a keen interest in, and responsibility to, Radcliffe" and would accept his and Dean Kerby-Miller's advice about her future responsibilities.[49] Subsequently, in 1956, she would accept a six-year term on Radcliffe's Administrative Board, saying, "Unlike most honors, it is sure to be instructive and I feel the need of learning more about the college with which I am affiliated."[50]

During her first semester, however, President Jordan took advantage of Du Bois's writing skills and requested that she draft a citation for Dr. Martha Eliot (Radcliffe '13), a former physician in Yale's Department of Pediatrics who was to be honored by the college for its seventy-fifth anniversary. Cora produced a draft document that Jordan thanked her for, saying, "I am finding it awfully easy to plagiarize what you have said but I am finding it extremely difficult to compress it into the required length. It is just too good."[51] Jordan seemed pleased with the selection of Du Bois for the Zemurray-Stone Professorship and in a letter to Seymour E. Harris, a professor of economics at Harvard who had requested information about her, he forwarded Cora's curriculum vitae, along with the remark, "May I add that I think she is quite a girl?"[52] Relations with Jordan were clearly very cordial. "Courteous" is the word Cora used in recounting these experiences years later. She remembered having to attend "dress-up luncheons with deans—all very polite and prettily dressed in hats and white gloves—but I never could really grasp what it was about, except that Radcliffe seemed to be a boarding school. . . . [And these events] had no, in my terms, professional functions."[53]

In the fall of 1954, when she began teaching at Harvard, Cora was about to turn fifty-one. The Zemurray-Stone Professorship would be the capstone to her unusual and remarkable career, but as already indicated, it came with certain strains. One of these was being a woman and a lesbian in an era in which the latter could not be publicly revealed. Close Harvard friends, such as the Kluckhohns and John and Beatrice Whiting—friends from her Yale days, when they were graduate students and she a postdoctoral fellow—knew and welcomed both Cora and Jeanne to Cambridge.[54] But for much of her tenure at Harvard and Radcliffe, Cora had to keep her personal life private. Furthermore, she knew that the FBI was still investigating her.

Teacher and Mentor

While a small handful of other Harvard anthropologists would become her good friends, Cora quickly surmised that the Department of Anthropology was largely "an aggregate of isolates."[55] The Peabody Museum, as already noted, did not lend itself to easy collegiality; it was not the Tin Bin that Cora had so relished during her graduate student days at Berkeley. This was a convenience in that social obligations were minimized, but it also left an intellectual vacuum. To the benefit of students, Cora filled this vacuum by nurturing—in her exacting and, at times, formidable manner—many who came her way. And during her first year, several remarkable ones did come her way.

James Gibbs and Laura Nader have already been mentioned in the context of the big introductory course for which they were teaching assistants. Both studied with Cora as well. Gibbs was enrolled in her course on friendship, for which he produced a publishable paper. He characterized Cora as "quite a mentor"—someone who treated her teaching fellows and graduate students as junior colleagues. "It was characteristic of her to be sensitive to our status," he recalled. "And she was the only faculty member to invite graduate students to her home—a warm inviting house," where he met Jeanne Taylor and where "Cora fixed a powerful martini." Gibbs also touched on a recurring theme—Cora's attentiveness to students' writing—but he felt that her mentoring went well beyond teaching information and attention to writing. "She looked at me as an individual" and tried to give advice. Cora once said, in her authoritative voice, "James Gibbs, you need to develop more tolerance for ambiguity." And on another occasion she told him, "There's more to life than anthropology." "I thought about Cora and that remark when I had prostate cancer in the 1990s," Gibbs added.[56]

Laura Nader took a reading course with Cora. She reported that when they would meet to discuss a set of readings, Cora would say, "Now, teach me what you learned." This was one of Cora's pedagogical techniques—turn the student into a teacher. Nader considered Du Bois to be generally self-effacing and self-critical, as well as particularly insightful about people. After returning from her dissertation fieldwork in Mexico, Nader bumped into Du Bois one day in the halls of the Peabody Museum, and Cora immediately said, "Let me take you to lunch." Over lunch, Cora interrogated Nader about her research and gave her advice about return culture shock. "Cora had a kind of detachment," Nader added, "yet she was also very understanding and insightful."[57]

Clifford and Hildred Geertz, who had just returned from doing fieldwork in Indonesia during Cora's first year at Harvard, came under her tutelage as they wrote their dissertations. With her expertise on Southeast Asia, Cora was a natural to be put on their dissertation committees even though she had not been at Harvard to help direct their fieldwork. They had both been part of a joint Harvard-MIT research project to study postwar change in Indonesia, specifically in a town in central Java known as "Modjokuto." Clifford Geertz's book *The Religion of Java* (1960), based on his dissertation, would become a classic in cultural anthropology and would launch him on a highly acclaimed career as one of the preeminent anthropologists of the second half of the twentieth century. Cora immediately recognized his brilliance but nonetheless tried to get him to write more concisely. (He wrote a 574-page dissertation.) According to Hildred

Geertz, Cora told Clifford that his thesis was way too long and that he must cut it down. Robert Jay (now professor emeritus of anthropology at Brown University and a fellow researcher on the Java project) reported that Clifford was not pleased with Cora's many editorial comments on his thesis and complained that he would never finish it if he had to keep revising, so she let it go.[58] "In the end, remarkably, Cora read it as it was, without [further] revisions."[59] And Cora became one of Clifford Geertz's champions with respect to procuring jobs and getting fellowships. In fact, at her recommendation, he would be invited to spend the 1958–59 year with Du Bois and other eminent anthropologists at Stanford's Center for Advanced Study in the Behavioral Sciences.

For the remainder of her life, Cora and Clifford Geertz would have a warm correspondence, and Geertz would send Cora a copy of each of his books with a personal inscription. For example, he sent her a copy of *Islam Observed* (1968) with a personal note, written while he was in Morocco, saying, "In case you were wondering what I'm up to these days, I offer this book. By now I don't think it should be necessary to tell you either the respect I have for you or the gratitude I feel toward you. I only wish we saw each other more often."[60] Cora responded, writing, "*Islam Observed* and the very kind note that accompanied it have warmed an aging heart not much given these days to warmth. As always I am delighted and enlightened by your insights that are ranging, humane and persuasive. I am equally captivated by the felicity of your writing."[61]

Du Bois, who had also served on Hildred Geertz's dissertation committee, would hear occasionally from her as well. For example, in 1974 Hildred wrote from Princeton, inquiring about prospective candidates for a position they had there. And she used the occasion to thank Cora for being an important role model. "I am constantly living up to the one you set for me," Geertz wrote. "It is challenging."[62] For some women graduate students, Cora provided a critical role model in an otherwise all-male university.

From the fall of 1954 into the early 1970s—even after her retirement from Harvard—Cora would mentor a large and diverse group of students.[63] (The voices of those who worked with her on her twelve-year project in Bhubaneswar, Odisha, India, will be reserved for the next chapter.) These former students invariably identified a similar set of characteristics that, for them, made Du Bois stand out at Harvard: She had presence; she was powerful, forceful, and strong—even formidable and intimidating to some—but also warm and nurturing; she was dignified and principled, straightforward, an acute observer and omnivorous learner, and a private person who opened her door to students, which is when they could observe her zest for living, her wit, and her sense of humor. As James Peacock (now the Kenan Distinguished Professor of Anthropology at the University of North Carolina) put it so evocatively, "Cora Du Bois had *presence*, which was commanding and also a bit adventuresome and humorous—a bit of Tallulah Bankhead–like presence but, of course, with academic standards and a firm code of honor."[64]

For a number of anthropology and social relations graduate students, Du Bois became a kind of guardian angel—the term that J. David Sapir (now professor emeritus of anthropology at the University of Virginia) used when describing how she took him on as an advisee when he could find no one else to oversee a linguistically oriented PhD dissertation.[65] Sapir's thesis was on West African languages, folklore, and culture, with a focus on the grammar of the Kujamaat Jóola of southern Senegal. This was not an area of expertise for Cora, but she frequently supported students with no clear academic sponsor—students whose interests did not fit the specific research interests of other faculty. Besides, she had known David as a small boy when his father, Edward Sapir, had supervised her National Research Council fellowship.

As Karl Heider, who became one of Cora's graduate student advisees and great fans, expressed it, "Cora took under her wing people who didn't fit." Heider had begun specializing in archaeology at Harvard but then shifted to material culture in New Guinea and was invited to be the ethnographer (*The Dugum Dani*, 1970) for Robert Gardener's acclaimed film project there, *Dead Birds*. Heider, too, was a graduate student without a clear academic sponsor and adviser. He had worked some with Kluckhohn, but Kluckhohn had died unexpectedly. Cora, Heider said, was like Kluckhohn in that she was generous in supervising students who did not fit the research agendas of other faculty. "Some of us were refugees," Heider and James Peacock both reported, and Cora, also somewhat an outsider at Harvard, came to their rescue.[66]

James Peacock's first advisor was William Caudill (a psychologist in the

Department of Social Relations and at the Harvard Medical School), but Caudill also died unexpectedly. When Peacock decided that he wanted to do his dissertation fieldwork in Indonesia, there was no one with whom to work. Du Bois's interests had shifted to India, and she had left for a year to explore research possibilities there. So Peacock undertook the study of Indonesia—its language and culture—on his own and then prepared a research proposal that Cora read and accepted when she returned from India. Following Peacock's sojourn in Indonesia, Du Bois invited him to give a guest lecture to her Peoples and Cultures of Southeast Asia course, which helped him to sort through his myriad field notes and begin to draft a thesis that she read carefully and commented on meticulously. The thesis became another important publication on postwar change in Indonesia, *Rites of Modernization: Symbolic and Social Aspects of Indonesian Proletarian Drama* (1968). As with Clifford Geertz, Cora admired Peacock's work and recommended him for an appointment at Princeton, saying in her letter of recommendation, in a wry fashion, "It would be, for James, a solid Tory experience." Later, when Peacock left Princeton for the University of North Carolina, Cora pithily noted, "You are crossing the Rubicon!"[67] Peacock appreciated the humorous side that underlay Cora Du Bois's commanding presence.

Jean Briggs (now professor emerita of anthropology, Memorial University, Newfoundland, and renowned for her book *Never in Anger* [1970]) was another such refugee, only her relationship with Du Bois was filled with a variety of hurdles that I will present in some length to give the full flavor of what it was like for some students to work with the, at times, irascible Cora Du Bois.

The relationship began when Briggs, at the recommendation of a fellow student, audited Cora's course on India. In the first lecture, Cora informed the students that her expertise on India was limited. "I am not a universal genius," she announced to the class. Briggs, who was deeply ambivalent about higher education, liked Du Bois's self-presentation, and so she approached Cora one day about doing a reading course in psychological anthropology with her. Cora's response was, "Can I buy you off with a bibliography?" Briggs said, "No." So Cora took Briggs to her office and questioned her about her academic experience—the research she had done with Kluckhohn, Alex Inkeles (professor of sociology in the Department of Social Relations), and others—and decreed that it was "a very rich background." Cora then gave Briggs an exercise to do, and Briggs's work passed muster. Next Cora gave her a research question—"Did Navajo childrearing follow Erik Erikson's paradigm?" After doing a lot of reading, Briggs phoned Cora to say that she could not answer the question. According to Briggs, Cora hung up on her and terminated the reading course.

Jean Briggs did not approach Du Bois again until it was time for her to do her dissertation fieldwork. She wanted to work in the Arctic with a remote group of Eskimos (today known as the Inuit), and there were no faculty in anthropology or social relations with that area specialty or research interest. Most of them, according to Briggs, were collecting disciples for their own projects, so in a state of nervousness, she phoned Cora. After Briggs made her request, there was a long silence, followed by Cora's dry voice saying, "Is it my name you want to use?" Briggs responded, "No. I want you." Du Bois took her on reluctantly. Briggs then sent Cora her first-year qualifying paper to read, which Cora "did not think much of." Jean's face must have shown disappointment because Cora's response was, "I knew you were intelligent, but I didn't expect you to be temperamental!"

The complex interpersonal relationship went on from there. Du Bois chaired Briggs's predoctoral oral examination and helped her get through that ordeal, but she was seriously concerned about sending a graduate student off to an Eskimo community where she could be a burden to people. "Cora gave me a stiff drink before telling me that I had no right to go—that there could be unanticipated negative effects, that I would be a burden to them for food, etc." Finally, Briggs and Du Bois reached an agreement: Briggs promised to leave if there were any kind of problem. "Neither of us realized that I could not get out once I was there," Briggs reported. As it turned out, the Eskimo families with whom Briggs lived competed for her because of the resources she brought with her, such as kerosene, and because she provided comic relief in an otherwise harsh environment.

During the early months of her fieldwork with Utku Eskimos in Chantrey Inlet on the northern rim of the American continent—"the most remote group of Eskimos that I could find on the map of the Canadian Arctic"—Briggs wrote a twelve-page letter to Du Bois, saying that she was totally confused by everything she was seeing and experiencing.[68] She had to wait six months for Du Bois's reply to reach her, but it was a reassuring letter in Cora's authoritative voice. "The fact that you are confused means that you are a good anthropologist," Cora wrote. "You can oversimplify when you come back, if necessary." This, Briggs reported, gave her the heart to continue her arduous fieldwork.

Upon her return to Harvard, Briggs presented Du Bois with a traditional thesis outline. Du Bois invited her home for a drink and a critique. "This looks very pedestrian," she announced. "Can you write flowingly?" (Cora asked this knowing that Briggs could speak evocatively about her life among the Eskimos.) "Just tell five anecdotes and string them together," Du Bois continued. "Of course, we'll have to pack the dissertation committee!" Briggs had a difficult time getting started on such a seemingly informal dissertation. "I couldn't take the first step alone into the void," she said. Once again, she telephoned Du Bois, who, after a long pause, said, "I guess I'll have to see you. Come on Thursday and try to be as cogent as possible."

To make a long story short, Briggs wrote an engaging, insightful, and nontraditional thesis in which she explored intimate interpersonal relationships and emotions among a small group of Eskimo families. It was a groundbreaking piece of work. There continued to be more painful moments along the way with Du Bois, such as when Briggs mentioned to her that she was having trouble with chapter 3. Cora's irritated response was, "You don't need a thesis adviser. You need a psychiatric social worker!" Understandably, Briggs was shaken by this remark. Ten years later, when their relationship had become one of friendship rather than student–thesis advisor, Cora alluded to that moment. "Out of the blue," Briggs reported, "Cora said, 'I hurt your feelings badly once, and I could have bitten my tongue off.'" With respect to Briggs's thesis, Du Bois was so impressed that she was instrumental in getting it published by Harvard University Press, and when the press tried to change the title, Cora supported the one that Briggs had given the book, *Never in Anger: Portrait of An Eskimo Family*. "Cora made my career," Briggs concluded.[69]

Cora Du Bois's relationship with Jean Briggs was not unique. Her teaching, advising, and mentoring often combined some degree of harshness and exactitude with nurturance and support. It was the "tough love" that she had experienced in childhood with her own mother, combined with her own high standards for clear thinking and graceful prose. There was more going on by way of complicating factors in Cora's life, however. Briggs's solicitation of Du Bois's help as a dissertation advisor came just when Cora was herself deeply immersed in research in India and was working with a significant number of other graduate students on that project. Cora was also completing her first decade at Harvard, was turning sixty, and was quite depressed—as evidenced by this self-portrait: "She was really quite a mean old bitch; although to the charitable and casual observer she often appeared only sad, severe, pre-occupied or maybe not very well—despite a vigorous and overfleshed body. At 60 she was still able, when she deemed the occasion demanded it, to turn on her old vivacity and the simulacrum of that former almost innocent and pure spontaneity. What had been a real reserve of charm was now a rather blunted instrument. The inner rot was clearer to herself, she thought and hoped, than it was to others."[70] This brutally critical self-portrait makes it clear that Cora Du Bois was not having an easy time at Harvard.

Private Life

Returning to Cora's first year in Cambridge, she and Jeanne Taylor began their private lives at the Kluckhohn house at 50 Fresh Pond Parkway, a nice residential area in the northwest section of town. To Robert Lowie, Cora wrote that she was "physically unprepared for the fact that Cambridge is really a vast industrial slum in which the residential enclaves are so small, so tight, and so ingrown."[71] But they settled in, and Cora concentrated on her teaching and myriad other responsibilities at Harvard and Radcliffe. In a September letter home, she described working at the Peabody Museum for most of a Saturday. "It is always tomb like, but on a Saturday a pin can be heard to drop two stories and six sections away. Furthermore it is all locked up."[72] But Cora and Jeanne soon began to have a stream of visitors—Jeanne's mother (who would come annually for a week or two), a niece and nephew of Jeanne's from Minnesota, OSS and Washington DC friends (including Julia and Paul Child), and new Cambridge friends. And, as already mentioned, Cora had begun to invite her teaching assistants and other graduate students to the house.

In a letter to her parents during these early years in Cambridge, Cora reflected on the irony in this very busy stage of her life:

One of the very odd aspects of our society is that the more competent (presumably) one becomes to do what one was trained to do (i.e., think and do research)—the less opportunity one has. One becomes a senior administrator (in government) or a senior professor (in universities). There seems to be no way of avoiding social responsibilities that are essentially irrelevant to one's trained capacities. And while that whole process goes on, there also accumulates a whole lifetime of human relationships—so that friends and colleagues are more numerous and make, therefore, an ever increasing load of human demands. It is awfully odd to be the kind of person I am at my age grade. Just when your life forces are diminishing, the demands on them reach a peak.[73]

At fifty, Cora had begun to experience eyesight problems but resisted wearing bifocals. "Why," she wrote in a letter to her parents, "this solitary symptom of physical vanity should plague me, only Freud knows." And, she added, menopause "continues troublesome," with periods of depression.[74] By her late fifties, Cora had partially capitulated to bifocals. She would bring two sets of glasses to the classroom—her preferred reading half glasses, which she could peer over to see her students while glancing at her lecture notes, and a pair of the less desirable bifocals. Cora's office was large enough to accommodate a chaise longue, which startled some students but which gave her a place to stretch out for short periods during her long days at work.

For Cora, life that first year at Harvard was extremely strenuous. However, in her private life she shared tasks with Jeanne, who was the one with a car and who did the grocery shopping and other such errands. (Cora, for whom parking at Harvard was a major inconvenience, gave up driving and used taxis and buses to get back and forth to work.) Cora, however, liked to do the cooking and to be in charge of meals, while Jeanne oversaw other household chores, such as hiring and overseeing housekeepers. Working in their garden was an activity that they both enjoyed and shared. Once they were established in Cambridge, Jeanne returned to painting, graphic design, and writing and illustrating children's books. She had already published a delightful book, *Child's Book of Carpentry* (1948), which introduced young girls and boys to different kinds of tools, showing them how to use specific tools to make footstools, chests, picture frames, and a chair.[75] Jeanne also attended art and literary events that Cora did not have time for, and she began to make a set of friends independent of Cora. One such friend was the poet and novelist May Sarton, who would become a celebrity during the women's movement of the 1970s and 1980s.

But the year was punctuated by a tragic event that required the Kluckhohns to return home sooner than expected and forced Cora and Jeanne to find another house to rent.[76] This move triggered Cora to begin looking for a house to buy, which would require selling her Georgetown home as well as clearing up her brother Claude's estate—the money that had been allocated to him in her father's will. (She would need all of these resources to begin to afford a down payment on a house in Cambridge, where faculty housing was limited and expensive.) Claude had long ago disappeared, but Cora hired detectives and made a final, unsuccessful effort to find him.[77] Cora also worked with a lawyer and became the "legal administratrix" of Claude's estate—worth some $10,000—under jurisdiction of the New Jersey Surrogate Court. "Should Claude or an established heir—closer than mother or sister—ever appear, I am both legally (and certainly morally) obligated," she wrote to her parents, "to restitute the inheritance plus interest from the time I assumed administrative responsibility."[78] In the spring of 1957 Cora and Jeanne found the perfect house—20 Coolidge Hill Road—located in a small residential area on the western edge of Cambridge and adjacent to the Mount Auburn cemetery, which would provide an expansive, park-like area in which to take walks. And it was easily accessible to Harvard Square by bus.

After laying out the financial side of the purchase in a letter to her parents, Cora described the house that would become her home for the remainder of her life. "It is a brick house (saves hideous painting costs), it has a largish, but manageable, and very private garden and terrace. It has a large living-dining room with fire place, a modern kitchen, a dry basement, 3 bedrooms [on the second floor], a studio for Jeanne on the third floor, a study for me and a small "maid's room" annex with bath and private entrance. . . . It is *really* very nice—and in a part of Cambridge that is safe from commercialization and whose value can only rise in my life time."[79]

Meanwhile, Cora was still financially involved with some of her Du Bois relatives in Europe. In the 1940s she had accepted as a godson the only son of her cousin Henri Du Bois and the grandson of her uncle Philippe, the brother who had enticed her father to South Africa as a young man. Cora set up a savings account for her godson, Gerald, that she planned to give him when he turned eighteen. Meanwhile, her aunt Wally—the one with whom she had stayed in Frankfurt after graduating from high school—sent Cora a letter about the Henri Du Bois's "precarious financial position," asking her to help with Gerald's education. As Cora reported to her parents,

> Fortunately I have a $1,500 savings account in New York that I have built up for Gerald—so I have written Wally saying I would send that as soon as she wished—but that it should be devoted to Gerald's education. It should see him through the Gymnasium in Geneva (another year and a half, I believe). Thereafter we shall see. Although I recognize that Gerald is only 16, the letters we have exchanged indicate that he is no more of a world-buster than his father, uncle, cousin or grandfather. I do not feel it is fair to prejudge, but he may well be a chip off that not very admirable Philippe Du Bois block. As mother knows as well as I, the Georges Du Bois branch of the family has helped carry the Philippe Du Bois branch for just about 70 years. Aunt Wally is, of course, a Trojan—just as Uncle Georges was. But the family fortunes, and good-fortune, are running out.[80]

Gerald, a handsome young man, did complete the gymnasium and obtained a law degree, after which he spent a year in New York with a financial firm and was admitted to an elite French graduate school of administration. He died at an early age in a plane crash in France, so his long-term capacities were never tested.

While finances were on her mind with respect to Claude's estate, the purchase of a house, and her godson's savings account, Cora also began preparing a new will. In a letter to her parents, she explained that her mother would have "first claim" and then Jeanne, "plus certain small bequests here and there. . . . I am pondering a trust situation for Jeanne and an ultimate disposal after her death. I have not yet decided between or among the European and American cousins on the one hand, or on the other hand leaving my resources to educational institutions like Peabody, Harvard Anthro Dept, Radcliffe, or Barnard, or Dept of Anthro at California—primarily for graduate students and research."[81] Cora was planning ahead, and as the principal breadwinner in her relationship with Jeanne, she wanted to make sure that Jeanne, ten years her junior, would have some financial security.

Life at Harvard also included spending time at Martha's Vineyard, one of the favorite spots for Harvard faculty to summer. Cora's friend and colleague John Whiting had grown up on a farm on West Tisbury Pond in Martha's Vineyard and retained part of the farm and the farmhouse for his own summers there. In the summer of 1956 he offered Cora and Jeanne the use of a cabin on the property for a vacation. In a letter to her parents, Cora reported that it was more appropriately called a "shack."

> Our shack was an old barn on which have been tacked a tiny bedroom, a tinier kitchen and a miniscule "head," as Jeanne nautically calls the john. We are about 6 feet from the pond and about 6 feet above it. . . . The shack is as primitive, as remote, and as dirty as we anticipated. J and I have had diligent bouts of scrubbing greasy kerosene stoves, pans and lamps; have about mastered the cranky kerosene ice box; have moved furniture (such as it is) all around and now like dogs circling in the grass before lying down, we feel quite settled in. The beach, a mile away, is superb! First it is absolutely private. Second, it is full of terns and tern chicks and tern eggs. Third, it is a beachcomber's delight. . . . There are thousands of other things to tell you about that make up an enchanting vacation![82]

The "shack" at Tisbury Pond became Jeanne and Cora's regular retreat for several weeks each summer.

In the summer of 1956 Cora returned to Martha's Vineyard to spend a week as May Sarton's guest—"this time to posh Edgartown."[83] Sarton, whom Cora mentioned with some regularity in her letters home, had, it seems, become more than just a friend. According to Sarton's biographers and her published letters, May Sarton and Cora Du Bois had become lovers, and they had a five-year tumultuous relationship.[84] The Cora Du Bois archives contain only evidence of a friendship, as indicated in references to Sarton in letters home and by a small handful of cordial letters and thank-you notes that Cora and Sarton exchanged over the years. As with most of her love relationships, Cora left only tantalizing fragments—an occasional journal entry or poem—but no love letters. This, as the feminist historian Estelle Freedman has noted in her essay "The Burning of Letters Continues," was characteristic of a period when love between women was still unsafe, especially for public women like Du Bois.[85]

Jeanne had brought Sarton to the house for drinks one evening during Cora's second semester at Harvard. According to Sarton, there was an immediate attraction between herself and Cora.[86] A portrait of a young Sarton shows her leaning forward intently, her long dark hair drawn back and her right elbow resting on her lap with a cigarette in hand. Everything about her looks intense, intelligent, and dramatic: she is wearing a dark green jacket over a bright orange sweater, with turquoise cuffs showing at the wrists, and turquoise pants. The background is red. This bold portrait by artist Polly Thayer is, coincidentally, owned by Harvard's Fogg Art Museum. Sarton was nine years younger than Cora, so one can well imagine Cora's pleasure in this younger woman's vivacious attention, particularly during a stressful first year at Harvard. Plus, Sarton was a published poet—poetry being a medium in which Cora had dabbled since childhood. The two women also had a European connection: like Cora's early years in France, Sarton had spent her early childhood in Belgium before her family fled to the United States as the Germans advanced during World War I.

Sarton has depicted her and Cora's relationship as passionate and tumultuous. "We fought like tigers, poetry against science," she would say.[87] Sarton was an emotionally expressive person. In a letter to her parents, Cora described her as follows: "May Sarton arrived with flowers and a book of her poetry. She is an effervescent and noisy person who always introduces zest."[88] She was also an emotionally needy person who aroused affection in others. As the literary critic Carolyn Heilbrun has written, "[Sarton] was able to arouse affection so often, so deeply, and so widely because she offered affection with so lavish a hand, and with so much humor and attention and excitement. She needed people, and was able to make that need evident; in fulfilling it, therefore, individuals, even if raged at, understood that they had served her in a meaningful way."[89] For a time, Cora would serve as Sarton's muse—her creative inspiration. And Sarton would become a passionate distraction for Cora, whose life at Harvard was stressful, as well as painful in ways that she had not yet fully identified.

Sarton asserted that it was their difference that made "the attraction between us magnetic and nourishing."[90] And, she rightly noted, "There is no point in trying to change Cora, any more than I can change fundamentally. But perhaps we can learn little by little to enjoy what we can give each other instead of merely suffering and raging!"[91] With Cora Du Bois, May Sarton was confronted with a formidable professor of anthropology who, both by temperament and by profession, had a preference to be "a distant observer of humankind." And yet she was someone capable of deep sympathy for and insight into others, as well as love. Sarton drew her into a relationship that was undoubtedly cathartic during her early years at Harvard. Furthermore, Sarton represented something that Cora had always admired—the ability to write evocative prose and poetry. Just a few years before meeting Sarton, Cora had made the following two entries in her journal:

JUNE 17, 1951

Reading Elizabeth Bowen's *The House in Paris*. Strange that at my age and with my degree of self-satisfaction I should envy anyone. But such sensitivity of observation, such imagination about people, and such ease in *disciplined use of language* is enviable. I wish my life had been shaped to such expressions and not to the rot I have just thought and worse yet thought worth writing. [Cora's self-denigration here coincides with her leaving the State Department and turning down the UC Berkeley job.]

APRIL 24, 1952

These notes are written less in the mood of information than of atmosphere, to use the term of E. M. Forester. Altho such writing as I have done so far, and all within the framework of my profession, have [*sic*] been informative in content and style; it now seems the better part of maturity to abandon such limitations and to state such things as seem true to me in atmospheric terms. This is a difficult, and probably impossible, reformulation of my experiences. The evocative use of language is a life's discipline in both reading and writing. It has not been mine.[92]

Early in her relationship with Sarton, Cora wrote a short piece in her journal that she entitled "The Actor and the Poet." In it, she lauded "Poetry's" capacity for "direct and spontaneous communication" over "the artificial and repetitive action of the Stage"—that is, the actor (or the professor/lecturer). Poetry, she wrote, "is communication between the creator and the receptive reader. Whether it is romantic, classical, intellectual or mystic, intuitive or rational, is of no consequence. It is above all direct."[93] Cora was clearly infatuated with poetry and her new friend, a poet, and was denigrating what she did—teaching (often on a stage). And although Sarton tended to cast her as "the scientist," Cora was, in fact, very much a humanistic anthropologist (see chapter 10).

Cora's liaison with Sarton had to be kept hidden, although obviously Jeanne Taylor knew about it and must have found it painful—something to which Sarton alluded in a 1958 letter to Cora.[94] Sarton, who pined for a more open relationship, moved in that same year from Cambridge to a small town, Nelson, in New Hampshire. She hoped to provide Cora a safe retreat and a place where they could spend time more openly together. "Here at Nelson I shall see you for the first time in a place which I cannot be 'asked to leave' or 'allowed to stay'—in which I am not helplessly in the power of an atmosphere created by others—Here I create the atmosphere—you can come or go as you choose but you *cannot* make me leave," Sarton wrote in her journal.[95] Sarton's move to Nelson, however, coincided with Cora's year (1958–59) to do research at Stanford's Center for Advanced Study in the Behavioral Sciences, where she was accompanied by Jeanne Taylor. Sarton was hurt and angry. Her poem "Der Abschied" (The farewell), she said, commemorated Cora's visit to Nelson to say good-bye.[96] It begins,

> Now frost has broken summer like a glass
> This house and I resume our conversations;
> The floors whisper a message as I pass,
> I wander up and down these empty rooms
> That have become my intimate relations,
> Brimmed with your presence where your absence blooms—
> And did you come at last, come home, to tell
> How all fulfillment tastes of a farewell?[97]

By 1960, after five years, Cora had terminated the intimate part of her relationship with May Sarton, to which Sarton responded with a poem of anguish, "Divorce of Lovers."[98] Cora's complex life at Harvard—combined with a semester at the University of Hawaii as the Carnegie visiting professor (1957), followed by a year at Stanford (1958-59), and then longitudinal research in India (1961-72)—would have made it difficult to maintain, in secrecy, a relationship with a demanding lover. Furthermore, Cora began to fear that she might lose Jeanne Taylor, her long-term partner in life.[99] Despite the breakup, Sarton, who had planned a world tour for the spring of 1962 to celebrate her fiftieth birthday, visited Cora in Bhubaneswar, Odisha, India, where Cora was engaged in a year of fieldwork. That trip inspired a number of Sarton poems about India. Further, both women exchanged playful verses about Indian wildlife, such as jackals, shrews, and geckos ("lizards" in the poems below).

One of Sarton's poems begins,

I am suddenly homesick for
The Indian night
And my dark cell
In Orissa
Where I was visited
By a white lizard
With emerald eyes[100]

And Cora wrote,

TO THE TAILOR'S LIZARD OF BHUBANESWAR
Little Brother
Did you lose in April
That resplendent rudder?
Little lizard, never mind!
When comes the rain in August
You will grow again
Another!

At the bottom of her handwritten verse, Cora noted, "To be scientifically accurate rains have no known influence on the growth of lizard tails, any more than fish tails influence the waves of the sea!"[101] It would seem that these two writers—one a poet, the other a scholar—were having fun.

In 1965 Sarton would publish what has become known as her "coming out" novel, *Mrs. Stevens Hears the Mermaids Singing*. In that book, according to Sarton, the main character, Hilary Stevens, a writer, is modeled on herself, and one of Stevens's lovers, Dorothea, is modeled on Du Bois.[102] Dorothea is depicted as ten years older than Hillary, "at the height of her powers, cynical, passionate, realistic. The anti-mystic by nature and by profession, for Dorothea was a sociologist. The attraction had been immediate, the attraction of opposites. The war had been immediate too. . . . Dorothea [had] an air of composure, an air of reason which she had fitted over a passionate temperament like a suit of armor."[103] In this brief sketch of Dorothea, Sarton manages to capture some of the essence of Cora Du Bois.

Carolyn Heilbrun—Sarton's literary executor and herself a prolific writer, literary critic, and a "first woman" (the first tenured woman in the English Department at Columbia)—seems to have been inspired by the Sarton–Du Bois affair for her satirical treatment of Harvard in her mystery *Death in a Tenured Position* (1981). Under the penname Amanda Cross, Heilbrun addressed the polemical issue of "first women" professors at Harvard, specifically mentioning Cora Du Bois as the Zemurray-Stone Professor and dedicating the book to May Sarton—not an accidental conjunction of names. Fortunately, however, unlike the central character in Heilbrun's mystery, who turns up dead under strange circumstances, Du Bois did not get killed off at Harvard but managed, as evidenced in the next chapter, to have a continuing productive career as teacher and scholar.

In summary, Cora Du Bois's early years at Harvard were both stimulating and trying, and her personal life was complex. She had moved into a new decade of life and into a celebrated position at Harvard and Radcliffe. The "first woman" position, however, made her feel, much of the time, like "just so much *baksheesh*"—a little something extra that the departments did not have to budget for and that her male colleagues could ignore.[104] One means of ignoring her was to not invite her to departmental meetings. Another was to treat her as if she were invisible. For example, on one occasion, when she was serving on the university Faculty Review

Advisory Committee to the Philips Brooks House (a Harvard residence), one of the housemasters "really tongue-lashed" the presence of women at Harvard. Cora reported, "The very pleasant chairman of that meeting went the rounds and finally I was asked what my opinion was, and I said, 'Well, obviously I don't agree.'"[105] Harvard of the 1950s and 1960s was not an easy setting for a woman, even one of Cora Du Bois's stature and formidable presence.

CHAPTER 9

Sociocultural Change in India

Modernization is again one of those superficial blanket terms that means little more than a contemporary effort to cope with new situations. Imperial Rome was "modernizing"; Renaissance Europe was modernizing; and so are all societies and cultures extant in the twentieth century. It is the situation and not the processes that have changed, and are changing. The changes are taking place from various cultural base lines, at different rates, and toward varied goals throughout the world.

—Cora Du Bois

Cora Du Bois's major research project while at Harvard was to investigate post–World War II sociocultural change in India following independence from Great Britain in 1947. The study of contemporary change in such a large, complex society, with its long heritage of literacy, was an extreme departure from her classic psychocultural study of nonliterate villagers on the remote island of Alor, Indonesia. Du Bois's wartime experiences had reoriented her interests toward the dramatic changes that were occurring in a postwar world of emerging new nations. She had also become convinced that "high cultures"—as opposed to small, remote, nonliterate societies—were the places to examine these processes of change "written large."[1] Accordingly, she developed at Harvard a seminar, Social Change, which carefully examined theories of modernization, as well as area courses on Southeast Asia and India. In lecture notes for her

Social Change seminar, she wrote the following explanation for her new research focus:

> There were other influences operative in changing my interests and focus of attention from non-literate cultures to high cultures. (1) Certainly the whole dramatic shift in the world power situation that occurred during and particularly after WWII must have influenced me. (2) Also—almost all of the academic disciplines, many of whose practitioners had been ripped out of our ivory towers, came to realize the limitations of our own disciplines in describing and hopefully explaining socio-cultural realties and processes. This was an era in which cross-disciplinary inquiries and cooperation were the order of the day. (3) Lastly—the inadequate knowledge of other cultures and societies and the changed position of the U.S. toward them as we shifted into the role of a major power—gave a great impetus to "area studies." The [area study] centers were and are largely interdisciplinary and focus primarily on centers of high culture.[2]

Area Studies

Du Bois's changed interests were first reflected in the area courses that she developed. She regularly alternated ones on India and Southeast Asia, the latter a two-course sequence entitled Peoples and Cultures of Southeast Asia: composed of The Buddhist World and The Islamic Area. In reflecting upon these courses in later life, Cora would say, in her frequently self-denigrating fashion, "Well, I got into giving area courses, and I alternated for a time, Southeast Asia and India. Really, I was not competent in the profound sense, but I was interested and had had just enough exposure to sop up what I read and understood pretty much what I read, but it was never in depth."[3] Du Bois, of course, had had more opportunities than the average professor to think broadly about both of these regions of the world and had published a book on Southeast Asia. Her in-depth field research experience had, it is true, been limited to a remote island in Indonesia. Soon, however, she would get more in-depth experience in India, but she was neither a Sanskrit scholar nor a Buddhist scholar, and in that sense she considered herself not "profoundly competent." To students, what was masterful about her courses was her ability to incorporate into lectures and required readings a broad spectrum of theory and research—from geography, linguistics, and prehistory to more contemporary history, economics, politics, religion, philosophy, and kinship. The more standard ethnographic works by anthropologists on tribal groups or rural villages were used but did not constitute such a course. As one of her former students put it, "The Southeast Asia course was very good and a different experience. It was not a trait-list course such as I had had at UC Berkeley as an undergraduate, and I appreciated Cora Du Bois's perspectives on international relations as well as ethnology. She was ahead of her time."[4]

In one sense, Du Bois was ahead of her time in having mastered such a broad spectrum of research materials and having the competence to introduce them—in a coherent and interesting fashion—into new courses at Harvard. In another sense, she was contemporaneous with her time. It was during World War II and its aftermath that language-based area programs were promulgated at American universities. In 1948, for example, Harvard established, with major funding from the Carnegie Corporation, the Russian Research Center with anthropologist Clyde Kluckhohn as its first director. In 1954 the university developed the Center for Middle Eastern Studies—the first of its kind in the United States—and in 1955 it founded the Center for East Asian Research (now the John King Fairbank Center for Chinese Studies). "America's [post–World War II] cultural hegemony strengthened the cause of Harvard's internationalism, much as British higher education took up remote places, people, and tongues during the apogee of the Empire."[5] Cora's area courses fit into this growing international focus at Harvard, but there was no suitable area program with which she could affiliate. Programs that focused on South Asia and Southeast Asia would be established elsewhere, at such universities as the University of Chicago, the University of Pennsylvania, UC Berkeley, and Cornell.

Had Du Bois gone to Berkeley, she would most likely have been drawn into the development of its area study centers—something that Alfred Kroeber had hinted at in his 1948 letter promoting her candidacy to the Department of Anthropology. But she would have had some ambivalence about doing so because she believed strongly in the separation of government intelligence research and university research. As we have seen,

Cora had had extensive experience with both endeavors, but intelligence research required secrecy and entailed government interference with "free and fearless inquiry"—the expression she used to address government-required loyalty oaths at universities. Following her experience with the World Health Organization and the Institute of International Education, she had become critical of research funded by "government agencies and wealthy foundations" that were often, as she put it, "staffed by ill-informed persons and guided by political considerations."[6] So Cora probably would have found it disagreeable to have to collaborate with either the Ford Foundation or the Carnegie Corporation, the principal funders of university area studies programs established during the Cold War era. The fact that many of these programs also had ties with the CIA and other government intelligence agencies would have been a total anathema to her.[7]

Fieldwork and Ethics in Anthropology

Du Bois never explicitly addressed, in writing, her position with respect to the infiltration of area studies programs by the CIA, and she was probably unaware of Clyde Kluckhohn's collaboration with that entity when he directed Harvard's Russian Research Center.[8] (Kluckhohn retired from that position in 1954, the year Cora joined Harvard.) From one anecdote reported by her Harvard anthropology colleague Irven DeVore, however, Du Bois's position with respect to the infiltration of the CIA into any academic endeavor is emphatically clear.

In 1963 two CIA agents approached DeVore, a new professor at Harvard, and offered to fund two of his graduate students who wanted to study nonhuman primates in Southeast Asia. The CIA knew that DeVore had received a large National Institutes of Health research grant to study nonhuman primate behavior in different parts of the world but that these particular students remained unfunded. If the students would collect certain kinds of information about village life while studying primates in Southeast Asia, the CIA agents assured DeVore, then they could be fully funded. DeVore was troubled. As a new and junior professor at Harvard, he said, he did not know how to handle this situation. On the one hand, he did not want to hurt his students' research opportunities, but on the other hand, he was uncertain about this kind of government collaboration. This, it should be remembered, was a period when opposition to the

Vietnam War and American involvement in Southeast Asia was growing. So DeVore sought advice from his senior colleague John Whiting, who, in turn, sent him to confer with Cora Du Bois.

That conversation with Du Bois, DeVore reported, was the first serious one he had had with her since his arrival at Harvard. It took place in her Peabody Museum office, with DeVore sitting on one side of her large desk and Cora on the other. After he explained the situation to her, Cora, he said, leaned across her desk, looked him squarely in the eye, and said in her most authoritative voice, "If I ever learn that any graduate students have taken money from the CIA, I'll personally see to it that they never graduate from Harvard." As DeVore put it, "Cora Du Bois's strength of character and firm opinion came through *very clearly*."[9]

At a time when people were not yet addressing the conflict of interest between covert intelligence research for the state and the principle of free and open inquiry in academe, Cora Du Bois had a clear position—one that she implemented during her research in India. In 1964 public allegations were made that MIT's Center for International Studies (CENIS) had CIA connections. The center had been deeply involved in economic planning and development in India since 1957.[10] These allegations produced a political fire in India that resulted in CENIS withdrawing from India the following year, but suspicions of U.S. covert intelligence programs under the guise of academic research and development projects remained prevalent for some years. Du Bois later addressed these circumstances and how she had handled them during her years of research in India:

In India, as elsewhere in the world, the question of one's integrity as a scholar may come under suspicion. The ineptitude of our Central Intelligence Agency, as well as the Chinese and Pakistan hostilities, have accentuated—fortunately only in a minor way—what I have come to consider the normal suspicions that I or my American colleagues are spies. Even after six years [of fieldwork in India] such rumors are current. Certainly I consider it desirable to leave my notes freely accessible to any [Indian] intelligence officer who may wish to examine them during my absence from my room [in the State Guest House, Bhubaneswar, India]. Such is my duty, and I feel that I should make no attempt to outwit him. I also believe that my policy of making my presence and objectives known to the highest officials has reduced gossip on this score. I have pursued a policy of making my arrivals and departures known by brief visits or letters, beginning with the state governor and working downward. Further, when gossip of spying [by any individuals under my direction] has reached me, stemming from persons of some status, I have made a point of tracing it to its source, of expressing my concern, and of asking for evidence—with assurances that, if any evidence exists, the culprit would be dismissed immediately. I consider covert "intelligence work" in any case disreputable, but *to pursue it under cover of academic research is an unpardonable betrayal of professional ethics.*[11]

While at Harvard, Du Bois never spoke publicly about these matters, nor did she address the Vietnam War in her courses on Southeast Asia. Furthermore, she did not assign her book on Southeast Asia, which would have made her position clear. There are at least two reasons for her silence, I suspect. First, she wanted to be viewed as an academic anthropologist, not as a former World War II intelligence officer or member of the State Department. Thus she preferred to keep these two parts of her life separate, and she made only occasional remarks about the latter over drinks in the privacy of her home. Second, she had to be cautious about what she said publicly because she knew that she was still under investigation by the FBI. Laura Nader, in her chapter in *The Cold War and The University*, makes a strong case for what she calls "the phantom factor" in anthropology during the Cold War era. Harvard had experienced its share of "Red Menace" purges, as had many other campuses, and many faculty had thereby been silenced. Cora Du Bois, as we have seen, was not a person who was easily intimidated or quieted, but her return to the groves of academe was, in part, an effort to remove herself from the painful experiences she had had with McCarthyism in Washington DC. Besides, she had already sacrificed a position at UC Berkeley by taking a public stand against the newly imposed loyalty oath there, and she probably did not want to become a target of controversy at Harvard.

Putting all of this together—and given Du Bois's position with respect to U.S. policy regarding the former French Indochina and the buildup of the Vietnam War during the 1960s—it is not surprising that she decided to initiate her major Harvard research project in India rather than in some part of Southeast Asia.

The Center for Advanced Study, Stanford

The prelude to Du Bois's research in India was a yearlong appointment (1958–59) at Stanford University's Center for Advanced Study in the Behavioral Sciences. Following four intensive years of teaching and catching up on anthropology at Harvard, it was a year that she could devote to thinking, writing, and planning. It also provided her a year of contact with a stimulating set of anthropologists who, unlike those at the Peabody Museum, were intellectually and socially engaged with one another, some of whom became her admirers. They included Edward Dozier, Fred Eggan, Clifford Geertz, Raymond Firth, George Murdock, David Schneider, and Melford Spiro. Geertz, whose PhD dissertation Du Bois had overseen, was already a close acquaintance. Melford Spiro (now professor emeritus of anthropology, UC San Diego) was someone she had met only briefly one summer when he was teaching a course at Harvard. Initially, Spiro reported, he had been "seduced by her wonderful voice" over the telephone into writing an article for a volume of the *American Anthropologist* (1955) that focused on American culture.[12] Subsequently, when they met at Harvard, Cora invited him to have lunch at the Harvard Faculty Club. It was a "very embarrassing" moment, Spiro said, when he—very much Cora's junior—could enter through the front door of the club whereas Cora had to enter through the back. Over lunch, "I was totally captivated by her in person," and "Cora became one of my favorite anthropologists, not because of her anthropology per se but *because of her person*."[13] As a graduate student, Spiro had studied Cora's book *The People of Alor*, but like many of her Harvard students, he found Cora herself a deeply engaging personality and someone with whom he wanted more contact.

Proximity of offices at Stanford allowed Spiro to drop by Du Bois's office for informal conversations. "I need not apologize (I hope)," he would write a year later, "for saying that I miss you very much, and would be willing to put up with much of the inanity of Palo Alto for the opportunity of being able to walk into your study at my convenience."[14] One of their topics of conversation was Spiro's proposed research in Southeast Asia. Cora recommended Sri Lanka or Burma as research sites, and when Spiro decided on Burma as a locus for investigating the psychological underpinnings of Burmese animism and Buddhism, Cora introduced him to friends of hers at the American embassy there. Conrad Bekker, who had known Cora from their days together in the OSS, told Spiro, "If you're a friend of Cora's, I'll do anything I can for you."[15]

Cora found Stanford's center a rich intellectual environment where she could contemplate research in India, work on a cross-cultural study of friendship, and edit a volume of the collected papers of Robert Lowie. Cora's longtime friend and mentor, Lowie, had died the year before she went to Stanford. Up to the time of his death on September 21, 1957, at the age of seventy-four, Lowie and Cora had carried on a lively correspondence. Knowing of their close relationship, the secretary of the Department of Anthropology at UC Berkeley notified Cora by telegram of his passing: "ROBERT DIED THIS AFTERNOON. CREMATION PRIVATE. MEMORIAL SERVICE LATER—POLLY."[16] Shortly thereafter, Cora drafted a letter of consolation to his widow, Luella Cole (Cy) Lowie, in which she expressed some of her special fondness for Robert. "You know how I feel about Robert," she wrote.

> He was not only 'my professor'—which is always a very special and treasured relationship—but he was also always a staunch friend. For almost 30 years I have long relied on his support and concern that were invariably available and disinterested. I shall miss him and his friendship—as will so many of his students. Even when I refused his guidance—for example when he wanted me to take the University of Oregon appointment—there was never any withdrawal of his concern. He was one of the few genuinely liberal and dispassionate men I have ever known and, needless to say, his students learned much from him that transcended anthropology.[17]

Later Cora incorporated some of her special feelings for Lowie into an obituary that she wrote for the journal *Science*.[18] At the time, however, she was grieving and unable to accept the request to write Lowie's obituary for the *American Anthropologist*. She responded to the editor, Walter Goldschmidt's, invitation, saying, "It is a saddening task and I would wish for my elders and betters [to do it] at this point—even though that may reflect a lingering infantilism."[19] Goldschmidt acquiesced but asked whether

Cora might consider editing a volume of Lowie's papers that would illustrate "the range and development of [his] thoughts on anthropology."[20] This Cora agreed to do. Clearly her competence and special relationship with Lowie were professionally recognized.

During a portion of her year at Stanford, Du Bois worked with Cy Lowie, going through Robert Lowie's hundreds of published and unpublished papers and selecting a representative sample for this special volume to honor him. The endeavor had a timely outcome. One year later the University of California Press published *Lowie's Selected Papers in Anthropology* (1960), edited by Cora Du Bois, thereby honoring one of the luminaries in twentieth-century American anthropology. As Goldschmidt put it in a congratulatory note to Cora, the volume was "a big task and a labor of love. . . . Not only are all of us who hold Robert's memory dear very deeply indebted to you, but so is all anthropology."[21]

Cora's cross-cultural study of friendship fared less well. She had held onto her students' papers from the yearlong graduate seminar on friendship that she taught during her first year at Harvard. With the students' permission, Cora had circulated the papers—totaling some 350 mimeographed pages—among several colleagues for their feedback. At Stanford she hoped to produce a theoretical framework for the cross-cultural study of friendship that would be a companion volume to one that incorporated the student papers. Although she drafted a book outline and several versions of a 135-page manuscript entitled "The Gratuitous Act: An Introduction to the Comparative Study of Friendship Patterns," she was dissatisfied with the outcome and decided not to proceed toward publication. At the end of the year she released her former students from the joint endeavor and encouraged them to publish their papers independently. Many years later a shortened version of Du Bois's manuscript would be published following a 1969 symposium, "The Comparative Sociology of Friendship," in which she participated at the Memorial University of Newfoundland. Cora turned over her "Gratuitous Act" manuscript to Elliott Leyton, the conference organizer, and he reduced it in length and incorporated it into an edited volume, *The Compact: Selected Dimensions of Friendship*—one of the first cross-cultural studies of friendship to be published.[22]

The Harvard-Bhubaneswar, India, Project

Du Bois's research in India began in 1961 when she received a two-year National Science Foundation research grant for a project entitled "Change and Stability in India," which enabled her to explore the suitability of Bhubaneswar, Odisha (formerly Orissa), as a site for a long-range study of sociocultural change in India.[23] As already mentioned, in the aftermath of World War II, private foundations and government agencies were supporting large-scale research projects in many emerging postcolonial nations of the world, and Harvard had its share of such enterprises during Cora's tenure there.[24] Du Bois's project was designed to be a smaller ethnographic study, based on repeated informal interviews and observations, as distinct from the larger modernization projects, to be discussed below, that some of her colleagues in the Department of Social Relations were undertaking that relied on collecting quantifiable data from highly structured interviews, questionnaires, and tests.

Why, one might ask, did Du Bois select the relatively unknown town of Bhubaneswar, located in one of India's least urbanized and, by most measures, poorest states? The answer is that it was a "double town"—a small Hindu temple town in eastern India that had recently been made the site of a new capital city in the state of Odisha. With India's independence from Great Britain in 1947, Odisha had become a new state, with its own language (Oriya) and the need for a capital city. Bhubaneswar had been selected by politicians for both symbolic and practical reasons: it was a sacred pilgrimage center known to a wide range of Hindus, and it also had enough government-owned land to accommodate the construction of a new town. Thus, for Cora, it provided the opportunity to examine the impact of a new, planned city of administration (the New Capital) on an ancient temple town (the Old Town), with two different sociopolitical hierarchies juxtaposed: a hierarchy of Brahmin priests who, in the Old Town, controlled a major Hindu temple complex, affiliated ashrams, and farmland; and a new hierarchy of government officials who, in the New Capital, staffed and managed the newly established state government. In addition, there were a set of rajas (princely rulers under the British) who still had some political influence, five villages that were being gradually incorporated into the city, and all the people and institutions required to build and maintain a new capital city. Bhubaneswar provided, therefore, an ideal microcosm for examining many of the forces of change and transformation that were occurring nationally as India became a new democratic state.

The First Stage of Research

In contrast to her several-months-long voyage by sea to Alor, Indonesia, in 1937, Du Bois arrived in India by plane in July 1961 and spent the 1961–62 academic year first tending to a myriad of government approval processes in New Delhi and Bhubaneswar and then beginning to establish her research project. Her first stop was Bombay, where, she noted, the monsoons were in "full force." Shortly after her arrival, she contacted Sachin Chaudhuri, the Bengali editor of the *Economic Weekly of Bombay*, "one of the best journals in the country," she reported in a letter home. Chaudhuri, to whom she brought a bottle of Scotch, had become, according to Cora, "for some odd reason the counsellor and father confessor of all the young American social scientists who come through Bombay. Within a half hour of my phoning him he trotted over to call. I was not prepared—a tall gaunt man in gauze diapers [dhoti], shirt tails out, wall-eyed, snaggle toothed, bare footed and chewing beetle. And then a sparkling intelligence, a sardonic and worldly humor, an international sophisticate. Surely only India could cast up someone like that! He is altogether charming and I look forward to dinner with him tomorrow night."[25]

From Bombay, Du Bois went to New Delhi to visit with government officials and to do some archival research on Odisha. In one of her weekly letters home, she wrote,

> This week my "news" is dull—even though considerable progress has been made. In the National Archives I am sitting in the stacks (air cooled) ploughing through a superb collection of Gazeteers. Most useful and instructive they are. . . . On the official front I have letters of introduction from Delhi nabobs to Orissa Nabobs: The governor, the chief minister, the chief secretary and the president of the university (here known as the vice-chancellor). I shall of course have to make a series of courtesy calls immediately upon arrival in Bhubaneswar. . . . Meanwhile I have dressed myself all up in finery and paid a brief call on

the Under-Secretary of Commerce, one Mr. Kanungo, who is an Orissa politician and who has also promised to bestir himself on my behalf. If 200 people promise assistance, one may actually come through. On the whole the officials have been very quick to see the significance of my proposed project and [have been supportive].[26]

At the time, field research in new, postcolonial nations was not possible without permission that involved elaborate procedures and clearances. As Du Bois would later write, "More than ever good briefing and tact are professional obligations. Today, in India at least, no anthropologist can hope to do field research without a reasonable knowledge of its bureaucratic regulations and, best of all, influential and helpful acquaintances in the government and universities."[27] Her experiences with the U.S. State Department and the World Health Organization were undoubtedly useful in knowing how to handle these elaborate bureaucratic processes. Cora succeeded in getting permission for her long-term research in India, and she established excellent relationships with government officials and university faculty in Bhubaneswar that enabled a coterie of American students to do research there with few bureaucratic impediments. Despite being a woman, Cora had high status in India as a Harvard professor. That status, together with her powerful and engaging personality, proved to be very effective.

By late August, Cora had arrived in Bhubaneswar and wrote about her first impressions of the town in a letter to her parents:

Now as to Bhubaneswar:—this is only the end of my second full day here—and today was actually spent in Cuttack (an hour's bus ride toward the north). My impressions are necessarily quick and superficial—*But!* The new capital area is a vast, sprawling, sterile artificiality. Big modern buildings rising here and there out of the brush, miles between places, *and no public transportation.* In only the last few years some tricycle rickshaw men have appeared on the scenes. Very few automobiles and those either private or official. A poverty stricken shopping center in very splashy new buildings—already beginning to run down. No movies, no recreation—visible, at least. I haven't yet been to the old temple town—that may be more alive. But the new town is really incredibly *un-vital*,—in appearance at least:—a structure housing people, not a community.[28]

Du Bois's first impressions were reasonably accurate. The New Capital was still very much a work in progress when she arrived in 1961. Bhubaneswar's population had grown from an estimated ten thousand to about forty thousand after becoming the site for a new capital city, and it was spread out over some thirteen square miles. It was a planned city on the British military cantonment model, with large government buildings and a marketplace that formed the town center and broad intersecting avenues that created neighborhood blocks with rows of Western-style housing for government officers and other employees. Houses, which had fenced yards and such modern amenities as electricity and running water, varied in size and were assigned to government officials based on their position in the government service hierarchy. It would, however, take decades for the town to fill in and begin to look somewhat urban. Odisha, in 1961, was one of the least urbanized states in India, having only one city (nearby Cuttack) with a population that exceeded one hundred thousand.[29]

By contrast, the Old Town was an oversized village consisting of irregular-sized houses densely clustered around a set of medieval Hindu temples—the most prominent of which was Lingaraj Temple. Lingaraj, with its sacred communal water tank, served as the town's center. Small lanes, which did not accommodate automobiles, spiraled outward from the temple and created a variety of caste-based neighborhoods. The Old Town stood in dramatic and symbolic contrast to the sprawling and much less densely populated New Capital. Furthermore, Old Town houses were built in a variety of styles, many with dirt floors and thatched roofs, and at that time they had no modern amenities, such as running water, electricity, or latrines connected to a sewer system.

During her first ten months of research in Bhubaneswar, and during subsequent visits, Du Bois was given permission by the chief secretary—"top man of civil service officials," as she put it in a letter to her parents—to have a room in the State Guest House. The State Guest House was then, and continues to be, a facility for government officials visiting on business in Odisha. While not fancy—no hot water or air conditioning, for instance—it provided Cora with reasonably comfortable accommodations and meals for this and subsequent fieldwork in Bhubaneswar. "Meals—noon and evening," she wrote, "with unfailing regularity are:—a small bowl of soup, a piece of fried fish, rice and *hot* greasy curries, and a pudding. *Not* a reducing diet. Even the complete absence of alcohol [Odisha was a dry state] won't cut my weight with all these carbohydrates."[30]

Soon after her arrival in Bhubaneswar, Du Bois began studying Oriya, the language of Odisha. "Oriya seems not too hard grammatically, and there are a few familiar cognates—since it is an Indo-European language," she wrote home. "The script is, of course, hideously complicated. . . . I have great difficulty driving myself to the inescapable dog work of memorizing and drilling."[31] Cora never became fluent in Oriya, but she kept up the instruction for many years, and she made contact with two Orissan linguists who successfully introduced some of her American students to the language.[32]

One of Du Bois's early observations about Bhubaneswar was that women were generally invisible. During her initial yearlong stay at the State Guest House, she only once observed another woman dining there with her husband. At the big weekly farmer's market, Cora saw a few village women who had accompanied their husbands with produce, but no middle- or upper-status women. "One very elegant town woman arrived, driving her own car and dressed in a flowing Punjabi pajama costume," Cora wrote.

> But her male servant got out to do the shopping. [At that time only men—husbands or male servants—did the public shopping.] . . . With the semi-purdah that women live in, no one except family and most intimate friends ever are invited to homes. And even the echelon of westernized officials do not seem to give dinner parties or have people to their homes—often I suspect because their wives are much more conservative than the men. . . . I'm going to have to struggle against being put in purdah myself. The officials, out of politeness, offer to come to the [guest] house to call or bring me data—a most unsatisfactory and inefficient courtesy from my view point.[33]

Although Du Bois's high status gave her access to men, she never achieved much access to women in this relatively conservative part of

India. Even when she did get invited to the homes of government officials, wives and other female kin remained in the background, usually in the kitchen, where they helped to prepare and serve food to their husbands and esteemed guests. Although purdah restrictions were less severe in the New Capital than in the Old Town, it was not until the 1980s that one began to see middle- and upper-status women in public. And even in the 1990s, many Old Town women were still in purdah.[34]

In coming to India to do research, Du Bois had shifted from one patriarchal setting, Harvard, to another, but she came to feel that Bhubaneswar was an amiable place to work. "Except for my usual bronchial infections and a certain lassitude as I readjust to heat and dietary changes," she wrote, "India agrees mightily with me, and I feel better here than in the, to me, wretched climate of New England and the incessant and disparate demands on my time. The climatic difficulties [in India] of which some Americans make so much and of which some pseudo-westernized Indians make even more, are not really a problem, at least, in Bhubaneswar."[35]

Du Bois's first experience with Bhubaneswar coming alive was in mid-September, when Ganesh Puja, a national holiday and festival, was celebrated throughout the city. Below is her description, in a letter home, of this event:

On the local front the main news has been the Ganesh Puja. Ganesh is Shiva's younger son. He has an elephant's head, four arms and a third eye on his forehead. He is the God of wisdom and good fortune. His worship is a national holiday and both families and all kinds of groups buy images for the occasion, get Brahmins to perform the necessary rituals (puja) and then there is a feast. I attended three or four of these affairs, but the one ritual I went through in full force was at the veterinary college (a singularly appropriate locale, I thought). I was the only European in a group of distinguished guests so there was nothing to do but enter into the spirit of the thing. Conch shells blowing, a skinny Brahmin in a loin cloth, only, from the temple, bowing, chanting, offering flowers and food to a large elephant idol (deity is the Indian English term) all set up in a tinsel frame and hung with flower wreathes. Black and red pigment was smeared on my throat and forehead, I snuffed camphor, tossed flowers, prostrated myself forehead to floor, ate some of the offertory food. In sum, lost whatever claim I might have left to a Christian soul and consumed enough germs to discombobulate the intestinal tract of a goat. (Mine did not even quiver.) In the evening the anthropology students gave a feast. Spread on a large slab of a banana leaf were piles of differently flavored rice, and a whole array of spicy curries and curds. Fingers of course [no eating utensils]. This "sumptuous repast" I learned had all been cooked in the temple kitchen of the Old Town from which the priests seem to run a sort of "take it out" restaurant service considered a great blessing to local housewives on festive occasions.

Anyhow, for the first time since I have been here, only a little more than three weeks, although it seems much longer, I had the impression that possibly a spark of liveliness might be hidden in the town and that possibly a few people would talk to and get along with a few other people. Like country towns years ago in the States you would see groups of youths under an electric light talking. Families were out walking, looking at the various shrines that had been erected for Ganesh, and critically comparing the esthetic merits of the various plaster figures. It seems there is considerable rivalry among groups to get the finest Ganesh possible and they hire artisans well in advance to make them.[36]

Ganesh Puja provided Du Bois with her first opportunity to do some participant observation in the larger community. For the most part, she had been preoccupied with meeting all the top government officials, from the governor and chief secretary down, as well as the Utkal University chancellor and members of the Department of Anthropology—all of whose support was critical to her research project. Bhubaneswar, as the new state capital, had become the center of formal education for the state of Odisha, and schools from the kindergarten level to a variety of colleges and a postgraduate university were being established. At the time, Utkal University was the top-ranking institution in town, and it was here that Cora would hire research assistants and begin to train graduate students in anthropology—all a very different enterprise from her solo ethnographic fieldwork among the villagers of Alor, Indonesia, in 1937–39. This research project was modeled more on Cora's experiences with interdisciplinary research teams during her years with the OSS and the State Department.

Longitudinal, Interdisciplinary Research

To study the transformation of an Indian town was a complex enterprise that required time and researchers with different interests and areas of expertise. Initially Du Bois had intended to set up a semipermanent research station in Bhubaneswar that would have a local director in situ during the periods when she was back in the United States teaching at Harvard. She quickly learned, after circulating a proposal among appropriate academic and government persons, that "the special interests of the individuals consulted would serve only to disperse the intent of the project and that administrative costs in both time and money would far exceed those spent on research. I settled for a looser and more independent enterprise, even though it increased my supervisory burdens."[37] This was a politic way of saying that there were competing special interests for what American dollars Du Bois could bring to the table.

For the next eleven years (1962–73) Du Bois would direct what became known as the Harvard-Bhubaneswar Project. Eight American graduate students and three Indian ones would complete PhD dissertations based on research in Bhubaneswar, and many others would benefit from serving as research assistants to Du Bois and to other project researchers in Bhubaneswar or from working with the Harvard-Bhubaneswar files in Cambridge, Massachusetts.[38] In her final report to the National Science Foundation in 1973, Cora wrote, "[At] a minimum some 80 Americans and Indians have derived varying amounts of direct benefits from exposure to the Harvard-Bhubaneswar project."[39] This is quite an astounding figure that reflects Du Bois's moral convictions as well as her commitment to research. She believed that it was important, when working in a community on whose goodwill one depended, to render that community some services in return. "The employment of local personnel is not only a research necessity, it is also a training potential," she wrote. "I have spent a disproportionate amount of time training Oriya students to collect data systematically, to analyze and present material cogently, and to note the implications of such material. I can only hope that the training and the financial support have been some small return for the assistance they and many other members of the community so generously contributed."[40]

Cora Du Bois became a teacher/guru to a set of Utkal University

20. Cora Du Bois being honored at Utkal University, Bhubaneswar, India, 1967. Cora Alice Du Bois Papers (SPEC.COLL.ETHG.D852c), Tozzer Library, Harvard College Library, Harvard University.

students with master's degrees in anthropology, directing their PhD dissertations based on research into different parts of the city that were being transformed.[41] Initially, working with local Oriya-speaking students presented a variety of challenges for Du Bois. Although these young men had been studying at the college and university level in English, their command of the language was "rudimentary," she reported, and their knowledge of the discipline of anthropology only "slight."[42] At the time, their university had no library with books and research journals to study, in an era before the Internet, and they had had little or no research experience. So Du Bois began training them in the rudiments of written English as well as in data collection, organization, and analysis.

Reflecting on this situation midway through her research in Bhubaneswar, Cora wrote, "The combination of these [my] expectations and [the students'] lack of competences produces a level of noise in our communications that at times approaches cacophony. This lack of communication, I believe, would never have occurred had I been working with illiterate tribal people, simply because mutual expectations would have been so different. I still regret the time it has taken me to understand what was happening, and I regret my frequent outbursts of bad temper. Now, at least, I hope we have reached a compromise in our expectations of each other."[43]

Given Du Bois's high standards for research and writing, it must have been a grueling experience, at the start, for both students and teacher. Nonetheless, three of the Indian students with whom she began work in 1961 completed their PhDs under her direction and achieved good positions. Harish Chandra Das, who studied the impact of socioeconomic change on two villages that had become suburbs of Bhubaneswar, became superintendent of the state museum in Bhubaneswar.[44] Jyotish Acharya investigated the growth of a slum area near the railroad line that divided the Old Town and the New Capital and became a college lecturer in geography at Sambalpur University in Odisha. And Manamohan Mahapatra studied changes in the structure of the Old Town Lingaraj Temple—a complex in which he had grown up and that he knew intimately as the son of a temple cook—and, subsequently, conducted a study of a Bauri outcaste community that resided on the periphery of the Old Town. Mahapatra became a lecturer in anthropology at BJB College in Bhubaneswar.[45] Despite some harshness that these and other students experienced with this demanding Harvard professor, they came to view her as a kind of guru—a spiritual teacher from whom they sought personal as well as academic advice. For many years, at least one of these former students kept a large garlanded photo of Du Bois in the entrance hall to his home.

Du Bois's first Harvard graduate student arrived during the second half of her initial year in Bhubaneswar. James Freeman (now professor emeritus of anthropology, San Jose State University, California) had been attracted to the Bhubaneswar project after taking a course with Cora. He felt "rescued by this extraordinary teacher" after "floundering" for a year or so as an anthropology student in the Department of Social Relations at Harvard. Du Bois impressed him as being well grounded theoretically and highly organized, plus he found her "open and giving."[46] She invited him to come investigate Bhubaneswar as a possible research site for his PhD dissertation. When Freeman arrived in the spring of 1962, Du Bois suggested that he consider studying the impact of urbanization on the temple village of Kapileswar—one of several villages being incorporated into the Bhubaneswar municipality. The result was a dissertation that examined the widening economic gap between upper-status and lower-status villagers as they became part of an urban center. A distillation of the dissertation became a well-known text in anthropology, *Scarcity and Opportunity in an Indian Village* (1977). "Modernization and urbanization," Freeman wrote, "far from alleviating the plight of the poor, have increased the income gap between them and the affluent."[47] The building of a new capital city had changed local politics and had benefited some caste groups over others.

Freeman credits Du Bois with teaching him how to become a good observer and careful ethnographer, as well as how to write clearly and concisely. "It was an extraordinary gift that Cora was in Bhubaneswar when I started fieldwork," Freeman reported.[48] Even after she returned to the United States, Cora continued to offer Freeman detailed guidance by letter—something that she did with all of her graduate students. Both Indian and American students were expected to send field notes monthly to Du Bois, who read and then filed them in her Annex—a wing of her home in Cambridge devoted to the growing Harvard-Bhubaneswar Project files. (Du Bois was told that the Peabody Museum did not have adequate space for this scholarly enterprise.) These files, together with a library of books on this part of India, became a resource for both undergraduate and graduate Harvard and MIT students interested in India, especially for those preparing to do research in Bhubaneswar.[49]

Research into Different Aspects of Sociocultural Change

To undertake the examination of such a complex setting as Bhubaneswar required many different personnel with training in a variety of fields. Over the course of the next eleven years, seven more American graduate students—some with spouses and children—would come to Bhubaneswar, but never more than two at a time. "[I]t has seemed both considerate and conciliatory to have never more than two graduate students in the community at one time and to have these students addressing themselves to different segments of the town's small but highly diversified population," Du Bois wrote.[50] Thus American graduate students with different areas of interest and expertise arrived for staggered two-year stays that were financed by their own research grants. Altogether, there were three anthropologists, two sociologists, one urban planner, and two religious studies specialists.

Peter Grenell (now general manager of the San Mateo County Harbor District in California), an MIT city planning student, and Richard Taub (now Paul Klapper Professor in the Social Sciences, University of Chicago), a sociology student in the Department of Social Relations at Harvard, had nonoverlapping research stays in the New Capital. Grenell investigated the politics of the planning process for the New Capital—who was making what decisions and why—whereas Taub focused on high-level government officials. Taub, like Freeman, had been seeking a professor at Harvard who was more empirically grounded than others to whom he had been exposed in the Department of Social Relations, and he found one in Cora Du Bois when he enrolled in her Social Change seminar. He had enrolled in it with some trepidation, he reported, because she had a reputation for being "a castrating, mean bitch," yet he found her to be "the nicest, fairest person he ever knew—warm and supportive in every way."[51] Cora invited Taub and his wife, Doris Leventhal Taub, a Radcliffe graduate who was interested in India and who had done her senior thesis with Du Bois, to join the Bhubaneswar project.

Once in Bhubaneswar, the Taubs were quickly befriended by a group of high-level Indian Administrative Service (IAS) officers—the administrative civil service of the executive branch of the Indian government—and their wives, who had recently been posted to the New Capital. They, like the Taubs, were new to this region of India. "We were all foreigners together," Taub reported.[52] These connections quickly gave Taub access to other high-level government officials, a study of whom became the basis for his PhD dissertation and then a book, *Bureaucrats under Stress: Administrators and Administration in an Indian State* (1969). Taub was able to get some seventy-six IAS officers, and other high-level government personnel, to undergo long, rigorous interviews that helped to illuminate how a modern government bureaucracy operated during a dramatic transfer of power—from a colonial to an independent political regime. With the advent of democratic politics and development needs, these civil servants experienced novel pressures combined with decreased status and power. Major personal and professional readjustments were required as this highly educated elite had to change its expectations from being members of the esteemed British Indian Civil Service to being civil servants more beholden to elected politicians.

Peter Grenell had been introduced to Du Bois by Myron Weiner, then the chair of the Department of Political Science at MIT and renowned for his work on political change in developing countries, including India. That introduction led to an invitation to join the Bhubaneswar project. In preparation, Grenell began visiting Du Bois's Annex to examine the Bhubaneswar files. Eleven a.m., he learned, was "sherry time"—the hour when Cora would invite him to share in a glass of sherry and conversation. "It was a revelation," Grenell recalls, "that this eminent person would come in and chat with me. We would have *real* conversations, and those times became an unusual extension of my undergraduate days at Antioch College [in Ohio]," where an informality of student-faculty relations prevailed.[53] Grenell, who had already had a year's experience in India as a Tata Institute fellow in Bombay, was a natural choice for the Bhubaneswar project. His work there provided a comprehensive look into how plans for Bhubaneswar's new planned city were conceptualized and implemented and the kinds of effects they had on the Old Town and surrounding villages. What made the New Capital particularly interesting, Grenell has written, was that it was "a deliberate effort at planned change. It was planned and built as a symbol of both Indian Independence and the determination to build a better life."[54]

Over the years the construction of the New Capital would have numerous effects on the Old Town, despite the consensus of planning agencies that the Old Town should be preserved as a national historic and cultural site of major importance, with its temples and sacred water tanks restored and maintained.[55] Nonetheless, a major question for the Bhubaneswar project concerned the extent to which religious institutions would prevail during a period of rapid urbanization and Western-style modernization. Taub's study of high-level government officials had suggested that there was little interest among that group in the Old Town, with its many temples, priests, monasteries, and ascetics, and that these highly educated

New Capital residents held unfavorable attitudes toward religion. David Miller (now professor emeritus of Religion, Concordia University, Montreal), a student of comparative religion at Harvard, learned otherwise. He spent two years in Bhubaneswar studying the twenty-two monastic orders (ashrams) in the Old Town and the some forty-one ascetics residing in them.[56] While Old Town temple rituals were declining during the 1960s and 1970s as members of the younger generation of priestly families received a secular education and found employment in the New Capital, traditional Hindu teaching orders (*sampradya*) and the teacher-disciple (*guru-shisya*) relationship remained strong. In other words, the status of Old Town temples and temple rituals had to be carefully distinguished from that of monasteries and the ascetics residing in them. Miller, in fact, discovered that numerous New Capital civil servants provided the main source of financial support for some Old Town monasteries, attended ceremonies, and sought advice from their Old Town gurus and that even seven of Taub's elite government informants were recorded on the lists of donors maintained by Old Town monasteries.[57]

Whereas there was a decline in the popularity of many Old Town temples during this era, James Preston (now professor emeritus of anthropology, State University of New York, Oneonta) found that a nearby temple complex in the city of Cuttack was flourishing. Preston, a graduate student in anthropology and religion at the Hartford Seminary in Connecticut, came to the Bhubaneswar project indirectly. His adviser, Bhabagrahi Misra, a native of Odisha who had received his PhD in folklore at Indiana University, had contacted Du Bois after learning of her research in Bhubaneswar. When Misra left the seminary to pursue a job back in Odisha, Du Bois, who had agreed to be an outside member of Preston's PhD dissertation committee, became his principal advisor and mentor.

Preston conducted ethnographic fieldwork in Cuttack, the preindependence capital of Odisha and the current-day commercial center, located twenty-five miles north of Bhubaneswar. There he studied a Hindu temple complex—Chandi Temple—that was expanding in its popularity. Why, with the development of the New Capital city, were Old Town and some village temples suffering, whereas in Cuttack, the largest population center in Odisha, a temple was gaining in popularity? Urbanization and modernization in this part of India were having different kinds of effects, contrary to the expectations of such Western theorists as Max Weber, Gunnar Myrdal, and Marion Levy Jr., all of whom had predicted that as societies like India modernized, they would become more secular.[58]

The explanation is, of course, multifaceted, but with India's independence and a wave of new political consciousness there had been a decline in the old temple patronage system. Rajas and priests became less powerful, particularly with the establishment of the Odisha Hindu Religious Endowments Commission to oversee temple disputes. In addition, there had been a rise of a strong mercantile class. In the case of Chandi Temple, its new patrons were local merchants, government officials, and other members of a rising urban elite. Instead of a hierarchy of Brahmin priests running the temple, there was one young, charismatic priest who welcomed religious and social change. Finally, the temple participated in the popular version of Durga Puja, the colorful worship of a mother goddess that had spread from Calcutta, West Bengal, to Cuttack and Bhubaneswar.[59]

Both David Miller and James Preston, the two members of the Bhubaneswar project whose focus was religious continuity and change in this part of India, credit Cora Du Bois with not only having supported their research but having forced them to write clearly and concisely. "There was to be no extraneous verbiage and jargon [in my dissertation]," Preston reported, "and she also forced me to be more focused and disciplined—a blessing."[60] The published version of Miller's dissertation was *Hindu Monastic Life: The Monks and Monasteries of Bhubaneswar* (1976) and for Preston, *Cult of the Goddess: Religious Change in a Hindu Temple* (1980).

Changing Family Life, Childrearing Practices, and Schooling

Two research projects that complemented each other were Alan Sable's (a former professor of sociology at UC Santa Cruz and counselor for gays and lesbians in San Francisco) study of schools in Bhubaneswar and my study of family organization and childrearing practices. Sable, a sociology student in the Department of Social Relations at Harvard, had spent a year in India as a Fulbright teacher and had "fallen in love with the country—with its color and its diversity." When he arrived at Harvard and learned of the Bhubaneswar project, he sought out Du Bois in her Peabody Museum office to discuss the possibility of joining the project and was quickly invited to do so. Cora, he said, "was very open to his interests" and to his idea of studying schools there—a critical area to investigate as Bhubaneswar became the locus of educational development for the state of Odisha.[61]

By 1965, when Sable began his research, there were twenty-nine Oriya-medium neighborhood schools in Bhubaneswar, ranging from the primary level through high school, and all children—whether residents of the Old Town, the New Capital, or incorporated villages—had access to schools for the first time. (There were also some private elite schools where instruction was in English.) Remarkably, Sable discovered, all the primary schools, regardless of location, facilities, and staff, had comparable "pass rates"—rates of children who passed the national certificate examinations. What varied dramatically were rates of attrition by socioeconomic status as measured by the father's employment. Nonetheless, Sable concluded, "Old Town and New Capital residents were found to share the same approach to education: pragmatism, flexibility, and rational planning; socio-economic and in some cases cultural background, rather than residence, was most important in determining educational opportunity, aspiration, and achievement."[62] Sable's dissertation research was published as *Paths through the Labyrinth: Educational Selection and Allocation in an Indian State Capital* (1977).

My introduction to Cora Du Bois and the Bhubaneswar project has already been described in the prologue. My project in India was to study a stratified sample of families from both parts of Bhubaneswar—the Old Town and the New Capital—in order to examine similarities and contrasts in child-rearing practices and in child development among infants and young children. At Du Bois's recommendation, I had been trained by Beatrice Whiting in the Six Culture Study methods of systematic, timed behavior observations of children and their caretakers.[63] While there were subtle differences between the rearing of children in middle- and in upper-status Old Town and New Capital families, there were also pervasive similarities. One of these was multiple childcare. In the Old Town, women had married into their husbands' multigenerational, patrilineal (joint) families in which sets of brothers and their wives, together with their parents, resided together. This produced a hierarchy of women, from mothers-in-law down to the youngest daughter-in-law. These women, who were in purdah, were expected to share all household tasks, including childcare. In addition to mothers and grandmothers, there were aunts, uncles, and cousins who also helped with childcare. Children were, accordingly, never left alone, and they had many caretakers and figures with whom to identify. The ideal outcome was to produce children who identified with the joint family as a whole and who would value its well-being over their own personal desires and interests.

New Capital middle- and upper-status families, on the other hand, were not formally "joint" in structure because branches of families had had to move to Bhubaneswar as men, who were civil servants, were transferred there. Nonetheless, mothers were not alone in rearing children. There was almost always a grandmother or some other relative, as well as servants, to help with childcare. While the joint family was still highly valued, children were growing up under conditions in which greater self-reliance and individual initiative were also valued.

In low-status families in both the Old Town and the New Capital, where both men and women worked outside the home in order to eke out a living, children were put to work at an early age. Girls became caretakers of younger children by the age of six. They also prepared meals, hauled water, and cleaned house in their mothers' absence. Boys also helped with childcare, ran errands, and did other outdoor work. As a consequence, few of these children were enrolled in school. My research, which involved observing children *inside* homes and courtyards, thus complemented Sable's study of school and school attrition. From this perspective, it was easy to understand why children from poor, low-status families had high attrition rates, if they ever attended school at all.

There were also significant gender differences in how Old Town and New Capital families valued schooling. As Sable had determined, Bhubaneswar residents' orientation to all these new public schools was highly pragmatic. How might a formal education help the family? What careers should sons pursue? Of what value was schooling to girls, who were expected to marry relatively young and become wives and mothers in a highly patriarchal society? Some schooling might be beneficial for arranging marriages, but too much would be problematic in a society where it was important for wives to be younger, less well educated, and subservient to their husband and their husband's family. Two years of research in Bhubaneswar allowed me to recognize these kinds of issues but not to know how they would be resolved.

In a series of follow-up studies with my sample of Bhubaneswar families, I discovered that all New Capital middle- and upper-status girls and some Old Town ones had been allowed to remain in school as long as they were passing exams. In many families, in fact, girls were outperforming their brothers. Such extended schooling for girls resulted in marriage crises for families that now had to find suitable grooms for older, educated, and potentially independent and professionally ambitious daughters. Schooling, it turned out, would have a major impact on gender and family systems in this part of India, but it required longitudinal research—from 1965 to 1989—to learn this.[64]

Concepts of Personhood

The eighth American graduate student member of the Bhubaneswar project was Richard Shweder (now William Claude Reavis Distinguished Service Professor of Human Development, University of Chicago). Shweder's initial interest in Bhubaneswar was to study issues of equality and inequality. He wanted to work in a society that inverted American principles and beliefs, and India, with its hierarchical caste system based on notions of social and religious inequality, seemed ideal. These interests resonated with those of Du Bois, whose own research was to investigate changes in values among different categories of Bhubaneswar residents. Hoping that Shweder would also do something related to changing values, in the summer of 1968 Du Bois financed a trip to Bhubaneswar for him and his wife, "to explore the place, muck around, make contacts and see if it was a site that might be appealing for Ph.D. [dissertation] research later."[65]

Du Bois had suggested that, while there, Shweder might investigate a form of devotional worship in Bhubaneswar known as Trinath Mela, an intercaste devotional songfest at which devotees share sacred food and ganja, or hemp. Cora was curious to learn more about this new popular form of worship that was yet another alternative to the more traditional temple worship. Shweder did look into the Trinath Mela and submitted field notes to the project files in Cora's Annex, but he did not view it as a suitable dissertation topic.

As Shweder, an anthropology student in social relations, prepared for longer research in India, his interests turned increasingly toward new work being done in cognitive anthropology and cognitive psychology. Both fields were using highly formalistic techniques for gathering and analyzing cultural and psychological data, and Du Bois was not an advocate of these new methodologies. She and Shweder engaged in lengthy and heated intellectual disputes from which, Shweder reported, he would emerge "sweating." "Cora," he said, "was tough, literate, and a no-nonsense person who was effective at argument and put-downs."[66] They also sparred over Shweder's "excessively jargon laden, overly academic writing and talking style. [H]er favorite model in those meetings was E.B. White and the *New Yorker*'s 'The Talk of the Town.' . . . Cora instilled a certain terror in me," Shweder said, but he was ultimately grateful that, in her "tough love" fashion, she had insisted on good writing.[67]

Ultimately, Shweder undertook research in the Old Town, where he used a sample of Brahmins to investigate "the deep semantic structures implicit in the Oriya lexicon of personality terms" and "the biasing influence of language on thought in the personality assessment process."[68] (Shweder's dissertation was entitled "Semantic Structures of Personality Assessment.") As a highly theoretical and formalistic enterprise, it did not fit well into the Bhubaneswar project's more ethnographic focus on sociocultural change. As a consequence, Shweder and Du Bois parted ways. He found another thesis advisor and Cora, in her 1973 final report to the National Science Foundation, wrote, "Mr. Shweder's interest turned increasingly to methodological problems. His use of Indian data has been largely illustrative and incidental. The principal investigator did not supervise his thesis."[69] Du Bois and Shweder reconciled some years later, when Shweder sent Cora several of his published papers that used Bhubaneswar data and she responded with warmth and appreciation.[70] As someone who had been an innovator in the 1930s culture and personality movement within anthropology, Du Bois's antipathy to Shweder's cognitive and linguistic study of personhood, using new methodologies, might seem surprising. The explanation may lie in Du Bois's changing perspectives toward her own discipline, the social sciences in general, and post–World War II studies of sociocultural change and "modernization."

A Critic of the Social Sciences and Modernization Theories

Cora Du Bois's return to academe in 1954 had coincided with the postwar expansion of higher education, stimulated in part by the 1944 GI Bill; an explosion in academic research and publications, much of it underwritten by government grants that supported postgraduate study; and an immense growth in the social sciences as the United States launched numerous technical assistance programs throughout the world. "It has been in these two post-war decades that the term *social sciences*, *behavioral sciences*, and even that noxious term, *social engineers*, came into use," Du Bois wrote.[71] All of these factors, she asserted, had had an impact on anthropology, a field that had attracted numerous veterans who, during the war, had been trained in foreign languages and cultures for overseas service. The result was a rapid growth in anthropology programs and PhD degrees awarded in the United States. "In 1947," Cora wrote, "there were some 500 members of the American Anthropological Association. Today [1972], there are some 5,000—in other words, about a ten fold increase."[72] What Cora had experienced as a relatively small and intimate profession, where people knew one another and could keep up with one another's research, had expanded into, in her terms, "a depersonalized profession." Another effect of this rapid expansion, Du Bois, believed, was "the flood of publications" and "the fragmentation of anthropology that once had the proud, if pretentious, goal of a unified study of man."[73]

In the postwar era, rapid change was occurring at home as well as in India, and not all of it was to Du Bois's liking. She became ambivalent about aspects of her own discipline and a critic of the social sciences in general. Nonetheless, she was "startled" one day when William Howells (chair of the Harvard Anthropology Department in the 1960s) told her that she was "one of the last humanists in anthropology."[74] Presumably he meant that she still had the holistic goals of an earlier generation of anthropologists, whereas the discipline was becoming increasingly specialized and technical. Ultimately, Du Bois would consider herself "a philosophical humanist," but at the time she was a hard-nosed ethnologist who believed that generalizations about the human condition should be based on careful fieldwork and that premature theory building and hypothesis testing should be avoided.[75] Her intellectual position brought her, at times, into conflict with some of her colleagues, even her good friend John Whiting.[76]

Whereas Whiting embraced the other social sciences, especially psychology and its quantitative methodologies, Du Bois had grown suspicious of them. She had come to believe that as a new world power the U.S. government was pouring funds into research that had neocolonial and military implications and led, she believed, to "culture-bound theories, concepts, and techniques irrelevant to the [culture] areas in which they operated."[77] In her 1966 vice presidential address to Section H (Anthropology) of the American Association for the Advancement of Science, for instance, she urged anthropologists to be wary of premature "theoretical formulations" and "rhetorics of persuasion." In that speech, she asked, "To what extent are we committed to a gradual understanding, empirically based, of other societies; and to what extent are culturally pre-determined techniques and rhetorics to form not only our own students, but our national and professional world view? Are we engaged in a clear-eyed, flexible, empathetic, unsystematic inquiry? Or have we decided that our knowledge, our techniques, and our rhetorics are so puissant that we can move 'ahead' confidently in the intellectual conquest of the thinking world. For the moment, I feel insecure in the latter alternative."[78]

The word left unmentioned above, but which became prominent in her subsequent speeches, was "modernization."[79] Du Bois was, in part, responding to the grand theories that had evolved early in the Cold War era about how to modernize "traditional" (formerly colonized) societies—through Western-style economic, political, and social psychological development—so that they would resemble the United States and be less susceptible to influences from the Soviet Union. Much of the modernization literature of that era sounds almost prophetic in its assumptions and goals—that is, "the West" was synonymous with modernity, and the rest of the world had to be brought up to those socioeconomic standards with the help of "value-free" social science and technology.[80] In some ways modernization theory resembled the nineteenth-century unilinear theorizing about the evolution of societies that Franz Boas had rejected, instead encouraging his students to do careful ethnographic research *before* theorizing—a tradition that Cora Du Bois was continuing. At Harvard, however, she was surrounded by such prominent modernization theorists as Talcott Parsons, Alex Inkeles, and David McClelland in the Department of Social Relations. Close by were W. W. Rostow, Myron Weiner, Lucian Pye, Daniel Lerner, Paul Rosenstein-Rodan, Max Millikan, Everett E. Hagen, and others at MIT's Center for International Studies. All had written seminal books during this era, and some would become advisers to Presidents Kennedy and Johnson, the State Department, and/or the National Security Commission.[81] In the words of one contemporary historian who has examined this era of American history, "Whether it was Talcott Parsons arguing that specific, universalistic, achievement-oriented values were the hallmark of modernity; or Daniel Lerner claiming that modernity resulted from exposure to mass media and communications technologies; or David McClelland declaring that a population with high *n*Ach (the psychological 'need for achievement') would create modernity; or Alex Inkeles claiming that the factory experience created 'modern' notions about family, life, and politics, modernization theorists agreed that modernization was a totalizing, monolithic phenomenon which again and again, regardless of time and place, worked the same basic results for the same basic reasons."[82]

Du Bois was prescient in her critiques of modernization theory and its applications to U.S. technical assistance programs around the world. "Most of these programs," she wrote in 1972, "were conceived and executed by one or another variety of technical specialists whose understanding of both specific peoples and of social theory was too often minimal or non-existent. . . . Much of this aid was associated with the new military posture of the United States as the arch-defender of democracy against communism. This meant that large allocations of government expenditures were dictated by the military bureaucracy whose power in official councils in no way diminished, even after the end of World War II hostilities."[83] These remarks are as relevant today as they were in the 1960s and 1970s.

In her courses on culture change at Harvard—variously titled Culture Change, Problems in Socio-Cultural Change, and Individual and Socio-Cultural Change—Du Bois was dispassionate and nonjudgmental about her colleagues' theories of modernization.[84] She simply introduced them as different kinds of models of sociocultural change that students should consider. Her course syllabi, which kept changing over time, make it clear,

however, that she was asking students to critically assess different defini-
tions and theories of modernization and to question the ways in which
they might be culture bound.[85] She also insisted that students consider
the historical contexts of sociocultural change and "modernization."

There was a synergy between Du Bois's courses on culture change, the
questions she asked students to consider about modernization theory,
and her own personal research project in Bhubaneswar. That project was
originally entitled, "Confrontation of Modern and Traditional Values
in a Changing Indian Town." Specifically, she was going to investigate
"the importance of explicit and implicit traditional values in retarding
or accelerating modernization."[86] Although Du Bois used this language
in her 1963 application to the National Science Foundation, within a few
years she had repudiated it. In the spring of 1967, for instance, Du Bois
was invited to give the Cooper Lecture at Swarthmore College—a lecture
entitled "An Anthropologist Looks at Modernization." After reviewing
her discipline's different approaches to the study of sociocultural change,
Du Bois shifted her attention to recent American history and the impact
of World War II on research. During the war, she said, the United States
"had been severely handicapped by its lack of knowledge about foreign
terrains in which its troops fought. When we emerged from that war we
were a major world power. We shifted—partially, at least—from fighting
to diplomacy. Here our ignorance of the subtle and intricate characteristics
of cultures became even more apparent than our ignorance of their terrains." In this context, Du Bois continued, "modernization" was "one of
those superficial blanket terms that means little more than a contemporary
effort to cope with new situations. Imperial Rome was 'modernizing';
Renaissance Europe was modernizing; and so are all societies and cultures [including the United States] extant in the twentieth century. It is
the situation and not the processes that have changed, and are changing.
The changes are taking place from various cultural base lines, at different
rates, and toward varied goals throughout the world."[87]

In the course of her research in India, Du Bois had become a critic
of the very model of modernization that she had used in her initial NSF
proposal. She acknowledged this in her 1970 presidential address to the
Association for Asian Studies, where she wrote, "I began the enterprise
[in Bhubaneswar] with ideas as naïve as secularization, urbanization,

modernization, value confrontations, etc., etc.: i.e., that whole armamentarium of rather loose catch-words derived from western social science. I did have sense enough, even in 1961, to recognize that catch-words and simple dichotomies are only preliminary ordering devices without analytic puissance."[88] By the time Du Bois had completed research in India in 1973—including collecting 240 values protocols—she had concluded that all of these were Western ethnocentric terms that tended to focus attention on structural differences and implied incompatibilities between the old and the new rather than upon *processes of adaptation.*[89] Tradition and modernity thereby became static and opposed categories—that is, to become "modern" required discarding old institutions and ways of life, something that was not happening in Bhubaneswar. Residents were, in fact, learning how to negotiate the new while retaining much of the old, whether it was the system of stratification (caste and class), political hierarchies, occupations, different forms of education, patrilineal kinship and family organization, or religious faith and practices. While not addressing every dimension of postcolonial, postindependence change in Bhubaneswar, an impossible task, the project had provided many useful insights into these multifarious processes of sociocultural change and adaptation.[90] As we shall see, the challenge for Du Bois was to synthesize all of this into her proposed capstone volume to the Harvard-Bhubaneswar, India, Project.

CHAPTER 10

Looking Inward

> It is true of course that in the pause before death
> one experiences a variety of physical and mental disabilities.
> On the other hand, there is no greater good fortune
> than to outlive regret for failures and gratification for
> success:—in sum, to achieve a dispassionate appraisal of
> oneself in one's era.
> I have reached this point.
> —Cora Du Bois

Cora Du Bois's journey into a more self-reflective stage of life did not begin immediately upon her retirement from Harvard, in 1969, at the age of sixty-five. There were still several years of research in India to complete, PhD theses to direct, and professional writing projects to pursue. In addition, she would preside over the two professional societies that were most important to her—the American Anthropological Association (1969) and the Association for Asian Studies (1970)—during politically turbulent times. The process of retiring from her appointment at Harvard, furthermore, turned out to be a somewhat disagreeable one. Not only was she asked to vacate her office in the Peabody Museum immediately, but, more significantly, she discovered that, despite her Swiss-German habits of thrift, her retirement benefits were inadequate to sustain her in her Cambridge home. Between her low salary (by comparison with her male colleagues) and her numerous unpaid leaves of absence to do research in India, she had not built up adequate funds in the Teachers Insurance and

Annuity Association, for which her Zemurray Professorship had made her eligible.[1] In a 1968 letter to her friend and anthropology colleague Melford Spiro, Cora wrote, "I am in the process of preparing for the 'retirement life crisis.' There are Ph.D. students to be seen through their rigmaroles. There are also stringent financial curtailments to be ascertained and then coped with."[2]

These economic stringencies were brought to the attention of the Council of Radcliffe in February 1969. The council was informed that if Radcliffe's retirement formula were strictly adhered to, "Miss Du Bois' pension would be $7,120 annually.[3] Mrs. Bunting [president of Radcliffe] said that since Miss Du Bois is in the unique position of being Radcliffe's only Faculty member, it had seemed appropriate to consult [Harvard's] Dean Ford to see what Harvard would do if Miss Du Bois were paid by the University. Dean Ford recommended that Radcliffe consider making a special arrangement to bring Miss Du Bois' retirement income up to the $10,000 level."[4] Accordingly, on February 3, 1969, the council voted to award Cora Du Bois a pension supplement so that her total income, including Social Security and her retirement annuity, would amount to $10,000 annually.[5] In addition, Du Bois arranged to continue doing some part-time teaching at Harvard for several more years to build up her retirement income.

Not a person given to complaint or self-pity, Du Bois did express some displeasure with this conclusion to her celebrated position at Harvard. For example, in a 1972 letter to Evon Vogt, a Harvard anthropology colleague whose office she was using in his absence, she wrote, "I try not to feel rejected and ill-used, knowing how tangential my position has been from the beginning and from which I have derived certain freedoms in the past."[6] But she did feel poorly treated. Nonetheless, she would publicly deny that her treatment by Harvard had anything to do with her gender.[7] In some handwritten "Biographical Notes" that she drafted in the 1970s, however, Du Bois wrote both more philosophically about her years at Harvard and more forthrightly about the ways in which being a woman was problematic.

The decade and a half (1954–1969) that I spent at Harvard was not a fortunate one for that institution or for me. [Nathan] Pusey was president of Harvard and Polly Bunting of Radcliffe. Neither could be called visionary leaders. On their behalf it should be noted that those fifteen years found the University entrapped by national disaffections not of their making. The increasing opposition to the Vietnam war split the faculty. Large numbers of young men crowded the graduate schools to escape the discriminatory draft. The younger faculty and the radicalized youth movement furthered disruption of educational goals. Government grants for research and fellowships placed a heavy administrative task on the university as well as on faculty and students. Like the federal and state governments, the growth of regulatory bureaucracies at Harvard were costly in money and time that might have been better spent. Paper work and manipulation eroded energies that might have been better spent on education and on less money-seeking self-advancement. The faculty found its autonomy eroded by "rights" rather than privileges of the radicalized student body and the controls of funding institutions. Increasingly the faculty was seduced by politically influential appointments of putative power on the national scene. . . .

Personally, as Radcliffe's only Professor (ROP or Ropy as some of my friends called me) I experienced [many] of the various stresses and strains of the situation at Harvard. I was approved by both the Departments of Anthropology and of Social Relations as the only [female] tenured, full-professor and accepted with varied grace by its faculties. However as an endowed chair at Radcliffe was pure gravy for the Departments [at Harvard]—no cost and extra teaching for the growing load of students—I was rarely included in departmental decisions arrived at fraternally and covertly. In the broader context of Radcliffe, I was not socially acceptable to deans who were loyal to old standards of being ladies devoted to female education. In the still broader aspects of Harvard I was rarely forgiven attitudes or faults [that were] forgiven [others] in the inner circles of what has come to be called male chauvinism. There were many occasions when my outspokenness was frowned upon as lacking delicacy and my gross disregard of social reciprocities was taken amiss by (I suspect) wives of the faculty invested in their husbands' careers. I was not gracious nor did I have the energy, time, and funds to reciprocate. Parenthetically, I was consistently underpaid compared to colleagues holding comparable appointments.[8]

This is as close as Du Bois ever came to acknowledging some of the gender discrimination that she had experienced at Harvard. Not only was she paid less than her male colleagues, but she was often excluded from departmental meetings and other faculty deliberations. Male colleagues viewed her as too outspoken and Radcliffe administrators deemed her not sufficiently ladylike. In addition, her unique position as Harvard's only woman professor was a social liability. She had no "wife" to handle the social side of academic life, and her domestic arrangements had to be kept private.

As we have seen, Cora's greatest satisfaction at Harvard came from teaching and working with students, many of whom came from some distance to celebrate her upon the occasion of her retirement in the spring of 1969. They organized a gala "surprise" party for her at 20 Coolidge Hill Road, her home in Cambridge. (In uncharacteristic fashion, Cora feigned surprise to satisfy those who had organized the party in her honor.) Former students who could not be there wrote warm tributes to their teacher-mentor. Some years later, Cora expressed these sentiments about her teaching role at Harvard: "At Harvard I am sure that I was a disappointment to both men and women who expected me to accept a reformer's role or provide leadership in that direction. For me, the outlet in that direction lay in teaching and support for those students who happened to come my way and showed promise in understanding my own search for rational humanism. There have been possibly a dozen that I influenced directly and another possible couple of dozen that I influenced indirectly—more, certainly, than I could have produced in childbirth, adoption, or cultism."[9]

There was, at the time, no critical mass of women in the Harvard academic community with whom Du Bois might have affiliated and been a leader, nor, as we shall see, was she inclined to be a feminist reformer.

War and Ethics

Before retiring from Harvard Du Bois had been elected president of the American Anthropological Association. This entailed a three-year period of service—first as vice president/president elect, then as president, and finally as a senior advisor to the Executive Board. Her year as president (1969) coincided with her last year of full-time teaching at Harvard and overlapped with her three-year term presiding over the Association for Asian Studies (AAS). In other words, she was very much in the public domain during this period—nationally recognized and presiding over two major American scholarly organizations. It is ironic that whereas at Harvard Du Bois was treated as an outsider by her male colleagues, on the national scene her scholarship and leadership skills were well recognized. As president of the AAA, she followed in the footsteps of her principal teachers and mentors—Franz Boas, Ruth Benedict, Alfred Kroeber, and Robert Lowie—and she became the fifth woman to hold the position since the association's founding in 1902.[10] Du Bois became the first woman to preside over the Association for Asian Studies.

In later years Du Bois reported that she had allowed her name to go forward as a nominee for these leadership positions because she knew that she was about to retire, that she had been working under a lot of pressure, and that she would "probably need a *decompression chamber* of some sort."[11] It is hard to imagine that presiding over these two organizations during a tumultuous period in American history that seriously disrupted both associations provided much of a decompression chamber. But just as she had assumed a leadership position in the OSS during World War II, Cora seems to have handled these situations with her usual composure, impartiality, and attention to detail.

The context was the growing opposition in the United States to the Vietnam War, which had been increasing since 1964 and which by the spring of 1969 had essentially closed down Harvard University for the semester and, in 1970, reached tragic heights with the shooting of Kent State students. Opposition to the war had repercussions in both of these professional societies. In 1966, for instance, the American Anthropological Association had passed the first of many resolutions against the war. By 1969 a "Radical Caucus" group had formed and issued, at the annual AAA business meeting, a set of proposed resolutions that would prohibit members from doing contract research for the U.S. government, especially proscribing any "'defense,' 'defense'-related, or foreign or domestic counterinsurgency research, contract or otherwise."[12] By March 1970 there had been a shift from proposed resolutions to highly public accusations against certain individual anthropologists who did research in Thailand. Some students at UCLA had broken into a professor's office and taken documents that allegedly implicated a number of Thai experts in unethical complicity in U.S. counterinsurgency programs in Thailand. They gave these documents to the Student Mobilization Committee to End the War in Vietnam, which published them in the *Student Mobilizer*. The documents were also sent to the chair of the AAA Committee on Ethics, who, together with another member of the committee, proceeded to publicly condemn the actions of numerous Thai experts without first informing them of the charges or giving them the opportunity to respond.[13] At this point debates within the AAA escalated: the association was divided over ethical issues pertaining to possible clandestine activities by fellow anthropologists and also by the ethical issues associated with purloined documents and public accusations based on them.

This was the political context during Du Bois's three-year term presiding over the AAA. Although, as we have seen, she was strongly opposed to any kind of clandestine research by anthropologists, she was equally opposed to McCarthy-era tactics in which some persons publicly accused others of inappropriate behavior without giving them a chance to defend themselves.[14] She was president the year that the Executive Board asserted that the charges by two members of the Ethics Committee were "inadequately verified" and, hence, premature and unfair. Furthermore, the board asserted, "The Chairman (Wolf) and a member (Jorgensen) of the Ethics Committee, in communicating this matter outside the Ethics Committee, went beyond the mandate of the Executive Board to that Committee and were speaking as individuals and not on behalf of the Committee or the Association." The board agreed, however, that if such clandestine research were going on in Thailand or elsewhere, it would be "a breach of the ethical standards of the Association."[15] Meanwhile, it instructed the Ethics Committee "to limit itself to its specific charge, narrowly interpreted, namely to present to the Board recommendations on its future role and functions, and to fulfill this charge without further collection of case materials or by any quasi-investigative activities."[16]

These admonitions did not stop several members of the Ethics

Committee from making further charges against individuals who worked in Thailand, and in the subsequent year Du Bois advised the incoming AAA president, George Foster, on how he might best handle these public accusations. She wrote,

> At least two courses seem open. The first might be an independent Board of Inquiry. . . . I am not sure this is the best procedure although there is precedent. . . . An alternative is to disqualify Wolf, Jorgensen and Berreman as members of the Ethics Committee because of their precipitous and injudic public statements. They might then be replaced pro tem by three members of the Executive Board. Since the Executive Board members are elected and since the Ethics Committee is responsible to the Board, this seems an adequate way to exercise Executive Board jurisdiction when members of one of its committees *qua* committee is not repudiated but pre-committed members are.
>
> Since feelings are rightly running high, a judicious statement in the next *Newsletter* seems indicated.[17]

The Executive Board implemented all of Du Bois's suggestions, and George Foster wrote to thank Cora for her "energetic and vigorous leadership" as president and for her "presence, friendship, and judicious advice [that] will be missed by all of us at future Board meetings."[18] The three members of the Ethics Committee resigned and were replaced, and a special ad hoc committee, headed by Margaret Mead, was established to investigate the entire affair. None of these efforts entirely calmed the waters, however. Tensions within the association, which mirrored those throughout the country, continued until the Vietnam War ended, only to be revived by two twenty-first-century U.S. wars, in Iraq and Afghanistan. These latter wars have engaged some anthropologists in U.S. military counterinsurgency operations and have, once again, raised many of the same ethical issues within the American Anthropological Association—issues about the importance of transparency and openness in anthropological research, the importance of not doing harm to those people studied, and the need for anthropological knowledge to circulate freely.[19]

During her presidency of the AAA, Cora Du Bois made her views on clandestine research very clear in the response she made to a representative of the International Research and Technology Corporation who had asked her to provide him with a list of anthropologists who specialized in South and Southeast Asian affairs. She was unwilling to cooperate with such a request and responded as follows:

> As I understand IR&T's situation, you wish to have a list of anthropologists specializing in South and Southeast Asian affairs who would provide guidance and/or undertake applied research in the field of population problems on behalf of AID as IR&T's funding agency. What is unclear is whether the persons doing research; 1) are free to publish their results independently of AID and IR&T; 2) may be requested to deal with classified materials; 3) have any share in setting up priorities; and 4) have any voice in policy decisions at any level.
>
> *In terms of professional standards and ethics, I personally would not be willing to accept research so-sponsored—even if the most acceptable answers to the foregoing questions were available.* Nevertheless, I thank you for asking me. Clearly, I cannot speak for my colleagues.
>
> If you wish to have a list of individual anthropologists who do not share my reservations and who have relevant professional competence, may I suggest that you draw up a mailing list of Fellows of the American Anthropological Association who have South and Southeast Asian area interests. In a rough way this can be done by consulting the annual Directory of Departments of Anthropology [published by the AAA]....
>
> I regret having to write you so equivocal a letter but in all frankness, I cannot do otherwise.[20]

Du Bois's letters to George Foster and to the International Research and Technology Corporation representative illustrate some of the polemics that anthropologists and their national association faced during an unpopular war. Du Bois helped guide the AAA through a difficult period while at the same time making very clear her own ethical principles—that anthropologists should *not* engage in clandestine research or research that could be used for purposes over which they did not have control. This was the kind of "applied" anthropology for which she had a certain antipathy. She considered it distinctly different from the type of research she had undertaken for the OSS during World War II that did not use anthropological fieldwork as a cover for other, clandestine purposes.[21] Unfortunately, she was forced to use her term as president to ameliorate tensions and crises within the association rather than to speak out clearly about her conviction that there should be a complete separation of intelligence work and academic functions—that classified work, such as the kind she had undertaken for the government during a full-scale war, should not continue after one returns to academe.[22]

One of Du Bois's accomplishments during this period of turmoil, however, was to preside over the restructuring of the AAA. Up until her presidency there had been two categories of membership—fellows (voting members approved by the Executive Board as qualified anthropologists) and members (nonvoting members, most of whom were students), with fellows in control of the association. Du Bois came to believe that the "student" category was "a vague designation extending from freshmen taking their first courses, through undergraduate majors, to doctoral candidates. The term and the status," she wrote, "include persons who are casually curious to those professionally dedicated."[23] The AAA, she asserted, was a group of professional colleagues regardless of age or status. Under Du Bois's leadership all AAA members became voting members. As Louise Lamphere (Distinguished Professor of Anthropology Emerita, University of New Mexico, and former AAA president) has put it, "This meant a huge transformation for the organization, making it much more democratic so that the membership could more clearly have a say in how anthropologists should respond to pressing social issues like the Vietnam War, sex discrimination, minority rights, etc."[24]

Du Bois's term as president of the AAS required walking a political tightrope similar to the one she had been on with the AAA. That association was also splintered by the same kinds of accusations and ethical debates (with some of the same players) as in the AAA—debates that resulted in the formation of a Concerned Asian Scholars group that met separately but concurrently with the annual meetings of the AAS in 1970 (during Cora's term as president) and in 1971.[25]

In later years, when Du Bois reflected back on these experiences, she reported in her often self-derogatory fashion, "I really have no taste for this sort of organizational thing. I don't think I was very successful at it . . . [but] I was terribly conscientious and when that was through, I was through."[26]

21. Portrait of Cora Du Bois in later life. Cora Alice Du Bois Papers (SPEC.COLL.ETHG. D852c), Tozzer Library, Harvard College Library, Harvard University.

Margaret Mead and Cora Du Bois: Public vs. Private Personas

Margaret Mead, as mentioned above, chaired the special AAA ad hoc committee to investigate "the Thai affair." The committee's report was presented at the association's annual meeting in New York in November 1971 and was "overwhelmingly rejected by the membership as a whitewash of the Association."[27] Mead, one of the elder stateswomen of the association, was undoubtedly displeased with this outcome. Shortly thereafter, in a January 1972 letter to Cora Du Bois purportedly written to respond to Du Bois's review of her most recent book, *Culture and Commitment: A Study of the Generation Gap* (1970),[28] Mead interjected the following paragraph into the midst of a letter otherwise devoted to explicating and defending her book against some of Du Bois's critiques: "Somehow you do always manage to sound more like an elder statesman than even your seniors. You know I wanted to have you chair the committee on the Thailand Controversy, I felt you were far better fitted for it than I, but apparently you had expressed views, while I had been out of the political arena at the time and so had not made any comments. But I thought you were the ideal person."[29] Mead was clearly unhappy with the outcome of the investigation *and* with Du Bois's review of her book. Hence this sudden attack on Du Bois's "statesmanship." Both women had commanding presences and both, as senior stateswomen of the association, were caught in the middle of an unpleasant political fight that they could not resolve.

Mead, however, always liked to be in the limelight, whereas Du Bois did not seek public attention.[30] Mead liked the role of reformer whereas Du Bois did not. In fact, Du Bois's review of *Culture and Commitment* and Mead's personal responses to it typify their very different orientations toward scholarship as well as their responses to the antiwar and civil rights demonstrations of the 1960s. In her review Du Bois began by praising Mead's prolific writings—her "excellent ethnographic monographs" and also her "series of readable and timely books [that] have, more than the writings of any anthropologist of her generation, brought the discipline into popular repute. In these she has been an ingenious syncretist, a diligent communicator and, despite her grounding in relativism, a firm moralist. By the same token, and to her honor, she is not necessarily consistent either within or between publications. Consistency can be left for petty minds."[31] There was an edge to this generally benign introduction.

Du Bois went on to summarize Mead's assumptions and arguments in the book, some of which she took issue with, asserting that Mead "had jeopardized her argument [in the third section of the book] in various ways" and that "her rhetoric of persuasion changes from generalizations based on illustrative insights to generalizations based on intuitive foresight and ethical judgments. I am not decrying," Cora continued, "out of social scientific purism, either generalizations based on supportive illustrations or intuitive foresight. I am sympathetic to Mead's implicit position that creative, humanistic thought is more interesting than pedantic rhetorics of proof. *But thought must be rigorous.*"[32] One can imagine the sparks that flew when Mead reached this point in reading Du Bois's review. Clarity and rigor had always been two of Du Bois's bêtes noires with respect to writing, and students' writings were not the only objects of her critiques. Throughout her career, Du Bois was a prolific reviewer of books, and many authors were the objects of both her praise and criticism. Mead, who often wrote for public consumption, tended at times to be more provocative than rigorous, and Du Bois, writing for an anthropological audience, called her on it in this instance.

One of Du Bois's criticisms concerned Mead's assertion that the world was in a "putative third evolutionary phase" of development with respect to intergenerational interaction, in which youths looked only to one another for answers rather than to their elders—that is, "the generation gap." Mead, the contemporary cultural commentator, viewed the events of the 1960s as a sign of irreversible change, whereas Du Bois, more a cultural historian, saw parallels with other moments in American history. Du Bois wrote,

> This is not to say that unprecedented changes have not occurred in some areas of human societies in the last thirty years. They have. And some may be irreversible. But do these changes really entail any more of a generation gap than have occurred in many other situations of the past? Is the much touted "generation gap" really so new or so much more extreme than were met in other eras and situations with present-oriented peer group responses which Mead herself sees as temporary and transitional? To my mind the present youth unrest lies in taking seriously traditional American values and goals as well as much of the social behavior including outbursts of violence. *The young reformists are thoroughly within the American tradition in their desire to see the benefits of the society more widely and equably distributed.* This is again simply a reassertion of the egalitarian ideals that have too often been forgotten in practice. The so-called generation gap should not be confused with genuine changes in technology, population, growth, pollution, etc. etc. The generation gap, if it exists at all, looks to me like a postfigurative [Mead's category] situation with a dash of peer group solidarity—but only a dash.
>
> The present young activists and reformists are looking for guidance to grandparents and great grandparents:—*inter alia* Mead and Marcuse; Marx, Hegel or even Thoreau; and in some cases to the turn of the century anarchists. The disparate responses of young people is a very mixed bag which produces in this elder, at least, all too frequently a sense of *déjà vu*.[33]

This "exchange" between two of the most renowned women anthropologists of their generation essentially concluded a long and uneasy relationship with one another. Mead died six years later, in 1976. Born only two years after Mead (Mead in 1901, Du Bois in 1903), Cora would say that they belonged to different centuries. Mead, having decided on a career in anthropology much sooner than Du Bois, was professionally senior to her. She was writing her PhD dissertation at Columbia when Cora was an MA student in history at the same institution. But in the end, Mead was a curator at the American Museum of Natural History and an adjunct professor at Columbia, whereas Du Bois had the more prestigious academic position—a named chair at Harvard. Du Bois was queried by one of Mead's biographers, Jane Howard, as to whether these different appointments might have bothered Mead.[34] "Could she have resented your being appointed—if my facts are correct—the first female full professor at Harvard?" Howard wrote. "How much did her adjunct status at Columbia bother her? Were her aggressive forays into the larger world in any sense a reaction to the lukewarm treatment she might have been given by her immediate colleagues?"[35] Du Bois responded to Howard, saying,

> This [the Zemurray Professorship at Harvard] raises a whole series of administrative facts and fictions that constitute a considerable historical digression that I still do not fully understand. The point is that in the narrow confines of the "Groves," it induced considerable gossip. Shortly after my appointment Margaret and I met for four or five days in a conference between California's educators and representatives of "applied anthropology" and other social disciplines. At that time I spoke to Mead about her outstanding status in comparison to mine for this "honor." She was gracious about the whole matter saying that she preferred her appointment as "adjunct professor" at Columbia (where I was also about to be appointed) and her ties to the American Museum of Natural History, where she had greater freedom and resources for research and writing. I have come to recognize that her judgment was correct and astute.[36]

Du Bois's relationship with Mead had remained uncomfortable ever since their 1937 "misunderstanding"—Cora's word—when she had turned down the invitation to join Mead and Bateson's research project in Bali.

Mead also seems to have viewed Du Bois as a rival for Ruth Benedict's attention and as a potential competitor in the culture and personality movement of the 1930s. In addition, she may have resented the friendship that had grown between Du Bois and Gregory Bateson (Mead's then husband) when they served together in Kandy, Ceylon, during the war. Following the war, when Cora was working for the State Department—"not a salubrious intellectual atmosphere," Cora would say—she liked to spend time with anthropology colleagues and friends in New York City. "I asked to spend an evening with Gregory and Margaret to talk shop. Margaret made it quite clear that I was not welcome. After that I saw her only in passing at professional meetings. We were both courteous but aloof."[37]

The correspondence with Jane Howard stimulated Du Bois to jot down a list, with paper and pencil, of some of the ways in which she considered herself different from Mead:

I am more private; less assured; more philosophic; more lazy; less "contemporary" than she was.

We belonged to different centuries although we were within a year or two of the same age.

She sought celebrity and achieved it. I sought privacy. She turned outward, I turned inward.[38]

As we shall see, Du Bois increasingly turned inward during this last stage of her life, whereas Mead remained on the public lecture circuit, did TV shows, and wrote regularly for *Redbook* magazine. Du Bois, by contrast, was a private person who had successfully acted on a large and public stage but who, unlike Mead, was not comfortable there.

When Mead died, Cora sent a letter of condolence to Mead's longtime research associate and companion, Rhoda Métraux. "It is to you possibly more than anyone else," she wrote, "that I want to extend my condolences and sympathy at Margaret's death. Your many years of professional and personal support must have been one of the ties she most needed and prized as she grew older. Your self-effacing loyalty and tact were evident possibly to relatively few."[39] Métraux replied, "Thank you for your letter. Very few people can have any understanding of Margaret [*sic*] and my relationship, as so few had of Margaret's and Ruth's [Benedict]."[40] This was as close as either woman, born in a different era, could come to naming what were lesbian, as well as professional, relationships. Cora would address this issue privately in her "Biographical Notes," to be discussed below.

Writing about India

After serving as president of two major professional societies, Cora was ready to turn inward and away from Harvard and her professional duties, but she still had several graduate students to shepherd through their PhD dissertations and degrees and her own book on the Bhubaneswar project to write. Part of her plan had always been to write a capstone volume that would synthesize this multifaceted project and address how Bhubaneswar, in microcosm, might throw light on "the difficulty of any new nation that is trying simultaneously to achieve social welfare measures and economic development in the context of political democracy."[41] It had been, indeed, an ambitious project that tried to understand, from the perspective of one community, how a young democracy was faring politically, economically, socially, and culturally in a post–World War II and postcolonial environment.

Cora Du Bois never wrote her book about India. Du Bois—a woman known for her intellectual prowess, penetrating prose, and decisiveness about important matters—had put herself into a state of "neurotic conflict" (her term) over the writing of a synthesis of the Bhubaneswar project, a book that would have served as an intellectual capstone to her years at Harvard. What had happened? She struggled with it for five or six years in the 1970s, producing elaborate outlines for a two-volume work, numerous notes, and several published and unpublished papers.[42] How could such a clear-minded and strong-willed woman, whose pen was always ready and decisive, become blocked? There were, I believe, a variety of contributing factors. Her book outlines and notes make it clear that she had turned the Bhubaneswar project into a massive theoretical and ethnographic enterprise that became difficult to accomplish. She wanted to address the many questionable methodological and theoretical issues in which, she believed, the social sciences were engaged—from reliance on ethnocentric surveys to the comparative method, a hallmark of anthropology, which she had come to believe gave preference to form over meaning. In notes attached to her book outline, Cora wrote,

Responses to questionnaires, however skillfully constructed, even for Euro-American society, seldom reveal much more than the stereotypes of what people think they think is important . . . but trivial in comparison to what they passionately believe or to how they actually behave. Any ethnographer knows the difference. . . . In India, I am convinced that quantitative data widely collected on western models is open to wide areas of inaccuracies, that questionnaires produce at best the respondent's sense of what either the interrogator or the national stereotype require. Courtesy, patriotism, and a display of sophistication commensurate with the respondent's schooling may separately and collectively require such responses.[43]

Du Bois's personal experience with trying to capture value changes in Bhubaneswar by using a systematic interview schedule had clearly colored her views on such research techniques. She had developed a lengthy values protocol that had been translated into Oriya and pretested before being administered to some 240 Bhubaneswar residents who represented new and old occupations.[44] The interview schedule tried to tap into people's changing views on education, occupational choices, religion, the extended family, arranged marriage, gender hierarchies, caste, and responsibilities of the government. Du Bois, however, distrusted the quantitative results and found the whole process distancing and unsuitable to her more ethnographic enterprise. Her critique of such methodologies anticipated many of the more humanistic concerns and approaches that came to dominate cultural anthropology by the 1980s, in part through the influence of her former student Clifford Geertz.[45]

Du Bois also intended to address scholars' tendencies to impose upon Indian society and culture such Western dualisms as "tradition vs. modernity," the "Great Tradition vs. Little Traditions," or the "Eastern vs. the Western mind," instead of recognizing India's enormous heterogeneity. Again, in notes attached to her book outline, Cora wrote,

Anyone who has spent intimate times in India has certainly come to at least two major conclusions. The first one is that, as in any other culture, the Intellectual (Great) Tradition has only a very limited, elite clientele. Whether schooled or illiterate the understanding of philosophic traditions is shot through with local interpretations and

re-interpretations. These have been called the Great and Little Traditions. This duality seems to me much too simple—as indeed are most
of these facile dualities which distract western thought and particularly
the social disciplines and the humanities. The "apperceptive mass" that
an Indian intellectual schooled in the West brings to bear on the vastly
varied intellectual tradition of India is both highly eclectic and skewed.
The Indian intellectual who has had minimal western schooling may
bring a quite different "apperceptive mass" to a different segment of
India's inexhaustible philosophy. The highly schooled Indian techni-
cian may have as his indigenous resource little more than versions of
the [Hindu] epics and puranas his educated but unschooled mother or
grandmother told him as a child. . . . The lower middle and low caste
unschooled groups may not even understand the intent symbolism of
a Car festival—or even recognize the word *sadhu*.[46]

Du Bois's proposed book was going to move well beyond a synthesis
of the Bhubaneswar project to a critique of many of the theoretical and
methodological approaches being generated in the social sciences during
the Cold War era. She had addressed some of them in public lectures but
none in print. I suspect that this was one source of her internal conflict.
Was she correct in her views or was she just unsympathetic with new
experimentation? And was she ready, as Harvard's first tenured woman
professor, to be overtly confrontational with many of her male colleagues
at Harvard and MIT, as well as with a variety of other scholars at South
Asian research centers around the country?

Never lacking in courage, Du Bois may, however, have lacked adequate
certitude at this stage of her career. Unlike her occasional adversary, Margaret Mead, Du Bois was much more cautious about what she put into
print. "Less assured" she had categorized herself in comparison with
Mead. When talking about India, Cora often mentioned the naiveté with
which she had begun research there. Had she learned enough to proceed
with such a mammoth book? Or was she, too, caught in what she viewed
as the complexity of Indian society and culture, which "left me feeling
the shallow naiveness of our own [American] materialism and the stupidity of our approach, internationally speaking?" "We just thought," she
continued, "if we transplanted our patterns and enough machinery and

enough technology that all would be well and India would be a democracy on its way to wealth and prosperity, or else we would have India under our thumbs because there has always been this in our foreign policy, our oscillation between do-gooders and exploitation, and neither worked."[47] Cora Du Bois, the former OSS intelligence officer and State Department official, wanted no part in this kind of approach to India. In a 1981 interview, Cora reported, "I would not consider that project a successful enterprise. Not for me. I learned a great deal but it was from such a base of naiveté that by the time I had learned a great deal I had only really begun to be at a [requisite] level of sophistication."[48]

The seemingly indomitable Cora Du Bois was feeling vulnerable—vulnerable intellectually and vulnerable as Harvard's celebrated Zemurray-Stone Professor, of whom important things were still expected, certainly this book as a suitable conclusion to her career there. Could she produce a book that would live up to what she considered an inflated reputation as Harvard's first tenured woman? "I don't think I was nearly as good as I was often appraised as being," she reported. "And really, I don't say this with false modesty. I know what I aspired to, what I did well and what I didn't do well, and my resort to expediencies of one sort or another."[49] This was Du Bois the self-critic speaking. She could be as hard on herself as she was on her students, and her standards for analysis and writing were immensely high. How was she going to live up to her own self-imposed standards, let alone the expectations she imagined others had for her?

There was yet another significant facet to Du Bois's "neurotic block." In the early 1970s, during this period of frustrated writing, she had become depressed and had begun to drink more. Alan Sable, one of the Bhubaneswar cohort, was working on his dissertation during this period and, when visiting Cora at her home for advice and direction, he observed her general depression and increased consumption of alcohol—something that she, herself, attested to in her "Biographical Notes." His thesis discussions, he reported, would frequently devolve into the sharing of drinks and stories. Cora, Sable felt, preferred him as a raconteur to a graduate student in need of help with his dissertation. On one such evening Jeanne Taylor, in a worried voice, told Sable, "Cora's not happy because she's not doing her work."[50] During this period of depression and inner turmoil,

Cora addressed, in her personal memoirs, one of her most deep-seated vulnerabilities—her sexuality. Entitling her remarks "The Testament of a Public and Private Person in the mid 20th Century," she began,

> The latter part of my life has been in a milieu of rather frenetic Freudianisms and crude "behavioral scientism." Privacy was not valued. The attacks on it by my associates were varied but insistent. Because any individual who has led a socially aberrant life, in my case a lesbian one, inevitably bears with gross discrepancies between his public and his private persona, it has seemed worthwhile to assemble in the last years of my life a running comment on those views I tried as far as possible in my prurient environment to keep to myself. Most of the comments, though not necessarily of experiences, belong to the last decades of that life. They were assembled after the full "enormity" of being a deviant in mid-20th century America [became] apparent to me. This record may have psychological implications beyond those I appreciate. But after all, anyone shaped in the image of even the finale of the Protestant Ethic must justify indiscretion. . . .
>
> What I do wish to state is that the professional, that is public, last years of my life were markedly uncreative and unproductive, largely because I found the grounds of emphasis [in anthropology] shifting underneath me. My private life, and the values I prized in it, were increasingly important to me. Simultaneously my public role was, disproportionately to my feelings about it, rewarded. I was locked in a conflict which I have chosen to phrase in these terms, but in whatever phrases they may be stated, are commonplace to all *neurotic* conflict. I prize that conflict as all neurotics do.[51]

Clearly, one source of Du Bois's inner turmoil was this divide between her public and private selves that had become increasingly burdensome. She complains here of attacks on her privacy—a privacy necessitated by who she was, a lesbian in an era of "frenetic Freudianisms," as she put it—that labeled her a deviant. For most of her lifetime, by keeping her "socially aberrant life" private, Du Bois had built—by means of her powerful personality, intellect, and drive—an immensely successful career in the public realm. Now, as she moved into retirement and the last stage of life, Du Bois found herself "locked in a neurotic conflict" over this split in her personhood. Writing her India book represented the public realm that, over time, she had come to value less than her private life. Cora Du Bois, as she moved into her seventies, was no longer disposed to have to maintain this split identity, and the book was one of the casualties of that struggle.

Du Bois was released from some of the professional guilt that she felt during this period when, quite independently, I proposed that the American members of the India cohort meet together and plan a joint volume on the Bhubaneswar project. (Cora would later remember this as having "turned over" the project to me.)[52] I applied for and received a small grant from the South Asia Regional Council, a subgroup of the Association for Asian Studies, which covered airfare for everyone to meet together for three days in Chicago. Richard Taub, one of the Bhubaneswar cohort and a professor at the University of Chicago, and his wife, Doris, offered their Chicago home as a meeting center-cum-hotel and restaurant, and Cora was invited to join us there in March 1976. She arrived with two large baskets of live lobsters from Boston that—accompanied by fresh asparagus, bread, and plenty of wine—we consumed with relish the first evening. It was a celebratory occasion to have Cora and all of her former U.S.-based Bhubaneswar project students—some with spouses—gathered together for the first time. That feast was followed by two full days of planning, the upshot of which was that each person agreed to contribute one or two chapters for the volume; we would solicit chapters from our Odishan colleagues; Cora would contribute an introduction; and I would serve as editor. Afterward Cora wrote to say, "That was a fine meeting on all scores. You make an excellent chairman:—efficient but not officious. It was a most productive meeting in terms of THE BOOK and in terms of human relations. The Taubies, of course, were superb hosts." In a footnote, Cora asked, "What is 'IT' to be called? Is it too early to start building a file of suggestions? I am *not* suggesting this but might the title be something along the lines—'Can Community Studies Throw New Light on India?' It is certainly the goal I hope for."[53]

Clearly Cora was engaged in the enterprise, but as the deadline for contributions to the Bhubaneswar volume neared, she sent me a letter saying, "I thought I ought to phone you but decided a letter would be less embarrassing to me. I am welching out on an introduction to the Bhubaneswar book. I can't tell you how abashed I am. More or less legitimate excuses could be mustered I suppose, but the real issue is that I have what can only be considered a neurotic block."[54] Once again, Cora could not face writing about the Bhubaneswar project. As editor, I drafted an introduction and a concluding section to the book and sent them to her for comments. In characteristic fashion, she returned eight pages of typed queries and suggestions. Du Bois the teacher and critic was still very much alive and well. *The Transformation of a Sacred Town: Bhubaneswar, India* was published in 1980 and dedicated to Cora Du Bois, who, meanwhile, had divested herself of all the Bhubaneswar files and books that had accumulated in her Annex since 1961. She had shipped them to the University of Chicago and turned her attention to other endeavors.

New Directions, Old Constraints

It is ironic that Du Bois's period of depression and private musings about her "deviant" sexual orientation coincided with the increased activism of women and gays and lesbians in the United States. Retired from Harvard and trapped in her book-writing project, she was in no position to follow these events, which had been spurred on by the antiwar and civil rights movements of the 1960s, nor to benefit from them. Furthermore, in the late 1960s, when women at Harvard had begun to organize, Cora declined to participate. This piqued her good friend, Beatrice Whiting, a long-term lecturer in the Department of Social Relations, where her husband, John Whiting, was a tenured professor. (In 1974 Beatrice Whiting—after twenty-two years as a lecturer—was finally made a full professor with tenure in the School of Education.) As Cora had discovered, even for someone like herself with a named professorship, Harvard had a deep-seated tradition of marginalizing women. Into the 1970s, most women at Harvard held minor, impermanent appointments as lecturers, research staff, and teaching fellows.[55] Organizing and putting pressure on the university was the only way to make some incremental change, and Beatrice Whiting sought Cora's leadership.[56]

As Whiting expressed it years later, "Cora was not a feminist and she did not believe that gender should be a consideration in appraising or rewarding intellectual performance. She often stated that she had not experienced discrimination at Harvard even though many of her colleagues and students tried to persuade her that perhaps this was the case.

As for privileges not granted women, she considered them trivial. . . . She remained aloof from the fray in the 1960s."[57] Whiting, however, understood that Cora's experiences with Red-baiting in Washington DC during the McCarthy era had made her turn away from political activism and that, furthermore, when Cora had arrived at Harvard, there had been "no critical mass of women" with whom to congregate. For Du Bois, Harvard had been a relatively lonely existence and one in which she believed she had to protect her personal life from potentially homophobic—a term invented in the 1960s—administrators, faculty, and staff. "An air of composure, an air of reason," as May Sarton had put it in her fictional account of Cora Du Bois, became her "suit of armor."[58]

Sarton, by contrast, had come out as a lesbian in the mid-1960s and had become a spokesperson for the women's and gay/lesbian movements of the 1970s and 1980s. Sarton became a celebrated poet and writer during that era and was in much demand as a speaker at women's conferences and programs around the country. Presumably, it was an easier transition to make for an independent writer like Sarton than for someone like Cora who had an academic reputation to uphold at a prestigious and highly patriarchal institution.

Du Bois's "suit of armor" affected her views on feminism well into the 1980s. On two different occasions when staying with Cora and Jeanne in Cambridge, I tried to explain my own engagement with feminism and women's studies, to little avail. Cora understood *gender* as a legitimate research category—one that she had been instrumental in promoting in her own early research—but not as a political agenda. On one occasion, when I returned to their home after an afternoon's visit with Beatrice Whiting, I had a note from Cora awaiting me that said, "Where have you been? Off, I suppose, talking women's lib with Bea." And in a 1984 letter to a former student, Antonia Mills (professor of First Nation Studies, University of Northern British Columbia), which she copied me on, Cora wrote, "I urge you—while you think about your book [on Beaver women]—to get in touch with Susan Seymour. She has built up a very considerable knowledge of research in women's roles and life styles in widely diverse societies around the world. I must stress that her interests are *not* NOW political but socio-cultural."[59] Research on women had met with Cora's approval but not political feminism.

Meanwhile, Cora's interests had turned to considerations of her own life and career and to reconceptualizing anthropology for herself. In one of her two final publications, "Some Anthropological Hindsights," she recounted her own journey in and out of anthropology and how she had come to view herself as a philosophical humanist.[60] She had, in a sense, come full circle from her intellectual origins in history and her early ambitions to write something comparable to Oswald Spengler's *Decline of the West*. If she had undertaken such a project at this stage of her life, it might have been entitled "The Rise and Fall of Culture-Bound Theories" or "Why Anthropology Is a Philosophical Humanism." It would have addressed all the problems that she saw in the post–World War II social sciences as the United States became a "neocolonial world power" and how some anthropologists' captivation with "the growth and successes of our Western ideologies" had "diverted attention from the question of what is pan-human and what are culture-specific generalities"—what she considered to be the principal raison d'être of the discipline.[61] Then Du Bois would have recounted some of what we knew about *Homo sapiens* and all that we did not know, but how we needed to proceed cautiously in building our base of knowledge, in full recognition of the dangers with cross-cultural translation and generalization. It would have been a cautionary tale.

"The Springtime of My Senility"

As Cora Du Bois entered her seventies, she began using the expression "I am in the springtime of my senility," which she attributed to Anne Morrow Lindbergh. As someone who was very concerned not to publish beyond having her full mental capacities, as she believed others had done, it was her way of indicating that she was slowing down both physically and mentally. Yet as someone who had defined her identity early on through the mastery of written English, she never stopped writing letters and making notes about her life and thoughts until she experienced a severe stroke in 1988, when she was eighty-four. She had experienced a variety of other severe health problems along the way—surgeries on a malignant colon in 1976 and on her lungs in 1979, both of which, she reported to Jeanne, made her "fuzzier in the head than usual." After the latter operation, she wrote, "I do seem to be regaining whatever stage of senility at 76 is appropriate."[62] Much of the time Cora was able to maintain a dispassionate appraisal of herself as she aged—a distanced perspective on herself and human affairs that she had cultivated since childhood. When asked, at age seventy-seven, to evaluate her life, Du Bois responded both modestly and dispassionately:

> I can't see anything to regret. In fact, I think I have been extraordinarily lucky. It wasn't my fault that I was lucky. Just that's the way the chips fell. During almost three-quarters or more of a century of the most tremendous upheavals and with so many anguishing and terrible things happening to the rest of the world, and here I sat and just paddled through without a quiver. It's just remarkable. I mean, I have early memories of World War I, World War II, the depression, all of the things that have gone on in this time and the horrors of the world events over the last 75 years or so. Really, I was unscathed, and sometimes I felt almost guilty about it. I mean that I should have had such a lucky, self-fulfilling life with no real effort or deprivations of anything on my part and none of the anguish that so large a part of the world's population has gone through. And I've seen some pretty horrible things in my life.[63]

It was eye surgery for a ripped retina in 1980, however, that in some ways was most devastating to Du Bois. The surgery, she reported, did not work and her "good right eye is now completely and irrevocably blind" and her "bad left eye remains limited and needs magnification for reading."[64] This made both reading and writing extremely difficult, but she persevered. Her penmanship, which had always been tiny and precise, now became large and the sentences less coherent. In these later years she increasingly relied on a private secretary, Eric Davis, to type her letters and other documents. As she explained to her cousin, Gérard Du Bois, "[Eric] is a gentle and understanding teacher at a private school in Boston. He can decipher my writing and gives me as much time as possible, including typing this note to you."[65]

Du Bois exchanged stories about aging with her close friend Margaret Read, a British social anthropologist. "Like you," Cora wrote to Read, "I deplore the absence of grey hair to signal that my hearing diminishes; that my recall especially for names if not for people is deplorable (it took me two days to recall Edmund Leach's [a renowned British anthropologist] name); and that eyesight is such that reading proceeds at a snail-like pace. And here I am fifteen years younger than you. I have always thought of myself as a slow developer but this transition from late middle age to old age has changed that illusion."[66]

Then Cora continued, in a more serious vein, to address "living with death":

It still astonishes me that I, at least, did not foresee this stage of "living with death." It is a phase of life as pronounced as childhood and adolescence. The prolonged middle stages of youth and maturity seem to block out the earlier and the ultimate phases of life. What most oppresses me at present is the task of clearing up the physical detritus of those intermediate years. Books and papers to be disposed of, the house and garden to be maintained, the disposal of trinkets and such funds as may remain after inflation, while trying to guard against an increasing dependency for an unforeseeable end.

I have not had your capacity for having continuing friends. Most of those I had are either gone or in a most painful state of senility which prohibits any meaningful communication. As for kin, I never really had or was prepared to cherish them as you did yours. The upshot is a retreat into seclusion with one exception, that I enjoy greatly having people come to me—rather than my going out to them. There are enough of those among the young [former students] to provide me still with frequent guests. But they too will disappear if I last too long and deteriorate much further.

Jeanne and I manage our relationship as amicably and with as much mutual concern as our very different temperaments and interests allow. She is ten years younger than I and has not yet entered the "terminal stage." She has, to my regret, given up painting but she has acquired a whole series of other "craft-like" interests, makes new acquaintances, and maintains a few life long ties of friendship and family. This is, for me, very reassuring.

This letter has become much too long winded. Do forgive me. It is such a pleasure to know that you are a friend to whom I can still communicate with some hope of understanding. The greatest discovery is that one can live with death without being unhappy—just retractive.[67]

I quote at length from this particular letter because of its richness. With regard to aging, Du Bois was evoking issues that have become commonplace in contemporary American culture and that now have an industry to address them, whether it be physical and/or mental decline, loss of independence, or a reduction in friends and family members. And "living with death," as Cora put it, has become a recognized stage of life.

Cora wrote this letter just a month before her seventy-fifth birthday. It is true that she had lived most of her life without "cherished kin." Her father, with whom she had a close and loving relationship as a child, had died when she was eighteen. Her problematic brother had disappeared, never to be found. And her antagonistic relationship with her mother had improved over the years, but it was never one of great warmth and mutual admiration. Symbolic of this, perhaps, is that the Cora Du Bois Papers at Harvard include no letters from her mother. However, in gratitude for all that her mother and stepfather had done for her during her years in Indonesia, she dedicated *The People of Alor* to them. By this stage of life, however, her mother and stepfather were deceased, as were all of her Du Bois and Schreiber aunts and uncles. Cora's Swiss godson had been killed in a plane accident, leaving only some Du Bois cousins in Switzerland and some Schreiber cousins in various parts of the United States with whom Cora had not remained in close contact during the later part of her demanding professional life. This situation, however, was about to change.

On October 26, 1978—Cora's seventy-fifth birthday—the doorbell rang at 20 Coolidge Hill Road. When Cora opened it, there stood two of the three Swiss cousins with whom she had lived in Frankfurt as an eighteen-year-old, together with two "newly discovered cousins," Gérard and Pat Du Bois. Gérard, a second cousin who had only recently become known to Cora but who resided in the United States, had written to her when updating the Du Bois family genealogy. He had discovered that he had a famous cousin at Harvard and contacted Cora for information about herself and her branch of the Du Bois family. Then, while in Switzerland visiting relatives and collecting more family data in the summer of 1978, he suggested, "facetiously," to Cora's three cousins that they pay a surprise visit to her for her upcoming seventy-fifth birthday. "Ruth declined; her husband, who had just retired from the post of Chief of Protocol in

22. Jeanne Taylor, Gérard Du Bois, and Cora Du Bois, 1980. Cora Alice Du Bois Papers (SPEC.COLL.ETHG.D852c), Tozzer Library, Harvard College Library, Harvard University.

Holland, was dying of cancer," Gérard reported. "But, typical of Du Bois spirit for adventure, Louison and Irene agreed." Jeanne, acting as Gérard's "mole," told Cora that some former students were coming to visit her that day and, in preparation, got out drinks and snacks. At 6:00 p.m. the front doorbell rang, and there were Cora's cousins. "Instantly, Cora recognized them, even after so many years," Gérard said. "Jeanne posted cheerful 'Welcome to Swiss cousins' posters, and for a few hours, happy memories were recalled."[68]

From that moment on, Cora had a coterie of devoted cousins in her life. Gérard and Pat Du Bois remained in continuous contact with her and Jeanne, visiting them in Cambridge with some regularity, writing letters, and sending gifts throughout the remainder of Cora's life. Cora reciprocated with warm letters of appreciation and gifts. Following her eightieth birthday, in a letter to her cousin Louison, thanking her for her "kind and heartwarming" wishes, Cora wrote,

I, too, wish that we were not an ocean apart. Gérard Du Bois flew up from Washington DC for lunch and a three-hour visit and then flew back. Poor Pat had to stay home to take care of three grandchildren who had chicken-pox. She did find time to send a torte and a charming and most skillfully made greeting card. Gérard brought wine and liqueur—it was a gay and vivacious though brief party on Oct. 26. The *big* celebration was a surprise party the evening of the 29th. Jeanne secretly invited seventeen of my favorite local friends for cocktails and a catered supper. I have not felt so gay since your famous visit for my 75th birthday—though we did miss Ruth.[69]

Cora also corresponded with two of her Schreiber cousins—her childhood playmate Henry and his older brother, Bill—both of whom, in their later years, lived in Minneapolis–St. Paul. In 1982 Cora wrote to Bill, explaining her poor health but saying that she was "fortunate in having a thoughtful housemate in Jeanne Taylor (who grew up in St. Paul!)."[70] She also sent Bill, who was in poorer health than she was, occasional checks to help support him in his old age. During this period Henry's daughter, Carol Bollinger, and her daughter, Anna, came to 20 Coolidge Road for a visit. Following that visit, Carol wrote an admiring note to Cora, saying, "Anna and I had a truly memorable visit with you! You are our most distinguished relative and I have always admired you and your many accomplishments. Most impressive to me is that you did what you wanted to do before such independence became, shall we say, 'socially acceptable.' . . . This visit gave us a chance to know the other more intimate side of Cora Du Bois a little better and we love you even more. Thank you for having us in Cambridge and for being our cousin."[71]

Her remarks to Margaret Read notwithstanding, Cora had a coterie of devoted kin, friends, and former students, and her and Jeanne's guest quarters were well used. Among their many visitors was Les Barnette, the former Lieutenant W. L. Barnette Jr. who became acting chief of Research and Analysis for the OSS in Ceylon when Cora was called home at the end of the war. Cora invited Julia and Paul Child, who now resided in Cambridge, to join them for dinner the night Barnette was in town. Afterward Barnette sent the following note: "Just to say I had a delightful dinner and evening and it seemed very much like old Ceylon times. Frankly, I was wondering what you'd produce for a dinner for Julia and I was so pleased that it was all so simple and yet delicious and that you had not been spending the entire day stirring and chopping and mincing and reducing. And also that delicious dry white wine, and you were smart enough to provide a second bottle."[72]

Cora, the principal cook in the household, was never intimidated by Julia Child's presence. To other friends, who had requested recipes from her in exchange for recaning a chair, Cora wrote, "Gwen suggests that your generosity might be modestly reciprocated if I send you some notes of a skill I am reputed to share with you both: COOKING, of course. I should warn you immediately that I am not a COOK. I couldn't write a sensible recipe to save my life. I find it impossible even to follow one to its bitter end. I am a Swiss bourgeoisie—which means that I shop carefully, cook economically, and improvise madly when it comes to remnants. The results can range from good to terrible—I never know." Cora concluded her note with an interesting comment—"Maybe it is risk more than result that is gratifying"—and attached some recipes.[73] She may have been a Swiss bourgeoisie, but she also came from an adventurous family. Improvised cooking may have been a suitable outlet for someone like Cora whose professional life had always been highly structured.

All kinds of people from the past turned up in Cambridge or contacted Cora by letter. One was Frank Orenstein, who knew Cora and Jeanne only remotely when they lived in Georgetown. He contacted Cora in 1977 after seeing an article in the *New Paltz (NY) Weekly* about the "Cora Du Bois sewer line" that was about to be dug up and replaced. He sent Cora a letter, along with a clipping of the article. "I had not heard of you in many years," he wrote, " and now I find in one and the same article that you have your very own sewer line named after you and that, alas, it is to be torn up. *Sic transit* . . . First those South Sea Islanders probably all writing their memoirs for television and complaining that you didn't understand them [a reference to Margaret Mead], and now this."[74] It was all tongue in cheek, of course. Cora responded in kind: "Despite repeated failures to establish genealogical connections between the Swiss Calvinists of Neuchatel [Switzerland] and the French Huguenots of New Paltz [New York], it was thoughtful of the latter to give my name to a sewer main. Jeanne

Taylor, whom you may remember, said rather wistfully when I showed her your letter, 'I wish *I* had a sewer main named for me.'"[75]

To other friends, Cora recounted the story of the "Cora Du Bois sewer line" with great delight. "But you will ask," she wrote, "'How did [the name] *Cora* get into this?' Well my mother was related to the Dutch Guliks of the Hudson Valley where Cora was a common diminutive of Cornelia. Well, blow me over, when I first got a copy of my birth certificate, which was dated 1903, I discovered that I had been baptized Cornelia Alice Du Bois. The Alice was for my Swiss god-mother who was my father's sister."[76] The name Cora, or Cornelia, had been for her maternal grandmother.

The need to settle her affairs during this stage of life, as well as fears of dependency, were two of the themes in Cora's letter to Margaret Read. The former she could handle, despite declining health and eyesight, but the latter was an increasingly difficult matter, especially for such a strong-willed woman who had led a life of independence. Du Bois had already divested herself of her India materials, but now she needed to address all of her other personal and professional papers and books and her financial affairs. Through her friendship with Nancy Schmidt, the former head librarian of Tozzer Library—the library associated with Harvard's Peabody Museum and Department of Anthropology—Cora gave her personal library and papers to Harvard, to be housed in Tozzer. In a 1984 letter to Gérard Du Bois, Cora explained, "In sum, I want to reduce my detritus; I have turned my library and my archives over to Harvard and wish to leave what [financial] residue may remain on my death to the Cora Du Bois Endowment Fund through the anthropological library at Harvard, thereby getting rid of my professional accumulation as well as my personal one."[77] The Cora Du Bois Endowment Fund serves today to help support graduate student research in anthropology.

The lengthy legal and bureaucratic process of making all of this happen created a certain amount of tension between Cora and Jeanne. I visited them during this period, and Cora explained that Jeanne was not happy with her because she, Jeanne, was not sufficiently included in the decision making. In fact, the only "letter" to Jeanne Taylor that is included in the Cora Du Bois Papers at Harvard is a rough and not entirely coherent note, handwritten on the evening of April 25, 1985, in which Cora apologized to Jeanne for her recent preoccupations. "For almost a year (if not longer)," she wrote, "I have made clear to myself and to you that I had completed whatever my life has been and death [would be] a release. . . . In my own self-centered life, my Sir Roger de Coverly syndrome [looking at life from a distance], I ignored [you] and inexcusably ignored that my death might follow rather than proceed yours. I suspect that even such a gross self-centered assumption would injure you. It did." Then Cora reminisced about their purchase of their home at 20 Coolidge Hill Road so many years before and how much they had loved the house and the garden and had worked together to make it their own.[78]

Similarly, only one note from Jeanne to Cora exists in the archives. It is undated but must have been written as Cora declined physically and mentally and Jeanne tried, with some difficulty, to improve communication with her. (Cora, Jeanne's note implies, resented having to be helped with anything, including doing the taxes.) In the note, Jeanne attributed communication problems to Cora's poor hearing, declining memory, alcohol consumption, and obsession with finances (what had always been her source of independence). Jeanne outlined several ways in which they could improve matters, which included more *written* communication, Cora's use of "that damnable hearing aid," and "that we hug each other as often as possible!" Jeanne concluded, "I do truly love you—I do truly want us to stop being so hard on each other—I do truly want our last years to be good and understanding & loving. And to do that, I think we both have to give more than a few inches—maybe even a foot! Let's try it!"[79]

After Cora's stroke, in 1988, communication was further hampered. "At first, it was doubtful that Cora would survive," Jeanne wrote.

In those first days she was lucid and quite calm; in fact, it was she who assured us that there was nothing to fear. . . . Cora stopped smoking in the hospital, and slowly regained her physical strength. But the stroke, probably followed in the next months by other lesser strokes, steadily destroyed her ability to find words for what she wanted to say. She would speak in long, grammatically elegant sentences, using carefully pronounced nonsense words or words displaced from the ones she intended. She knew this was happening, and the struggle to articulate and to stay in touch often exhausted and disheartened her. Yet she never gave up on the effort.[80]

One of Cora's former students, Antonia Mills, came, with two of her children, to visit Cora in the year following her stroke. She found Cora looking physically fit and very energetic. Over lunch, Cora wanted to talk about all kinds of things. She talked and gestured animatedly as Jeanne translated for her. "It made her a more dynamic person who used gestures and exclamations more to augment what she was trying to communicate," Mills reported. "She was remarkably engaged in the conversation/interaction in a new kind of dynamic because of the truly remarkable word associations that emerged." Cora expressed concern for Mills being a single parent. She talked about the respect and honor that she had received in India and how she had felt poorly treated at the time of her retirement from Harvard. But most significantly, she spoke about the lesbian conference that she and Jeanne had attended at Yale. "Through facial expressions and tone of voice, Cora communicated enthusiasm about it," Mills reported.[81] The stroke, which had negatively affected Cora's prime mode of personhood—her facility with the English language—seems to have released some emotions and alternative ways of communicating. Perhaps it had also helped her move past the stigmatized self-concept that she had carried with her for so many years.

Cora Du Bois died on April 7, 1991, at the age of eighty-seven, in a nursing home where, the preceding year, Jeanne had had to move her after Cora had fallen and broken a hip. "Her anger with all the indignities of age," Jeanne wrote, "was matched by as many hours of philosophical equanimity, in which she would survey the whole of the human scene with a benign relish of its many ironies. Her sentences may have been hard to make out, but nonetheless she made many things—her fierce hold on life, her unending and kindly curiosity, the dispassionate breadth of her view—very clear.... I expected her to fight [the move to a nursing home], but instead she seemed to take it up as a kind of venture, almost as if this were a field trip into yet another curious new society."[82]

Cora Du Bois's remarkable journey through much of the twentieth century had come to an end. It had been filled with adventure and with unprecedented accomplishments in the world of government service and of academe. She had been a "first woman" in both realms—as chief of Research and Analysis for the OSS/Southeast Asia Command during World War II and as a tenured woman professor at Harvard.

She demonstrated courage by standing up for civil liberties during the
McCarthy era, in particular by refusing to sign a loyalty oath in the state
of California (and thereby losing her dream job at UC Berkeley, where
she would have become the first woman professor of anthropology). Not
a reformer by temperament, Du Bois was always a woman of principle,
as exemplified early on by her resigning from the student Honor Board
at Barnard when she believed that a fellow student had been unjustly
expelled from the college. In later years, she displayed her ethical principles by objecting to Harvard graduate students receiving funding from
the CIA, by instilling in her students strong fieldwork ethics, and in the way
she tried to handle complex ethical issues that arose when she presided
over two major professional associations during the Vietnam War. Du
Bois began life as a somewhat lonely and awkward girl who liked being a
removed observer of humankind but matured into a formidable woman
whose powerful mind, insatiable curiosity, and commanding presence
helped take her on an exceptional journey. While not intending to be a
leader or a woman of renown, she became one.

NOTES

Prologue

1. The other woman was Cecilia Payne-Gaposchkin, professor of astronomy, who came up through the ranks at Harvard and was advanced to rank of professor in 1956, two years after Du Bois's appointment.
2. At the time John W. M. Whiting was a professor of anthropology in the Department of Social Relations, and his wife, Beatrice B. Whiting, was a lecturer. Together they had instigated and developed systematic observation techniques for the cross-cultural study of children and their families in what has become known as the Six Culture Study (see, e.g., Whiting and Whiting, *Children of Six Cultures*).

1. Tomgirl

Epigraph: Quoted from a family memoir prepared by George Straub, one of Cora's first cousins on her mother's side (hereafter cited as "Straub memoir"). Carol Schreiber Bollinger, Straub's niece, made the memoir available to me.

1. JW, Session I, Pt. 1, p. 8.
2. CDBH, Box 10.
3. Mark Weber, "Boer War Remembered."
4. CDBH, Box 80.
5. Jean Jules Phillipe Du Bois obituary, *Perth Amboy Evening News*, January 13, 1922.
6. See Mark Weber, "Boer War Remembered"; and Van Onselen, *New Babylon, New Nineveh*.
7. Straub memoir.
8. Gérard Du Bois (one of Cora Du Bois's cousins), personal communication.
9. Jean Du Bois obituary, *Perth Amboy Evening News*, January 13, 1922.
10. Cora Du Bois's cousin, Gérard Du Bois, kindly provided me with a copy of the family genealogy that he had updated: "Notice Généalogique de la Famille Du Boz dit Du Bois," Supplément, 1986. A copy also resides with the CDBH.
11. Thanks to the hospitality of Helga Kaussler-Du Bois, my husband and I had the pleasure of staying at La Maison Du Bois and being shown through the different rooms of this old Du Bois residence and atelier.
12. Straub memoir.
13. Straub memoir.
14. Straub memoir.
15. "Biographical Notes," CDBH, Box 11.
16. CDBH, Box 79.

17. Cora Du Bois gave these letters to her cousin Gérard Du Bois, who entrusted them to me.

18. JW, Session I, Pt. 1, pp. 7–8.

19. JW, Session I, Pt. 1, p. 8.

20. "Biographical Notes," CDBH, Box 11.

21. JW, Session I, Pt. 1, p. 2.

22. Family letters in author's possession.

23. "Biographical Notes," CDBH, Box 11.

24. Family letters in author's possession.

25. Family letters in author's possession.

26. St Quentin lay at the heart of the war zone after 1916, when the Germans integrated it into the Hindenburg Line—a vast system of defenses that they built in northeast France. Much of the population was evacuated and the town was systematically looted, with industrial equipment removed or destroyed and nearly 80 percent of its buildings damaged. See "Saint-Quentin, Aisne," *Wikipedia*, last modified February 4, 2014, en.wikipedia.org/wiki/Saint-Quentin,_Aisne.

27. Hays, *From Cooperation to Complicity*.

28. Jean Du Bois obituary, *Perth Amboy Evening News*, January 13, 1922.

29. Sequine-LeVine, *Perth Amboy*.

30. Straub memoir.

31. JW, Session I, Pt. 1.

32. JW, Session I, Pt. 1, p. 8; see also "Miscellaneous Notes," CDBH, Box 11.

33. CDBH, Box 19.

34. CDBH, Box 19.

35. CDBH, Box 19.

36. Carol Bollinger, personal communication, reporting memories about her father's (Henry Schreiber) tales regarding his cousin Cora Du Bois and her parents.

37. Straub memoir, p. 10.

38. Straub memoir.

39. JW, Session I, Pt. 1, p. 1.

40. JW, Session I, Pt. 1, p. 7.

41. Jean Du Bois letters in author's possession.

42. JW, Session I, Pt. 1, p. 7.

43. Cora Du Bois, personal communication; see Seymour, "Cora Du Bois."

44. Addison and Steele, *Days with Sir Roger de Coverley*, 2–3.

45. CDBH, Box 10.

46. JW, Session I, Pt. 1, p. 10.

47. CDBH, Box 1.

48. CDBH, Box 79.

49. JW, Session I, Pt. 1; Straub memoir. Jean Du Bois's passport indicates that he took a trip to France in 1915.

50. CDBH, Box 11.

51. JW, Session I, Pt. 1, p. 3.

52. JW, Session I, Pt. 1, pp. 11–12.

53. CDBH, Box 11.

54. This poem was signed D. V. Dorm, a pseudonym that Cora Du Bois sometimes used for her poetry. CDBH, Box 11.

55. I am appreciative of help in analyzing these poems from my colleague Jill Benton, professor emerita of English and world literature, Pitzer College.

56. "Lesbian" is the label that Cora Du Bois used for herself in "Biographical Notes," CDBH, Box 11.

57. JW, Session I, Pt. 1, p. 3.

58. Cora Du Bois never married, and her later diaries made it clear that in college, and subsequently, she dated women, not men.

59. JW, Session I, Pt. 1, p. 3.

60. Evidence comes from Du Bois's post–World War II journals, CDBH, Box 11.

61. CDBH, Box 11.

62. October 25, 1921, letter home, CDBH, Box 1.

63. November 3, 1921, letter home, CDBH, Box 1.

64. October 28, 1921, letter home, CDBH, Box 1.

65. November 3, 1921, letter home, CDBH, Box 1.

66. November 3, 1921, letter home, CDBH, Box 1.

67. January 1, 1922, letter home, CDBH, Box 1.

68. January 1, 1922, letter home, CDBH, Box 1.

69. October 25, 1921, letter home, CDBH, Box 1.

70. January 1, 1922, letter home, CDBH, Box 1.

71. Jean Du Bois to Cora Du Bois, December 1, 1921, CDBH, Box 1.

72. January 1, 1922, letter home, CDBH, Box 1.

73. January 1, 1922, letter home, CDBH, Box 1.

74. CDBH, Box 1.

75. "Biographical Notes," CDBH, Box 11.

2. Escape and Resolve

Epigraph: Lapsley, *Margaret Mead and Ruth Benedict*, 226.

1. JW, Session I, Pt. 1, p. 8.

2. "Stigmatized" is the word that Du Bois used in old age in "Biographical Notes," CDBH, Box 4.

3. CDBH, Box 10. This is also mentioned in JW, Session I.

4. The money that Claude inherited from his father's estate remained in probate until the 1950s, when Cora hired detectives to search for Claude. When he was not found, she was able to have him legally declared dead and to have the money released to her mother.

5. CDBH, Box 11. The delay in attending high school put Cora in what today would be considered a normal age cohort. She was not quite fourteen when she began high school, and she graduated from high school at age seventeen.

6. "Biographical Notes," CDBH, Box 11.

7. See Goldin, "America's Graduation from High School."

8. "Biographical Notes," CDBH, Box 11.

9. Mead's mother and grandmother were active in the suffragist movement.

10. See Mead, *Culture and Commitment*.

11. See Rosenberg, *Changing the Subject*, 12; Goldin, "America's Graduation from High School."

12. JW, Session I, Pt. 1, p. 16.

13. CDBH, Box 1.

14. CDBH, Box 1 (emphasis added).

15. "Biographical Notes," CDBH, Box 11.

16. JW, Session I, Pt. 1, pp. 16–17.

17. JW, Session I, Pt. 1, p. 18.

18. Rosenberg, *Changing the Subject*.

19. "Biographical Notes," CDBH, Box 11.

20. JW, Session I, Pt. 1, pp. 9–10.

21. JW, Session I, Pt. 1, p. 10.

22. CDBH, Box 10.

23. JW, Session I, Pt. 1, pp. 9–10.

24. 1926–28 diary, CDBH, Box 10. In this diary, for some reason, Du Bois refers to Virginia Wittens as "Virginia Riese."

25. 1926–28 diary, CDBH, Box 10.

26. 1926–28 diary, CDBH, Box 10.

27. See Du Bois, "The Dominant Value Profile of American Culture."

28. 1926–28 diary, CDBH, Box 10.

29. 1926–28 diary, CDBH, Box 10.

30. 1926–28 diary, CDBH, Box 10.

31. CDBH, Box 35.

32. See, e.g., D'Emilio and Freedman, *Intimate Matters*; and Faderman, *Odd Girls and Twilight Lovers*.

33. See Banner, *Intertwined Lives*, 31–32.

34. See Smith-Rosenberg, "Discourses of Sexuality and Subjectivity," 270–73.

35. D'Emilio and Freedman, *Intimate Matters*, 193–94.

36. See Freedman, *Maternal Justice*; Smith-Rosenberg, "Discourses of Sexuality and Subjectivity," 272; and, regarding Dean Gildersleeve, Rosenberg, *Changing the Subject*, 169–70.

37. See Mead, *Blackberry Winter*.

38. 1926–28 diary, CDBH, Box 10.

39. Rosenberg, *Changing the Subject*, 167.

40. Rosenberg, *Changing the Subject*, 169–70.

41. Rosenberg, *Changing the Subject*; Banner, *Intertwined Lives*.

42. 1926–28 diaries, CDBH, Box 10.

43. 1926–28 diaries, CDBH, Box 10.

44. 1926–28 diaries, CDBH, Box 10.

45. 1926–28 diaries, CDBH, Box 10.

46. 1926–28 diaries, CDBH, Box 10.

47. Letter to Mattie Du Bois, 1926, CDBH, Box 1.

48. *Camp Fire Girls Newsletter*, May 1927.

49. "Biographical Notes," CDBH, Box 11.

50. Memorandum regarding the estate of Jean J. P. Du Bois, October 27, 1926, CDBH, Box 1.

51. Barnard was the first liberal arts college to provide a permanent position in anthropology when it hired Reichard in 1923. Rosenberg, *Changing the Subject*, 154.

52. Du Bois's college course notes, CDBH, Box 35.

53. "Biographical Notes," CDBH, Box 11; and JW, Session I, Pt. 2, p. 5.

54. JW, Session I, Pt. 2, pp. 5, 8–10; "Intellectual History," outline for lecture, Brandeis University, February 1965, CDBH, Box 73 (hereafter cited as "Intellectual History").

55. JW, Session I, Pt. 2, pp. 5, 8–10; "Intellectual History," CDBH, Box 73.

56. "Intellectual History," CDBH, Box 73 (italics added).

57. Benedict, "Anthropology and the Abnormal," 60.

58. Class notes, CDBH, Box 35.

59. "The Ekoi and How They Share the Religious Complex of 16th Century Europe," paper submitted to Anthropology 4 (Barnard College), April 27, 1927, pp. 2–3, CDBH, Box 35.

60. "Intellectual History," CDBH, Box 73.

61. "Biographical Notes," CDBH, Box 11.

62. "Biographical Notes," CDBH, Box 11.

63. "Intellectual History," CDBH, Box 73.

64. "Intellectual History," CDBH, Box 73.

65. 1928–29 diary, CDBH, Box 10.

66. 1928–29 diary, CDBH, Box 10.

67. 1928–29 diary, CDBH, Box 10.

68. 1928–29 diary, CDBH, Box 10.

69. 1928–29 diary, CDBH, Box 10.

70. 1928–29 diary, CDBH, Box 10.

71. 1928–29 diary, CDBH, Box 10.

72. 1928–29 diary, CDBH, Box 10.

73. Du Bois later wrote that, for Boas, women were "daughters and handmaidens, emotionally"; "men were sons to play with." "Biographical Notes," CDBH, Box 11.

74. "Intellectual History," CDBH, Box 73.

75. Cora Du Bois to Susan Seymour, February 1986, in preparation for Seymour, "Cora Du Bois"; copy in author's possession.

76. "Biographical Notes," CDBH, Box 78.

77. 1926–28 diary, CDBH, Box 10.

78. CDBH, Box 11.

3. Becoming an Anthropologist

Epigraph: Excerpt from A. L. Kroeber, letter of recommendation for Cora Du Bois, December 9, 1932, RDA, "Du Bois, Cora 1928–1938," Series 4, Subseries 4, Box 51, CU-23.

1. Cora Du Bois, personal communication.

2. January 12, 1929, letter home, CDBH, Box 1.

3. See T. Kroeber, *Alfred Kroeber*; and Jacknis, "First Boasian."

4. The museum was housed on campus once again when new buildings for it and the Department of Anthropology were erected in 1959. At that time the museum was named in honor of Robert Lowie.

5. This is a compilation of Du Bois's remarks from two interviews: JW, Session I, Pt. 1; and Lawrence C. Kelly, interview with Cora Du Bois, CDBH, Box 11.

6. JW, Session I, Pt. 1, p. 3.

7. JW, Session I, Pt. 1, p. 3; and Kelly interview, p. 3, CDBH, Box 11.

8. Kelly, interview, p. 4, CDBH, Box 11.

9. T. Kroeber, *Alfred Kroeber*, 263.

10. January 31, 1929, letter home, CDBH, Box 2.

11. JW, Session I, Pt. 1, pp. 3–4.

12. January 20, 1929, letter home, CDBH, Box 2. Dorothy Demetracopoulou was better known as Dorothy D. Lee, the author of the popular book *Freedom and Culture: Essays* (1959).

13. JW, Session I, Pt. 1, p. 4.

14. "Intellectual History," CDBH, Box 73.

15. March 2, 1929, letter home, CDBH, Box 2.

16. Du Bois, "Tolowa Notes."

17. "Intellectual History," CDBH, Box 73.

18. "Intellectual History," CDBH, Box 73.

19. May 9, 1929, letter home, CDBH, Box 2.

20. May 9, 1929, letter home, CDBH, Box 2.

21. Du Bois to Kroeber, May 18, 1929, RDA, "Du Bois, Cora 1928–1938," Series 4, Subseries 4, Box 51, CU-23.

22. Although Du Bois indicated in a July 3, 1929, letter home that she had administered these tests, she seems not to have published the results.

23. May 15, 1929, letter home, CDBH, Box 2.

24. June 16, 1929, letter home, CDBH, Box 2.

25. Du Bois, "A Paiute Prophet Died in Nevada."

26. Du Bois and Demetracopoulou, "Wintu Myths"; Du Bois and Demetracopoulou, "Study of Wintu Mythology"; and Du Bois, "A Paiute Prophet Died in Nevada."

27. "Intellectual History," CDBH, Box 73.

28. "Intellectual History," CDBH, Box 73.

29. "Intellectual History," CDBH, Box 73.

30. Beals, "Fifty Years in Anthropology."

31. See A. L. Kroeber, *Anthropology*, 255; and Steward, *Alfred Kroeber*.

32. "Intellectual History," CDBH, Box 73.

33. "Intellectual History," CDBH, Box 73.

34. "Intellectual History," CDBH, Box 73.

35. JW, Session I, Pt. 1, pp. 3–5.

36. November 11, 1929, letter home, CDBH, Box 4.

37. November (undated) 1932 letter home, CDBH, Box 4.

38. May 5, 1930, letter home, CDBH, Box 3.

39. January 21, 1929, diary entry, CDBH, Box 10.

40. May 22, 1930, diary entry, CDBH, Box 10 (emphasis added).

41. "Emily H. Huntington, Economics: Berkeley," University of California: In Memoriam, 1989, edited by David Krogh, Calisphere, http://content.cdlib.org/view?docId=hb4p30063r&doc.view=frames&chunk.id=div00024&toc.depth=1&toc.id=&brand=calisphere.

42. "Emily H. Huntington, Economics: Berkeley."

43. CDBH, Box 11.

44. February 8, 1931, letter home, CDBH, Box 3.

45. January 6, 1931, letter home, CDBH, Box 3.

46. September 5, 1929, letter home, CDBH, Box 3.

47. Du Bois, "Some Anthropological Hindsights."

48. March 17, 1930, letter home, CDBH, Box 3.

49. June 14, 1930, letter home, CDBH, Box 3.

50. June 19, 1930, journal entry, CDBH, Box 10.

51. March 12, 1929, letter home, CDBH, Box 2.

52. August 25, 1930, letter home, CDBH, Box 2.

53. Du Bois to Benedict, January 10, 1931, RFB.

54. Benedict to Du Bois, January 17, 1931, RFB.

55. August 29, 1931, letter home, CDBH, Box 2.

56. Du Bois, "Wintu Ethnography," 1–2.

57. Du Bois, "Wintu Ethnography," 118.

58. April 28, 1930, letter home, CDBH, Box 3.

59. Cora Du Bois, personal communication, quoted in Seymour, "Cora Du Bois."

60. Cora Du Bois, "Girls' Adolescence Observances in North America" (PhD diss., Department of Anthropology, University of California, Berkeley, 1932), 69.

61. "Intellectual History," CDBH, Box 73. See A. L. Kroeber, "Stimulus Diffusion."

62. October 7, 1932, letter home, CDBH, Box 4.

63. October 7, 1932, letter home, CDBH, Box 4.

64. Excerpt from A. L. Kroeber, letter of recommendation for Cora Du Bois, December 9, 1932, RDA, "Du Bois, Cora 1928–1938," Series 4, Subseries 4, Box 51, CU-23.

65. Rossiter, *Women Scientists in America*.

66. Rossiter, *Women Scientists in America*, 58–63.

67. See Lepowsky, "Charlotte Gower and the Subterranean History of Anthropology." Lepowsky, after considerable research, discovered that Gower had gone to China

to teach, had been captured, in 1941, by the Japanese in Hong Kong, where she was interned for four years, and then joined the CIA after the war.

68. There were thirteen women of Cora Du Bois's cohort who earned PhDs in anthropology during the 1920s and 1930s: Cora Du Bois (UC Berkeley 1932), Frederica de Laguna (Columbia 1933), Charlotte Gower (Chicago 1928), Jane Richardson Hanks (UC Berkeley 1938), Isabel Kelly (UC Berkeley 1932), Margaret Lantis (UC Berkeley 1939), Ruth Landes (Columbia 1935), Dorothy Demetracopoulou Lee (UC Berkeley 1931), Katharine Luomala (UC Berkeley 1936), Margaret Mead (Columbia 1928), Laura Thompson (UC Berkeley 1933), Gertrude Doniger Toffelmier (UC Berkeley 1936), and Gene Weltfish (Columbia 1950). Weltfish completed her doctoral exams in 1929, but because of a prohibitive $4,000 cost to publish her dissertation, did not receive her formal degree until 1950.

69. Sabra Lee (one of Dorothy Lee's daughters), personal communication.

70. Rossiter, *Women Scientists in America*.

71. Kerns, *Scenes from the High Desert*, 262.

72. JW, Session I, Pt. 1, p. 10.

73. January 25, 1934, letter home, CDBH, Box 4.

74. "Modern Cults among the Oregon Indians," research proposal submitted to the Social Research Council, 1934, CDBH, Box 40.

75. May 22, 1933, letter home, CDBH, Box 40.

76. February 17, 1934, letter home, CDBH, Box 40.

77. July 31, 1933, letter home, CDBH, Box 40.

78. Du Bois to Kroeber, July 31, 1933, RDA, "Du Bois, Cora 1928–1938," Series 4, Subseries 4, Box 51, CU-23.

79. August 22, 1933, letter home, CDBH, Box 40.

80. Du Bois to Benedict, August 22, 1933, RFB.

81. "Scurrilous Sketches," CDBH, Box 4.

82. August 7, 1933, letter home, CDBH, Box 11.

83. Du Bois, *Lowie's Selected Papers in Anthropology*.

84. Du Bois to Benedict, May 24, 1934, RFB.

85. April 14, 1935, letter home, CDBH, Box 11.

4. Culture and Personality

Epigraph: LeVine, "Culture and Personality Studies," 809.

1. JW, Session II, Pt. 1, p. 12.

2. Darnell, *Edward Sapir*, 320.

3. Fellowship application submitted to the National Research Council by Cora Du Bois, RDA and RFB (emphasis added).

4. Stocking, "Polarity and Plurality," 53 (emphasis added).

5. Boas, "Psychological Problems in Anthropology," 372–81.

6. A. L. Kroeber, "The Superorganic."

7. A. L. Kroeber, "The Superorganic," 180, 189.

8. Sapir, "Do We Need a Superorganic?," 443.

9. Darnell, *Edward Sapir*, 147–50.

10. Darnell, *Edward Sapir*, 336.

11. Mead, *Coming of Age in Samoa*, 11.

12. For a good discussion of the controversy about Mead's research, see Lutkehaus, *Margaret Mead*.

13. Lutkehaus, *Margaret Mead*, 87.

14. Benedict, *Patterns of Culture*, 46.

15. Benedict, *Patterns of Culture*, 46.

16. Benedict, *Patterns of Culture*, 254–55.

17. A. L. Kroeber, Review of *Patterns of Culture*.

18. Du Bois to Kroeber, January 18, 1935, RDA, "Du Bois, Cora 1928–1938," Series 4, Subseries 4, Box 5.

19. Kelly interview, p. 8, CDBH, Box 11.

20. Du Bois to Kroeber, January 18, 1935, RDA, "Du Bois, Cora 1928–1938," Series 4, Subseries 4, Box 5.

21. There is considerable correspondence for this period between Du Bois and Kroeber, who as chair of the Anthropology Department presumably used a secretary who kept and filed copies of all letters. Hence, that correspondence is archived in the Records of the Department of Anthropology (RDA). By contrast, most of Du Bois's correspondence with Lowie was of a personal nature and was not handled by the Department of Anthropology. It is archived with the Robert Harry Lowie Papers (RHL).

22. Triplett, "Harvard Psychology," 240.

23. See, e.g., Kluckhohn and Murray, *Personality in Nature, Society, and Culture*.

24. Du Bois to Kroeber, October 12, 1935, RDA.

25. Murray, *Explorations in Personality*, xi.

26. Kelly interview, p. 7, CDBH, Box 11.

27. Murray, *Explorations in Personality*, 530.

28. Du Bois to Kroeber, October 12, 1935, RDA.

29. JW, Session II, Pt. 1, pp. 12–13.

30. Kroeber to Du Bois, October 30, 1935, RDA.

31. A. L. Kroeber to the Board of National Research Fellowships in the Biological Sciences, January 18, 1935, RDA.

32. Du Bois to Kroeber, November 15, 1935, RDA.

33. Kroeber to Du Bois, November 23, 1935, RDA.

34. Lowie to Du Bois, October [?], 1935, RHL (italics added).

35. Lowie to William F. Ogburn, October 3, 1935, RHL.

36. Du Bois to Kroeber, October 12, 1935, RDA.

37. Du Bois to Kroeber, November 15, 1935, RDA.

38. Cora Du Bois, research proposal, "Sex Differences in Relation to Cultural Determinants," RDA.

39. Kroeber to Du Bois, November 23, 1935, RDA.

40. Lowie to Du Bois, November 20, 1935, RHL.

41. Kroeber to Du Bois, November 23, 1935, RDA (italics added).

42. January 25, 1936, letter home, CDBH, Box 5.

43. Du Bois to Kroeber, January 21, 1936, RDA.

44. Kroeber to Du Bois, January 28, 1936, RDA.

45. Du Bois to Kroeber, January 21, 1936, RDA.

46. CDBH, Box 40.

47. Du Bois, *People of Alor*, v.

48. Kelly interview, p. 9, CDBH, Box 11.

49. Du Bois, "Some Anthropological Perspectives on Psychoanalysis," 248.

50. Du Bois, "Some Anthropological Perspectives on Psychoanalysis," 249.

51. Du Bois to Lowie, April 24, 1936, RHL.

52. Du Bois to Lowie, April 24, 1936, RHL.

53. Du Bois to Lowie, December 14, 1936, RHL.

54. Du Bois to Lowie, March 6, 1937, RHL.

55. Lowie, *History of Ethnological Theory*, viii.

56. Du Bois to Lowie, June 30, 1936, RHL.

57. Du Bois to Kroeber, June 30, 1936, RDA.

58. Kelly interview, pp. 10–11, CDBH, Box 11.

59. Kardiner, *Individual and His Society*, 2.

60. Kardiner, *Individual and His Society*, 237 (italics added).

61. See Strauss and Quinn, *Cognitive Theory of Cultural Meaning*.

62. Kardiner, *Individual and His Society*, 446–50.

63. See Barnouw, *Culture and Personality*; Bock, *Psychological Anthropology*; LeVine, *Culture, Behavior, and Personality*; Whiting, *Six Cultures*; Whiting and Whiting, *Children of Six Cultures*.

64. Kardiner, *Individual and His Society*, 84–85.

65. Irvine, *Edward Sapir*, 181–82 (brackets are in the original).

66. Du Bois to Kroeber, June 30, 1936, RDA.

67. Du Bois, *People of Alor*, v.

68. Du Bois, *People of Alor*, v.

69. JW, Session II, Pt. 1, pp. 15–16.

70. Undated letter to Du Bois's mother, CDBH, Box 5.

5. A Pioneer

Epigraph: Hortense Powdermaker, Review of *The People of Alor*.

1. Du Bois to Benedict, July 26, 1938, RFB.

2. Until her three-year fieldwork expedition with Gregory Bateson to Bali (1936–39), Mead had spent relatively short periods doing fieldwork: nine months in Samoa (1925–26), six months on Manus (1928–29), and eight months among the Arapesh in New Guinea (1931–32), followed by a few weeks each among the Mundugumor, the Chambri, and the Iatmul in New Guinea.

3. Mead to Du Bois, June 29, 1937, CDBH, Box 25.

4. Mead to Du Bois, June 29, 1937, CDBH, Box 25.

5. Mead to Du Bois, June 29, 1937, CDBH, Box 25.

6. October 11, 1937, letter home, CDBH, Box 7.

7. Du Bois to Lowie, April 6, 1937, RHL.

8. September 25, 1937, letter home, CDBH, Box 7.

9. Du Bois to Jane and Julian Steward, March 29, 1938, CDBH, Box 31.

10. November 8, 1937, letter home, CDBH, Box 7.

11. November 8, 1937, letter home, CDBH, Box 7.

12. Du Bois to Jane and Julian Steward, March 29, 1938, CDBH, Box 31.

13. Claire Holt would also become a research assistant to Margaret Mead and would help found the Modern Indonesian Project at Cornell University.

14. December 21, 1937, letter home, CDBH, Box 7.

15. December 28, 1937, letter home, CDBH, Box 7.

16. Du Bois to Jane and Julian Steward, March 29, 1938, CDBH, Box 31.

17. Mead to Benedict, December 25, 1937, in Caffrey and Francis, *To Cherish the Life of the World*, 273-75.

18. Du Bois to Jane and Julian Steward, March 29, 1938, CDBH, Box 31.

19. Du Bois to Jane and Julian Steward, March 29, 1938, CDBH, Box 31.

20. Du Bois to Jane and Julian Steward, March 29, 1938, CDBH, Box 31.

21. Du Bois, *People of Alor*, vii.

22. Du Bois, *People of Alor*, viii.

23. Du Bois, *People of Alor*, vii.

24. Du Bois, *People of Alor*, viii-ix.

25. March 22, 1938, letter home, CDBH, Box 7.

26. Du Bois to Jane and Julian Steward, March 29, 1938, CDBH, Box 31.

27. March 22, 1938, letter home, CDBH, Box 7.

28. See chapter 8, note 31.

29. Du Bois to Jane and Julian Steward, March 29, 1938, CDBH, Box 31.

30. Du Bois to Benedict, September 19, 1938, RFB.

31. Du Bois to Jane and Julian Steward, March 29, 1938, CDBH, Box 31.

32. Du Bois, "Why People Quarrel in Alor," 91.

33. Du Bois to Benedict, March 6, 1938, RFB.

34. Du Bois to Benedict, March 6, 1938, RFB.

35. Du Bois to Benedict, March 21, 1938, RFB.

36. Du Bois to Kroeber, July 21, 1938, RDA.

37. Du Bois to Kroeber, July 21, 1938, RDA.

38. Du Bois to Kroeber, July 21, 1938, RDA.

39. May 30, 1938, letter home, CDBH, Box 7.

40. See, e.g., A. L. Kroeber, *Anthropology*, 589.

41. Rohner, De Walt, and Ness, "Ethnographer Bias in Cross-Cultural Research," 275-308.

42. Du Bois to Benedict, March 21, 1938, RDA.

43. Du Bois to Benedict, March 21, 1938, RDA.

44. Du Bois, "Comments on Alorese Economy," unpublished notes, CDBH, Box 50.

45. Du Bois, "How They Pay Debts in Alor."

46. Du Bois to Kardiner, April 12, 1938, CDBH, Box 23.

47. Du Bois to Jane and Julian Steward, March 29, 1938, CDBH, Box 31.

48. March 22, 1938, letter home, CDBH, Box 7.

49. CDBH, Box 52.

50. Du Bois, *People of Alor*, 24.

51. Du Bois to Kardiner, April 12, 1938, CDBH, Box 23.

52. Du Bois to Kardiner, April 12, 1938, CDBH, Box 23.

53. Du Bois, "Attitudes towards Food and Hunger in Alor," 248.

54. Du Bois to Benedict, March 21, 1938, RFB.

55. Du Bois, *People of Alor*, 162.

56. Du Bois to Benedict, July 26, 1938, RFB.

57. Du Bois to Benedict, July 26, 1938, RFB.

58. Du Bois to Lowie, September 19, 1938, RHL.

59. Du Bois, *People of Alor*, 154.

60. Du Bois to Kroeber, July 21, 1938, RDA.

61. Kroeber to Du Bois, October 12, 1938, RDA.

62. Du Bois to Kroeber, December 15, 1938, RDA (emphasis on "searching for . . ." added).

63. Du Bois to Kroeber, December 15, 1938, RDA.

64. Du Bois to Kroeber, December 15, 1938, RDA.

65. Hetty Baets (one of Nicolspeyer's daughters), personal communication. I am grateful for Ms. Baets's translation, from Dutch to English, of her mother's tribute to Cora Du Bois.

66. Du Bois to Lowie, May 1, 1939, RHL.

67. Du Bois to Lowie, May 1, 1939, RHL.

68. Emilie Wellfelt, personal communication. Wellfelt has been working with some 237 artifacts that Du Bois collected in Alor at the request of Dr. Walter Kandern, the former director of the Gothenburg Museum of World Culture in Gothenburg, Sweden. In 2006 Wellfelt took photographs of all the museum artifacts to Alor to discuss with Atimelang villagers. See Wellfelt, "Returning to Alor."

69. Du Bois to Jane and Julian Steward, March 29, 1938, CDBH, Box 31.

70. Lapsley, *Margaret Mead and Ruth Benedict*, 281.

71. From a cross-cultural perspective, exclusive mother caretaking is rare. Weisner and Gallimore, in "My Brother's Keeper," found, using holocultural ratings for 150 small-scale societies, that in only 3 percent of the cases were infants exclusively nurtured by mothers.

72. Du Bois, *People of Alor*, 421–22 (emphasis added).

73. Du Bois, *People of Alor*, 251.

74. Du Bois, *People of Alor*, 51.

75. Du Bois, "Attitudes towards Food and Hunger in Alor," 244.

76. Du Bois to Lowie, May 1, 1939, RHL.

77. Du Bois, *People of Alor*, 53.

78. Kardiner's analyses appear at the end of each of the autobiographies that were published as part 3 of *People of Alor* (1944). The book also includes a chapter (chapter 18, pp 548–51) by Kardiner entitled "Conclusions to the Autobiographies."

79. Du Bois to Benedict, February 2, 1940, RFB.

80. Excerpts from chapter 22, by Emil Oberholzer, in Du Bois, *People of Alor*, 596–99.

81. Du Bois, *People of Alor*, 589.

82. Du Bois, *People of Alor*, 584–85.

83. S. D. Porteus to Du Bois, November 8, 1939, CDBH, Box 22. Most of this letter is reprinted in Du Bois, *People of Alor*, chap. 19.

84. Du Bois, *People of Alor*, 95.

85. Du Bois, *People of Alor*, 563.

86. Du Bois, *People of Alor*, 78.

87. Du Bois, *People of Alor*, 78.

88. Du Bois, *People of Alor*, 4.

89. Powdermaker, Review of *The People of Alor*.

90. See, e.g., Munroe and Gauvain, "Cross-Cultural Study of Children's Learning and Socialization"; and LeVine, "Ethnographic Studies of Childhood."

91. Undated letter home, CDBH, Box 5.

92. In her correspondence with Benedict, Du Bois made it clear that both she and Benedict had doubts about Kardiner's coherence of thinking and writing. In a February 2, 1940, letter to Benedict, Cora wrote, "I may go back to K's first and third portion of his book and try to work out with some semblance of coherence what is constructive in that jumble"; RFB. Du Bois was also having to deal with Kardiner's questionable ethics. For example, he tried to publish her Alorese material in his own book, *The Psychological Frontiers of Society* (1945), *before* she had had a chance to publish her own ethnography, *The People of Alor* (1944).

93. Du Bois to Benedict, October 17, 1939, RFB.

94. Sonia Hodsen, telephone interview by author, October 12, 2008.

95. Du Bois to Lowie, June 11, 1941, RHL.

96. Horace Gregory was a writer and literary critic who also taught at Sarah Lawrence College when Du Bois was there.

97. CDBH, Box 11.

6. World War II and the OSS

Epigraph: Excerpt from the 1946 Exceptional Civilian Award, and supporting documents, presented to Cora Du Bois on May 6, 1946. NARA, RG 263, CIA Personnel Records, Box 152.

1. Quoted in B. Smith, *Shadow Warriors*, 55.

2. R. Smith, *OSS*, 1.

3. See, e.g., Winks, *Cloak and Gown*, for an account of the number of Yale scholars involved in intelligence work during and after the Second World War.

4. R. Smith, *OSS*, 17.

5. Undated (early June 1942) letter home, CDBH, Box 6.

6. See, e.g., B. Smith, *Shadow Warriors*; Winks, *Cloak and Gown*; McIntosh, *Sisterhood of Spies*; and R. Smith, *OSS*.

7. B. Smith, *Shadow Warriors*, 361.

8. Winks, *Cloak and Gown*, 113. In 2008 the previously classified files of OSS intelligence officers were released for the first time and some twenty-four thousand people were identified for all the different branches of the OSS.

9. R. Smith, *OSS*, 13.

10. David Donovan, interview, July 20, 1995, quoted in McIntosh, *Sisterhood of Spies*, 11.

11. See McIntosh, *Sisterhood of Spies*.

12. JW, Session III, Pt. 2, p. 7.

13. The R&A reports are housed in the National Archives in Washington DC (NARA).

14. June 2, 1942, letter home, CDBH, Box 6.

15. Steward, *Handbook of South American Indians*.

16. July 4, 1942, letter home, CDBH, Box 6.

17. Kelly interview, p. 16, CDBH, Box 11.

18. Hyatt, *Franz Boas, Social Activist*, 146.

19. Quoted in Price, *Anthropological Intelligence*, 28.

20. Price, *Anthropological Intelligence*, 37. Also see Price for a good review of what many anthropologists were doing during the war.

21. See, e.g., CEAUSSIC's October 14, 2009, "Final Report on the Army's Human Terrain System Proof of Concept Program," submitted to the Executive Board of the American Anthropological Association, http://www.aaanet.org/cmtes/commissions/ceaussic /upload/ceaussic_hts_final_report.pdf.

22. R. Smith, *OSS*, 29–30.

23. JW, Session II, Pt. 1, p. 1.

24. August 6, 1942, letter home, CDBH, Box 6.

25. May 29, 1939, letter home, CDBH, Box 7.

26. Kelly interview, pp. 15–16, CDBH, Box 11.

27. Kelly interview, pp. 15–16, CDBH, Box 11.

28. Ruth Benedict to Margaret Harding, University of Minnesota Press, September 22, 1942, RFB.

29. Du Bois to Benedict, September 26, 1942, RFB.

30. Price, *Anthropological Intelligence*, 30. In an unpublished manuscript about applied anthropology, Du Bois rejected that label for her government service during and after the war. She viewed those years as "patriotic" ones, not ones in which she was engaged in anthropology. As an anthropologist, she wrote, "[m]y goals were those of an observer rather than an activist." "Applied Anthropology," ca. 1982, CDBH, Box 78.

31. January 8, 1943, letter home, CDBH, Box 6.

32. February 19, 1943, letter home, CDBH, Box 6.

33. Undated letter home (1944, written on board ship), CDBH, Box 6.

34. JW, Session III, Pt. 1, p. 3.

35. McIntosh, *Sisterhood of Spies*, 209.

36. JW, Session III, Pt. 1, p. 4.

37. McIntosh, *Sisterhood of Spies*, 210.

38. Roosevelt and Karlow, *War Report*.

39. See E. Taylor, *Awakening from History*, for a detailed description of Donovan's negotiations with Mountbatten.

40. E. Taylor, *Awakening from History*, 394.

41. NARA, RG 226, Entry 139, Box 194, Folder 2575.

42. NARA, RG 226, Entry 154, Box 127, Folder 2222 (emphasis added).

43. NARA, RG 226, Entry 146, Box 82, Folder 1175.

44. June 6, 1944, letter home, CDBH, Box 6.

45. NARA, RG 226, Entry 1, Box 29, Folder 11 (emphasis added).

46. NARA, RG 226, Entry 146, Box 82, Folder 1179.

47. NARA, RG 226, Entry 110, Box 052, Folder 1H.

48. Guy Martin, interview by author, May 7, 2007, Georgetown, Washington DC.

49. NARA, RG 226, Entry 1, Box 29, Folder 11.

50. NARA, RG 226, Entry 154, Box 128, Folder 2246.

51. Elizabeth P. McIntosh, interview by author, May 6, 2007, Woodbridge VA.

52. December 19, 1944, letter home, CDBH, Box 6.

53. NARA, RG 226, Entry 99, Box 74.

54. "Report of Operations, Office of Strategic Services, India-Burma Theater," September 14, 1945, NARA, RG 226, Entry 154, Box 127, Folder 2221.

55. Roosevelt and Karlow, *War Report*.

56. "Report of Operations, Office of Strategic Services, India-Burma Theater," September 14, 1945, pp. 403–4, NARA, RG 226, Entry 154, Box 127, Folder 2221.

57. Colonel Richard P. Heppner to The Director, OSS, "History of OSS/SEAC," February 19, 1945, NARA, M1642, Roll 55, Frames 712–36.

58. McIntosh, *Sisterhood of Spies*, 212.

59. Du Bois to Fahs, August 22, 1944, "OSS General Correspondence," NARA, RG 226, Entry 1, Box 29 (emphasis added).

60. Du Bois to Donovan, memo regarding the reorganization of R&A/SEAC, January 18, 1945, NARA, RG 226, Entry 146, Box 82, Folder 1175 (emphasis added).

61. See McIntosh, *Sisterhood of Spies*, 191–96.

62. NARA, RG 226, Entry 53, Box 2.

63. Incoming #2, R&A/SEAC Outpost Letter 41, May 21, 1945, NARA, RG 226, Entry 53, Box 2.

64. Cited in supporting documents for the Exceptional Service Award presented to Cora Du Bois, NARA, RG 263, CIA Personnel Records, Box 152.

65. Winks, *Cloak and Gown*, 56.

66. Martin, interview by author, May 7, 2007, Georgetown, Washington DC.

67. Quoted in Fitch, *Appetite for Life*, 190–91.

68. Fitch, *Appetite for Life*, 190–91.

69. Fitch, *Appetite for Life*, 186.

70. Quoted in Lipset, *Gregory Bateson*, 174.

71. July 5, 1944, letter home, CDBH, Box 6.

72. May 11, 1944, letter home, CDBH, Box 6.

73. December 19, 1944, letter home, CDBH, Box 6.

74. Colonel Richard P. Heppner to the Director, OSS, "History of OSS/SEAC," February 19, 1945, p. 20, NARA, MI642, Roll 55, Frames 712–36.

75. Du Bois to Robert Lowie, July 13, 1945, RHL.

76. Price, *Anthropological Intelligence*.

77. NARA, RG 226, Entry 154, Box 72.

78. NARA, RG 226, Entry 53, Box 2.

79. Du Bois and La Barre would occasionally correspond. In one such letter La Barre wrote, "I, too, can scarcely believe in everything that happened in Ceylon so long ago. . . . The cloak-and-dagger days do not die!" CDBH, Box 24.

80. E. Taylor, *Awakening from History*, 365n40.

81. McIntosh, *Sisterhood of Spies*, 217.

82. Jeanne Taylor, unpublished partial memoir about her life during the war.

83. Taylor, unpublished memoir.

84. Letter sent by Julia McWilliams Child to her family after arriving in Kandy, cited in McIntosh, *Sisterhood of Spies*, 211.

85. May 16, 1945, letter home, CDBH, Box 6.

86. July 13, 1945, letter home, CDBH, Box 6.

87. Du Bois to Fahs, August 22, 1944, NARA, RG 226, Box 20.

88. NARA, RG 226, Entry 1, Box 22, Folder 10 (emphasis added).

89. Incoming #2, Outpost Letter 44, June 16, 1945, NARA, RG 226, Entry 53, Box 2.

90. NARA, RG 226, Entry 154, Box 127.

91. NARA, RG 226, Entry 154, Box 128 (emphasis added).

92. Du Bois's comment on Davies, "American Policy in Asia," NARA, MI642, Reel 41. Also cited in Reynolds, *Thailand's Secret War*, 221.

93. Du Bois to Heppner, June 29, 1944, NARA, RG 226, Entry 110, Box 51, Folder 510.

94. NARA, RG 226, Entry 53, Box 2.

95. Colonel Richard P. Heppner to the Director, OSS, "History of OSS/SEAC," February 19, 1945, NARA, MI642, Roll 55, Frames 712–36. See also Reynolds, "Opening the Wedge"; and Reynolds, *Thailand's Secret War*.

96. JW, Session III, Pt. 1, p. 5.

97. R&A/SEAC Mission Letter #1, NARA, RG 226, Entry 53, Box 2.

98. Wells to Du Bois, Outpost Letter, NARA, RG 226, Entry 154, Box 128.

99. September 2, 1945, letter home, CDBH, Box 6.

100. R&A/SEAC Mission Letter #4, NARA, RG 226, Entry 53, Box 2.

101. JW, Session III, Pt. 1, pp. 7–8.

7. The Cold War Era

Epigraph: Excerpt from Cora Du Bois to UC Berkeley president Sproul, September 1950, regarding the California Loyalty Oath, CDBH, Box 18.

1. Du Bois to Lowie, July 13, 1945, RHL.

2. September 2, 1945, letter home, CDBH, Box 6.

3. Du Bois to Lowie, July 13, 1945, RHL.

4. NARA, RG 226, Entry 1, Box 2, Folder 23.

5. NARA, RG 226, Entry 1, Box 2, Folder 23.

6. B. Smith, *Shadow Warriors*, 390–91.

7. Hoover had considered Donovan's intelligence operation a threat from the start, and he did his best to undermine Donovan's OSS operations and his postwar chances of continuing on in the government. See, e.g., Waller, *Wild Bill Donovan*.

8. In July 1947 Truman signed the National Security Act of 1947 that created a unified Department of Defense, the Central Intelligence Agency, and the National Security Council.

9. Outgoing letter from Washington, October 8, 1945, NARA, RG 226, Entry 53, Box 2.

10. Outgoing letter from Washington, October 8, 1945, NARA, RG 226, Entry 53, Box 2.

11. Cited in Winks, *Cloak and Gown*, 115.

12. See, e.g., B. Smith, *Shadow Warriors*; and Winks, *Cloak and Gown*.

13. B. Smith, *Shadow Warriors*, 388.

14. By 1964–65, the recruitment of anthropologists for counterinsurgency work had become an explosive topic within the discipline and within the American Anthropology Association. See, e.g., Nader, "Phantom Factor."

15. Winks, *Cloak and Gown*; and Chomsky et al., *Cold War and the University*.

16. November 16, 1945, letter home, CDBH, Box 6.

17. I am indebted to Jeanne Taylor's niece, Lisa Schlingerman, for providing me with a copy of Jeanne Taylor's resume and for information about her family. Also see Crump, *Minnesota Prints and Printmakers*, regarding Taylor's art.

18. "To J.T.," CDBH, Box 11.

19. February 23, 1946, letter home, CDBH, Box 6.

20. May 22, 1946, letter home, CDBH, Box 6.

21. March 15, 1946, letter home, CDBH, Box 6.

22. March 15, 1946, letter home, CDBH, Box 6.

23. May 22, 1946, letter home, CDBH, Box 6.

24. May 22, 1946, letter home, CDBH, Box 6.

25. Quoted in Fitch, *Appetite for Life*, 193.

26. Child, *My Life in France*, 107.

27. Child, *My Life in France*, 107.

28. Memorial Day 1946, letter home, CDBH, Box 6.

29. Du Bois to Richard Bicknell (Du Bois's stepfather), January 13, 1947, CDBH, Box 6.

30. April 14, 1947, letter home, CDBH, Box 6.

31. Memorial Day 1946, letter home, CDBH, Box 6.

32. June 23, 1947, letter home, CDBH, Box 6.

33. Beisner, *Dean Acheson*, 51.

34. Beisner, *Dean Acheson*.

35. "The Situation in Southeast Asia," October 7, 1949, speech delivered to a Department of State conference called by Phil Jessup, pp. 7–8, CDBH, Box 66 (emphasis added). Also mentioned in Beisner, *Dean Acheson*, 192.

36. Beisner, *Dean Acheson*, 186.

37. Beisner, *Dean Acheson*, 173.

38. Beisner, *Dean Acheson*, 174–75.

39. Beisner, *Dean Acheson*, 43. See also T. White, *In Search of History*.

40. "The Situation in Southeast Asia," speech, pp. 1–2, CDBH, Box 66 (emphasis added).

41. "The Situation in Southeast Asia," speech, pp. 1–2, CDBH, Box 66.

42. Du Bois, *Social Forces in Southeast Asia*, 42.

43. Du Bois, *Social Forces in Southeast Asia*, 27.

44. Du Bois, *Social Forces in Southeast Asia*, 52.

45. Thailand, it should be noted, was never colonized by Europeans. It was, however, occupied by the Japanese during World War II.

46. "Sociologic Factors in the Far East," lecture to the Department of the Army Intelligence Division, Strategic Intelligence School, April 26, 1949, pp. 6–7, CDBH, Box 66.

47. Du Bois, *Social Forces in Southeast Asia*, 43.

48. Du Bois, *Social Forces in Southeast Asia*, 54.

49. Du Bois, *Social Forces in Southeast Asia*, 3.

50. "The Situation in Southeast Asia," speech, pp. 1–2, CDBH, Box 66.

51. Beisner, *Dean Acheson*, 487.

52. Kennan, for example, resigned from the State Department in 1950 and took a position at the Institute of Advanced Study at Princeton University. Other Asian specialists, such as John Paton Davies Jr., John Stewart Service, and John Carter Vincent, were all purged from the State Department during the McCarthy era.

53. Beisner, *Dean Acheson*, 484–85.

54. Colbert, *Southeast Asia in International Politics*, 198.

55. McNamara, *In Retrospect*, 32 (emphasis added).

56. NARA, RG 59, Entry 205K, Box 118.

57. NARA, RG 59, Entry 205K, Box 118.

58. Beisner, *Dean Acheson*, 61.

59. April 14, 1947, letter home, CDBH, Box 6.

60. Beisner, *Dean Acheson*, 286; see also Johnson, *Lavender Scare*.

61. Beisner, *Dean Acheson*, 286–87.

62. Beisner, *Dean Acheson*, 303; also see "Executive Order 9835," *Wikipedia*, last modified April 30, 2014, http://en.wikipedia.org/wiki/Executive_Order_9835.

63. Jeanne Taylor's niece, Lisa A. Schlingerman, has kindly provided me with a copy of this letter as well as with Jeanne's notes that try to reconstruct her interrogations.

64. CDBH, Box 18 (emphasis added).

65. Under the Freedom of Information and Privacy Acts, David H. Price was able to acquire most of the FBI files on Cora Du Bois for his book *Threatening Anthropology:*

McCarthyism and the FBI's Surveillance of Activist Anthropologists. I am indebted to him for making Du Bois's FBI file available to me.

66. Cora Du Bois, FBI File No. 121–8038, June 7, 1948.

67. Cora Du Bois, FBI File No. 121–8038, June 25, 1948.

68. McIntosh, *Sisterhood of Spies*, 219. Also see Foster, *Unamerican Lady*; and Conant, *Covert Affair*.

69. Cora Du Bois, FBI File No. 121–8038, September 1, 1953. A copy of this 1948 interrogation was included in the file for a new investigation that the FBI initiated in 1953.

70. B. Smith, *Shadow Warriors*; Waller, *Wild Bill Donovan*.

71. Ruth Benedict and Gene Weltfish, for example, had published a pamphlet, *Races of Mankind* (1943), during the war that was distributed among the armed forces to try to enhance understanding among men and women of different ethnicities who were fighting together. It argued strenuously against racial inequities in the United States, Nazi Germany, and elsewhere. Weltfish was subpoenaed by Senator McCarthy during his witch hunt, and Benedict also would have been had she not died first. Subsequently, Weltfish would be dismissed by Columbia University. Price, *Threatening Anthropology*, 24, 112–13.

72. Price, *Threatening Anthropology*, 294.

73. Beisner, *Dean Acheson*, 304.

74. Johnson, *Lavender Scare*, 75.

75. See, e.g., Theoharis, *Abuse of Power*; Theoharis, *The FBI*; Theoharis, *From the Secret Files of J. Edgar Hoover*; and Morro, "Who Knew What."

76. Price, *Threatening Anthropology*, 15.

77. Cora Du Bois, FBI file 121 8038-10, April 5, 1948. There had been much political turmoil during Du Bois's year teaching at Hunter College, from which she tried to keep herself removed, but by 1939 an instructors' union had been formed that had some communist membership. See Schrecker, *No Ivory Tower*.

78. Cora Du Bois, FBI file 121-4442, July 29, 1948. This boss probably was John Carter Vincent, director of Far Eastern Affairs, State Department, at the time.

79. Cora Du Bois, FBI file 138-1830-17, September 1, 1953.

80. Cora Du Bois, FBI file 41305, September 14, 1953.

81. Cora Du Bois, FBI file 41305, September 14, 1953.

82. There is no saved audio recording of the Wheeling speech, but it is generally agreed that McCarthy held up a piece of paper that he claimed had such names on it and that he made these accusations against Dean Acheson and the State Department. "Joseph McCarthy," *Wikipedia*, last modified May 30, 2014, http://en.wikipedia.org/wiki /Joseph_McCarthy.

83. Cora Du Bois, FBI file 138-1830, September 1, 1953.

84. Du Bois to Lowie, March 25, 1948, RHL.

85. For example, John Carter Vincent, one of the country's leading China specialists and the director of Far Eastern Affairs when Cora was in the State Department, was transferred to Switzerland to get him out of McCarthy's way. He was recalled in

1952 for an investigation and ultimately suspended. John Paxton Davies Jr., another China expert, went through nine loyalty board reviews before being sacked. And John Stewart Service, another China expert, was fired by Acheson in 1951.

86. Du Bois to George Foster, September 21, 1981, CDBH, Box 20.
87. JW, Session III, Pt. 1.
88. Kelly interview, CDBH, Box 11.
89. Caffrey, *Ruth Benedict*, 337.
90. Du Bois, Contributions to *Ruth Fulton Benedict*, 12–13.
91. Caffrey, *Ruth Benedict*, 278.
92. "Scurrilous Sketches," CDBH, Box 4.
93. Price, *Threatening Anthropology*, 112.
94. Grace Buzaljko, unpublished paper on Kroeber and his women students, 1984, in author's possession; Kerns, *Scenes from the High Desert*, 260.
95. A. L. Kroeber to Ted McCown, November 5, 1948, RDA.
96. Du Bois to Lowie, December 13, 1949, CDBH, Box 18.
97. For example, when leaving Alor, in a May 29, 1939, letter to her parents, Cora wrote, "I consider it [an offer from Sarah Lawrence] a good stop gap. My heart's desire is still a job in the Univ. of Calif. . . . I don't want to put off too long my favorite fantasy of a house in Berkeley." CDBH, Box 5.
98. Kelly interview, p. 19, CDBH, Box 11.
99. Cora Du Bois to President Sproul, February 20, 1950, RDA.
100. Du Bois to Lowie, December 13, 1949, RHL.
101. JW, Session III, Pt. 1, p. 10 (emphasis added).
102. Du Bois to George Foster, September 21, 1981, CDBH, Box 20.
103. "Resolution Adopted by the Regents of the University of California," April 21, 1950, *The Loyalty Oath Controversy, University of California 1949-1951*, University of California History Digital Archives, http://sunsite.berkeley.edu/~ucalhist/archives_exhibits /loyaltyoath/regent_resolution.html.
104. CDBH, Box 18 (emphasis added).
105. CDBH, Box 18.
106. CDBH, Box 18.
107. See Schrecker, *No Ivory Tower*, 117–18.
108. Edward C. Tolman to UC president Robert G. Sproul, July 18, 1950, in *Loyalty Oath Controversy*, http://sunsite.berkeley.edu/~ucalhist/archives_exhibits/loyaltyoath/tolman .html.
109. Schrecker, *No Ivory Tower*.
110. Du Bois to Ted McCown, November 7, 1950, CDBH, Box 18.
111. Kelly interview, p. 19, CDBH, Box 11.
112. It was not until October 1952, in *Tolman v. Underhill*, that the Supreme Court of California ruled that "university personnel cannot properly be required to execute any other oath or declaration relating to loyalty other than that prescribed for all state employees." The nonsigners were ordered to be reinstated. "Expanded Timeline: Events of the Loyalty Oath Controversy and Historical Background," in *Loyalty Oath Controversy*,

http://sunsite.berkeley.edu/~ucalhist/archives_exhibits/loyaltyoath/timeline1951
_1956.html.

113. Du Bois to President Sproul, July 30, 1951, CDBH, Box 18.

114. September 15, 1952, journal entry, CDBH, Box 40.

115. February 17, 1951, journal entry, CDBH, Box 40.

116. Du Bois, "Some Anthropological Hindsights," 3.

117. Kelly interview, p. 20, CDBH, Box 11.

118. Cora Du Bois, FBI file HQ 138–1830, June 26, 1953.

119. Child, *My Life in France*, 195–97; also see Conant, *Covert Affair*.

8. Harvard

Epigraphs: James Gibbs, interview by author, November 19, 2007; James Peacock, personal communication, January 20, 2007.

1. Kelly interview, p. 20, CDBH, Box 11.

2. WJK, Box 40.

3. WJK, Box 40 (emphasis added).

4. WJK, Box 40.

5. As mentioned in the prologue, note 1, Cecilia Payne-Gaposchkin, a professor of astronomy, was the first woman *within* Harvard to be promoted to full professor with tenure, but that occurred two years after Du Bois's appointment as the Zemurray-Stone Professor. In fact, both Helen Maud Cam's and Du Bois's appointments seem to have helped trigger some changes for women instructors at Harvard. Cam had a short-term, trial appointment as the first Zemurray-Stone Professor.

6. Howells, *A Century to Celebrate*.

7. JW, Session IV, Pt. 1, p. 8.

8. *Harvard Crimson*, September 28, 1964, p. 1.

9. "Radcliffe College," *Wikipedia*, last modified June 2, 2014, http://en.wikipedia.org/wiki/Radcliffe_College.

10. Bernice Brown Cronkhite, dean of Radcliffe College, to Samuel Zemurray, September 26, 1944, WJK.

11. Cronkhite to Zemurray, September 26, 1944, WJK.

12. Bentinck-Smith and Stouffer, *Harvard University*, 579.

13. "Draft Proposals for a Radcliffe Professorship in the Faculty of Arts and Sciences of Harvard University," final agreement, June 6, 1947, WJK (emphasis added).

14. W. K. Jordan to Mr. Samuel Zemurray, February 14, 1947, WJK.

15. Edwin G. Boring, chairman, Department of Psychology, to President Jordan, June 16, 1947, WJK.

16. Kelly interview, p. 22, CDBH, Box 11.

17. W. K. Jordan, S. E. Thorne, and G. Constable, "Helen Maud Cam: Memorial Minutes Adopted by the Faculty of Arts and Sciences," Harvard University, November 12, 1968, WJK.

18. Jordan to Du Bois, December 11, 1953, WJK.

19. Professor Rogers to President Jordan, October 2, 1953, WJK.

20. WJK.

21. WJK.

22. Du Bois to Jordan, February 10, 1954, WJK.

23. Dean Bundy to Du Bois, December 24, 1953, WJK.

24. Du Bois to parents, May 6, 1954, CDBH, Box 6.

25. JW, Session IV, Pt. 1, p. 1.

26. A number of former anthropology graduate students whom I interviewed volunteered this observation.

27. Keller and Keller, *Making Harvard Modern*, 216.

28. Several male former anthropology graduate students independently characterized the Peabody Museum this way in their interviews with me. They knew that some professors were there because of their independent wealth or connections. Over the years, a few women had been hired—e.g., Alice Cunningham Fletcher and Harriet Silliman Cosgrove—as museum ethnologists or archaeologists, but they did not have professorial status. The Maya art expert Tatiana Prokouriakoff would become a museum curator in 1958 and was a friend of Du Bois, but she also did not have professorial status.

29. JW, Session IV, Pt. 1, p. 3.

30. Dr. Sarah Nerlove, program director, Partnerships for Innovation Program, National Science Foundation, personal communication.

31. Du Bois credited Ruth Benedict for first using the term "culture shock" and asserted that by 1940 it was so widely used that it needed no citation. See Golde, *Women in the Field*, 11. The Institute for International Education published a short article by Du Bois entitled "Culture Shock," in *To Strengthen World Freedom*, Special Publications Series, no. 1, December 1951. And years later the term would be attributed to her in a letter to the *Washington Post*, September 3, 1978.

32. JW, Session IV, Pt. 1, p. 2.

33. Du Bois, *Foreign Students and Higher Education*, 62–65.

34. James Gibbs, for example, was enrolled in that course, and his research paper on blood-brotherhood in two African societies became one of his first publications. See Gibbs, "Compensatory Blood-Brotherhood."

35. JW, Session IV, Pt. 1, p. 3.

36. Karl Heider, interview by author, November 18, 2006.

37. James Siegel, email correspondence, December 6, 2001.

38. Gibbs, interview by author, November 19, 2007, plus follow-up email correspondence.

39. Laura Nader, interview by author, April 2, 2007.

40. Du Bois to Lowie, May 3, 1955, RHL.

41. Sam Smith, "Practicing Anthropology without a License," speech delivered to the One Hundredth Anniversary Conference of the Berkeley School of Anthropology, June 21, 2006, http://samsmithessays.blogspot.com/2006/06/practicing-anthropology-without.html.

42. Nader, interview by author, April 2, 2007.

43. Robert Le Vine (chairman), Susan Seymour, Evon Z. Vogt Jr., Beatrice Whiting, and John W. M. Whiting, "Cora Du Bois," Memorial Minute Adopted by the Faculty of Arts and Sciences, Harvard University, October 20, 1992, *Harvard University Gazette* 88, no. 14 (December 4, 1992).

44. Gibbs, interview by author, November 19, 2007, plus follow-up email correspondence.

45. Du Bois "Appendix to the Preface of 1944," *People of Alor* (1960 ed.), pp. xiv–xv.

46. Du Bois to Lowie, May 3, 1955, RHL.

47. Kelly interview, p. 22, CDBH, Box 11.

48. Jordan to Du Bois, May 24, 1955, WJK.

49. Du Bois to Jordan, May 28, 1955, WJK.

50. Du Bois to Jordan, June 30, 1956, WJK.

51. Jordan to Du Bois, November 5, 1954, WJK.

52. Jordan to Harris, February 9, 1955, WJK.

53. JW, Session IV, Pt. 1, p. 7.

54. John W. M. Whiting and Beatrice B. Whiting came to Harvard with the developmental psychologist Robert R. Sears, director of the Laboratory of Human Development in the Graduate School of Education. John Whiting came as an associate professor and Beatrice Whiting as a research associate. In 1953 John Whiting succeeded Sears as the director of Human Development when Sears moved to Stanford. In 1962 John Whiting moved to the Faculty of Arts and Sciences as a professor of anthropology. Beatrice Whiting remained in the position of research associate, despite her collaborative research with John Whiting and her many publications. It was not until the feminist movement of the 1970s that she was finally given a professorship in the Graduate School of Education at Harvard.

55. JW, Session IV, Pt. 1, p. 6.

56. Gibbs, interview by author, November 19, 2007, plus follow-up email correspondence.

57. Nader, interview by author, April 2, 2007.

58. Robert Jay, interview by author, May 3, 2008.

59. Hildred Geertz, interview by author, June 28, 2008. Unfortunately, Clifford Geertz had recently died, so I was not able to interview him personally, but I have had access to his correspondence with Cora Du Bois.

60. Clifford Geertz to Du Bois, November 13, 1968, CDBH, Box 31.

61. Du Bois to Clifford Geertz, December 19, 1968, CDBH, Box 31.

62. Hildred Geertz to Du Bois, 1974, CDBH, Box 21.

63. I was able to interview thirty-seven of Cora Du Bois's former students, who have been identified and thanked in the preface.

64. James Peacock, personal communication, January 20, 2007.

65. J. David Sapir, interview by author, March 19, 2008.

66. Karl Heider and James Peacock, joint interview by author, November 18, 2006.

67. Heider and Peacock, joint interview by author, November 18, 2006; and James Peacock, personal communications, January 20–21, 2007.

68. Briggs, "Kapluna Daughter," 19.

69. Jean Briggs, interview by author, September 20, 2008.

70. Undated, from "Biographical Notes," CDBH, Box 11.

71. Du Bois to Lowie, May 3, 1955, letter from RHL.

72. September 10, 1954, letter home, CDBH, Box 6.

73. November 14, 1957, letter home, CDBH, Box 6.

74. May 6, 1954, letter home, CDBH, Box 6.

75. Thanks to Jeanne Taylor's niece, Lisa Schlingerman, I learned about the carpentry book and other children's book manuscripts—with such wonderful titles as "Drawing in Bed" and "The Third Black Cat"—that Jeanne worked on in Cambridge.

76. Clyde and Florence Kluckhohn's son Richard shot and killed a woman in Durham, North Carolina, while he was on a business trip. A graduate of the University of Chicago, Richard was working as an acquisitions editor for Row, Peterson Publishers and staying at a hotel in Durham while trying to procure book manuscripts from Duke and University of North Carolina faculty. According to his testimony, he was "dry firing" his gun out the window and had no idea that it was loaded and that it had fired and hit someone. Needless to say, the event created a dramatic and painful episode for the Kluckhohns, who returned from California and used their Cambridge house as a base from which to travel to Raleigh, North Carolina, where their son was tried for second-degree murder and found guilty of involuntary manslaughter.

77. Cora Du Bois, personal communication.

78. October 10, 1957, letter home, CDBH, Box 6.

79. August 4, 1957, letter home, CDBH, Box 6.

80. October 10, 1957, letter home, CDBH, Box 6.

81. November 9, 1956, letter home, CDBH, Box 6.

82. July 11, 1956, letter home, CDBH, Box 6.

83. August 13, 1956, letter home, CDBH, Box 6.

84. See Peters, *May Sarton*; Sherman, *May Sarton: Among the Usual Days*; and Sherman, *May Sarton: Selected Letters*.

85. Freedman, "Burning of Letters Continues."

86. Peters, *May Sarton*, 203.

87. May Sarton, "I See Myself as a Builder of Bridges," interview by Neila C. Seshachari, *Weber Studies* 9, no. 2 (Spring/Summer 1992), http://weberstudies.weber.edu/archiveA .htm.

88. October 30, 1955, letter home, CDBH, Box 6.

89. Heilbrun, *Last Gift of Time*, 87.

90. Sarton to Judith Matlack, June 6, 1957, in Sherman, *May Sarton: Selected Letters*, 59.

91. Sarton to Judith Matlack, June 6, 1957, in Sherman, *May Sarton: Selected Letters*, 59.

92. 1952–63 Journal, CDBH, Box 11.

93. "The Actor and the Poet," October 22, 1957, CDBH, Box 40.

94. In a September 1958 letter to Du Bois, Sarton makes it clear that the status of Jeanne Taylor had become painful for both of them. See Sherman, *May Sarton: Selected Letters*, 73.

95. Sherman, *May Sarton: Selected Letters*, 74.

96. Sherman, *May Sarton: Selected Letters*, 74.

97. Sarton, *Cloud, Stone, Sun, Vine*.

98. Sherman, *May Sarton: Selected Letters*, 289.

99. Sherman, *May Sarton: Selected Letters*, 73.

100. Sarton, *Collected Poems*.

101. CDBH, Box 11.

102. Peters, *May Sarton*, 255.

103. Sarton, *Mrs. Stevens Hears the Mermaids Singing*, 162–63.

104. JW, Session IV, Pt. 1, p. 2.

105. JW, Session IV, Pt. 1, p. 9.

9. Sociocultural Change in India

Epigraph: Cora Du Bois, "An Anthropologist Looks at Modernization," Cooper Lecture, Swarthmore College, April 7, 1967 (unpublished), CDBH, Box 73.

1. Notes for October 10, 1966, lecture to Social Relations 205, CDBH, Box 55.

2. Notes for October 10, 1966, lecture to Social Relations 205, CDBH, Box 55.

3. JW, Session IV, Pt. 1, p. 13.

4. Ben Finney, professor emeritus, University of Hawaii at Manoa, interview by author, July 18, 2008.

5. Keller and Keller, *Making Harvard Modern*, 416.

6. Du Bois, "Some Anthropological Hindsights," 3.

7. See, e.g., Diamond, *Compromised Campus*; and Cumings, *Parallax Visions*.

8. Diamond, *Compromised Campus*; Nader, "Phantom Factor," 112–13.

9. Irven DeVore, interview by author, October 27, 2006.

10. Engerman, " West Meets East," 214–15.

11. Du Bois, "Studies in an Indian Town," 224–25 (emphasis added).

12. That issue of the *American Anthropologist*, vol. 57, no. 6, December 1955, was a special issue entitled "The U.S.A. as Anthropologists See It" and included articles by many distinguished anthropologists. Spiro's article was "The Acculturation of American Ethnic Groups" and Cora Du Bois's was "The Dominant Value Profile of American Culture."

13. Melford Spiro, interview by author, April 15, 2008.

14. Spiro to Du Bois, January 30, 1960, CDBH, Box 31.

15. Spiro, interview by author, April 15, 2008.

16. CDBH, Box 24.

17. Undated draft of letter to Cy Lowie, CDBH, Box 2.

18. See Du Bois, "Robert H. Lowie, Anthropologist."

19. Du Bois to Goldschmidt, October 24, 1957, CDBH, Box 21.

20. Goldschmidt to Du Bois, October 29, 1957 CDBH, Box 21.

21. Goldschmidt to Du Bois, September 27, 1960, CDBH, Box 21.

22. See Du Bois, "Gratuitous Act."

23. Interim Report on NSF Grant 17913, September 1962, CDBC, Box 1, Folder 7. The initial NSF grant was followed by a series of two- and three-year grants that covered

Du Bois's expenses and that of research assistants for another eleven years. Her American PhD students had to procure their own grants for research in Bhubaneswar.

24. Examples are the Harvard-MIT project on modernization in Indonesia (chapter 8); the Alex Inkeles study of modernization in five countries, including India (Inkeles, *Becoming Modern*; Inkeles, *Exploring Individual Modernity*); Evon Vogt's long-term research project in Chiapas, Mexico (Vogt, *Zinacantán*); Beatrice B. Whiting and John W. M. Whiting's Six Culture Study of childrearing (Whiting, *Six Cultures*; Whiting and Whiting, *Children of Six Cultures*); Irven DeVore's Harvard-Kalahari project (see, e.g., Lee and DeVore, *Man the Hunter*); and David McClelland's cross-cultural "need for achievement" (*n*Ach) projects (McClelland, *Achieving Society*).

25. July 18, 1961, letter home, CDBC, Box 14, Folder 3.

26. August 6, 1961, letter home, CDBC, Box 14, Folder 3.

27. Du Bois, "Studies in an Indian Town," 224.

28. August 23, 1961, letter home, CDBC, Box 14, Folder 3.

29. Grenell, "The Setting," 11.

30. August 23, 1961, letter home, CDBC, Box 14, Folder 3.

31. August 29, 1961, letter home, CDBC, Box 14, Folder 3.

32. They were Dr. D. P. Pattanayak, the director of the Linguistic Institute of the Deccan College in Pune, Maharashtra, and Gagan N. Dash, a graduate student at Santiniketan University in Kolkata. Together, Pattanayak and Dash would publish *Conversational Oriya* (1972), based on the lessons they prepared for Du Bois's American students.

33. August 29, 1961, letter home, CDBC, Box 14, Folder 3.

34. See Seymour, *Women, Family, and Childcare in India*. In 1965–67 I was the only woman who shopped at the New Capital farmer's market.

35. Du Bois, "Studies in an Indian Town," 234.

36. September 16, 1961, letter home, CDBC, Box 14, Folder 3.

37. Du Bois, "Studies in an Indian Town," 225–26.

38. Technically, only seven of the eight graduate researchers completed PhD degrees. Peter Grenell submitted a draft of his dissertation to the Department of Urban Development at MIT but never finalized it. He was drawn away by job opportunities that did not require the degree.

39. "Summary and Appraisal of the Harvard-Bhubaneswar Project, Orissa, India: 1961–1973," CDBC, Box 6, Folder 17.

40. Du Bois, "Studies in an Indian Town," 226.

41. With the support and collaboration of Professor A. Aiyappan, then the chair of the Department of Anthropology at Utkal University, Du Bois immediately had a set of anthropology students and colleagues with whom to work.

42. Du Bois, "Studies in an Indian Town," 231.

43. Du Bois, "Studies in an Indian Town," 231.

44. Das, "Economy of an Urbanizing Village."

45. Mahapatra, "Lingaraj Temple."

46. James Freeman, interview by author, November 16, 2006.

47. Freeman, "Widening Economic Gap," 185.

48. Freeman, interview by author, November 16, 2006.

49. Today the Harvard-Bhubaneswar files and books reside in the Cora Alice Du Bois Papers, Special Collections, University of Chicago Library (CDBC).

50. Du Bois, "Studies in an Indian Town," 226.

51. Richard Taub, interview by author, April 27, 2008.

52. Taub, interview by author, April 27, 2008.

53. Peter Grenell, interview by author, January 20, 2008.

54. Grenell, "Planning the New Capital," 31.

55. Grenell, "Planning the New Capital," 44.

56. See Miller and Wertz, *Hindu Monastic Life*.

57. Miller and Wertz, *Hindu Monastic Life*; also see Miller, "Religious Institutions and Political Elites."

58. See, e.g., Max Weber, *Religion of India*; Gunnar Myrdal, *Asian Drama*; and Levy, *Modernization and the Structure of Societies*.

59. See Freeman and Preston, "Two Urbanizing Orissan Temples."

60. James Preston, interview by author, January 18, 2008.

61. Alan Sable, interview by author, August 7, 2007.

62. Sable, "Indian Education," 181.

63. See, e.g., Whiting, *Six Cultures*.

64. See Seymour, *Women, Family, and Childcare in India*.

65. Richard Shweder, interview by author, June 16, 2008.

66. Shweder, interview by author, June 16, 2008.

67. Richard Shweder, personal communication, October 29, 2011.

68. Shweder, personal communication, October 29, 2011.

69. "Summary and Appraisal of the Harvard-Bhubaneswar Project, Orissa, India: 1961–1973," National Science Foundation, p. 5, CDBC, Box 6, Folder 17.

70. Shweder to Du Bois, March 13, 1984, and Du Bois reply, April 20, 1984, CDBH, Box 29.

71. Cora Du Bois, "Perspectives on Recent American Anthropology," revision of a lecture given to the Department of Sociology and Anthropology, University of North Carolina in Greensboro, April 1972, p. 9, CDBH, Box 77 (emphasis added).

72. Du Bois, "Perspectives on Recent American Anthropology," lecture, pp. 10–11, CDBH, Box 77.

73. Du Bois, "Perspectives on Recent American Anthropology," lecture, p. 12, CDBH, Box 77.

74. January 26, 1963, journal entry, CDBH, Box 40.

75. Du Bois, "Some Anthropological Hindsights," 9.

76. Roy D'Andrade (professor emeritus of anthropology, UC San Diego), for example, in a March 2007 interview, related how a heated debate between Du Bois and Whiting had nearly upset passage of his preliminary oral examinations for the PhD in social relations at Harvard. D'Andrade, who became an eminent cognitive anthropologist, had listed Southeast Asia as his geographic/cultural area of expertise for these exams. What he knew of the ethnographic literature, he reported, came from reading bits

and pieces of the Human Relations Area Files, not from taking a course with Du Bois or working with a reading list for Southeast Asia. Du Bois was put on his examination committee and began asking him some general questions that he could not answer. Things went from bad to worse, and eventually D'Andrade was asked to leave the room while the committee deliberated. Du Bois and Whiting, he later learned, had argued for a considerable time about the extent to which anthropology students in the Department of Social Relations should be well grounded in the ethnographic literature of a region of the world. (Students in the Department of Anthropology were responsible for two regions of the world.) D'Andrade passed his exams, but without honors.

77. Du Bois, "Some Anthropological Hindsights," 8.

78. Cora Du Bois, "The Ethnographer and the Social Scientist," vice presidential address to Section H, American Association for the Advancement of Science, December 29, 1966, CDBH, Box 73.

79. For instance, Du Bois gave the Cooper Lecture, entitled "An Anthropologist Looks at Modernization," at Swarthmore College in April 1967; CDBH, Box 73.

80. See, e.g., Latham, *Modernization as Ideology*.

81. Examples are Parsons and Shils, *Toward a General Theory of Action*; Parsons, *Societies*; Parsons, *Structure and Process in Modern Societies*; Lerner, *Passing of Traditional Society*; Inkeles, *Becoming Modern*; McClelland, *Achieving Society*; Rostow, *Stages of Economic Growth*; Weiner, *Modernization*; and Pye, *Politics, Personality, and Nation Building*.

82. Gilman, "Modernization Theory," 50.

83. Du Bois, "Perspectives on Recent American Anthropology," lecture, CDBH, Box 77.

84. James Peacock, who took the course with Du Bois in the early 1960s, reported that she was never critical of her highly theoretical colleagues. Personal communication, November 17, 2011.

85. Course syllabus for Social Relations 229b, Individual & Socio-Cultural Change, Spring 1964, CDBH, Box 59.

86. Application for Research Grant from National Science Foundation, February 1, 1963, p. 1, CDBC, Box 6, Folder 1 (emphasis added).

87. Du Bois, "An Anthropologist Looks at Modernization," lecture, pp. 13–14, CDBH, Box 73.

88. Du Bois, "Presidential Address to the Association for Asian Studies," 4.

89. Du Bois had discarded her own personal contribution to the project—the study of changing values among 240 subjects who represented new and old occupations in Bhubaneswar. She had developed—"after lengthy consultations with persons knowledgeable about values research"—a lengthy values protocol that was translated into Oriya and pretested, after which Cora recruited and trained twenty Orissan interviewers "whose status, rapport and/or competence was suitable to the proposed sample of twenty persons in twelve salient socio-cultural categories." "Summary and Appraisal of the Harvard-Bhubaneswar Project, Orissa, India: 1961–1973," National Science Foundation, p. 11, CDBC Box 6, Folder 17. This was Du Bois's excursion into

a new research methodology that produced quantitative data requiring computerized statistical analyses—a process that she found distancing and that produced outcomes in which she did not have confidence.

90. Du Bois wrote two unpublished papers about some of these processes. "Traditional Orientations and Occupational Choices in an Indian Triple Town" laid out clearly the economic changes that were occurring and why they varied by social status (i.e., caste) and by residence in the Old Town, the New Capital, or one of the five villages that had been incorporated into this new city of administration. The other was "Paths to Modernization: Temple and Government in a Town of Eastern India." Here Du Bois outlined the numerous parallels that existed between the ancient Hindu Lingaraj Temple complex of the Old Town and the recently established government bureaucracy of the New Capital. Both were hierarchical institutions, she argued, characterized by social distance, inefficiency, internal factionalism, and impersonal authority. "My intent," Du Bois wrote, "is to search out the paths open from the old to the new institutions for persons who are living through the changes taking place." The paths were generally horizontal—some individuals moved from one status position in the older system to a comparable position in the newer system. For instance, members of literate castes (Brahmins and Karens) moved into middle- and high-level civil service positions, whereas outcaste Sweepers became salaried janitors for New Capital buildings and homes. Some Old Town Brahmin families kept a foot in each system by educating one son for the new civil service system and another for temple service. Entrepreneurs tended to be migrants from outside Odisha or Old Town and village residents who had a caste occupation needed in the New Capital, such as Washermen who opened laundry services or Barbers who set up hair salons. An expanding urban population had many service needs that had not been part of the planning process. CDBC, Box 11, Folder 8.

10. Looking Inward

Epigraph: Excerpt from Cora Du Bois, "Statement of Thanks," November 16, 1984, for the Thomas Jefferson/Distinguished Service Award in International Anthropology, Denver, author's personal copy.

1. In addition, because Du Bois had not built up enough years of teaching at Harvard to be eligible for a sabbatical leave, her year at Stanford (1958–59) and a semester at the University of Hawaii (1957) were leaves of absence without pay. W. K. Jordan to Cora Du Bois, January 7, 1957, WJK.

2. Du Bois to Spiro, October 22, 1968, CDBH, Box 29.

3. Du Bois's list of home expenses (mortgage, tax, heat, etc.) for 1959 came to $6,152.50. A decade later, the $7,000 pension might have barely covered those expenses but would not have covered food, travel, etc. She feared that she might have to give up her home. CDBH, Box 11.

4. Council of Radcliffe College, February 3, 1969, minutes, Schlesinger Library, Radcliffe Institute, Cambridge MA.

5. Council of Radcliffe College, February 3, 1969, minutes.

6. Du Bois to Vogt, October 1971, CDBH, Box 31.

7. Cora Du Bois and Beatrice Whiting, personal communications. Also see Robert A. LeVine (chair), Susan Seymour, Evon Z. Vogt, Jr., Beatrice B. Whiting, and John W. M. Whiting, "Cora Du Bois," Memorial Minute Adopted by the Faculty of the Arts and Sciences, Harvard University, October 20, 1992, *Harvard University Gazette* 88, no. 14 (December 4, 1992).

8. "Biographical Notes," June 5, 1978, CDBH, Box 4.

9. Notes for 1981 interview sessions with Judith Walzer, CDBH, Box 4.

10. The women who preceded Du Bois as president of the AAA were Elsie Clews Parsons (1941), Ruth Benedict (1947), Margaret Mead (1960), and Frederica de Laguna (1967).

11. JW, Session IV, Pt. 2, p. 1 (emphasis added).

12. See Lewis, "Radical Transformation of Anthropology," 212.

13. See Hill, "Committee on Ethics."

14. See, e.g., Herbert Phillips, "Between the Tiger and the Crocodile: Scholarly Ethics and Government Research in Thailand," unpublished book manuscript regarding this and related issues, Bancroft Library, University of California, Berkeley.

15. "Statement of the Executive Board of the AAA," *Bulletins of AAA*, Annual Report, 1969.

16. "Statement of the Executive Board of the AAA," *Bulletins of AAA*, Annual Report, 1969.

17. Du Bois to Foster, May 14, 1970, AAA, Box 109.

18. Foster to Du Bois, November 26, 1969, CDBH, Box 20.

19. See American Anthropological Association, 2012 Statement on Ethics, AAA Ethics Blog, http://ethics.aaanet.org.

20. Du Bois to Humpstone, September 16, 1969, AAA, Box 110 (emphasis added).

21. In several instances anthropologists did use archaeological or ethnographic fieldwork as a cover for intelligence work in other parts of the world during World War II. See Price, *Anthropological Intelligence*.

22. See Cumings, *Parallax Visions*, for an excellent discussion of these issues.

23. Cora Du Bois, "Statement by the President," *Newsletter of the American Anthropological Association* 10, no. 5 (May 1969): 1.

24. Louise Lamphere, personal communication.

25. Berreman, "Social Responsibility of the Anthropologist," 9.

26. JW, Session IV, Pt. 2, p. 1.

27. Hill, "Committee on Ethics."

28. Du Bois, Review of *Culture and Commitment*.

29. Mead to Du Bois, January 13, 1972, CDBH, Box 26.

30. See Lutkehaus, *Margaret Mead*.

31. Du Bois, Review of *Culture and Commitment*, 1291.

32. Du Bois, Review of *Culture and Commitment*, 1291 (emphasis added).

33. Du Bois, Review of *Culture and Commitment*, 1292–93 (emphasis added).

34. Howard, *Margaret Mead*.

35. Howard to Du Bois, February 10, 1981, CDBH, Box 26.

36. Du Bois to Howard, March 2, 1981, CDBH, Box 26.

37. Du Bois's handwritten draft of a response to Howard's set of inquiries about Margaret Mead, CDBH, Box 26.

38. Undated, handwritten notes by Du Bois, CDBH, Box 26.

39. Du Bois to Métraux, November 20, 1978 CDBH, Box 26.

40. Métraux to Du Bois, December 17, 1978, CDBH, Box 26.

41. Handwritten notes attached to Du Bois's 1967 Interim NSF Report, CDBC, Box 6, Folder 1.

42. The one published paper was Du Bois, "Studies in an Indian Town." Also see chapter 9, note 90, regarding two of Du Bois's unpublished papers on India.

43. Notes attached to Bhubaneswar, India, book outline, CDBC.

44. See chapter 9, note 89.

45. Geertz's *The Interpretation of Culture* (1973) had an enormous impact on theory and methods in cultural anthropology. See, e.g., Peacock's tribute to Geertz, "Geertz's Concept of Culture in Historical Context." It is also important to note that the "crisis" in the study and representation of other peoples and cultures helped to spawn the Society for Cultural Anthropology in 1983 (a subsociety of the American Anthropological Association) and its own journal, *Cultural Anthropology*, in 1986.

46. Notes attached to Bhubaneswar, India, book outline, CDBC.

47. JW, Session IV, Pt. 2, p. 6.

48. JW, Session IV, Pt. 2, pp. 6–7.

49. JW, Session IV, Pt. 2, p. 9.

50. Alan Sable, interviews by author, August 2007 and August 2008.

51. "Biographical Notes," CDBH, Box 11.

52. JW, Session IV, Pt. 2, p. 6.

53. Du Bois to Seymour, March 26, 1976, CDBC.

54. Du Bois to Seymour, October 31, 1977, CDBC.

55. See Keller and Keller, *Making Harvard Modern*.

56. Beatrice Whiting, personal communication.

57. Beatrice Whiting, 1991 draft of Harvard memorial minute for Cora Du Bois, copy in author's possession.

58. Sarton, *Mrs. Stevens Hears the Mermaids Singing*, 162–63.

59. Du Bois to Mills, June 6, 1984, CDBH, Box 26.

60. See Du Bois, "Some Anthropological Hindsights." The other publication was Du Bois, "Anthropology in Context."

61. Du Bois, "Some Anthropological Hindsights," 8.

62. "Biographical Notes," CDBH, Box 11.

63. JW, Session 4, Pt. 1, pp. 7–8.

64. Cora Du Bois, personal communication.

65. Cora Du Bois to Pat and Gérard Du Bois, December 21, 1984, CDBH, Box 19.

66. Du Bois to Read, September 28, 1978, CDBH, Box 28.

67. Du Bois to Read, September 28, 1978, CDBH, Box 28.

68. Gérard Du Bois, personal communication.

69. Cora Du Bois to Louison Du Bois, November 11, 1983, courtesy of Gérard Du Bois.

70. Du Bois to Bill Schreiber, December 10, 1982, CDBH, Box 8.

71. Bollinger to Du Bois, August 16, 1982, CDBH, Box 8.

72. Barnette to Cora and Jeanne, April 7, 1976, CDBH, Box 17.

73. Du Bois to Phil and Louise, July 10, 1977, CDBH, Box 17.

74. Orenstein to Du Bois, June 1, 1977, CDBH, Box 27 (emphasis added).

75. Du Bois to Orenstein, June 7, 1977, CDBH, Box 27. The branch of unrelated Du Boises that Cora refers to here was established in New Paltz, New York, by 1705. A historical "Du Bois House" exists from that period that, according to plaques, served as a fort-cum-inn/tavern and safe haven in case of attack. Carol Schreiber Bollinger (Cora Du Bois's cousin), personal communication.

76. Du Bois to Phyllis Hind, January 21, 1980, CDBH, Box 22 (emphasis added).

77. Cora Du Bois to Pat and Gérard Du Bois, December 21, 1984, courtesy of Gérard Du Bois. Jeanne Taylor was the immediate beneficiary of Du Bois's house and financial resources until the time of her death. (Jeanne died one year after Cora.)

78. "Addendum for JT," Miscellaneous Notes, CDBH, Box 11.

79. "Dearest Cora," CDBH, Box 11.

80. Jeanne Taylor to friends, May 1, 1991, personal communication.

81. Antonia Mills, interview by author, November 29, 2007, and subsequent email communications.

82. Jeanne Taylor to friends, May 1, 1991, personal communication.

BIBLIOGRAPHY

Archives and Manuscripts

AAA   Papers of the American Anthropological Association. National Anthropological Archives, Smithsonian Institution, Washington DC.

CDBC   Cora Du Bois Papers (1961–72). Special Collections Research Center, University of Chicago Library, University of Chicago, Chicago IL. (Permission granted by the trustees of the Cora Du Bois Revocable Trust.)

CDBH   Cora Alice Du Bois Papers (SPEC.COLL.ETHG.D 852C). Tozzer Library, Harvard College Library, Harvard University, Cambridge MA.

FBI   Federal Bureau of Investigation, Washington DC.

JW   Judith Walzer. "An Oral History of Tenured Women in the Faculty of Arts and Sciences at Harvard University." Murray Center, Schlesinger Library, Radcliffe Institute, Cambridge MA.

NARA   U.S. National Archives and Records Administration, Washington DC.

RDA   Records of the Department of Anthropology, 1901– (Collection No. CU-23). University Archives, University of California, Berkeley CA.

RFB   Ruth Fulton Benedict Papers (1905–48). Archives and Special Collections, Vassar College, Poughkeepsie NY.

RHL   Robert Harry Lowie Papers (1872–1968) (BANC MSS C-B 927). Bancroft Library, University of California, Berkeley CA.

WJK   Wilbur Kitchener Jordan, Records of the President of Radcliffe College, 1943–60. Radcliffe College Archives, Schlesinger Library, Radcliffe Institute, Cambridge MA.

Published Works

Addison, Joseph, and Richard Steele. *Days with Sir Roger de Coverley*. New York: Globusz, 2001.

Banner, Lois W. *Intertwined Lives: Margaret Mead, Ruth Benedict, and Their Circle*. New York: Knopf, 2003.

Barnouw, Victor. *Culture and Personality*. 4th ed. Homewood IL: Dorsey Press, 1985.

Beals, Ralph. "Fifty Years in Anthropology." *Annual Reviews in Anthropology* 11 (1982): 1–23.

Beisner, Robert L. *Dean Acheson: A Life in the Cold War*. New York: Oxford University Press, 2006.

Benedict, Ruth. "Anthropology and the Abnormal." *Journal of General Psychology* 10, no. 2 (1934): 59–82.

———. *Patterns of Culture*. New York: Houghton Mifflin, 1934.

Bentinck-Smith, William, and Elizabeth Stouffer. *Harvard University: History of Named Chairs: Sketches of Donors and Donations*. Vol. 1. Cambridge MA: Secretary to the University, 1991.

Berreman, Gerald D. "The Social Responsibility of the Anthropologist." In *To See Ourselves: Anthropology and Modern Social Issues*, edited by Thomas Weaver, 8–9. Glenview IL: Scott, Foresman, 1973.

Boas, Franz. *The Mind of Primitive Man*. New York: Macmillan, 1911.

——. "Psychological Problems in Anthropology." *American Journal of Psychology* 21, no.3 (1910): 371–84.

Bock, Philip K. *Psychological Anthropology*. Westport CT: Praeger, 1994.

Briggs, Jean. "Kapluna Daughter." In *Women in the Field: Anthropological Experiences*, edited by Peggy Golde, 19–46. Chicago: Aldine Press, 1970.

——. *Never in Anger: Portrait of an Eskimo Family*. Cambridge MA: Harvard University Press, 1970.

Caffrey, Margaret M. *Ruth Benedict: Stranger in This Land*. Austin: University of Texas Press, 1989.

Caffrey, Margaret M., and Patricia A. Francis, eds. *To Cherish the Life of the World: Selected Letters of Margaret Mead*. New York: Perseus Books, 2006.

Child, Julia. *My Life in France*. New York: Knopf, 2006.

Chomsky, Noam, Ira Katznelson, R. C. Lewontin, David Montgomery, Laura Nader, Richard Ohmann, Ray Siever, Immanuel Wallerstein, and Howard Zinn. *The Cold War and the University: Toward an Intellectual History of the Postwar Years*. New York: New Press, 1997.

Colbert, Evelyn. *Southeast Asia in International Politics 1941–1956*. Ithaca NY: Cornell University Press, 1977.

Conant, Jennet. *A Covert Affair: Julia Child and Paul Child in the OSS*. New York: Simon and Schuster, 2011.

Cross, Amanda [Carolyn Heilbrun]. *Death in a Tenured Position*. New York: Dutton, 1981.

Crump, Robert L. *Minnesota Prints and Printmakers, 1900–1945*. St. Paul: Minnesota Historical Society Press, 2009.

Cumings, Bruce. *Parallax Visions: Making Sense of American–East Asian Relations at the End of the Century*. Durham NC: Duke University Press, 1999.

Darnell, Regna. *Edward Sapir: Linguist, Anthropologist, Humanist*. Berkeley: University of California Press, 1990.

Das, Harish C. "The Economy of an Urbanizing Village." In Seymour, *Transformation of a Sacred Town*, 212–33.

D'Emilio, John, and Estelle B. Freedman. *Intimate Matters: A History of Sexuality in America*. New York: Harper & Row, 1988.

Diamond, Sigmund. *Compromised Campus: The Collaboration of Universities with the Intelligence Community, 1945–1955*. New York: Oxford University Press, 1992.

Du Bois, Cora. "Alorese." Chapter 5 in *The Psychological Frontiers of Society*, by Abram Kardiner, with the collaboration of Ralph Linton, Cora Du Bois, and James West. New York: Columbia University Press, 1945.

———. "Anthropology in Context." In *Crisis in Anthropology: View from Spring Hill, 1980*, edited by E. Adamson Hoebel, Richard Currier, and Susan Kaiser, 13–22. New York: Garland, 1982.

———. "Attitudes towards Food and Hunger in Alor." In *Personal Character and Cultural Milieu*, edited by Douglas G. Haring, 241–53. New York: Syracuse University Press, 1956. First published in *Language, Culture and Personality: Essays in Memory of Edward Sapir*, edited by Leslie Spier. Menasha WI: Memorial Publication Fund, 1941.

———. Contributions to *Ruth Fulton Benedict: A Memorial*, 12–13. New York: Viking Fund, 1949.

———. "The Dominant Value Profile of American Culture." *American Anthropologist* 57, no. 6, pt. 1 (1955): 1232–39.

———. *The 1870 Ghost Dance*. Anthropological Records, vol. 3, pt. 1. Berkeley: University of California Press, 1939. Republished with an introduction by Thomas Buckley. Lincoln: University of Nebraska Press, 2007.

———. *The Feather Cult of the Middle Columbia*. General Series in Anthropology, no. 7. Menasha WI: George Banta, 1938.

———. *Foreign Students and Higher Education in the United States*. Washington DC: American Council on Education, 1956.

———. "The Gratuitous Act: An Introduction to the Comparative Study of Friendship Patterns." In *The Compact: Selected Dimensions of Friendship*, edited by Elliott Leyton, 15–32. Newfoundland Social and Economic Papers No. 3. St. Johns: Institute of Social and Economic Research, Memorial University of Newfoundland, 1974.

———. "How They Pay Debts in Alor." *Asia*, September 1941, 483–86.

———. "How to Make a Totem Pole for Your Camp." *Camp Fire Girls Newsletter*, May 1927.

———, ed. *Lowie's Selected Papers in Anthropology*. Berkeley: University of California Press, 1960.

———. "A Paiute Prophet Died in Nevada." *California Monthly* 40 (April 1935): 9–11.

———. *The People of Alor: A Social Psychological Study of an East Indian Island*. Minneapolis: University of Minnesota Press, 1944. Reissued by Harvard University Press, 1960, with a new appendix to the preface.

———. "Presidential Address to the Association for Asian Studies." *Asian Studies Professional Review* 1, no. 2 (Spring 1972): .1–11.

———. Review of *Culture and Commitment*, by Margaret Mead. *American Anthropologist* 73, no. 6 (1971): 1292–93.

———. "Robert H. Lowie, Anthropologist." *Science* 127, no. 3291 (January 24, 1958): 181–82.

———. *Social Forces in Southeast Asia*. Cambridge MA: Harvard University Press, 1959. Originally published by University of Minnesota Press, 1949.

———. "Some Anthropological Hindsights." *Annual Review of Anthropology* 9 (1980): 1–13.

———. "Some Anthropological Perspectives on Psychoanalysis." *Psychoanalytic Review* 24, no. 3 (1937): 246–63.

———. "Studies in an Indian Town." In *Women in the Field: Anthropological Experiences*, edited by Peggy Golde, 221–36. Chicago: Aldine, 1970.

———. "Tolowa Notes." *American Anthropologist* 34, no.2 (1932): 248–62.

———. "Wealth Concept as an Integrative Factor in Tolowa-Tututni Culture." In *Essays in Anthropology: Presented to A. L. Kroeber in Celebration of His Sixtieth Birthday, June 11*, edited by Robert H. Lowie, 49–65. Berkeley: University of California Press, 1936.

———. "Why People Quarrel in Alor." *Asia*, February 1941, 91–94.

———. "Wintu Ethnography." *University of California Publications in American Archaeology and Ethnology* 36, no. 1 (1935): 1–148.

Du Bois, Cora, and Dorothy Demetracopoulou. "Study of Wintu Mythology." *Journal of American Folklore* 45, no. 178 (1932): 375–500.

———. "Wintu Myths." *University of California Publications in American Archaeology and Ethnology* 28, no. 5 (1931): 279–403.

Engerman, David C. "West Meets East: The Center for International Studies and Indian Economic Development." In *Staging Growth: Modernization, Development, and the Global Cold War*, edited by David C. Engerman, Nils Gilman, Mark H. Haefele, and Michael E. Latham, 199–224. Amherst: University of Massachusetts Press, 2003.

Erikson, Erik. *Childhood and Society*. New York: W. W. Norton, 1950.

———. *Identity, Youth and Crisis*. New York: W. W. Norton, 1968.

———. *Young Man Luther*. New York: W. W. Norton, 1958.

Faderman, Lillian. *Odd Girls and Twilight Lovers: A History of Lesbian Life in Twentieth-Century America*. New York: Columbia University Press, 1991.

Fitch, Noel Riley. *Appetite for Life: The Biography of Julia Child*. New York: Doubleday, 1997.

Foster, Jane. *An Unamerican Lady*. London: Sidgwick and Jackson, 1980.

Frazer, James. *The Golden Bough: A Study in Magic and Religion*. 2 vols. New York: Macmillan, 1890, 1894.

Freedman, Estelle E. "The Burning of Letters Continues." In *Feminism, Sexuality, and Politics: Essays by Estelle B. Freedman*, 159–73. Chapel Hill: University of North Carolina Press, 2006.

———. *Maternal Justice: Miriam Van Waters and the Female Reform Tradition*. Chicago: University of Chicago Press, 1996.

Freeman, James M. *Scarcity and Opportunity in An Indian Village*. Menlo Park CA: Cummings, 1977.

———. 1980. "The Widening Economic Gap: An Urban Indian Example." In Seymour, *Transformation of a Sacred Town*, 185–215.

Freeman, James M., and James Preston. "Two Urbanizing Orissan Temples." In Seymour, *Transformation of a Sacred Town*, 97–117.

Freud, Sigmund. *Totem and Taboo*. Translated by A. A. Brill. New York: Moffat, Yard, 1918. Originally published in German in 1913.

Gacs, Ute, A. Kahn, J. McIntyre, and R. Weinberg, eds. *Women Anthropologists: A Biographical Dictionary*. New York: Greenwood Press, 1988.

Gibbs, James. "Compensatory Blood-Brotherhood: Comparative Analysis of Institutional Friendship in Two African Societies." *Proceedings of the Minnesota Academy of Science* 30 (1962): 57–74.

Geertz, Clifford. *The Interpretation of Cultures*. New York: Basic Books, 1973.

———. *Islam Observed: Religious Development in Morocco and Indonesia*. New Haven CT: Yale University Press, 1968.

———. *The Religion of Java*. Glencoe IL: Free Press, 1960.

Gilman, Nils. "Modernization Theory, the Highest Stage of American Intellectual History." In *Staging Growth: Modernization, Development, and the Global Cold War*, edited by David C. Engerman, Nils Gilman, Mark H. Haefele, and Michael E. Latham, 47-80. Amherst: University of Massachusetts Press, 2003.

Golde, Peggy, ed. *Women in the Field: Anthropological Experiences*. Chicago: Aldine Press, 1970.

Goldin, Claudia. "America's Graduation from High School: The Evolution and Spread of Secondary Schooling in the Twentieth Century." *Journal of Economic History* 58, no. 2 (1998): 345-74.

Goldstein, Robert Justin. "Prelude to McCarthyism: The Making of a Blacklist." *Prologue* (U.S. National Archives) 38, no. 3 (Fall 2006). http://www.archives.gov/publications /prologue/2006/fall/agloso.html.

Grenell, Peter. "Planning the New Capital of Bhubaneswar." In Seymour, *Transformation of a Sacred Town*, 31-66.

———. "The Setting." In Seymour, *Transformation of a Sacred Town*, 9-30.

Hays, Peter. *From Cooperation to Complicity: Degussa in the Third Reich*. New York: Cambridge University Press, 2007.

Heider, Karl. *The Dugum Dani: A Papuan Culture in the Highlands of West New Guinea*. New York: Wenner-Gren Foundation for Anthropological Research, 1970.

Heilbrun, Carolyn G. *The Last Gift of Time: Life beyond Sixty*. New York: Ballantine Books, 1997.

Hill, James N. "The Committee on Ethics: Past Present, and Future." In *Handbook on Ethical Issues in Anthropology*, edited by Joan Cassell and Sue-Ellen Jacobs, 11-19. Washington DC: American Anthropological Association, 1987.

Horney, Karen. "The Problem of Feminine Masochism." *Psychoanalytic Review* 22, no. 3 (1935): 241-57.

Howard, Jane. *Margaret Mead: A Life*. New York: Ballantine Books, 1984.

Howells, Dorothy Elia. *A Century to Celebrate: Radcliffe College, 1879-1979*. Cambridge MA: Radcliffe College, 1978.

Hyatt, Marshall. *Franz Boas, Social Activist: The Dynamics of Ethnicity*. New York: Greenwood Press, 1990.

Inkeles, Alex. *Becoming Modern: Individual Change in Six Developing Countries*. Cambridge MA: Harvard University Press, 1974.

———. *Exploring Individual Modernity*. New York: Columbia University Press, 1983.

Irvine, Judith T. *Edward Sapir: The Psychology of Culture: A Course of Lectures*. New York: Mouton de Gruyter, 1994.

Jacknis, Ira. "The First Boasian: Alfred Kroeber and Franz Boas, 1896-1905." *American Anthropologist* 104, no. 2 (2002): 520-32.

Johnson, David K. *The Lavender Scare: The Cold War Persecution of Gays and Lesbians in the Federal Government*. Chicago: University of Chicago Press, 2004.

Kardiner, Abram. *The Individual and His Society: The Psychodynamics of Primitive Social Organization*. 1939. Reprint, New York: Columbia University Press, 1955.

Kardiner, Abram, with the collaboration of Cora Du Bois, Ralph Linton, and James West. *The Psychological Frontiers of Society*. New York: Columbia University Press 1945.

Keller, Morton, and Phyllis Keller. *Making Harvard Modern: The Rise of America's University*. New York: Oxford University Press, 2001.

Kerns, Virginia. *Scenes from the High Desert: Julian Steward's Life and Theory*. Urbana: University of Illinois Press, 2003.

Kidder, Alfred V. *An Introduction to the Study of Southwestern Archaeology*. New Haven CT: Yale University Press, 1924.

Kluckhohn, Clyde, and Henry A. Murray, eds. *Personality in Nature, Society, and Culture*. New York: Knopf, 1948.

Kroeber, Alfred L. *Anthropology: Race, Language, Culture, Psychology, Prehistory*. New York: Harcourt, Brace, 1948.

———. *Configurations of Culture Growth*. Berkeley: University of California Press, 1944.

———. *Handbook of the Indians of California*. Smithsonian Institution, Bureau of American Ethnology, Bulletin 78. Washington DC: Government Printing Office, 1925.

———. Review of *Patterns of Culture*, by Ruth Benedict. *American Anthropologist* 37, no.4 (1935): 689–90.

———. "Stimulus Diffusion." *American Anthropologist* 42, no. 1 (1940): 1–20.

———. "The Superorganic." *American Anthropologist* 19, no. 2 (1917): 163–213.

Kroeber, Theodora. *Alfred Kroeber: A Personal Configuration*. Berkeley: University of California Press, 1970.

Lapsley, Hilary. *Margaret Mead and Ruth Benedict: The Kinship of Women*. Amherst: University of Massachusetts Press, 1999.

Latham, Michael E. *Modernization as Ideology: American Social Science and "Nation Building" in the Kennedy Era*. Chapel Hill: University of North Carolina Press, 2000.

Lee, Dorothy Demetracopoulou. *Freedom and Culture: Essays*. Englewood Cliffs NJ: Prentice-Hall, 1959.

Lee, Richard, and Irven DeVore, eds. *Man the Hunter*. Chicago: Aldine, 1968.

Lepowsky, Maria. "Charlotte Gower and the Subterranean History of Anthropology." In *In Excluded Ancestors, Inventible Traditions: Essays toward a More Inclusive History of Anthropology*, edited by Richard Handler, 123–65. Madison: University of Wisconsin Press, 2000.

Lerner, Daniel. *The Passing of Traditional Society: Modernizing the Middle East*. New York: Free Press, 1958.

LeVine, Robert A. "Culture and Personality Studies, 1918–1960: Myth and History." *Journal of Personality* 69, no. 6 (2001): 803–18.

———. *Culture, Behavior, and Personality*. New York: Aldine, 1973.

———. "Ethnographic Studies of Childhood." *American Anthropologist* 109, no. 2 (2007): 247–60.

Levy, Marion J., Jr. *Modernization and the Structure of Societies*. Princeton NJ: Princeton University Press, 1966.

Lewis, Herbert S. "The Radical Transformation of Anthropology: History Seen through the Annual Meetings of the American Anthropological Association, 1955–2005." Academia.edu. www.wisc.academia.edu/HerbertLewis.

Leyton, Elliott, ed. *The Compact: Selected Dimensions of Friendship*. St John's: Institute of Social and Economic Research, Memorial University of Newfoundland, 1974.

Lipset, David. *Gregory Bateson: The Legacy of a Scientist*. Englewood Cliffs NJ: Prentice Hall, 1980.

Lowie, Robert H. *The History of Ethnological Theory*. New York: Farrar and Rinehart, 1937.

———. "Reflections on Goldenweiser's 'Recent Trends in American Anthropology.'" *American Anthropologist* 43, no. 2 (1941): 151–63.

Lutkehaus, Nancy. *Margaret Mead: The Making of an American Icon*. Princeton NJ: Princeton University Press, 2008.

Mahapatra, Manamohan. "Lingaraj Temple: Its Structure and Change, ca. 1900–1976." In Seymour, *Transformation of a Sacred Town*, 69–81.

Malinowski, Bronislaw. *Sex and Repression in Savage Society*. London: Routledge and Kegan Paul, 1927.

———. *The Sexual Lives of Savages in Northwestern Melanesia*. London: Routledge, 1929.

McClelland, David C. *The Achieving Society*. New York: Free Press, 1967.

McIntosh, Elizabeth P. *The Sisterhood of Spies: The Women of the OSS*. Annapolis MD: Naval Institute Press, 1998.

McNamara, Robert M. *In Retrospect: The Tragedy and Lessons of Vietnam*. New York: Random House, 1995.

Mead, Margaret. *Blackberry Winter: My Earlier Years*. New York: Morrow, 1972.

———. *Coming of Age in Samoa: A Psychological Study of Primitive Youth for Western Civilization*. New York: Blue Ribbon Books, 1928.

———. *Culture and Commitment: A Study of the Generation Gap*. New York: American Museum/Doubleday, 1970.

———. *Sex and Temperament in Three Primitive Societies*. New York: Morrow, 1935.

Miller, David M. "Religious Institutions and Political Elites in Bhubaneswar." In Seymour, *Transformation of a Sacred Town*, 83–95.

Miller, David M., and Dorothy C. Wertz. *Hindu Monastic Life: The Monks and Monasteries of Bhubaneswar*. Montreal: McGill-Queen's University Press, 1976.

Morro, Anthony. "Who Knew What, and When, at the FBI." *New York Times*, May 28, 1978.

Munroe, Robert L., and Mary Gauvain. "The Cross-Cultural Study of Children's Learning and Socialization: A Short History." In *The Anthropology of Learning in Childhood*, edited by David F. Lancy, John Bock, and Suzanne Gaskins, 35–63. Lanham MD: Alta Mira Press, 2010.

Murray, Henry A. *Explorations in Personality: A Clinical and Experimental Study of Fifty Men of College Age*. New York: Oxford University Press, 1938.

Myrdal, Gunnar. *Asian Drama: An Inquiry into the Poverty of Nations*. New York: Pantheon, 1968.

Nader, Laura. "The Phantom Factor: Impact of the Cold War on Anthropology." In *The Cold War and the University: Toward an Intellectual History of the Postwar Years*, edited by Noam Chomsky et al., 107–46. New York: New Press, 1997.

Parsons, Talcott. *Societies: Evolutionary and Comparative Perspectives*. Englewood Cliffs, NJ: Prentice-Hall, 1966.

———. *Structure and Process in Modern Societies*. Glencoe IL: Free Press, 1960.

Parsons, Talcott, and Edward C. T. Shils, eds. *Toward a General Theory of Action*. Cambridge MA: Harvard University Press, 1951.

Pattanayak, D. P., and G. N. Dash. *Conversational Oriya*. Mysore, India: Sulakshana Pattanayak, 1972.

Peacock, James. "Geertz's Concept of Culture in Historical Context: How He Saved the Day and Maybe the Century." In *Clifford Geertz by His Colleagues*, edited by Richard A. Shweder and Byron Good, 52–62. Chicago: University of Chicago Press, 2005.

———. *Rites of Modernization: Symbolic and Social Aspects of Indonesian Proletarian Drama*. Chicago: University of Chicago Press, 1968.

Peters, Margot. *May Sarton: A Biography*. New York: Knopf, 1997.

Powdermaker, Hortense. Review of *The People of Alor: A Social Psychological Study of an East Indian Island*, by Cora Du Bois. *American Anthropologist* 47, no.1 (1945): 155–61.

Preston, James. *Cult of the Goddess: Religious Change in a Hindu Temple*. New Delhi: Vikas, 1980.

Price, David H. *Anthropological Intelligence: The Deployment and Neglect of American Anthropology in the Second World War*. Durham NC: Duke University Press, 2008.

———. *Threatening Anthropology: McCarthyism and the FBI's Surveillance of Activist Anthropologists*. Durham NC: Duke University Press, 2004.

Pye, Lucian. *Politics, Personality, and Nation Building: Burma's Search for Identity*. New Haven CT: Yale University Press, 1962.

Radin, Paul. *Crashing Thunder: The Autobiography of a Winnebago Indian*. New York: Appleton, 1926.

———. *Primitive Man as Philosopher*. New York: Appleton, 1927.

Reynolds, E. Bruce. "Opening the Wedge: The OSS in Thailand." In *The Secrets War: The Office of Strategic Services in World War II*, edited by G. C. Chalou, 328–49. Washington DC: NARA, 1992.

———. *Thailand's Secret War: The Free Thai, OSS, and SOE during World War II*. New York: Cambridge University Press, 2005.

Rohner, Ronald P., Billie R. DeWalt, and Robert C. Ness. "Ethnographer Bias in Cross-Cultural Research: An Empirical Study." *Behavior Science Notes* 8 (1973): 275–317.

Roosevelt, Kermit, and S. Peter Karlow. *War Report: Office of Strategic Services (OSS)*. Vol. 2. Prepared by History Project, Strategic Services Unit, Office of the Assistant Secretary of War, War Department. Washington DC: GPO, 1949.

Rosenberg, Rosalind. *Changing the Subject: How Women of Columbia Shaped the Way We Think about Sex and Politics*. New York: Columbia University Press, 2004.

Rossiter, Margaret W. *Women Scientists in America: Struggles and Strategies to 1940*. Baltimore: Johns Hopkins University Press, 1982.

Rostow, W. W. *The Stages of Economic Growth: A Non-Communist Manifesto*. New York: Cambridge University Press, 1960.

Sable, Alan. "Indian Education: A View from the Bottom Up." In Seymour, *Transformation of a Sacred Town*, 157–82.

———. *Paths through the Labyrinth: Educational Selection and Allocation in an Indian State Capital*. New Delhi: S. Chand, 1977.

Sanford, R. Nevitt, Theodor W. Adorno, Else Frenkel-Burnswik, and Daniel Levinson. *The Authoritarian Personality*. New York: Norton, 1950.

Sapir, Edward. "Do We Need a Superorganic?" *American Anthropologist* 19, no. 3 (1917): 441–47.

Sarton, May. *Cloud, Stone, Sun, Vine*. New York: Norton, 1961.

———. *Collected Poems, 1930–1973*. New York: Norton, 1974.

———. "I See Myself as a Builder of Bridges." Interview by Neila C. Seshachari. *Weber Studies* 9, no. 2 (Spring/Summer 1992). http://weberstudies.weber.edu/archiveA.htm.

———. *Mrs. Stevens Hears the Mermaids Singing*. New York: Norton, 1965.

Schrecker, Ellen W. *No Ivory Tower: McCarthyism and the Universities*. New York: Oxford University Press, 1986.

Sequine-LeVine, Joan. *Perth Amboy*. Images of America. Charleston SC: Arcadia Publishing, 1996.

Seymour, Susan C. "Cora Du Bois." In *Women Anthropologists: A Biographical Dictionary*, edited by Ute Gacs et al., 72–79. New York: Greenwood Press, 1988.

———, ed. *The Transformation of a Sacred Town: Bhubaneswar, India*. Boulder CO: Westview Press, 1980.

———. *Women, Family, and Childcare in India: A World in Transition*. New York: Cambridge University Press, 1999.

Sherman, Susan. *May Sarton: Among the Usual Days: A Portrait*. New York: Norton, 1993.

———, ed. *May Sarton: Selected Letters, 1955–1995*. New York: Norton, 2002.

Smith, Bradley F. *The Shadow Warriors: O.S.S. and the Origins of the C.I.A.* New York: Basic Books, 1983.

Smith, R. Harris. *OSS: The Secret History of America's First Central Intelligence Agency*. Berkeley: University of California Press, 1972.

Smith-Rosenberg, Carroll. "Discourses of Sexuality and Subjectivity: The New Woman, 1870–1936." In *Hidden from History: Reclaiming the Gay & Lesbian Past*, edited by Martin B. Duberman, Martha Vicinus, and George Chauncey Jr., 270–73. New York: Penguin, 1990.

Spengler, Oswald. *The Decline of the West*. New York: Knopf, 1926.

Steward, Julian H. *Alfred Kroeber, 1876–1969: A Biographical Memoir*. Washington DC: National Academy of Sciences, 1962.

———, ed. *Handbook of South American Indians*. Washington DC: Smithsonian Institution, Bureau of American Ethnology, 1946–59.

Stocking, George W., Jr. "Polarity and Plurality: Franz Boas as a Psychological Anthropologist." In *Delimiting Anthropology: Occasional Essays and Reflections*, 49–62. Madison: University of Wisconsin Press, 2001.

Strauss, Claudia, and Naomi Quinn. *A Cognitive Theory of Cultural Meaning*. New York: Cambridge University Press, 1997.

Taub, Richard. *Bureaucrats under Stress: Administrators and Administration in an Indian State*. Berkeley: University of California Press, 1969.

Taylor, Edmond. *Awakening from History*. Boston: Gambit, 1969.

Taylor, Jeanne. *Child's Book of Carpentry*. New York: Greenberg, 1948.

Theoharis, Athan G. *Abuse of Power: How Cold War Surveillance and Secrecy Policy Shaped the Response to 9/11*. Philadelphia: Temple University Press, 2001.

———. *The FBI: A Comprehensive Reference Guide*. Phoenix: Oryx Press, 1999.

———. *From the Secret Files of J. Edgar Hoover*. Chicago: I. R. Dee, 1993.

Triplett, Rodney G. "Harvard Psychology, the Psychology Clinic, and Henry A. Murray: A Case Study in the Establishment of Disciplinary Boundaries." In *Science at Harvard University: Historical Perspectives*, edited by Clark A. Elliott and Margaret W. Rossiter, 223–50. Bethlehem PA: Lehigh University Press, 1992.

Van Onselen, Charles. *New Babylon, New Nineveh: Everyday Life on the Witwatersrand, 1886–1914*. Johannesburg: Jonathan Ball, 2001.

Vogt, Evon Z. *Zinacantán: A Maya Community in the Highlands of Chiapas*. Cambridge MA: Belknap Press of Harvard University Press, 1969.

Waller, Douglas. *Wild Bill Donovan: The Spymaster Who Created the OSS and Modern American Espionage*. New York: Free Press, 2011.

Weber, Mark. "The Boer War Remembered." *Journal of Historical Review* 18, no. 3 (1999): 14–27. http://www.ihr.org/jhr/v18/v18n3p14_Weber.html.

Weber, Max. *The Religion of India*. Glencoe IL: Free Press, 1958.

Weiner, Myron, ed. *Modernization: The Dynamics of Growth*. New York: Basic Books, 1966.

Weisner, Thomas S., and Ronald Gallimore. "My Brother's Keeper: Child and Sibling Caretaking." *Current Anthropology* 18, no. 2 (1977): 169–90.

Wellfelt, Emilie. "Returning to Alor: Retrospective Documentation of the Cora Du Bois Collection at the Museum of World Culture, Gothenburg, Sweden. *Indonesia and the Malay World* 37, no. 108 (July 2009): 183–202.

White, Robert W. *The Abnormal Personality*. New York: Ronald Press, 1964.

White, Theodore H. *In Search of History: A Personal Adventure*. New York: Harper and Row, 1978.

Whiting, Beatrice B., ed. *Six Cultures: Studies of Child Rearing*. New York: Wiley, 1963.

Whiting, Beatrice B., and John W. M. Whiting. *Children of Six Cultures: A Psycho-Cultural Analysis*. Cambridge MA: Harvard University Press, 1975.

Winks, Robin W. *Cloak and Gown: Scholars in the Secret War, 1939–1961*. New Haven CT: Yale University Press, 1961.

the Alorese (*continued*)
systems for, 142, 147–48; as infants
and children, 157–60, 161–62,
163–64; marriages and divorces for,
147, 148, 149–50; as medicine men,
140; as mothers, 157, 158–59, 160,
163; participant observations and,
145–50; physical appearances of, *141*,
141–42; seminars about, 156–57, 164;
wealth and prestige systems for, 138,
145–50; as women, 146, 147, 148–49,
150, 155–56, 162, 163
Alorese language. *See* Abui language
American Anthropological Association
(AAA): and ethics regarding counterinsurgencies and intelligence, 173,
321–25, 367n14; meetings for, 91, 173;
memberships and, 232, 312, 325, 326;
monographs and, 99; presidents for,
320–21, 322–25, 380n10; Society for
Cultural Anthropology and, 381n45
American Anthropologist, 77, 105–6, 110,
164, 290, 291, 375n12
American Ethnological Society (AES),
177
American Museum of Natural History,
60–61, 73, 95, 329
anthropologists: American Anthropological Association for, 91, 173, 232,
320–25; *American Anthropologist* for,
77, 105–6, 290, 291, 375n12; candida-
cies and nominations for, 253–54,
254–56, 257; regarding culture and
personality studies, 104–11, 119–20,
121–26, 128–29, 152–54; as curators,
71, 72, 73, 256, 329; debates and, xiv,
105–6, 377–78n76; diaries and journals concerning, 50–51, 65, 68; and
ethics regarding counterinsurgencies
and intelligence, 173, 286–90, 321–25,
364n20, 367n14, 380n21; fellowships for, 101, 102–4, 111–17, 120, 258;
feminists as, 44, 148; humanists

as, 280, 312–13, 339; investigations
and, 231–32, 233–34, 237; concerning
models and theories, 83, 104–11, 119–
20, 121–26, 128–29, 312–13; patriotism
of, 173, 364n30; during postwar
era, 312, 320–25, 339; at Stanford
University, 268, 280, 290–92;
women as, 95–97, 171, 253–56, *257*,
262, 263, 329, 358n68; World Health
Organization and, 237, 241. *See also*
fieldwork; Harvard University; lecturers; professors; Zemurray-Stone
Professorship
anthropology: applied anthropology
as, 241, 324, 329, 364n30; Franz
Boas and, xiii, 60, 104–5, 173; correspondence about, 152–53; courses
and lectures about, 104, 105, 122,
156–57, 260–62, 314–15; cultural
anthropology as, 145–50, 152–53, 267,
332, 381n45; culture and personality
movement within, xiv, 3, 81, 88, 102,
105, 107–11, 113, 116; development
of, xiii–xiv, 104–5; ideas and theories
concerning, 104–11, 121, 122–23,
126–28, 151, 163–64, 313–15; Margaret
Mead concerning, xiii, 95, 107, 108,
118–19, 326–31; phantom factor and,
289; PhD requirements for, 81–82;
postwar era and, 312, 321–25, 339;
psychological anthropology as, xi–
xii, 63–64, 98, 105; research and, xiv,
103, 152–53, 321–24; women and, xiii,
95–97, 355n51, 357–58nn67–68
"Anthropology and the Abnormal"
(Benedict), 63
Anthropology Society of Washington, 96
anticolonialism, 197–201, 205, 207,
218–21
anticommunism, 219, 223, 224, 225, 231,
234, 236, 248
applied anthropology, 241, 324, 329,
364n30

Du Bois, Claude (*continued*)
schooling of, 15, 17, 19, 21, 27, 28, 29,
43; behavior and character of, 18, 24,
26, 29; bequests and inheritance for,
43, 45, 60, 275, 353n4

Du Bois, Cora: family and genealogy
of, 3–4, *5, 6, 7, 8,* 9–13, 342, 345–46,
351nn10–11, 382n75; birth and child-
hood of, xiii, 1–3, 7, *8,* 13, *14,* 15–24, *25,*
26–29; early education and school-
ing of, 17–18, 19, 21–23, 26, 27, 28, 30,
43–45, 353n5; adolescence of, 30, *31,*
32–41; gender and sexual identity
of, xv, 33, 43, 52, 54–55, 56–57, 112,
233; as lesbian, xv, 35, 232, 263–64,
266, 335, 353n56; intellectual and
personal growth of, 42–43, 48–51,
56–57; as student, 46–48, 51–52, *53,*
60–61, 63–65, 68–69, 70–90, 91–95;
as companion and partner, xv, 87,
88–89, 192, 210, *211,* 212, 280, 281,
343, *343,* 346–48, 374n94; in love
affairs and relationships, 88–89,
121, 166, 277–79, 280–82, 374n94; as
research assistant, 97–99, 100; as
teacher, xxi–xxii, 166–73, 300–304,
305, 307–8, 310, 311, 320, 336–37;
as a "first woman," xiii, 263, 348;
accomplishments and career of,
xi–xii, xiii, xiv–xv, xxi, 51, 65–69,
348–49; awards and honors for, xxi,
90, 101, 102–4, 202, 203, 204, 265; as
writer, xvi, xxiii–xxiv, 36–39, 43, 59,
188–92, 198, 339–42; articles, papers,
and publications by, 77, 80, 89–90,
93, 217, 222, 379n90; fellowships and
grants for, 100–101, 102–4, 111–17,
120, 258, 293, 300, 311, 315, 375–
76n23; manuscripts and memoirs
by, 89, 92, 121, 164, 176–77, 292, 335,
364n30; presentations and seminars
by, 120, 121–24, 126, 129, 156–57, 164,
284–85; lectures and speeches by,

122, 219–21, 260, 313, 315, 378n79;
as chief, xi, xiv–xv, 172, 182–92, *184,
186,* 196–204, *203,* 210, *211, 235;*
organizational memberships and,
170, 177, 228, 233, 237, 240–41, 320–
21, 322–25; public and private life of,
xv–xvi, xxiii, 57, 264–66, 327, 330–31,
334–36; parties and social life for,
85–86, 87, 195–97, 212, 214, 256, 274,
320, 342–44, *343;* ambivalence and
skepticism of, 49–50, 51, 246, 311–16;
self-deprecation by, 42, 171, 246, 273,
279, 285, 320, 325, 334; self-reflection
by, 50–51, 65, 86–87, 99, 186–87, 274,
318–20, 335; retirement of, 317–18,
320, *326,* 348; bequests, inheritance, and wills concerning, 45, 46,
59–60, 85, 276–77, 346; depression,
ill-health, and death of, 274, 334–35,
339, 340, 344, 346, 347, 348. *See also*
Zemurray-Stone Professorship
—Works: "Culture Shock," 372n31; "The
Dominant Value Profile of American
Culture," 375n12; *The 1870 Ghost
Dance,* 38, 98; *The Feather Cult of Middle Columbia,* 98; *Foreign Students and
Higher Education in the United States,*
247; "The Gratuitous Act," 292;
"How to Make a Totem Pole for Your
Camp," 59; *Lowie's Selected Papers
in Anthropology,* 292; *Social Forces in
Southeast Asia,* 210, 219–20, 223, 264;
"Some Anthropological Hind-
sights," 339; "Some Anthropological
Perspectives on Psychoanalysis,"
122; "The Wealth Concept as an
Integration Integrative Factor in
Tolowa-Tututni Culture," 101; "Win-
ter Ethnography," 92–93. See also
The People of Alor

Du Bois, Georges, 10–11, 36, 40, 134,
216, 276

Du Bois, Gerald, 275–76

126, 127; Oedipus complex and, 108, 122, 123; *Totem and Taboo* by, 104, 111, 122–23

Freudianism. *See* Freud, Sigmund, Freudianism and

friendships: with Alice, 18–19, 37–38; with Eleanor "Nell" Barnes, 121, 166; with Ruth Benedict, 106, 165; in correspondence and letters, 165–66, 277, 291–92, 341; courses and studies regarding, 260, 266, 292; diaries and journals concerning, 52, 86–87, 277; with Claire Holt, 135; with Alfred Kroeber, 75, 106; with Robert Lowie, 165–66, 206, 291–92; with Margaret Mead, 106, 166; poems and poetry about, 30, 32–34, 52, 54–55; with Margaret Read, 340–41; same-sex relationships as, 34, 48, 49, 52, 54–55, 87–89; with Edward Sapir, 106; with May Sarton, 275, 277–78; with Nancy Schmidt, 346; with Susan Seymour, xxiii, xxiv–xxv; with Sister Fay, 27, 29, 33; student cohorts as, 75–76, 95–96; with Edmond Taylor, 195. *See also* relationships

funding: for area studies, 209, 286, 287; from Carnegie Corporation, 286, 287; Carnegie Foundation for the Advancement of Teaching and, 247; from Central Intelligence Agency, 287–88; correspondence and letters regarding, 99–100, 121; endowments as, 252–53, 346; for expeditions and fieldwork, 121, 129–30, 131, 145; Ford Foundation and, 209, 247, 287; for museums, 71; for research, 71, 99–100, 121, 129–30, 131, 287–88, 346; from Rockefeller Foundation, 106; through Social Science Council, 130; stipends as, 97, 100; trust funds as, 45. *See also* financing; grants

Ganesh Puja, 298–99

Gardener, Robert, 269

gays, 232–33, 337

Geertz, Clifford, 267–68, 332, 373n59, 381n45

Geertz, Hildred, 267–68

gender: differences concerning, 162–63, 309–10; discrimination and politics concerning, 183–87, 259, 263, 318–20, 337–38; ethnography regarding, 118–19; identities regarding, 33, 57; research and, 338

genealogies: and family of Cora Du Bois, 3–4, 5, 6, 7, 8, 9–13, 342, 345–46, 351nn10–11, 382n75; kinship systems from, 142, 147–48

German language, 78, 81, 85

Germany: Berlin in, 65–66, 67–68, 104; Frankfurt am Main in, 10, 11, 15, 36–37, 39–41; Heidelberg in, 3–4, 65–68; World War I and, 19–20, 29, 352n26

Ghost Dance, 38, 64, 97–98

Gibbs, James Lowell, 261–62, 263–64, 266–67, 372n34

Gifford, Edward Winslow, 72

Gildersleeve, Virginia, 48, 56, 57

girls, 147, 158, 162–63, 309–10

Goldschmidt, Walter, 291–92

governments: bureaucracies and, 16, 294–95, 304–5, 314, 379n90; grants and funding from, 287–88, 293, 312, 319

Gower, Charlotte. *See* Chapman, Charlotte Gower

grants: for fieldwork and research, 101, 130, 247, 287–88, 293, 304, 319, 375–76n23; from governments, 287–88, 293, 312, 319; for students, 287–88, 304, 336, 376n23. *See also* financing; funding

"The Gratuitous Act" (Du Bois), 292

Great Britain, 7, 180–81, 190, 198–99, 221, 284, 293

instructorships. *See* teaching
intelligence: agents for, 187–88, 200,
201; analyses of, 173–74; covertness
and, 288–89; ethics concerning counterinsurgencies and, 173, 286–90,
321–25, 367n14, 380n21; ethnography
as, 380n21; personnel and staff for,
170–71, 173–74, 183, 188–90, 199,
201, 202–4, *203*, 207, 208–9; and
research during postwar era, 207–10,
286–90, 321–25, 367n7; and research
during World War II, 181, 187, 315,
324, 380n21; from Southeast Asia
Command, 187–88; trips concerning,
29, 352n49; during World War I, 29,
352n49
intelligence organizations. *See* Office of
Strategic Services (OSS)
Interim Research Intelligence Service,
208, 210
International Research and Technology
Corporation (IR&T), 323–24
interrogations, 226–27, 229–31, 368n63,
369n69
interviews: autobiographies as, 158, 159,
160, 163; with informants, 77; interrogations as, 226–27, 229–31, 368n63,
369n69; for investigations, 233–34,
236; concerning McCarthyism and
Red Scare, 237–38; about Peabody
Museum of Archaeology and Ethnology, 372n28; for research and studies,
114, 332, 378–79n89; with students,
114, 165, 286, 372n28, 373n63, 377–
78n76; concerning women, 185
Inuits, 104, 271–72
investigations: regarding communism
and Communist Party, 225–28, 231,
233–34, 236, 247–48; interrogations
and interviews for, 226–27, 229–
31, 233–34, 236, 368n63, 369n69;
concerning loyalty, 225, 228–29,
231–32, 247–48, 370n85; within State

Department, 225–27, 228–29, 231–34,
236, 237, 369–70n85
IPR. *See* Institute of Pacific Relations
(IPR)
IR&T. *See* International Research and
Technology Corporation (IR&T)

Japan, 168, 197, 198, 199, 200, 201, 220,
264, 368n45
Jessup, Philip C., 217–18
Jessup Commission, 217–18, 219, 222,
234, 236
jobs: in anthropology, 95–97; in chemical factories, 15, 19–20, 29; chief as,
xiv, xv, 172, 182–87, *184*, *186*, 202–3,
210, *211*, 215, 344; with Institute of
International Education, 247, 255;
labor as, 146–47, 148, 157, 159, 162,
163; letters regarding positions and,
99, 174, 175–76, 177–78, 181–84, 185,
202–3, 206, 215, 224, 370n97; with
Office of Strategic Services, xiv–xv,
169–72, 174, 175–76, 181–87, *184*,
186, 188; and positions as research
and teaching assistants, 97–99, 100,
261–62, 266–67, 300, 361n13, 376n23;
and positions with Southeast Asia
Command, 177–78, 181–87, 188;
during postwar era, 206, 224, 246;
with Southeast Asia Branch Division
of Research for the Far East, xv,
210, 212, 215; teaching as position
and, 156, 164, 165, 206, 320, 369n77,
379n1. *See also* employment
Johnson, David K., 232
Jordan, Wilbur Kitchener, 250, 252–53,
255, 265–66
Josselin de Jong, J. P. B. de, 134–35, 143
journalists, 195, 224, 262
Journal of American Folklore, 91–92
journals, private: after fieldwork, 165;
concerning friendships and relationships, 35, 86–87, 277, 280; language

Marshall, George C., 217

Martin, Guy, 185, 192, 203

Massachusetts: Boston Psychoanalytic Society in, 114, 116; Boston Psychopathic Hospital in, 101, 103, 115–17, 120, 122; Martha's Vineyard in, 277; Massachusetts Institute of Technology in, 288, 305, 376n24, 376n38. *See also* Cambridge MA

Massachusetts Institute of Technology (MIT), 288, 305, 376n24, 376n38

May, George, 192

McCarthy, Joseph, 225, 236, 368n52, 369n71, 369n82, 369n85

McCarthyism. *See* Red Scare

McClelland, David, 314, 376n24

McCormack, Alfred, 208–9

McCown, Theodore, 244–45

McIntosh, Elizabeth P., 185, 188

McNamara, Robert S., 223

McWilliams, Julia. *See* Child, Julia (née McWilliams)

Mead, Margaret: American Anthropological Association and, 323, 326, 380n10; American Museum of Natural History appointment for, 60–61, 95, 329; anthropology and, xiii, 95, 107, 108, 118–19, 326–31; correspondence and letters concerning, 117, 118–19, 132–33, 136, 156–57, 326–27, 329, 330; death of, 329, 330; ethnography and, 118–19, 327; feminism and, 44, 354n9; field notes and fieldwork by, 60, 64–65, 107, 132, 133, 135–36, 360n2; fieldwork advice from, 132, 133, 135–36; friendships and relationships with, 106, 132–33, 135–36, 156–57, 166, 326–31; "the generation gap" and, 44–45, 328; as lesbian, 57, 330–31; PhD for, 61, 329; psychoanalysis and, 112; research and studies by, 107, 117, 118–19, 132,

133, 327–28, 359n12; research assistants for, 330, 361n13

—Works: *Coming of Age in Samoa*, 107, 110; *Culture and Commitment*, 326, 327–28; *Sex and Temperament in Three Primitive Societies*, 110, 117, 118

Melanesia, 63, 107, 108, 112, 118, 119, 143

men: anthropology jobs for, 95; in Bhubaneswar, 297; Franz Boas regarding, 355n73; dates with, 34, 58, 353n58; friendships and, 32, 33–34; gayness as sexual orientation for, 232–33; gender differences and, 162–63, 309–10; at Harvard University, 251, 252, 254, 259, 261–64, 282–83, 319–20; labor and work by, 146–47, 148, 162; as students, 251, 261–63, 372n28; studies about, 114–15, 117, 118; tests regarding, 162; in wealth and prestige systems, 138, 145–50

mentors: Ruth Benedict as, xi, 68, 91–92; Cora Du Bois as advisor and, 266–73, 306, 320; Robert Lowie as, 206, 291; Edward Sapir as advisor and, 101, 105, 111, 112, 113, 120, 124, 269

Métraux, Rhoda, 330

Miles, Milton E., 181

Miller, David M., 306, 307

Mills, Antonia, 338, 348

Milton, John, 32, 33–34

The Mind of Primitive Man (Boas), 60, 104

Minh, Ho Chi, 234

Misra, Bhabagrahi, 306

mistrustfulness. *See* distrustfulness

MIT. *See* Massachusetts Institute of Technology (MIT)

modal personality, xi, 84, 162, 163

modernization, 284, 293, 303, 305–7, 313–16, 376n24, 378n79, 379n90

monographs: *1890 Ghost Dance* as, 64; *The 1870 Ghost Dance* as, 38, 98;

fieldwork and, 80–81, 82, 90, 92–93; PhDs concerning, 82, 99

Mooney, James, 64

Most Noble Order of the Crown of Thailand, xxi, 202

mothers, 157, 158–59, 160, 163, 362n71

Mountbatten, Louis. *See* Mountbatten of Burma, Earl

Mountbatten of Burma, Earl, xiv–xv, 178, 179, 180, 181, 185, *186*, 190

movements: concerning culture and personality studies, xiv, 3, 81, 88, 102, 105, 107–11, 113, 116; gayness, feminism, and women's rights as, 33, 44, 275, 337–38, 373n54; Ghost Dance as, 97–98; concerning independence and nationalism, 198–201, 219, 220, 221, 234

Mrs. Stevens Hears the Mermaids Singing (Sarton), 282

Murray, Henry A., 111, 113–15, 120

Museum of Natural History. *See* American Museum of Natural History

museums: American Museum of Natural History as, 60–61, 73, 95, 329; Bishop Museum as, 91; Chateau des Monts as, 9; curators for, 71, 72, 73, 256, 329, 372n28; in Heidelberg, 66–67; Museum of World Culture as, 362n68; Peabody Museum of Archaeology and Ethnology as, 71, 96, 256, 259, 273, 346, 372n28; Phoebe A. Hearst Museum of Anthropology as, 71, 356n4; Royal Ethnographic Museum as, 104; Smithsonian Institution as, 192

My Life in France (Child), 214

mythology, 80, 89–90, 91–92

Nader, Laura, 262, 263, 266, 267, 289

(NARA). *See* National Archives and Records Administration (NARA)

National Archives and Records Administration (NARA), 364n13

nationalism, 197, 198, 199–201, 219, 220, 221, 234

National Research Council (NRC), 101, 102–4

National Science Foundation (NSF), 293, 300, 311, 315, 375–76n23

National Security Act of 1947, 367n8

Native Americans: Ghost Dance movement and, 97–98; homosexuality and, 63; papers about, 101; at Second Annual Indian Congress, 58; shamans as, 79–80, 83, 93, 97, 101, 103, 119, 151, 152; Tolowa as, 77, 101; Wintu as, 76, 77–81, 92–93

Nerlove, Sarah, 372n30

Netherlands, 134–35

Netherlands East Indies: Bali in, 132–33, 135–36, 152, 157, 193, 329, 360n2; Batavia in, 135; Java in, 135, 267–68; intelligence concerning, 174; Kalabahi in, 136–37, 264. *See also* Alor (Netherlands East Indies)

Never in Anger (Briggs), 270, 272

New Capital (Bhubaneswar, Odisha, India), 295–96, 298, 304–6, 308–10, 376n34, 379n90

New Guinea, 108, 175–76

New York City NY: American Museum of Natural History in, 60–61, 73, 95, 329; Bellevue Hospital in, 120–21; Brooklyn in, 3, 7, 11–13, 21; Carnegie Corporation of New York in, 286, 287; fellowship orientation in, 111–13; homes in, 121; Hunter College in, 125–26, 369n77; New York Psychoanalytic Society in, 120, 121–24, 126; New York University in, 120; Sarah Lawrence College in, 156, 164, 165, 172, 206, 363n96; youth culture and, 56–57. *See also* Columbia University

operations, 187–88, 189, 193, 199, 200–
    201, 207–8. *See also* Office of Strategic
    Services
organizations, professional: American
    Anthropological Association as, 91,
    99, 173, 232, 320–21, 322–25, 381n45;
    American Ethnological Society as,
    177; Association for Asian Studies
    as, 321, 325, 336; East Indies Institute
    of America as, 170, 177; Institute of
    Pacific Relations as, 228, 233, 234;
    Society for Applied Anthropology as,
    177; Society for Cultural Anthro-
    pology as, 381n45; World Health
    Organization as, 237, 240–41
Orissa (India). *See* Bhubaneswar (Odi-
    sha, India)
Oriya language, 297, 332, 376n32, 378n89
oss. *See* Office of Strategic Services (oss)

papers: critiques for writing and,
    xxi, xxiii–xxiv, 47, 307, 311, 327–
    28; on feminine masochism, 118;
    friendship in, 292; regarding
    Harvard-Bhubaneswar Project and
    India, 311, 331, 379n90, 381n42;
    about Alfred Kroeber, 370n94; about
    mythology, 91–92; about Native
    Americans and the Wintu, 91–92,
    101; concerning psychiatry, 104;
    about psychological anthropology,
    63–64; about societies, 372n34; about
    suicide, 119; "The Superorganic" as,
    105–6; about women, 370n94
Parsons, Elsie Clews, 99, 380n10
Parsons, Talcott, xxiv, 265, 314
participant observations: 145–50, 299.
    See also ethnography; fieldwork
partners, xv, 87–89, 192, 210, *211*, 212,
    213, 281, 330–31, *343*
paternalism, 68, 74, 75, 355n73
patriotism, 172–74, 207, 233, 364n30

Pattanayak, D. P., 376n32
Patterns of Culture (Benedict), 61, 63,
    104, 109–10
Payne-Gaposchkin, Cecilia, 254, 351n1
    (prologue), 371n5
Peabody Museum of Archaeology and
    Ethnology, 71, 96, 256, 259, 273, 346,
    372n28
Peacock, James, 269–70, 378n84, 381n45
pen names. *See* pseudonyms
Pentecostalism, 79–80
The People of Alor (Du Bois): autobiog-
    raphies and, 158–59, 363n78; data
    and analyses for, xiv, 154, 160–64,
    363n78; distrustfulness and, 159–60;
    letters concerning, 164, 176, 177,
    363n92; observations and research
    for, 129–30, 142–54, 155–56, 157–60;
    prefaces for, 129, 138, 264; psy-
    chological anthropology and, xi;
    publications of, 164, 176, 264
People's Republic of China (PRC), 218
personalities. *See* culture and personal-
    ity studies
personality types: basic personality
    as, 126–28, 163–64; in cultures and
    societies, 97–98, 101, 109–10; modal
    personality as, xi, 84, 162, 163
personnel: agents as, 187–88, 200–201;
    and employees with State Depart-
    ment, 216–17, 225–27; memos about,
    188–89, 190, 201; for Office of
    Strategic Services, 170–71, 174, 178,
    184, 186, 203, 203–4; for Research
    and Analysis Branch, 170–71, 173–74,
    203–4, 207; for Southeast Asia Com-
    mand, 188–89, 190, *203*, 203–4; and
    students with Harvard-Bhubaneswar
    Project, xv, xxii–xxiii, 300–311, *301*,
    334, 336–37, 376n23. *See also* staff
Perth Amboy NJ, 20–21, 22, *25*, 26, 43–44,
    45

PhDs: Ruth Benedict and, 60; dissertations for, 65–66, 81–82, 93–94, 99, 135, 269, 358n68; Cora Du Bois and, 81–82, 90, 92–95; exams for, 81, 90, 92, 94–95, 358n68, 377–78n76; Harvard-Bhubaneswar Project dissertations and, 300, 303, 304–5, 307, 308, 310, 376n38; Alfred Kroeber and, 71; Robert Lowie and, 73; Margaret Mead and, 61, 329; Henry Murray and, 113; Elsie Parsons and, 99, 380n10; Paul Radin and, 84; requirements for, 81–82; for women, 95–97, 358n68

Phoebe A. Hearst Museum of Anthropology, 71, 356n4

photographs, 86, 134, 144, 362n68

poems: adolescence and, 30, 32–34, 69; analysis and examination of, 33–34, 353n55; for Eleanor "Nell" Barnes, 88–89; Christmas in, 29; Continental Divide, 69; about life's transitions, 166–67; love, friendships, and relationships in, 30, 32–34, 52, 54–55, 280, 281; pseudonyms for, 353n54; Jeanne Taylor and, 212, *213*; about wars, 29. *See also* poetry

poetry, 278, 280. *See also* poems

Porteus, Stanley, 162

Porteus Maze tests, 162

postwar era: anthropology and anthropologists during, 312, 320–25, 339; anticolonialism and, 205, 207, 218–21; area studies during, 209–10, 285–87; employment and jobs during, 206, 224, 246; foreign policy during, xv, 199–200, 217–24; India and, 284, 288–89, 293–311, 331–34; Indonesia and, 267, 270; intelligence and research during, 207–10, 286–90, 321–25, 367n7; journals and, 246, 353n60; letters and memos concerning, 190, 202, 206, 207; social

sciences and, 311, 312–13, 333, 339; sociocultural changes during, 267, 270, 284–85, 293–311, 331–32; State Department during, xiii, xv, 208–10, 216–17, 222, 225, 229, 232–34, 236; United States and, 314, 315, 321–22, 339. *See also* Cold War

Powdermaker, Hortense, 164

PRC. *See* People's Republic of China (PRC)

Prestes, Luís Carlos, 228, 230

Preston, James, 306–7

Price, David H., 232, 368–69n65

Pridi Banomyong, 200

Primitive Man as Philosopher (Radin), 84

Prince, Morton, 113

professorships. *See* appointments; Zemurray-Stone Professorship

programs: area studies as, 209–10, 285–87; funding for, 209, 286, 287; concerning health, 240–41; letters concerning studies and, 68–69, 75, 91, 92, 94–95; regarding loyalty, 224–25, 232; for studies and PhDs, xiii, 46, 81–82, 209–10, 286–87, 312

Prokouriakoff, Tatiana, 372n28

pseudonyms, 282, 353n54

psychiatrists, 111, 121–24, 160–61. *See also* Horney, Karen; Kardiner, Abram

psychiatry, 97–98, 101, 104, 110, 120–21

psychoanalysis, 55–56, 83, 102, 111, 112, 115, 116, 122–23

psychological anthropology, xi–xii, 63–64, 98, 105. *See also* culture and personality studies

The Psychological Frontiers of Society (Kardiner), 363n92

psychology: ideas and theories concerning, 107, 108, 110–11, 127–28, 151, 162, 163–64; of institutions, 108, 127–28, 151, 152, 160–62, 163–64; lectures about, 104, 105, 122–23, 156–57; concerning observations and research,

sociocultural change: courses and seminars about, 284–85, 314–15; Harvard-Bhubaneswar Project and, xi–xii, xv, xxii, 293–94, 300–311, 315–16, 331–32, 378–79nn89–90; master's thesis about, 64; during postwar era, 267, 270, 284–85, 293–311, 331–32. *See also* modernization

"Some Anthropological Hindsights" (Du Bois), 339

"Some Anthropological Perspectives on Psychoanalysis" (Du Bois), 122

South Asia Regional Council (SARC), 336

Southeast Asia: Allied Forces in, 180–81, 198–201, 222; anticolonialism and, 197–201, 218–21; Burma in, 290–91; China in, 180, 218, 369–70n78; Cold War and, 218, 219, 223; colonialism and nationalism concerning, 189, 190, 197, 198–201, 219–21; courses and lectures about, 219–21, 260, 270, 284, 285–86, 289; foreign policy regarding, 197–200, 217–24; Great Britain and, 180–81, 190, 198–99, 221; Indochina in, xv, 221–23, 289; Japan and, 197, 198, 199, 200, 201, 220; research in, 287–88, 290–91; Thailand in, 198, 199–201, 202, 322, 323, 326–27, 368n45; United States and, 180–81, 189, 190, 197–201, 287–88; as World War II theater, 181, 183, 187, 189–90, 199

Southeast Asia Branch of the Division of Research for the Far East: chiefs for, xv, 210, *211, 235*; investigations and, 233–34, 236, 237, 369n78, 369–70n85. *See also* Research and Analysis Branch (R&A)

Southeast Asia Command (SEAC): agents with, 187–88, 200–201; associ-ates, personnel, and staff for, 178, 183, 185, 187–89, 190, 192–97, 199, 201, 202–4; Gregory Bateson with, 193, 195, 330; chiefs for, xi, xiv, 172, 182–92, *184, 186*, 196–204, *203*, 344; Julia Child with, xv, xxv, 178, 179, 182, 192–94, 195, 210; Paul Child with, xxv, 182, 192, 210, 212; com-munications with, 188–92, 197–98, 199–200, 201; Cora Du Bois with, xi, xiv–xv, 172, 177, 178–80, 181–204, *184, 186, 203*; establishment and purpose of, 180–81, 187–88; headquarters for, 179–80, *184, 186*; jobs and positions with, 177–78, 181–87, 188; in Kandy, xi, xiv–xv, 178, 179–80, 181–203, *184, 186*; Weston La Barre with, 194–95, 366n79; David Mandelbaum with, 194; Earl Mountbatten of Burma with, xiv–xv, 178, 179, 180, 181, 185, *186*, 190; operations of, 187–88, 189, 193, 199, 200–201; parties and social life concerning, 195–97; reports from, 188, 191, 197–98; Edmond Taylor with, 195; Jeanne Taylor with, 182, 192, 195–96, 210, 212; women with, xi, xiv–xv, 178, 179, 181–87, *184, 186*. *See also* Research and Analysis Branch (R&A)

Southeast Asia Institute. *See* East Indies Institute of America

Spectator, 26

speeches, 217, 219, 220–21, 222, 236, 313, 369n82. *See also* lectures

Spengler, Oswald, 69, 72–73

Spier, Leslie, 82

Spiro, Melford E., 290–91, 318; "The Acculturation of American Ethnic Groups," 375n12

Sproul, Robert Gordon, 239–40, 242–43, 244, 245–46

Sri Lanka. *See* Ceylon

staff: agents as, 187–88, 200–201; letters and memos concerning, 188–89, 190, 199, 202–3, 206, 208–9; for Office of

Edited and with introductions by
Jennifer S. H. Brown and Susan Elaine
Gray

*Excavating Nauvoo: The Mormons and
the Rise of Historical Archaeology in
America*
Benjamin C. Pykles
Foreword by Robert L. Schuyler

*Cultural Negotiations: The Role of
Women in the Founding of Americanist
Archaeology*
David L. Browman

*Homo Imperii: A History of Physical
Anthropology in Russia*
Marina Mogilner

*American Anthropology and Company:
Historical Explorations*
Stephen O. Murray

*Racial Science in Hitler's New Europe,
1938–1945*
Edited by Anton Weiss-Wendt and
Rory Yeomans

*Cora Du Bois: Anthropologist,
Diplomat, Agent*
Susan C. Seymour

*Before Boas: The Genesis of Ethnography
and Ethnology in the German
Enlightenment*
Han F. Vermeulen

To order or obtain more information on these or other University of Nebraska
Press titles, visit www.nebraskapress.unl.edu.